The Rise of China

AN *International*
Security READER

EDITED BY

Michael E. Brown
Owen R. Coté, Jr.
Sean M. Lynn-Jones
and Steven E. Miller

THE MIT PRESS
CAMBRIDGE, MASSACHUSETTS
LONDON, ENGLAND

The contents of this book were first published in **International Security** (ISSN 0162–2889), a publication of The MIT Press under sponsorship of the Belfer Center for Science and International Affairs at Harvard University. Copyright in each of the following articles is owned jointly by the President and Fellows of Harvard College and the Massachusetts Institute of Technology.

Avery Goldstein, "Great Expectations: Interpreting China's Arrival," 22:3 (Winter 1997/98); Erica Strecker Downs and Phillip C. Saunders, "Legitimacy and the Limits of Nationalism: China and the Diaoyu Islands," 23:3 (Winter 1998/99); John Wilson Lewis and Xue Litai, "China's Search for a Modern Air Force," 24:1 (Summer 1999); David Shambaugh, "China's Military Views the World: Ambivalent Security," 24:3 (Winter 1999/2000). Thomas J. Christensen, "China, the U.S.-Japan Alliance, and the Security Dilemma in East Asia," 23:4 (Spring 1999); Robert S. Ross, "The Geography of the Peace: East Asia in the Twenty-first Century," 23:4 (Spring 1999); David Shambaugh, "Containment or Engagement in China? Calculating Beijing's Responses," 21:2 (Fall 1996); Gerald Segal, "East Asia and the 'Constrainment' of China," 20:4 (Spring 1996).

Library of Congress Cataloging-in-Publication Data

The Rise of China / edited by Michael E. Brown . . . [et al.]
   p. cm. — (An international security reader)
  Includes bibliographical references.
  ISBN 0-262-52276-4
  1. United States—Military policy. 2. National Security—United States. 3. Security, International.
  I. Brown, Michael E. II. International security readers

DS779.27 .R57 2000
327.51—dc21   00-033948

Contents

The Contributors

MICHAEL E. BROWN teaches in and is Director of Research for the National Security Studies Program, Edmund A. Walsh School of Foreign Service, Georgetown University, and is Editor of *International Security*.

OWEN R. COTÉ, JR., is Associate Director of the Security Studies Program at the Massachusetts Institute of Technology and Editor of *International Security*.

SEAN M. LYNN-JONES is Editor of *International Security* and a Research Associate at the Belfer Center for Science and International Affairs (BCSIA), Harvard University.

STEVEN E. MILLER is the Editor-in-Chief of *International Security* and Director of the International Security Program at BCSIA.

THOMAS J. CHRISTENSEN is Associate Professor of Political Science and a member of the Security Studies Program at the Massachusetts Institute of Techonology.

ERICA STRECKER DOWNS is a Ph.D. candidate in the Politics Department at Princeton University.

AVERY GOLDSTEIN is Professor of Political Science and Director of the Christopher H. Browne Center for International Politics at the University of Pennsylvania.

JOHN WILSON LEWIS is William Haas Professor of Chinese Politics at Stanford University.

XUE LITAI is a Research Associate with the Project on Peace and Cooperation in the Asia-Pacific Region at the Center for International Security and Cooperation, Stanford University.

ROBERT S. ROSS is Professor of Political Science at Boston College and a Member of the Executive Committee at the Fairbank Center for East Asian Research at Harvard University.

PHILLIP C. SAUNDERS is a Ph.D. candidate at the Woodrow Wilson School of Public and International Affairs, Princeton University.

GERALD SEGAL was Director of Studies at the International Institute for Strategic Studies in London at the time of his tragic and untimely death in November 1999.

DAVID SHAMBAUGH is Professor of Political Science and International Affairs and Director of the China Policy Program at George Washington University and a non-resident Senior Fellow in the Foreign Policy Studies Program at the Brookings Institution.

Acknowledgments

The editors gratefully acknowledge the assistance that has made this book possible. A deep debt is owed to all those at the Belfer Center for Science and International Affairs (BCSIA), Harvard University, who have played an editorial role at *International Security*. We are grateful for support from the Carnegie Corporation of New York. Special thanks go to Diane McCree, Chris Smith, Melanie Winograd, and Meara Keegan Zaheer at BCSIA for their invaluable help in preparing this volume for publication.

Preface | *Sean M. Lynn-Jones*

Dramatic increases in China's economic and political power were among the most important changes in international politics during the 1980s and 1990s. China's vast territory and huge population had made China a potential superpower for decades, but this potential did not come close to being realized until China embarked on an ambitious program of economic reform and modernization in the 1970s and 1980s. China's gross domestic product (GDP) more than quadrupled between 1978 and 1999. Other economic indicators, such as levels of trade and foreign reserves, also leapt upward. At the same time, China began to modernize its armed forces and bought advanced weapons from other countries.

The apparent rise of China has stimulated many debates among scholars, policymakers, and journalists. At least four themes have been prominent in these debates about the implications of China's rise. First, how large are China's economic and military capabilities? Some observers have extrapolated from recent trends and concluded that China will become a superpower of unprecedented proportions early in the twenty-first century. Lee Kuan Yew, former prime minister of Singapore, has declared that "it's not possible to pretend that [China] is just another big player. This is the biggest player in the history of man."[1] Others argue that China threatens to become a hegemonic power in East Asia.[2] But some analysts are more skeptical about the extent of the increase in China's power. Gerald Segal, for example, argues that China's economic growth is overstated by misleading statistics. In his view, China is actually "a second-rank middle power" that should not be regarded as a potential superpower. "In fact," he argues, "China is better understood as a theoretical power—a country that has promised to deliver for much of the last 150 years but has consistently disappointed."[3] This debate suggests that many assessments of Chinese capabilities depend on projections of current economic trends that may or may not continue.

Second, what does the growth of Chinese power (if it is growing) imply for the peace and stability of the international system? Some theorists of international relations argue that rise of a new great power often leads to war, either because the rising power uses force to change the international system to suit its interests or because the existing leading power launches a preventive war

---

1. Lee Kuan Yew, as quoted in Samuel P. Huntington, *The Clash of Civilizations and the Remaking of World Order* (New York: Simon and Schuster, 1996), p. 231.
2. Denny Roy, "Hegemon on the Horizon? China's Threat to East Asian Security," *International Security*, Vol. 19, No. 1 (Summer 1995), pp. 149–168.
3. Gerald Segal, "Does China Matter?" *Foreign Affairs*, Vol. 78, No. 5 (September/October 1999), p. 24.

to preserve its position while it still has the capabilities to do so.[4] This theoretical perspective implies that conflict—and perhaps war—is likely between the United States and China. Other observers, however, might point to the peaceful end of the U.S.-Soviet rivalry as evidence that great powers can rise and decline without provoking major wars.

Third, what are China's intentions? Does it seek to aggressively challenge and change the international system? There is no consensus on these questions. Some observers argue that China will, at most, seek greater influence in East Asia. Unlike the Soviet Union, it will not engage in a global ideological competition with the United States. Other, more pessimistic, observers argue that China has shown a propensity to use force, believes it has been the victim of repeated acts of aggression and humiliation, and will eventually assert its territorial claims to Taiwan, the Spratly Islands, and the Diaoyu (Senkaku) Islands. This pessimistic analysis suggests that China will be drawn into conflict with the United States because Washington will attempt to protect Taiwan from Chinese threats and will clash with China on Beijing's other territorial claims.

Fourth, how should the United States—and other countries—respond to China's growing power? During the mid-1990s, American commentators debated whether the United States should pursue a policy of containment or engagement toward China. Although the content of these two alternatives was often unclear, containment usually implied treating China as a potential military adversary, attempting to limit its economic growth, restricting its access to militarily significant technologies, punishing China for violating human rights, and strengthening U.S. alliances and military capabilities that are at least potentially directed against China. Engagement, on the other hand, entails continuing economic interaction with China and efforts to give China "a seat at the table" in important international institutions. Proponents of engagement hope that these policies will encourage China to liberalize internally and to avoid aggressive international behavior. While scholars and analysts have debated the merits of these approaches, U.S. policy has included elements of each.

This book includes essays that address these themes in detail. The first four essays in this volume present perspectives on China's power and China's

---

4. For important examples of "power transition" and "hegemonic transition" theories, see A.F.K. Organski and Jacek Kugler, *The War Ledger* (Chicago: University of Chicago Press, 1980; Robert Gilpin, *War and Change in World Politics* (Cambridge: Cambridge University Press, 1981); and Jacek Kugler and Douglas Lemke, eds., *Parity and War: Evaluations and Extensions of* The War Ledger (Ann Arbor: University of Michigan Press, 1996).

attitudes toward the world. They carefully consider China's aggregate capabilities, military power, apparent intentions, and perceptions of the world. Taken together, they offer a nuanced account of China's rise and its implications.

In "Great Expectations: Interpreting China's Arrival," Avery Goldstein considers the implications of China's increasing political, economic, and military power. He argues that objective measures suggest that China's increase in capabilities remains modest and that future increases may not be as large as many observers expect. Goldstein also suggests that China's rising power need not threaten international stability.

Statistics suggest that China's power has increased dramatically. China's GDP doubled in the 1980s and more than doubled in the 1990s. Its trade surplus and reserves of foreign exchange grew as it expanded its exports of consumer products. Goldstein notes, however, that China's military power has not increased dramatically. In the 1990s, increased military spending often went to fund operations and maintenance, not to procurement of more advanced weapons. Moreover, most of China's forces are not trained and equipped for modern, high technology warfare. China has begun to import advanced weapons, but it may not be able to integrate these weapons into its forces and use them effectively.

Goldstein argues that China's military capabilities must be assessed by comparing them to those of Beijing's likely adversaries: the ASEAN (Association of South-East Asian Nations) states; Taiwan; Japan; and the United States. These countries have more experience with advanced weapons and, in most cases, have enhanced their military capabilities in response to China's military buildup. ASEAN and Taiwan may not be able to defeat China, but their forces would make it very difficult and costly for China to launch offensive military operations in the South China Sea or across the Taiwan Strait. China's capabilities lag far behind those of the United States, but Beijing's modernization has denied Washington the option of decisive and risk-free military intervention in East Asia.

Given the limits on China's power, why have many observers concluded that China is rapidly rising to great-power status? Goldstein offers five answers. First, historically China has been cast in the role of a great power, even when it lacked the requisite capabilities. China was depicted as a great power during World War II and the Cold War, thereby creating a sense of unfulfilled expectations.

Second, China's recent growth seems especially impressive because it began from such a low baseline. China was an extremely poor country at the end of the 1970s and its armed forces remained backward. China's growth was more rapid because it began from a low starting point, creating the impression that it could continue until China joined the ranks of the leading powers.

Third, China's military modernization programs indicate that China is planning to project its power and influence. Beijing is acquiring ballistic missiles, strategic nuclear warheads, and air and naval forces that are traditional tools of great powers eager to project their power.

Fourth, a change in the method of calculating China's GDP has exaggerated the increase in China's economic power. In 1993, the International Monetary Fund began calculating GDP on the basis of purchasing power parity (PPP) instead of current exchange rates. As a result, China jumped from tenth to third on the list of the world's largest economies, trailing only Japan and the United States. Although this change was not just a statistical quirk, because the PPP method more accurately reflected China's economic vitality, it gave the impression of an even more rapid ascent by China.

Finally, the return of confrontational diplomacy and military threats between China and Taiwan in 1995 and 1996 added to the impression that China had replaced the Soviet Union as the principal military threat to the United States.

As its economy has grown during the 1980s and 1990s, China has begun to see itself as a more significant player in international economic diplomacy. Goldstein points out that China has sought to gain entry into the World Trade Organization (WTO) on its own terms and has resisted U.S. economic pressure. Beijing also has perceived itself as more militarily secure since the end of the Cold War; it no longer needs to cultivate one superpower as an ally against the other.

Assessing China's actual, as opposed to perceived, capabilities is complicated by the absence of recent "power tests"—crises and wars that provide an opportunity to assess capabilities and determination. Such tests were frequent in the early Cold War (e.g., the Korean War, crises in the Taiwan Strait) but have been rare since China's 1979 invasion of Vietnam. China's 1996 military coercion against Taiwan suggests that China is prepared to use force to prevent Taiwanese independence but also reveals that China's power-projection capabilities are weak.

To assess the implications of China's rising power, Goldstein examines the claims of five theoretical perspectives: theories of changing power relations, the significance of regime type, the role of international institutions, the effects of economic interdependence, and the strategic consequences of the nuclear revolution. These theoretical perspectives offer conflicting predictions. Some theories of changing power relations, for example, predict that major war between China and the United States is likely, whereas theories of economic interdependence imply that China's continued rise may be peaceful.

Goldstein concludes that China's military capabilities will continue to lag behind those of other major states—particularly those of the United States. Despite its rapid economic modernization, China will not be able to deploy technologically advanced forces for several decades, because it lacks the requisite scientific infrastructure. Nevertheless, China will increase its capabilities and is likely to come into conflict with other states. The open question is whether these conflicts will lead to war. Although many theories predict conflict between China and other powerful states, these theories do not specify the intensity of that conflict and many of them suggest ways of ameliorating it. Goldstein thus suggests that most observers have been too alarmist about the rise of China. He contends that the worst-case scenario may be a "manageable, if undesirable, cold war."

Many observers have wondered whether rising nationalist sentiment in China will lead Beijing to adopt a more assertive foreign policy. In "Legitimacy and the Limits of Nationalism: China and the Diaoyu Islands," Erica Strecker Downs and Phillip Saunders consider whether China is becoming increasingly nationalistic. Downs and Saunders examine China's behavior in China's 1990 and 1996 disputes with Japan over the Diaoyu (Senkaku) Islands. They find that China adopted restrained policies and placed economic developmemt ahead of stridently nationalist goals.

Downs and Saunders note that the Chinese government now relies on nationalism and economic performance to maintain its legitimacy, because communist ideology has collapsed as a legitimating force. These sources of legitimacy sometimes come into conflict. Excessive nationalism may imperil China's access to international markets, and excessive dependence on foreign markets and investment may undermine the Communist Party's nationalist credentials. China's government must carefully manage this dilemma.

The Diaoyu Islands, claimed by China, Taiwan, and Japan, are uninhabited but are adjacent to potential oil reserves in the East China Sea. China argues that these islands should have reverted to Beijing's control after World War II, but Japan regained "administrative rights" to the islands when the United States returned Okinawa to Japan in 1972. The United States has not taken a position on the sovereignty issue.

In 1990, a crisis over the Diaoyus arose when the Japanese Maritime Safety Agency prepared to recognize officially a lighthouse that had been erected on the islands by a right-wing Japanese group. China protested that such recognition would infringe on its sovereignty. During the ensuing war of words, Taiwanese boats attempted to reach the islands and Chinese protesters held anti-Japanese demonstrations in Hong Kong, Taiwan, and the United States. The Chinese government, however, banned demonstrations and engaged in restrained diplomacy with Japan, which had been one of the first countries to restore economic ties with China after the Tianamen Square riots of 1989.

In 1996 Japanese right-wingers erected a second lighthouse and a Japanese flag on the Diaoyu Islands. Japan's foreign minister reiterated Japan's claim to the islands. China issued stern warnings and called upon Japan to control the right-wing groups, but refused to let the dispute jeopardize Sino-Japanese relations and trade. Anti-Japanese demonstrations erupted in Hong Kong and Taiwan, but the Chinese government prevented demonstrations in China. Many Chinese wrote letters and signed petitions demanding a more assertive Chinese posture, but the government again was willing to emphasize economic development over strident nationalism.

Downs and Saunders argue that China's economic interests will lead Beijing to pursue policies of restraint over Taiwan and the Spratly Islands. Although developments such as major economic failure or Japanese and U.S. attempts to contain China might cause the Chinese government to conclude that it has nothing to lose by embracing strident nationalism instead of economic performance, for now at least, "Chinese nationalism is cause for concern, but not yet cause for alarm."

One hallmark of a great power is its ability to deploy advanced weapons. China has spent half a century attempting to build an effective, modern air force, but these efforts have failed repeatedly. In "China's Search for a Modern Air Force," John Wilson Lewis and Xue Litai review the history of China's air force to determine why China's efforts have failed and what policies China might pursue in the future. They find that China's failures took place for different reasons during different periods, making it harder for China to draw and apply useful lessons. China has again asserted its desire to deploy a modern air force, but it may not be able to achieve this goal.

China first attempted to acquire a combat-ready air force during the Korean War, when Chinese forces suffered heavy casualties due to U.S. air raids. For the next twenty-five years, China continued to try to manufacture and operate Soviet-designed aircraft. These efforts failed as a result of poor planning, lack of resources, and the priority given to building strategic nuclear forces. China's air force also neglected pilot training in the chaos of the Cultural Revolution. At the same time, aircraft designers and engineers were persecuted as ideological enemies. As a result, in the mid-1970s China had a fleet of poorly designed aircraft with serious technical problems, as well as pilots who flew poorly and rarely hit their targets.

Under Deng Xiaoping in the late 1970s China tried to revitalize its air force. Deng declared that the air force would receive a higher priority, but these efforts failed. China's continued commitment to self-reliance meant that it refused to buy advanced aircraft from other countries. By 1988, roughly half of China's aircraft, missiles, and radar systems were not operational.

The 1991 Gulf War against Iraq prompted China to rethink its doctrine for aerial warfare and to make more vigorous efforts to catch up with the United States and other advanced industrial countries. China's air force embraced more offensive concepts of air operations, while combining them with the establishment of a national air defense network. These doctrinal changes have been accompanied by a reduction in aircraft and personnel. Many obsolete planes have been retired. China is now trying to create the technical and infrastructure base for upgrading its air force, while simultaneously buying advanced foreign aircraft from Russia. Beijing has yet to train pilots capable of fighting high-technology wars; only 20.7 percent of its air officers are college graduates. After 1996, when Taiwan became the focus of China's military planning, Beijing accorded additional priority to modernizing its air forces and enhancing its conventional forces more generally.

Why does China continue to attempt to develop a modern air force when its potential adversaries have huge advantages in producing and using advanced combat aircraft? Lewis and Xue point out that China's leaders feel that China must have a modern air force to become a modern military power, that China must respond to aerial threats, that having conventional air power reinforces nuclear deterrence, and that an effective air force will be critical in any future confrontations with Taiwan—or any other high-technology war. It remains unclear whether these arguments and aspirations for a modern air force will be translated into reality.

In "China's Military Views the World: Ambivalent Security" David Shambaugh examines the beliefs and attitudes of China's People's Liberation Army (PLA). Given the growing power of China, it is particularly important to understand how China's military perceives the current international situation. Shambaugh finds that the PLA continues to see numerous latent security threats, even though China is apparently in the midst of a period of unprecedented peace. PLA commentators are particularly worried about the predominance of the United States.

Shambaugh begins by noting that it is difficult to gather information on the PLA's worldview. High-ranking generals rarely meet with foreigners and most have had little interaction with the outside world. There are, however, more opportunities for interaction with the next generation of China's military leaders, many of whom have spent time abroad and speak foreign languages. Because it is impossible to meet with many of China's highest-ranking military officers, PLA books and periodicals are the most important source of information on the PLA's views. It is also possible to interview some intelligence officers, military attachés, and personnel at military colleges.

Shambaugh finds that the Chinese military is deeply ambivalent about China's national security. On the one hand, China now has normal diplomatic relations with its neighbors and its borders are peaceful. Relations with Russia are at their best since the 1950s. China's continued economic growth and military modernization should make it even more secure. On the other hand, China's military worries about China's declining influence over North Korea, India's acquisition of nuclear weapons, political tensions with Taiwan, and, above all, U.S. capabilities and willingness to project military power globally.

PLA observers were particularly concerned by the U.S. advanced weapons used during the 1999 Kosovo Conflict. They were impressed by how the accuracy of U.S. advanced, long-range weapons had improved since the 1990–91 Gulf War. Such capabilities could be used against a Chinese army that historically has prepared for traditional ground combat with its enemies. On the other hand, Chinese observers also noted that Yugoslavia was able to hide many of its forces, and that China would be even better positioned to limit damage and absorb U.S. attacks. However, another lesson of the Kosovo conflict is that Taiwan would be able to hide its forces from Chinese attack.

The United States is the greatest security concern for PLA leaders. Chinese military leaders regard the United States as hegemonic and expansionist—as do most of China's civilian leaders. Chinese military leaders hope and expect that other countries will resist and prevent U.S. hegemony. They believe that the United States is trying to prevent any reunification between Taiwan and mainland China. They also resent U.S. alliances and regard them as directed against China.

In Northeast Asia, China's military continues to distrust Japan and remains suspicious of potential Japanese militarist tendencies. Chinese military commentators believe that the U.S.-Japan alliance is an attempt to contain China and they are particularly alarmed by Japan's participation in U.S. theater missile defense (TMD) programs. China does not believe that North Korea is on the verge of collapse and has opposed U.S. attempts to put pressure on the Pyongyang regime.

To the north, China has demilitarized its border with Russian, demarcated the boundary, and increased Sino-Russian cooperation directed against the United States. Much of this cooperation consists of rhetorical statements denouncing U.S. "hegemonism" but Russia also has increased its arms sales to China. Some Chinese military analysts, however, continue to be suspicious of Russia's long-term objectives.

In Southeast Asia, Chinese military commentators have devoted little attention to the ASEAN Regional Forum. Such institutions are seen not as attempts to promote cooperative security, but as potential instruments to disrupt U.S. hegemony and the U.S.-Japan alliance.

Few PLA analysts have written about South Asia, but India's May 1998 nuclear tests stimulated Chinese military officers to criticize India for its hegemonic aspirations and to note that India's conventional forces have grown stronger.

Shambaugh concludes that China's military continues to perceive many sources of instability and threats, even though China's objective security situation has not been better for over 50 years. The United States should attempt to engage PLA officers at all levels in an attempt to understand and potentially change their outlook. Nevertheless, Americans should not delude themselves about the depth of Chinese suspicion of the United States. "Competitive coexistence" is the most realistic relationship that the United States and China can probably achieve.

The next section of essays in this volume examines how China's increasing power and diplomatic assertiveness will influence the stability of the Asia-Pacific region and relations between Beijing and Washington. These issues have stimulated vigorous debate, and many scholars and analysts have argued that the rise of China is just one of many factors that will make the Asia-Pacific region increasingly insecure.[5]

---

5. See, for example, Aaron L. Friedberg, "Ripe for Rivalry: Prospects for Peace in a Multipolar Asia," and Richard K. Betts, "Wealth, Power, and Instability: East Asia and the United States after the Cold War," both in *International Security*, Vol. 18, No. 3 (Winter 1993/94), pp. 5–33; 34–77.

In "China, the U.S.-Japan Alliance, and the Security Dilemma in East Asia," Thomas Christensen argues that there is a particularly intense security dilemma among the leading powers of the Asia-Pacific region.[6] Historical memories and ethnic hatred exacerbate the security dilemma between China and Japan. The relationship between China and Taiwan creates a situation where even defensive military preparations are seen as having offensive purposes, further intensifying the security dilemma. In these circumstances, almost any change in the U.S.-Japan alliance will provoke Chinese opposition and potentially destabilize the region.

China's fears of Japan reflect a deep distrust of Japanese intentions. Chinese observers are concerned that Japan's failure to acknowledge and accept guilt for the 1937 Nanjing massacre and other atrocities will eventually make younger Japanese generations willing to increase Japan's military power. These Chinese fears are exacerbated by China's nationalist dislike of Japan and the role that anti-Japanese nationalism has played in legitimizing the Chinese Communist Party. Although their assessments are not couched in emotional or nationalistic terms, Chinese defense analysts worry about Japan's growing military strength and the potential for a future buildup.

According to Christensen, China believes that the U.S.-Japan security alliance is the critical factor in restraining the growth of Japanese military power. Beijing's leading defense experts fear any change in the alliance. If the alliance breaks down, Japan may decide to act unilaterally and expand its armed forces. If, on the other hand, strengthening the U.S-Japan alliance requires Japan to assume a larger share of its defense burdens, China would worry that an expanded Japanese military would threaten Chinese security. In particular, China fears that revitalization of the U.S.-Japan alliance might require Japan to offer greater support for U.S. military operations near Taiwan. China also has reacted negatively to Japanese plans to send peacekeeping forces to other countries and to cooperate with the United States in the development of TMD.

Christensen argues that the relationship between mainland China and Taiwan creates an unusual and pernicious security dilemma in East Asia. Most scholars agree that security dilemmas become more intense when two potentially hostile countries deploy offensive forces and less severe when they have defensive capabilities. In the China-Taiwan relationship, however, Taiwanese

6. For a critique of Christensen's arguments, and Christensen's response, see Jennifer M. Lind and Thomas J. Christensen, "Correspondence: Spirals, Security, and Stability in East Asia," *International Security*, Vol. 24, No. 4 (Spring 2000), pp. 190–200.

deployments of defensive forces exacerbate the security dilemma, because Beijing sees such defensive capabilities as an attempt to prepare for Taiwanese independence.

China's concerns about Taiwan influence its security relationship with Japan, according to Christensen, because Beijing fears that Japanese and U.S. deployments of TMD would reduce China's ability to coerce Taiwan with ballistic missiles. In a future crisis in the Taiwan Strait, Washington might ask Tokyo to deploy ship-based TMD systems to protect Taiwan against the threat from Chinese missiles. China would be particularly opposed to Japan's role in such a crisis, given the legacy of distrust between Beijing and Tokyo. China's leaders would have similar concerns if Japan assisted in minesweeping operations in response to a potential Chinese attempt to blockade Taiwan by laying mines around the island.

Christensen argues that the China-Japan security dilemma will be hard to defuse because Chinese leaders and analysts do not recognize that Japanese military policies may reflect fears of China. Other Chinese analysts even contend that China's growing power may enable it to coerce Japan into accommodating China. Either attitude will make it hard to resolve the security dilemma between the two countries. Christensen notes, however, that China's emerging interest in multilateral security forums such as the ASEAN Regional Forum provides grounds for moderate optimism about the potential for ameliorating the China-Japan security dilemma.

Christensen recommends that the United States maintain its presence in Japan, because this presence helps to stabilize East Asia. Japan should assume new responsibilities in the alliance, including logistics support, base access, and minesweeping, but the United States should maintain sufficient capabilities so that it does not have to rely on Japanese assistance. The United States and Japan should not exclude Taiwan from the scope of the U.S.-Japan alliance. This approach may help to deter Chinese military actions against Taiwan. The United States also should not encourage Japan to develop TMD, because this would provoke China. Instead, the United States should develop TMD independently, reserving for the future the possibility of reconsidering joint development with Japan.

Christensen observes that East Asia's security dilemmas may ease in the coming decades. Tokyo and Beijing may improve their bilateral ties, particularly as new generations come to power in each country. Regional confidence-building measures may increase transparency and reduce suspicion. In the short run, however, U.S. policies to maintain the U.S.-Japan alliance without provoking China will play the most important role in maintaining stability in East Asia.

Robert Ross offers a more optimistic analysis of the prospects for peace between China and other states. His "The Geography of the Peace: East Asia in the Twenty-First Century" argues that geography will play a central role in shaping great power competition in the Asia-Pacific region—and whether that competition remains peaceful. Ross argues that geography ensures that the Asia-Pacific region will remain bipolar and peaceful, with China and the United States as the two great powers.

Ross contends that East Asia is bipolar because China is an established regional power and the United States is a global superpower but only a regional power in East Asia. China dominates mainland East Asia and the United States dominates maritime East Asia. No other country can become a great power in East Asia. Russia's population lies far to the west of its East Asian regions and it has had difficulty projecting its strategic power to the Asia-Pacific region. Japan lacks the size and resources to be a regional great power. It depends too much on other great powers—particularly the United States—to aspire to great-power status.

According to Ross, China and the United States will be rivals in the bipolar East Asia of the twenty-first century. He argues that it is misleading to label China a "rising" power; China is already a great power in the East Asian region. It could only destabilize the region by challenging U.S. maritime supremacy, which no other East Asian country could do. China's vast size, natural resources (e.g., coal and oil), and population endow it with the prerequisites for strategic autonomy.

Because the United States is separated from East Asia by the Pacific Ocean and surrounded by weak neighbors, it can develop military power in isolation and project it into East Asia. It has considerable natural resources and a vibrant economy that depends little on foreign trade.

Ross argues that the Chinese-U.S. competition in East Asia resembles the U.S.-Soviet competition during the Cold War. In both bipolar rivalries, a land power competed with a maritime power for influence in a region of global geopolitical significance. In each rivalry, each competing state had the capabilities to challenge the vital interests of the other.

In Ross's view, the U.S.-Chinese competition is likely to be a stable bipolar rivalry. The competition exhibits the features one would expect in a bipolar system. China has balanced against the United States by abandoning its Marxist economic ideology to pursue pragmatic economic policies. It has improved its relations with most of its neighbors and compromised with the United States on many issues. For its part, the United States continues to maintain substantial forces in East Asia and has revitalized its alliance with Japan. U.S. defense spending continues at high levels, despite the end of the Cold War. Because the structure of the regional system is bipolar, smaller states do not matter very much. China and the United States can tolerate free-riding by their allies. And because the U.S. and Chinese spheres of influence are geographically distinct and separated by water, each can intervene in its own sphere without threatening the other. During the Cold War in Europe, by contrast, Soviet interventions in Eastern Europe threatened neighboring Western Europe and increased tensions.

The stability of the competition between the United States and China is further enhanced by the fact that the two countries—thanks to geography—have complementary interests in East Asia. The United States seeks to dominate the region's shipping lanes so that that it can maintain access to regional markets and resources. It can accomplish this task without threatening China because East Asia has many island nations that offer the United States allies and bases. The U.S. margin of naval superiority over China is large and probably growing, but it lacks the capability or desire for major land wars in Asia. Thus the United States benefits from the status quo, can defend it relatively easily, and has no incentives to challenge it by, for example, attempting to project land power onto the Asian mainland.

China's primary geopolitical interest is to secure its land borders. Recently, it has been remarkably successful in reducing land-based threats, but the fact that China borders on Russia means that this problem can never be eliminated. Throughout history, the main threats to China have come from the land; maritime powers like Britain imposed humiliations, but did not threaten to invade or occupy China. China will thus continue to pursue a continental strategy. It will find it difficult to challenge U.S. naval supremacy.

Ross argues that the security dilemma between the United States and China is likely to remain mild. The superiority of the United States at sea, and of China on land, gives each power a defensive advantage in its own theater and makes it hard to take offensive action in the other's theater. China and the United States can increase their own security without reducing the other's security.

There are three East Asian flashpoints that could trigger conflict between the United States and China: the Spratly Islands, Korea, and Taiwan. Of these, the Spratly Islands is the least important, because China lacks the means or the interest to occupy these islands in the South China Sea. Korea and Taiwan, however, could become major sources of tension. Both are exceptions to the general stability of the U.S.-Chinese maritime-continental rivalry. The Korean Peninsula is the only place on the Asian mainland where the United States has retained land forces. Fortunately, the status quo—reinforced by U.S. nuclear deterrence—has remained stable for almost half a century. The problem may be resolved eventually by Korean unification and the withdrawal of American troops. Taiwan is also a geographical anomaly because it lies in the Chinese continental theater and the U.S. maritime theater. However, Taiwan is not a vital strategic interest of the United States and it is likely that Washington and Beijing will be able to continue to manage this issue.

Ross concludes that if the United States avoids the temptation to withdraw from East Asia, and if China continues to pursue limited aims, there is no reason why the bipolar East Asian system cannot remain stable well into the twenty-first century. There is no guarantee that the two countries will achieve this outcome, but geography creates the possibility of avoiding a new Cold War in East Asia.

The final two essays in this volume examine the debate over how to respond to China's changing power and policies. The two sides in this debate are usually described as proponents of "containment" or "engagement." The former school favors a harder line toward China, whereas the latter prefers accommodation.

In "Containment or Engagement of China? Calculating Beijing's Responses" David Shambaugh considers how China is likely to respond to policies of containment or engagement. He examines the domestic factors that will shape Chinese policies and concludes that the best, although imperfect, option for Asian and Western governments is engagement.

Shambaugh recalls that the United States tried to contain China between 1950 and 1971, when President Richard Nixon adopted a policy of engagement, although he did not use that label. Analysts and commentators are again debating these two alternatives. Almost all the participants in this debate assume that China will inexorably grow to become a superpower. Most also fail to take into account how China will change in respond to whatever policy the United States chooses. Shambaugh points out that both these viewpoints are debatable. Domestic instability or an economic slowdown could interrupt China's drive for superpower status. And China's international environment will almost certainly influence the evolution of China's internal politics and society.

Shambaugh recognizes that China's rise may cause international instability and conflict. The rise of new, dissatisfied great powers historically has provoked major wars. China fits the profile of a rising, ambitious great power that wants to change the international status quo. Moreover, it has shown itself willing to use force against its neighbors, having fought more border wars than any country since 1945.

In Shambaugh's view, whether China forcefully challenges the international status quo or behaves by established rules and norms will depend on domestic factors in China. He identifies three sets of important factors: China's domestic politics, the decision-making milieu, and the elite's worldview.

Shambaugh argues that three elements of China's domestic politics will influence Beijing's foreign policy. First, the succession politics following the death of Deng Xiaoping will include factional struggles in which Chinese leaders will find it hard to make international concessions or compromises. As they struggle to retain or enhance their political standing following Deng's death, Chinese politicians will not be able to adopt a soft line against "hegemony" or "imperialism." China will thus be unwilling to be flexible on issues such as Hong Kong, Taiwan, and the South China Sea.

Second, the fragility of China's political system and its potential inability to address the political, social, and economic demands generated by rapid economic modernization increase Chinese leaders' suspicion of foreign demands for domestic change in areas such as human rights and intellectual property. At a time when China's citizens seek continued economic growth and improved social services, Beijing regards foreign requests for internal change as subversion.

Third, the devolution of central political control to subnational actors and units has reduced China's ability to comply with international agreements. The growing autonomy of local and regional authorities has made it more difficult for China to enforce compliance with international agreements on, for example, trade, transfers of weapons, and software piracy. Nevertheless, the central authorities retain firm control over the military and the making of national security policy.

Shambaugh finds that the institutional milieu in which China's leaders operate is an important source of China's foreign policy. Power is concentrated in the hands of a few leaders in the Politburo and the Central Military Commission. There are few, if any, opportunities for domestic lobbying or input from the National People's Congress. As a result, pressures from the bureaucracy and interest groups do not shape Chinese policies, but policy options may be narrowed.

In China's decision-making milieu, the worldview of political leaders clearly plays a crucial role in shaping Chinese foreign policy. In Shambaugh's view, this worldview is based on the socialization of key policymakers, the impact of the 1989 Tianamen Square demonstrations, and Chinese nationalism. He points out that many members of China's current elite were trained in the Soviet Union during the 1950s. They do not see Russia as a threat and have sought to improve Sino-Russian relations. The 1989 Tianamen Square demonstrations, as well as the global collapse of communist governments during that year, have increased the Chinese elite's fear of instability and given it a siege mentality. Nationalism is probably the most important element shaping the worldview of Chinese leaders. Shambaugh argues that China's nationalism combines arrogance with insecurity about China's place in the world. It thus produces an assertive yet defensive worldview.

How will these various domestic factors shape China's foreign policy? Shambaugh concludes that China will remain preoccupied with domestic issues and will not undertake major international initiatives. Beijing will often be truculent and suspicious in its dealings with the West. China will regard U.S. policies of engagement as covert attempts at containment. China's leaders will resist U.S. attempts to persuade China to accept international norms and multilateral institutions, unless China receives worthwhile financial incentives. A containment policy, however, would fare even worse. It would confirm Chinese suspicions of U.S. motives and provoke China to refuse to cooperate on most issues. Containment would not improve human rights or stimulate civil society in China. Shambaugh recalls that the United States tried to contain China from 1949 until 1971. The policy failed then and should not be resurrected now. Engagement will be difficult, but there is no other choice.

Gerald Segal's "East Asia and the 'Constrainment' of China" analyzes how East Asia should respond to China's growing power. So far, the debate on this issue has been between proponents of "engagement" and "containment." Segal argues that these categories are inadequate. He suggests that engagement with China is a necessary, but insufficient, first step. China's neighbors and other powers also must defend their interests by constraining China. The question is whether they have the will to adopt such a policy of "constrainment."

Segal contends that China is weaker than it appears at first glance. Statistics on its territory, population, and economic growth conceal its massive social problems and weak leadership. China's economy depends on continued access to foreign markets and technology. Other East Asia states, particularly Japan, may be able to manage a growing China.

Whatever the objective prospects, Segal sees little evidence that East Asian states have the will to balance against China. East Asia is fragmented. Some countries may tend to lean toward China because they have substantial ethnic Chinese populations. The Koreas view their relationship with China through the narrow prism of the issue of their unification. In Northeast Asia, the issue of North Korean nuclear weapons is intimately related to policy toward China. In Southeast Asia, the issue is not salient at all. There are no strong regional security institutions that might serve as a basis for common policies against China.

Proponents of engagement with China claim that balancing China is unnecessary because China will be restrained by economic interdependence. This school of thought suggests that China's dependence on the international economy will prevent it from becoming too assertive or aggressive toward its neighbors. Segal points out that ASEAN's engagement with China has not prevented Chinese military actions against the Philippines in the Spratly Islands. He suggests that the lesson of these events is that engagement is not sufficient to restrain China. At least some states in East Asia seem to share this conclusion. China did moderate its behavior in the South China Sea in late 1995 after it became clear that other states might begin to balance against it.

Segal concludes that China will pursue a complex and uncertain foreign policy, plagued by internal divisions and invocations of intense nationalism to forge domestic unity. It is not very constrained by economic interdependence, but its behavior probably can be moderated by concerted external pressure. Other states, in East Asia and beyond, will have to maintain such pressure in order for it to be effective.

The essays in this volume do not cover every topic related to the rise of China. As this book goes to press, China's entry into the World Trade Organization and the continuing tension over Taiwan's apparent aspirations for independence have taken center stage in Sino-American relations. Other issues will continue to emerge as China asserts its newfound power. We hope, however, that the book's overview of many aspects of China's rise will provide a useful introduction to these topics.

Part I:
Assessing China's Capabilities and Intentions

Great Expectations | *Avery Goldstein*
Interpreting China's Arrival

It has become nearly conventional wisdom that China is the post–Cold War world's emerging great power that poses the most difficult questions for the future of international security. Whether scholars, pundits, and policymakers are interested in environmental impact, human rights, economic affairs, or traditional military-security issues, most who think about the dynamics of the international system in the twenty-first century believe it essential to consider the rise of China and its implications.[1] This article focuses mainly on the military-security dimensions of this topic, exploring the basis for claims about China's growing power and the expectations about its significance that are rooted in relevant strands of international relations theory.

Perhaps the interest in China's international role should not be altogether surprising, inasmuch as it has long been a country with three of the least malleable attributes required for membership in the great power club—vast territory, rich resources, and a large population. And, in the course of the past century, other key requirements for international influence have been successively added. By the mid-twentieth century, the victory of the Chinese Communist Party (CCP) resolved a century-long pattern of internal political disunity and ended a series of varied foreign encroachments on China's sovereignty. During the Cold War, the new regime's leaders gradually enhanced

Avery Goldstein is Associate Professor of Political Science and Director of the Christopher H. Browne Center for International Politics at the University of Pennsylvania. He is the author of From Bandwagon to Balance-of-Power Politics: Structural Constraints and Politics in China, 1949–1978 *(Stanford, Calif.: Stanford University Press, 1991), and is completing a study entitled* Deterrence and Security in a Changing World: China, Britain, France, and the Enduring Legacy of the Nuclear Revolution.

I would like to thank Jean-Marc F. Blanchard, Thomas J. Christensen, and the anonymous reviewers for *International Security* who provided helpful comments on various drafts of this article.

1. The new wave of scholarly interest in East Asian security and China emerged in about 1993. Just two years earlier, such matters received relatively short shrift in one of the first serious comprehensive overviews of the post–Cold War world landscape. See Robert J. Art, "A Defensible Defense: America's Grand Strategy after the Cold War," *International Security*, Vol. 15, No. 3 (Spring 1991), pp. 5–53. Capturing the spirit of the recent "China-mania," the February 18, 1996, *New York Times Magazine* carried as its cover story, "The 21st Century Starts Here: China Booms. The World Holds Its Breath," by Ian Buruma, Seth Faison, and Fareed Zakaria. The editors of *International Security*, sensitive to market demand, have published an edited volume of selected articles entitled *East Asian Security*, whose largest section is a collection of major articles under the heading, "The Implications of the Rise of China." Michael E. Brown, Sean M. Lynn-Jones, and Steven E. Miller eds., *East Asian Security* (Cambridge, Mass.: MIT Press, 1996).

International Security, Vol. 22, No. 3 (Winter 1997/98), pp. 36–73
© 1997 by the President and Fellows of Harvard College and the Massachusetts Institute of Technology.

their international prestige and eventually overcame attempts at diplomatic isolation to assume their role as the sole legitimate representatives of the Chinese state in key international bodies, most notably the United Nations Security Council. In addition, during the Cold War the CCP invested heavily in the rapid development of the modern era's military badges of great power status—nuclear warheads and the ballistic missiles to deliver them.

Into the last decade of the Cold War, however, China remained a "candidate" great power because the communist regime had failed in its efforts to promote domestic development that could provide the basis for comprehensive economic and military clout at world-class levels. A vast army supplied with obsolete conventional, and crude nuclear, weaponry left China as one of a group of second-ranking powers, and among them perhaps the least capable.[2] But beginning in 1979, while the Soviet Union was retrenching internationally and then imploding, new leaders in Beijing were initiating a series of sweeping reforms that would result in high-speed growth—both quantitative expansion and qualitative improvements.[3] By the end of the Cold War, China was more than a decade into an economic takeoff that led many to reach the seemingly inescapable conclusion that the country was destined finally to add the last pieces to its great power puzzle. Beijing would have the wealth and expertise to be a leading player in international economic affairs, assets that might also provide the foundation for a large, first-class military capability. In short order, many who had comfortably spoken about a Chinese great power some time in the future began to worry about the implications of a China sooner, rather than later, having the ability to pursue its own interests more aggressively. Often, those thinking about this prospect believed it spelled trouble for international security, at least in the East Asian region and perhaps beyond.[4]

---

2. See Avery Goldstein, "Robust and Affordable Security: Some Lessons from the Second-Ranking Powers During the Cold War," *Journal of Strategic Studies*, Vol. 15, No. 4 (December 1992), pp. 478–479, 519.

3. For concise accounts of China's reforms, see Harry Harding, *China's Second Revolution* (Washington, D.C.: Brookings Institution, 1987); Kenneth Lieberthal, *Governing China* (New York: W.W. Norton, 1995); and Nicholas R. Lardy, *China in the World Economy* (Washington, D.C.: Institute for International Economics, 1994).

4. On the increased importance of China for U.S. foreign policy, see then-U.S. Secretary of State Warren Christopher's May 1996 speech to a joint meeting of the Council on Foreign Relations, the Asia Society, the National Committee on U.S.-China Relations, and *Business Week*. "'American Interests and the U.S.-China Relationship' Address by Warren Christopher," *Federal Department and Agency Documents*, May 17, 1996, *Federal Document Clearing House*, from NEXIS Library, Lexis/Nexis, Reed Elsevier (hereafter NEXIS). For samples of the emerging scholarly literature, see Aaron L. Friedberg, "Ripe for Rivalry: Prospects for Peace in a Multipolar Asia," *International Security*, Vol. 18, No. 3 (Winter 1993/94), pp. 5–33; Richard K. Betts, "Wealth, Power, and Instability: East Asia and the United States after the Cold War," *International Security*, Vol. 18, No. 3 (Winter

In this article, I analyze the conventional wisdom. First, I examine its basis. In what sense has China's power been increasing? To what extent do the claims of a rapidly rising China reflect reality as opposed to perceptions? What accounts for divergence between objective indicators and judgments about China's power? I then consider the key interpretive question: What are the expected consequences of China's rising power, whatever the pace at which it is increasing, for international security? My analysis (1) indicates that the recent increases in China's capabilities most important for international security, especially military power, have thus far been modest; (2) explains why expectations for great gains in the foreseeable future may well be exaggerated; and (3) acknowledges that although international relations theory provides persuasive reasons to expect China's growing power to increase the frequency and intensity of international conflicts, it also suggests ways to manage such conflicts and, perhaps most important, suggests why dire scenarios involving major war are unnecessarily alarmist.

Several caveats are in order. First, the core topic of this article, "power," is a highly contested term, and the debate about its meaning cannot possibly be resolved in this space.[5] Second, and perhaps ironically, in this case it is easier to deal with the theoretical-interpretive issues than with the empirical ones. The CCP has changed much about the way it runs China since it initiated its reform program, but it has not warmly embraced the notion of transparency in the military-security realm.[6] Third, the accuracy of assessments of China's

---

1993/94), pp. 34–77; Denny Roy, "Hegemon on the Horizon: China's Threat to East Asian Security," *International Security*, Vol. 19, No. 1 (Summer 1994), pp. 149–168; Michael G. Gallagher, "China's Illusory Threat to the South China Sea," *International Security*, Vol. 19, No. 1 (Summer 1994), pp. 169–194; Richard Bernstein and Ross H. Munro, *The Coming Conflict with China* (New York: Alfred A. Knopf, 1997); and Andrew J. Nathan and Robert S. Ross, *The Great Wall and the Empty Fortress: China's Search for Security* (New York: W.W. Norton, 1997).
5. For a brief introduction to the debate and references to some of the key positions, see William Curti Wohlforth, *The Elusive Balance* (Ithaca, N.Y.: Cornell University Press, 1993), especially pp. 3–10.
6. On the strategic rationale for China resisting transparency, see Goldstein, "Robust and Affordable Security," pp. 485–491, 500–503; Alastair Iain Johnston, "China's New 'Old Thinking': The Concept of Limited Deterrence," *International Security*, Vol. 20, No. 3 (Winter 1995/96), p. 31, fn. 92. China's Defense White Paper in 1995 was an unrevealing disappointment. The PLA has reportedly begun a more forthcoming draft for release in late 1997. See "White Paper—China: Arms Control and Disarmament," Xinhua News Agency, November 16, 1995, from NEXIS; Banning N. Garrett and Bonnie S. Glaser, "Chinese Perspectives on Nuclear Arms Control," *International Security*, Vol. 20, No. 3 (Winter 1995/96), pp. 43–78; Christopher Bluth, "Beijing's Attitude to Arms Control," *Jane's Intelligence Review*, July 1996, pp. 328–329; and Barbara Opall, "Skeptics Doubt Value of PLA White Paper," *Defense News*, December 9, 1996, p. 3, from NEXIS. Nevertheless, since 1979 Western scholars have been better able to interview relevant policymakers, Chinese academics, and military personnel, to gather the increasing volume of Chinese publications, as well as to obtain many imperfectly controlled "internal-circulation-only (*neibu*)" materials often discovered on the shelves of China's bookstores.

growing power, and thus its potential significance for international security, depends upon a variable only loosely connected to current patterns of economic and military growth—the country's future political coherence. Until the violent crackdown on demonstrators in 1989, few China experts concerned themselves with the possible collapse of the communist regime or disintegration of the nation-state. In the immediate wake of the events in Tiananmen Square, speculation about such extreme outcomes was rampant. But the success of the CCP in weathering the domestic and international pressures it faced in 1989 and 1990 has again shifted the balance, so that by the late 1990s most expect gradual rather than convulsive political change for China as it moves into the post–Deng Xiaoping era. The sobering experience of the unexpected collapse of the Soviet empire, however, has weakened whatever confidence political scientists may have had in their ability to anticipate the evolution of even ostensibly well-entrenched regimes. Thus heavily qualified rather than firm predictions are the order of the day.[7] Although close consideration of China's internal politics falls outside the scope of this article, it must be acknowledged that analysis of an international system in which a more powerful China plays a leading role may well be taking for granted answers to questions about the country's political coherence that are at least as vexing as those about its economic and military capabilities.

Interpreting China's Power

Although an assessment of China's power might seem a methodologically straightforward exercise, even if it is one that faces serious practical problems, there are important differences in the meaning conveyed by references to China's economic and military might at the end of the twentieth century. Some discuss its power in absolute terms. Such descriptions provide a snapshot of the quantity or quality of current Chinese capabilities (e.g., standard of living, trade volume, military assets). Given the country's huge population, it has long been easy for numbers alone to suggest the importance of patterns of consumption, expenditure, or military personnel without much apparent need for further elaboration. But for analysts whose interest in China has been piqued

---

7. For competing perspectives, see Jack Goldstone, "The Coming Chinese Collapse," *Foreign Policy*, No. 99 (Summer 1995), pp. 35–53; Huang Yasheng, "Why China Will Not Collapse," *Foreign Policy*, No. 99 (Summer 1995), pp. 54–68; Arthur Waldron, "After Deng the Deluge: China's Next Leap Forward," *Foreign Affairs*, Vol. 74, No. 3 (September/October 1995), pp. 148–153; and Richard Baum, "China after Deng: Ten Scenarios in Search of Reality," *China Quarterly*, No. 145 (March 1996), pp. 153–175.

by recent developments, this sort of static, absolute measurement of capabilities is not of much use. For those interested in changes in China's power, relative assessments are essential.

Broadly speaking, there are two ways to distinguish work that discusses power in relative, as opposed to absolute, terms. The first is whether the analysis is national or international in scope. A national assessment is one in which the analyst draws comparisons between a state's current and past capabilities, the sort of developmental story often told in the area studies literature. An international assessment is one in which the analyst draws comparisons between one state's capabilities and those of other states, the sort of "great game" story often told in various genres of the international relations literature. A second broad distinction can be made within the realm of international assessments. They may entail either synchronic comparison of current capabilities relative to other states (depicting a current balance of power, for example), or diachronic comparison that traces changes in such relations over time (depicting the rise and fall of great powers).

ESTIMATED POWER

Those familiar with the literature on the Chinese "miracle" will recognize that, with a few important exceptions discussed below, it chronicles China's growing power by describing the country's current capabilities, implicitly suggesting their impressiveness, or more often by identifying significant changes relative to China's own past. These accounts set forth measures of what William Wohlforth has termed "estimated power," that is, looking at indicators that many believe are the building blocks of international influence.[8] The two most important sets of indicators in the Chinese case have been economic and military statistics.

Economic statistics that describe the size or growth rate of China's aggregate and per capita gross domestic product (GDP) as well as the expanding volume and changing composition of China's international trade provide a startling picture of transformation since 1978. During the 1980s, China's GDP doubled, and by the mid-1990s was doubling again.[9] Although per capita levels remain low, here too statistics reveal increases that only partly reflect the fundamental

---

8. William C. Wohlforth, "The Perception of Power: Russia in the Pre-1914 Balance," *World Politics,* Vol. 39, No. 3 (April 1987), pp. 353–381.

9. See Lieberthal, *Governing China,* p. 126; also "Statistical Communiqué of the State Statistical Bureau of the People's Republic of China," released annually each March and available in *Beijing Review.*

improvements in the standard of living of most of China's citizens—changes better captured by statistics that detail patterns of consumer behavior.[10] Over the same time span, China's trade volume ballooned from \$38.2 billion to more than \$250 billion.[11] Equally impressive, the composition of imports and exports shifted during the reform era as China went from being an exporter of raw materials and importer of foodstuffs to being an exporter of labor-intensive consumer goods and an importer of industrial products.[12] Moreover, a string of trade surpluses led to stunning increases in the country's foreign exchange reserves.[13] In short, statistics indicate a remarkable increase in the quantity of China's involvement in international trade and an equally remarkable change in the quality of this involvement, as the country was transformed from a reluctant, small-scale international economic actor into an eager, larger-scale participant playing the role other East Asian export-led growth economies had pioneered.

The focus on China's emerging military capabilities lagged behind the interest in economic performance. Certainly, those specializing in the Chinese military wrote about basic changes in force structure and doctrine that were initiated in the early 1980s,[14] but only in the early 1990s did a broader community begin to pay attention to the indicators suggesting quantitative increases and qualitative improvements in China's military capabilities.

---

10. See Dong Li and Alec M. Gallup, "In Search of the Chinese Consumer," *China Business Review,* Vol. 22, No. 5 (September 1995), p. 19, from NEXIS; "Diversifying Consumer Purchases in China," *COMLINE Daily News Electronics,* June 18, 1996, from NEXIS. Even so, a substantial fraction of the Chinese population remains mired in poverty. See Patrick E. Tyler, "In China's Outlands, Poorest Grow Poorer," *New York Times,* October 26, 1996, p. A1, from NEXIS.
11. See Lardy, *China in the World Economy,* p. 2; "China Confident in Fulfilling Foreign Trade Target for This Year," Xinhua News Agency, July 9, 1996, from NEXIS.
12. Lardy, *China in the World Economy,* pp. 29–33.
13. From roughly \$15 billion at the end of the 1980s, China's foreign exchange reserves reached \$84.3 billion by August 1996, ranking China fifth in the world. Its reserves topped \$100 billion by November 1996 and were headed for \$150 billion by mid-1997. See Nicholas R. Lardy, "The Future of China," *NBR Analysis,* Vol. 3, No. 3 (August 1992), p. 7; "China's Forex Reserves Not Too High—Official," Reuters, November 30, 1996, from Clari.world.asia.china.biz, ClariNet Communications (hereafter Clari.china.biz); "China Growth Seen at 9.8 Pct, Reserves at \$140 Bln," Reuters, June 3, 1997, Clari.china.biz.
14. See Paul H.B. Godwin, *The Chinese Defense Establishment: Continuity and Change in the 1980s* (Boulder, Colo.: Westview Press, 1983); Harlan Jencks, "'People's War under Modern Conditions': Wishful Thinking, National Suicide, or Effective Deterrent?" *China Quarterly,* No. 98 (June 1984); Paul H.B. Godwin, "The Chinese Defense Establishment in Transition: The Passing of a Revolutionary Army?" in A. Doak Barnett and Ralph N. Clough, eds., *Modernizing China* (Boulder, Colo.: Westview Press, 1986); Charles D. Lovejoy and Bruce W. Watson, eds., *China's Military Reforms* (Boulder, Colo.: Westview Press, 1986); Ellis Joffe, *The Chinese Army after Mao* (Cambridge, Mass.: Harvard University Press, 1987); and Larry M. Wortzell, ed., *China's Military Modernization* (New York: Greenwood Press, 1988).

ESTIMATING CHINA'S MILITARY POWER. Following a decade during which the People's Liberation Army's (PLA) budgets were kept relatively low as domestic economic development was accorded highest priority, beginning in 1989 China's government announced a succession of large peacetime increases in military spending.[15] Although part of the increase was, as Beijing claimed, designed to offset the effects of inflation and a decade of relative neglect, most analysts concluded that the official increase, combined with the many hidden sources of PLA revenue that comprise its funding base, reflected a serious effort to upgrade China's armed forces.[16]

Nevertheless, the significance of the increase in resources devoted to military modernization is sometimes exaggerated in estimates of the various unofficial revenues, such as earnings from China's international arms sales and PLA commercial enterprises. The annual cash value of China's arms exports in the first half of the 1990s actually "dropped significantly from levels posted in the late 1980s" (as high as $3.1 billion) to a level of roughly $1.2 billion.[17] Earnings from the PLA's commercial activities probably generate between $1.2 and $1.8 billion annually, more than the officially announced figure (less than $1 billion) but significantly lower than the $5–$20 billion used to posit total PLA budgets in excess of $50 billion.[18] Moreover, although a thriving military business complex provides hidden revenues, it also exacts hidden costs, spreading corruption within the military, diverting the PLA's attention from its principal

15. On the reduced PLA budgets of the 1980s, see Paul H.B. Godwin, "Force Projection and China's National Military Strategy," in C. Dennison Lane, Mark Weisenbloom, and Dimon Liu, eds., *Chinese Military Modernization* (New York: Kegan Paul International, 1996), p. 77.
16. Figures on China's military spending range from the low official report of about $8 billion to foreign estimates exceeding $100 billion. For discussion of the technical and practical complexities of calculating China's defense spending that result in such conflicting results, see "China's Military Expenditure," *The Military Balance 1995–1996* (London: International Institute for Strategic Studies [IISS] and Oxford University Press, 1995), pp. 270–275. See also David Shambaugh, "Growing Strong: China's Challenge to Asian Security," *Survival*, Vol. 36, No. 2 (Summer 1994), p. 54; Shaoguang Wang, "Estimating China's Defence Expenditure: Some Evidence from Chinese Sources," *China Quarterly*, No. 147 (September 1996), pp. 889–911; the estimates regularly published in the U.S. Arms Control and Disarmament Agency's *World Military Expenditures and Arms Transfers* (Washington, D.C.: U.S. Government Printing Office); and Stockholm International Peace Research Institute, *SIPRI Yearbook* (New York: Oxford University Press).
17. Bates Gill, "The Impact of Economic Reform upon Chinese Defense Production," in Lane, Weisenbloom, and Liu, *Chinese Military Modernization*, pp. 153–154; and John Frankenstein and Bates Gill, "Current and Future Challenges Facing Chinese Defence Industries," *China Quarterly*, No. 146 (June 1996), p. 426.
18. Tai Ming Cheung, "China's Entrepreneurial Army: The Structure, Activities, and Economic Returns of the Military Business Complex," in Lane, Weisenbloom, and Liu, *Chinese Military Modernization*, pp. 184–187. For the higher-end estimates, see Solomon M. Karmel, "The Chinese Military's Hunt for Profits," *Foreign Policy*, No. 107 (Summer 1997), p. 106; and Bernstein and Monroe, *The Coming Conflict with China*, p. 72.

responsibility of readying itself for possible armed conflict, and redirecting the focus of China's defense industry away from strategically important military, to economically profitable civilian, production.[19] And whatever the precise level of China's military spending during the late 1990s may be, so far at least, much of the inflation-adjusted annual increases of roughly 4 percent has gone to operations and maintenance, not weapons procurement.[20]

Improvements in the PLA's deployed capabilities, as well as increases in its budget, seemed to point in the same direction. China's military spending has supported a program of force modernization consistent with the shift in doctrine that began in the early 1980s when Beijing heavily discounted the likelihood of major, potentially nuclear, war with the hostile Soviet superpower. The new view, formally articulated by the Central Military Commission in 1985, stressed instead the need to prepare to fight limited, local wars, for which neither the People's War doctrine of protracted national resistance nor China's small nuclear arsenal would be very useful.[21] During the late 1980s, the PLA began to revamp itself in line with this change in strategic outlook. The most dramatic tangible results emerged only in the 1990s, however, when the breathtaking demonstration of advanced Western military technology in the Gulf War, and the intensification of regional disputes in locations beyond the PLA's largely continental range of operation, provided strong incentives for accelerating a modernization program that increasingly emphasized the importance of "limited war under high-technology conditions."[22] At the same time, the continuing strength of China's growing economy and the availability of advanced armaments from an economically strapped Russian military industry provided a golden opportunity to act on these incentives.[23] The result was the

---

19. See Cheung, "China's Entrepreneurial Army"; Arthur S. Ding, "China's Defence Finance: Content, Process, and Administration," *China Quarterly*, No. 146 (June 1996), pp. 428–442; and Gill, "The Impact of Economic Reform," pp. 150–152. On the difficulties posed by China's Soviet legacy of a well-insulated military-industrial complex, see Eric Arnett, "Military Technology: The Case of China," *SIPRI Yearbook 1995: Armaments, Disarmament, and International Security* (New York: Oxford University Press, 1995), pp. 359–386.

20. Michael D. Swaine, "Don't Demonize China; Rhetoric about Its Military Might Doesn't Reflect Reality," *Washington Post*, May 18, 1997, p. C1, from NEXIS. See also Frankenstein and Gill, "Current and Future Challenges," pp. 411, 420–421. A good case can be made for total budget estimates in the $30 billion range. See "China's Military Expenditure," pp. 270–275.

21. For an overview of these doctrinal shifts, see Nan Li, "The PLA's Evolving Warfighting Doctrine, Strategy, and Tactics, 1985–1995: A Chinese Perspective," *China Quarterly*, No. 146 (June 1996), pp. 443–463; and Paul H.B. Godwin, "From Continent to Periphery: PLA Doctrine, Strategy, and Capabilities Towards 2000," *China Quarterly*, No. 146 (June 1996), pp. 464–487.

22. Li, "The PLA's Evolving Warfighting Doctrine," p. 448; and Godwin, "From Continent to Periphery," pp. 472–473.

23. See Godwin, "Force Projection," pp. 79–81.

emergence of what have been labeled "pockets of excellence" within the ground, air, and naval forces of the PLA. The wave of modernization that began in the 1980s initially focused on the organization of elite units, so-called rapid-response or fist forces, that are better supplied and take the lead in using more advanced equipment to master the techniques of combined arms and joint service operations. Analysts estimated that by the mid-1990s, between 15 and 25 percent of the PLA (i.e., several hundred thousand troops) was comprised of such elite forces designed for airborne and marine assaults as well as ground attack missions.[24] There are questions, however, about just how much of an improvement this ostensibly dramatic reorganization represented. Two U.S. Defense Department Asia analysts have argued, for example, that widely publicized exercises demonstrating new weapons and techniques (such as the simultaneous deployment of forces from multiple services and their use of multiple categories of armaments) should not be mistaken for the existence of a well-trained force with the doctrinal understanding and command-and-control capabilities essential to genuinely effective combined arms operations. Enduring shortcomings in the PLA's ability to coordinate tactical air power with quickly evolving ground or sea operations also cast doubt on the actual capabilities of China's new elite units.[25]

China's military modernization has also entailed a determined effort at reequipping its forces. In this process, as in other aspects of the military's modernization, the immediate goal has been to create pockets of excellence; comprehensive modernization remains a distant goal to be achieved perhaps in the middle of the next century.[26] The most noteworthy aspect of the procurement effort has been the selective purchase of equipment from abroad for the PLA Air Force (PLAAF) and Navy (PLAN) to quickly compensate for the most serious shortcomings in China's military capabilities and, if possible, to catalyze the production of better indigenously produced equipment.[27] What

---

24. Chong-pin Lin, "The Power Projection Capabilities of the People's Liberation Army," in Lane, Weisenbloom, and Liu, *Chinese Military Modernization*, pp. 110–111; and Godwin, "From Continent to Periphery," pp. 469–470, 482.
25. Dennis J. Blasko, Philip T. Klapakis, and John F. Corbett Jr., "Training Tomorrow's PLA: A Mixed Bag of Tricks," *China Quarterly*, No. 146 (June 1996), pp. 488, 517; also Dennis Blasko, "Better Late than Never: Non-Equipment Aspects of PLA Ground Force Modernization," in Lane, Weisenbloom, and Liu, *Chinese Military Modernization*, pp. 125–143, especially pp. 130–135; David Shambaugh, "Growing Strong," p. 53; and Godwin, "Force Projection," pp. 83–86.
26. Godwin, "From Continent to Periphery," p. 484.
27. New equipment for the ground forces has apparently been assigned a lower priority than air, naval, and ballistic missile forces. See Blasko, "Better Late than Never," p. 126.

have been the key improvements in the PLA's equipment, and to what extent have these increased China's military power?

Air Forces. In the 1990s the PLAAF has begun to overhaul a fleet dominated by thousands of obsolete, first- and second-generation fighter aircraft based on 1950s' Soviet designs (the MiG 19–based J-6 and MiG 21–based J-7), with an eye to improving both the combat effectiveness and the range of forces that would have to play a key role in projecting China's power across the Taiwan Straits or in the South China Sea.[28] The long-standing weaknesses of China's aircraft industry limited Beijing's ability to rely on indigenous production of modern fighters and bombers, and even to improve existing platforms without foreign assistance. Plans in the 1980s to upgrade China's J-8 with modern avionics supplied by the United States were dealt a serious blow by the sanctions imposed following the Tiananmen Square incident in June 1989. Shortly afterward, however, the collapse of the Soviet Union and diplomatic fence-mending with Russia gave China the opportunity to obtain advanced aircraft from a new major supplier. Beijing purchased 24 Su-27 fighters (designated J-11 in China) in 1991, and another 22 in 1995, and in 1996 reached agreement to coproduce additional batches of Su-27s, totaling perhaps 200, possibly including the upgraded Su-30MK or Su-37 versions.[29] In addition to providing the PLAAF with its first truly modern (i.e., fourth-generation) fighter aircraft, Russia also supplied China with a package of advanced capabilities, including Sorbtsiya ECM jamming pods and AA-10 Alamo and AA-11 Archer infrared-guided air-to-air missiles with helmet-mounted sighting.[30] Complementing the infusion of Russian equipment was the apparently imminent

---

28. In September 1996 Taiwan's deputy chief of the General Staff estimated that only about one-quarter of China's air force was operational (Barbara Opall, "China Boosts Air Combat Capabilities," *Defense News,* September 2, 1996, p. 3, from NEXIS). There have also been reports that China had ceased operating its nuclear strategic bombers (Barbara Starr, "China Could 'Overwhelm' Regional Missile Shield," *Jane's Defence Weekly,* Vol. 27, No. 16 (April 23, 1997), p. 16, from NEXIS). Production of the most obsolete aircraft was sharply reduced during the 1980s (Frankenstein and Gill, "Current and Future Challenges," pp. 412–413). Other upgraded Chinese aircraft— the J-7MG, J-8II, and the FC-1 (being codeveloped with Pakistan)—may continue production mainly for the export market (Richard D. Fisher, "The Accelerating Modernization of China's Military," *Heritage Foundation Reports,* June 2, 1997, from NEXIS).
29. "Arms Exports to China Assessed, Moscow" Itar-Tass, April 22, 1997, from FBIS-TAC-97–112; and Fisher, "Accelerating Modernization."
30. See Fisher, "Accelerating Modernization"; and Richard D. Fisher, "China's Purchase of Russian Fighters: A Challenge to the U.S.," *Heritage Foundation Reports,* July 31, 1996, from NEXIS. The upgraded version of the Su-27, if produced, may be fitted with the even more advanced Russian AA-12 air-to-air missile (Robert Karniol, "China Is Poised to Buy Third Batch of Su-27s," *Jane's Defence Weekly,* Vol. 25, No. 17 [April 24, 1996], p. 10, from NEXIS).

production of the Chinese J-10 aircraft, whose design benefited from cooperation with Israel Aircraft Industries and its work on the canceled Lavi project.[31]

Compared with the fighters available to the PLAAF just a decade earlier, deployment of Su-27s and J-10s constitutes a dramatic upgrade in capabilities, and may yield a contingent of several hundred genuinely modern aircraft early in the next decade. But questions remain about whether this promise will be fulfilled. China's track record in aircraft manufacturing is poor, in part explaining its current turn to imports despite an enduring preference for self-reliance. It is also unclear whether China's military and defense industry has the ability to maintain the advanced equipment it is importing and coproducing.[32] At a minimum, such problems cast doubt on the PLAAF's ability to smoothly translate new equipment purchases into *operational* pockets of excellence, especially given that the latter will depend also on adequate training of personnel and the integration of better equipment with revised doctrine for its use.

In addition to procuring of well-equipped fighter aircraft, in the 1990s the PLAAF has sought to purchase both AWACS and in-flight refueling systems, which are essential if China is to project its increased power any significant distance beyond its coastline. Once again, the PLAAF has looked abroad to fill these gaps in its capabilities. In-flight refueling technology has reportedly been obtained from Israel, Iran, or Pakistan; and China has begun modifying aircraft to serve as tankers.[33] After protracted negotiations, China has also agreed to

---

31. Godwin, "From Continent to Periphery," p. 480; Fisher, "Accelerating Modernization," especially n. 60; and Chong-pin Lin, "The Military Balance in the Taiwan Straits," *China Quarterly*, No. 146 (June 1996), pp. 587–588. The U.S. Office of Naval Intelligence believes this multirole fighter "may be more maneuverable than the U.S. F/A-18 E/F" but with "less sophisticated radar and countermeasures." The J-10 is expected to be deployed in significant numbers by the middle of the next decade. See "China Develops Stealthy Multi-role Fighter," *Jane's Defence Weekly*, Vol. 27, No. 9 (March 5, 1997), p. 3, from NEXIS.

32. The enduring shortcomings of China's military industry are in part a legacy of the Maoist era practice of "copy production" and "reverse engineering" (Gill, "The Impact of Economic Reform," pp. 147–149; see also Frankenstein and Gill, "Current and Future Challenges," pp. 414–415; and Lin, "Power Projection Capabilities," p. 107). On challenges facing China's indigenous combat aircraft industry, including quality control, limited funding, and competition from Russian imports, see Gill, "The Impact of Economic Reform," pp. 152–153. Such problems also raise doubts about China's ability to bring to fruition the XXJ advanced stealth multirole fighter program projected for sometime in the second decade of the twenty-first century (Joseph C. Anselmo, "China's Military Seeks Great Leap Forward," *Aviation Week and Space Technology*, Vol. 146, No. 20 [May 12, 1997, p. 68], from NEXIS).

33. See Lin, "The Military Balance in the Taiwan Straits," p. 587; Lin, "Power Projection Capabilities," p. 104; David Shambaugh "China's Military in Transition: Politics, Professionalism, Procurement, and Power Projection," *China Quarterly*, No. 146 (June 1996), p. 293; and Opall, "China Boosts Air Combat Capabilities." China is reported to have modified up to five of its H-6 bombers to refuel J-8II Finback fighters; U.S. intelligence reportedly estimates China may convert up to twenty

purchase an AWACS system from Israel that will marry its Falcon radar to the Russian Il-76, a platform with which the PLAAF already has experience.[34] Deployment of this equipment will provide China with the potential to sustain air operations throughout the most plausible theaters of engagement in East Asia. Mastering the techniques of in-flight refueling, however, involves much more than the construction of tankers and modification of aircraft.[35] Translating this potential into a usable capability will require substantial training of personnel and exercises sure to tax the PLA's capacity to maintain and repair this equipment.

Naval Forces. China's navy, too, is in the process of selective modernization focused on deploying vessels that have greater range, are more survivable, and carry more lethal weapons systems than the largely obsolete, vulnerable, coastal defense force that China possessed at the end of the Cold War.[36] Shortcomings in China's shipbuilding industry, as in its aircraft industry, help explain the extent to which the current naval modernization effort has depended on the import of foreign equipment and technology while attempts are made to combine it with or adapt it for indigenous production.

By the mid-1990s key improvements in PLAN equipment included the upgrading of two of China's seventeen aging Luda-class destroyers and its twenty-nine Jianghu-class frigates,[37] along with the introduction of at least two new Luhu-class destroyers and five Jiangwei-class frigates that incorporate significant elements of Western propulsion and weapons technologies.[38] Perhaps most significant was the announcement in December 1996 that China

H-6 bombers into air-to-air refueling aircraft; China's SU-27s are not modified for air-to-air refueling, but this capability could be acquired later. Fisher, "China's Purchase of Russian Fighters."

34. "Russia and Israel to Supply Airborne Radar to China," *BBC Summary of World Broadcasts*, May 20, 1997, from NEXIS. Between one and four such AWACS systems, at $250 million apiece, may be assembled for China by Elta, an Israel Aircraft Industry subsidiary ("AWACS for China," *Defense and Foreign Affairs Strategic Policy*, March 1997, p. 19, from NEXIS).

35. See Shambaugh, "China's Military in Transition," p. 295; Godwin, "From Continent to Periphery," pp. 478–480; and Godwin, "Force Projection," p. 86.

36. The goal is to transform the PLA Navy, in successive steps, from a white-water, to a green-water, to a blue-water force. On China's naval plans, see John Downing, "China's Evolving Maritime Strategy," Parts 1 and 2, *Jane's Intelligence Review*, Vol. 8, No. 2 (March 1, 1996), pp. 129–133, and Vol. 8, No. 4 (April 1, 1996), pp. 186–191; "PLANs for the Predictable Future," *Jane's Intelligence Review*, Vol. 3, No. 5 (May 1, 1996), p. 6, from NEXIS.

37. Upgrades included "C901 SSM launchers, improved missile and gun fire control electronics suites, a towed variable-depth sonar system and improved torpedo capabilities...[and] facilities for...Z-9a helicopters." (Godwin, "From Continent to Periphery," pp. 474–475); see also Frankenstein and Gill, "Current and Future Challenges," pp. 416–417.

38. These include U.S.-built General Electric turbine engines, French Crotale surface-to-air missile systems, C801 ship-to-ship missiles based on the French Exocet, and improved antisubmarine capabilities based on Italian torpedo launchers and torpedoes along with French Dauphin-2-based Z-9A helicopters. (Godwin, "From Continent to Periphery," pp. 474–475.)

would purchase from Russia two Sovremennyi-class guided missile destroyers, a larger, less vulnerable, and much more lethal ship than any in the PLAN's inventory.[39] The PLAN also improved its ability to sustain its forces at sea by deploying additional, more sophisticated oilers and storeships (especially the Dayun-class for vertical replenishment); furthermore, it enhanced its ability to transport troops and undertake amphibious landings with the addition of the Qiongsha attack transport and a small number of newer Yukan- and Yuting-class LSTs (landing ships, tank).[40]

Complementing its improvement in the surface fleet, China also has begun to replace its obsolete and noisy Romeo-class conventional and unreliable Han-class nuclear attack submarines. China has imported from Russia four (and reportedly plans to purchase as many as sixteen more) Kilo-class conventional submarines (two of which are the advanced "project 636" version rated by the U.S. Office of Naval Intelligence as comparably quiet to the Los Angeles–class SSN). Beijing has also begun production of its indigenous Song-class vessel (not yet as quiet as the most advanced Kilos) and continues development of a replacement for the troubled Han-class SSN, although it appears this may take at least another decade.[41]

As a result of these efforts, China's navy is beginning to deploy a range of modern forces that will enable it to undertake operations in regional conflicts at ever greater distances from the mainland. Again, issues of training and maintenance will partly determine whether this potential is realized. Moreover, even within these naval pockets of excellence, the surface fleet is, with few exceptions, still fitted with inadequate air and missile defense systems.[42] This vulnerability not only constrains the PLAN's ability to project power, but also helps explain the apparent delay, if not cancellation, of China's plans to purchase or construct an aircraft carrier.[43] The enormous investment (procure-

---

39. Carrying "a balanced suite of weapons: 8 SS-N-22 anti-ship missiles [additional quantities of these 'Sunburn' missiles may be sold to China for retrofitting on other destroyers and frigates], 44 surface-to-air missiles, and one anti-submarine warfare helicopter, plus advanced radar, sonar, and systems to defend against incoming missiles and torpedoes," the Sovremennyi-class destroyers allegedly can disable aircraft carriers and other surface ships, even those armed with advanced Aegis systems (Fisher, "Accelerating Modernization"; "Russian-Chinese Military-Technical Cooperation Background," Itar-Tass, April 22, 1997; and Anselmo, "China's Military Seeks Great Leap Forward.")
40. Godwin, "From Continent to Periphery," pp. 475–476.
41. Ibid., pp. 476–478.
42. Godwin, "Force Projection," pp. 87–88.
43. If China decides to build an aircraft carrier in the near future, it would most likely be in the 40,000-ton range and serve mainly as a project for mastering construction techniques and for training exercises in preparation for a genuine capability several decades into the next century. See Godwin, "From Continent to Periphery," p. 480; and Godwin, "Force Projection," pp. 96–97.

ment, maintenance costs, and personnel training) required to deploy an aircraft carrier battle group, which must include surface and submarine forces for the carrier's protection, makes it an unattractive proposition unless its prospects for survival are good. To the extent that China's land-based air force, by combining longer-range aircraft, in-flight refueling, and AWACS-assisted command and control, is able to extend the range of its operations and deliver its punch in the regions most important to China for the foreseeable future, the opportunity costs of rushing to deploy a potentially vulnerable carrier are likely to appear forbiddingly high.

Ballistic Missile Forces. In addition to modernizing its air and naval forces, during the 1990s China continued to invest in a well-established, comprehensive ballistic missile program that has been given preference by Beijing since the mid-1950s. With an eye to improving survivability and target coverage, and foiling anticipated missile defenses, China has pushed ahead with development of a second generation of long-range nuclear-armed intercontinental ballistic missiles (DF-31, DF-41) and a submarine-launched ballistic missile (JL-2) that will most likely be fitted with multiple warhead packages; these programs, however, are unlikely to bear fruit before the end of the century.[44] Until then, China's intercontinental nuclear ballistic missile arsenal will be limited to its five to fifteen first-generation, liquid-fueled ICBMs (the DF-5). The key area of growth in China's missile capabilities during the 1990s has instead been the deployment of increasing numbers of medium- and shorter-range, mobile, conventional (or dual-capable) ballistic missiles (DF-11, DF-15, DF-21). Beyond increasing the numbers of such missiles available for regional contingencies, Beijing has continued its efforts to improve their accuracy by incorporating data from global-positioning satellite systems and providing warheads with terminal guidance packages (with obvious potential applications to future intercontinental-range systems). China may also be pursuing advanced guidance and ramjet technologies from Russia and Israel in order to develop long-range, supersonic cruise missiles.[45] And despite Beijing's vocifer-

44. See Alastair I. Johnston, "Prospects for Chinese Nuclear Force Modernization: Limited Deterrence versus Multilateral Arms Control," *China Quarterly*, No. 146 (June 1996), pp. 548–576, especially pp. 562–563; also Johnston, "China's New 'Old Thinking'"; James A. Lamson and Wyn Q. Bowen, "'One Arrow, Three Stars': China's MIRV Programme," Parts 1 and 2, *Jane's Intelligence Review*, Vol. 9, No. 5 (May 1, 1997), p. 216ff., and Vol. 9, No. 6 (June 1, 1997), p. 266ff., from NEXIS; Godwin, "From Continent to Periphery," pp. 482–484; Wyn Q. Bowen and Stanley Shephard, "Living under the Red Missile Threat," *Jane's Intelligence Review*, Vol. 8, No. 12 (December 1, 1996), p. 560ff., from NEXIS.
45. See Bowen and Shephard, "Living under the Red Missile Threat"; and Fisher, "Accelerating Modernization."

ous opposition to the deployment of ballistic missile defenses by its prospective adversaries, China has purchased 100 Russian SA-10 surface-to-air missiles comparable to early versions of the U.S. Patriot system, and may be attempting to combine the SA-10 technology with that derived from a Patriot missile allegedly purchased from Israel to synthesize an improved HQ-9 SAM system.[46]

In short, compared with the legacy of the Maoist era, by the mid-1990s China's military profile—like its economic profile—was being dramatically transformed. But the importance of such a national assessment for international security is not self-evident. Most of the concern among policymakers outside China, and most of the interest among scholars (reflected in the various theoretical perspectives presented below) depends on the significance of changes in capabilities in relative terms that entail international comparisons, especially those that track changes in relative standing over time. How are China's military capabilities changing relative to those of its potential adversaries? In this respect, the PLA's power has also grown, although to an extent that continues to be significantly limited by ongoing improvement in the forces deployed by other regional actors.

Military Balances. Unlike the situation during the Cold War, the most important contingencies for the use of China's military no longer entail ground engagements on the Asian mainland[47] (aside from the possible use of the PLA as a last-ditch internal security prop for the communist regime[48]). Today's active disputes and most plausible confrontations lie across the sea (in decreasing order of importance) with the rival regime on Taiwan, with Southeast Asian states making claims in the Spratly Islands, and with Japan over the disputed Diaoyu (Senkaku) Islands. As such, China's military power should be measured against four prospective adversaries—the ASEAN (Association of Southeast Asian Nations) states with competing claims in the South China Sea; Taiwan; Japan; and because it has the ability and sometimes the interest to intervene in the region, the United States. A full evaluation of the rapidly

---

46. Ibid. China is also deploying Russian built S-300 air defense systems around Beijing and at the Wuhu and Suixi air bases for the PLAAF's Su-27s (Opall, "China Boosts Air Combat Capabilities").

47. This is good given that ground-force modernization has been modest at best. See Blasko, "Better Late than Never," p. 141.

48. China's People's Armed Police (PAP) have been revamped to be better able to play this role in any future domestic crisis, though as long as it remains willing, the PLA (especially its crack fist-, or rapid-reaction, units) is today probably more able than ever to ensure internal security. On the roles of the PLA and PAP, see Tai Ming Cheung, "The People's Armed Police: First Line of Defence," *China Quarterly*, No. 146 (June 1996), pp. 525–547.

changing dimensions of each of these military balances is not the purpose of this article. Nevertheless, some important general points can briefly be set forth.

The 1990s' phase of China's military modernization is lifting the PLA from what has been a position of near impotence against all but the smallest of its regional adversaries. The PLAAF's contingent of better-armed modern fighter aircraft, when combined with the range-extending effects of in-flight refueling and AWACS capabilities, together with the PLAN's strengthened contingent of missile destroyers, frigates, and submarines for which the PLAAF can provide a measure of air cover, should at least ensure China an edge over any individual ASEAN state it might face in the South China Sea. That said, many of the ASEAN states, although possessing forces smaller than those China will be able to deploy, have more experience with their modern air and naval equipment, and almost all have been augmenting their capabilities in response to China's programs. In this effort, the United States is usually the preferred source for prized modern fighters (especially F-16s and F-18s); but like China, the ASEAN states can now also tap the Russian (or French) market, as some already have.[49] More important, if China were to confront not isolated ASEAN adversaries, but a coalition, this would diminish the prospects for the decisive air superiority necessary for it to project naval power in the region. Given its quantitative edge (when one includes less-modern equipment), a determined China could most likely still prevail, but at a terrific cost—both military and diplomatic. As in most of the other plausible contingencies discussed here, without a high probability of success, it is unlikely that the PLA would be eager to put at risk its best new equipment—the few gems in its pockets of excellence—needed to ensure victory.[50]

---

49. See Michael G. Gallagher, "China's Illusory Threat to the South China Sea"; Godwin, "Force Projection," pp. 78, 90–91; Godwin, "From Continent to Periphery," p. 485; and Michael Klare, "East Asia's Militaries Muscle Up: East Asia's New-found Riches Are Purchasing the Latest High-tech Weapons," *Bulletin of the Atomic Scientists*, Vol. 53, No. 1 (January 11, 1997), p. 56ff, from NEXIS. See also "Philippines Studying Russian Offer of MiG-29s," Reuters, March 7, 1997, from NEXIS; "Russia Offers Its Jetfighters to Indonesia," UPI, June 9, 1997, Clari.tw.defense (hereafter Clari.defense), from ClariNet Communications. ASEAN air forces now include the following modern combat aircraft: Malaysia (8 F/A-18C/D, 18 MiG-29s); Thailand (36 F-16A); Singapore (17 F-16A); Indonesia (11 F-16A); and Vietnam (3 Su-27, 3 more on order).
50. See Gill, "The Impact of Economic Reform," pp. 160–161. China could of course find itself facing a coalition that included not just ASEAN members but also forces from Australia, New Zealand, and Britain who conduct exercises with Singapore and Malaysia under the Five-Power Defense Arrangement (Godwin, "Force Projection," p. 91). Intervention by extraregional powers, especially the United States and Japan, would doom Chinese operations in the South China Sea. See Lin, "Power Projection Capabilities," pp. 113–114.

Against Taiwan the effects of Beijing's military buildup have in large measure been offset by Taipei's efforts geared specifically to dealing with a potential PLA threat. During the 1990s, as China was selectively modernizing its air, naval, and ballistic missile forces in ways that make long-range operations in and across the Taiwan Straits technically more feasible, Taiwan substantially upgraded its military capabilities. While the PLAAF is deploying Su-27s, Taiwan is deploying a fleet of modern fighters comprised of 150 F-16s, 60 Mirage 2000s, and 130 domestically produced F-16–based Indigenous Defense Fighters supported by E2C Hawkeye AWACS. While the PLAN is deploying more sophisticated destroyers, frigates, and submarines, Taiwan is upgrading its surface fleet by adding at least 20 modern U.S., French, and indigenously produced frigates and improving its ship- and land-based antisubmarine warfare capabilities.[51] And while China's Second Artillery is deploying more numerous and more sophisticated missiles that place the entire theater within range, Taiwan is deploying ever more sophisticated, if inevitably imperfect, ballistic missile defenses.[52]

The point is not that Taiwan would easily be able to defeat an increasingly modern PLA assault. The point instead is that Taiwan's sustained military modernization will make it very costly for the PLA to prevail, even if others (most important the United States) choose not to intervene, something about which China cannot be certain. Beijing's political motivation to ensure Taiwan's reunification with the mainland may lead it to opt for military action, even if it means risking a substantial fraction of its best forces. But with the competitive modernization of forces on both sides of the Taiwan Straits, the direct military option is not becoming much more attractive than it was in the recent past. Despite increases in the PLA's absolute power, the smaller shifts in its power relative to Taiwan mean that the more plausible approaches remain for Beijing to rely on continued diplomatic and economic pressure, and when that

---

51. See Godwin, "From Continent to Periphery," p. 485, Godwin, "Force Projection," pp. 92–94; Lin, "The Military Balance in the Taiwan Straits," pp. 580–583; and John W. Garver, "The PLA as an Interest Group in Chinese Foreign Policy," in Lane, Weisenbloom, and Liu, *Chinese Military Modernization,* pp. 260–261. Taiwan is taking delivery of the Mirage 2000–5 and a version of the F-16A/B, called the F-16 MLU (midlife upgrade), reportedly "nearly as good" as the F-16 D/C. See "Taiwan to Take Delivery of Five More U.S. F-16s," *Deutsche Presse-Agentur,* May 15, 1997, from NEXIS.
52. They include post–Gulf War upgraded U.S. Patriot systems and the indigenously developed and improved Tiangong SAM systems. See Bowen and Shepherd, "Living under the Red Missile Threat"; and Lin, "The Military Balance in the Taiwan Straits," p. 579.

seems to be failing to use limited, indirect military action in attempts to deter or compel the regime in Taipei, as was evident in 1995 and 1996.[53] China's other potential adversaries that provide a benchmark for measuring the significance of the PLA's improved military capabilities are Japan and the United States. Either or both might confront China if Beijing's actions were judged a threat to their vital interests in the region. Japan's concerns center not only on the territorial dispute over the Diaoyu Islands, but also on the potential threat to shipping lanes in East and Southeast Asia (including the Malacca and Taiwan Straits), and more generally on the consequences of possible Chinese regional hegemony. Other than the Diaoyu Islands dispute, U.S. interests are similar to Japan's and can be broadly defined as preserving regional stability, ensuring freedom of the seas, and preventing the use of force to alter the status quo. When Japan or the United States provides the benchmark for assessing the PLA, the balance of capabilities is simple and clear. Compared with the current, and especially anticipated future, modernized air and naval forces of Japan or the United States, the PLA will remain outclassed well into the next century even if China's current round of military modernization proceeds smoothly.[54] Nevertheless, this direct force comparison may not be all that matters. Although China's military modernization is not increasing the PLA's power to the point where it can expect to prevail against better-equipped Japanese and American forces, it is providing China with the power to make it much more dangerous for either state to intervene in regional disputes. The deployment of well-armed Su-27s, Sovremennyi destroyers, and Kilo-class submarines will not turn the waters of East Asia into a Chinese lake, but it will mean that even the United States can no longer expect easily (i.e., at minimal cost) to dominate in limited conventional military engagements. Combined with China's improving ballistic missile forces, the ability to preclude swift, decisive outside intervention, and to require its most potent adversary to run

---

53. See Lin, "The Military Balance in the Taiwan Straits," pp. 591–595; and Lin, "Power Projection Capabilities," pp. 111–113.
54. Japan continues its own program of selective modernization and will be adding about 130 F-2 (formerly FSX) fighters to an air force that already possess 180 F-15Cs. See Chen Lineng, "The Japanese Self-Defense Forces Are Marching toward the 21st Century," *Guoji Zhanwang* (*World Outlook*), No. 2 (February 8, 1996), pp. 18–20, FBIS-CHI-96-085, May 1, 1996; and Swaine, "Don't Demonize China." For an account of the awesome capabilities at the disposal of the key units for American force projection in East Asia, the U.S. Pacific Fleet, especially its Seventh Fleet, see the weekly update of its web pages, http://www.cpf.navy.mil/pages/factfile/cpftoday.htm and http://www.c7f.yokipc.navy.mil/index.html. For a review that questions the durability of the U.S. military advantage, see Fisher, "China's Purchase of Russian Fighters."

the risk of nuclear escalation, may be all that Beijing needs in confrontations over interests it deems vital.

In sum, the increases in China's actual capabilities, compared with its own recent past and relative to others, are noteworthy, but remain limited in important respects. The recent surge in interest and concern with China's allegedly rapid rise appears to be driven more by changes in what Wohlforth labels "perceived" power than the more modest changes in "estimated" power.

PERCEIVED POWER

Four factors have helped create the perception that China is in the process of a *swift* rise to great power status—historical context, the low starting point for the current period of economic and military growth, the systems in which military modernization has been concentrated, and catalytic events.

First, history has established an expectation that China is a country in some sense deserving of a place in the ranks of the great powers. Part of this expectation is rooted in China's role as a regional hegemon during much of its imperial history. Another part is rooted in the anointing of China as at least a candidate great power by other states during the mid-twentieth century. During World War II, mainly at the behest of the Roosevelt administration, China was initially included as one of the big four allies to participate in summits planning grand strategy to defeat the Axis. The divergence between this lofty formal status and the reality of China's power limitations clearly bothered Britain's prime minister, Winston Churchill, and ultimately China's wartime great power role lost most of its substance.[55] Yet after the war the fiction of the Republic of China's (ROC) government-in-exile as a great power endured in the symbolic form of its seat allegedly representing China on the UN Security Council—again a status based on U.S. support rather than tangible capabilities. And when the People's Republic of China replaced the ROC as the internationally recognized representative of China in the early 1970s, the government in Beijing was once more anointed a great power in the emerging international system, again by a U.S. government that believed its strategic interests were served by bolstering China's status, the country's deficient economy and obso-

---

55. Churchill was shocked at the Americans' inflated perception of China. See Herbert Feis, *The China Tangle* (Princeton, N.J.: Princeton University Press, 1972), p. 11. Allied policy eventually adjusted to the reality of the limited military clout of Chiang Kai-shek's China. China was simply to be discouraged from seeking a separate peace with Japan in order to ensure that large numbers of Japanese troops would remain tied down in operations on the Chinese mainland.

lete military equipment notwithstanding.[56] As a consequence of history, then, "great power China" had become what cognitive theorists term "an unfilled concept," and one with deep roots; analysts were prepared to accept evidence that the promise was at last being realized.[57] In such circumstances, there may be an inclination to exaggerate the significance of limited data—whether economic statistics or military deployments.

A second influence on perceptions has been the low level from which China's economic and military growth began.[58] China's recent economic expansion has been impressive, but the perception of breathtaking change has also been enhanced in part because the opening of the country in 1979 enabled observers to pierce the veil of Maoist propaganda and grasp just how impoverished China had remained during the first thirty years of communist rule. As the Dengist reformers more successfully tapped what many believed were China's inherent economic strengths, it was easy to conclude that this was the beginning of a period during which the country's potential would be realized, rather than a brief surge resulting from extraordinary policies and efforts that could not be sustained. Confidence in China's growth trajectory was bolstered when the CCP not only succeeded in riding out the storm of international outrage that followed its suppression of domestic protests in 1989 and survived the collapse of communism in the former Soviet empire, but also accelerated its promotion of a market-based economy and posted the high growth rates and expanding trade volumes that have drawn attention in the mid-1990s.

Although many had been unaware of China's true economic conditions during the Maoist era, few harbored illusions about the backward state of China's armed forces before Deng's reforms. The dismal state of the PLA in the late 1970s, however, merely provided a stark background that highlighted the significance of each initiative in the current round of military modernization. In addition, unlike the Soviet Union, which had tapped a huge proportion of its stagnant economy in a desperate attempt to stay in the game of superpower military competition, the relatively small fraction of national

56. See Kenneth N. Waltz, *Theory of International Politics* (Menlo Park, Calif.: Addison-Wesley, 1979), p. 130. Ironically, perhaps, China's role in the event of a war with the Soviets would—as in World War II—almost certainly have been to tie down the enemy's forces on a second front.
57. On unfilled concepts, see Robert Jervis, "Hypotheses on Misperception," *World Politics*, Vol. 20, No. 3 (April 1968), pp. 454–479. The opening subheading ("This Time It Is Real") for Nicholas Kristof's *Foreign Affairs* article reflects this long-standing expectation. In "The Rise of China," *Foreign Affairs*, Vol. 72, No. 5 (November/December 1993), pp. 59–74.
58. See Wohlforth, "The Perception of Power," p. 374.

wealth devoted to China's PLA (even when the highest estimates for budgets are used), together with robust economic expansion, suggested the sustainability of its military modernization at a pace that would narrow the gap between China and the world's leading powers.[59] That this military growth spurt became most pronounced in the 1990s, when other major powers were implementing post–Cold War defense reductions, only enhanced its apparent significance.

A third factor affecting perceptions is the extent to which military modernization has focused on the development of capabilities that would empower China to play a more active international role.[60] Beijing's efforts to modernize ballistic missiles and strategic nuclear warheads, and to fashion a usable power projection capability by reorganizing and reequipping its air and naval forces, suggest that the PLA is not being developed merely to fulfill the minimal requirements of dissuasion by territorial self-defense and deterrence. Instead, although realization of its goals might be years away, the military investment program appears to target the sorts of capabilities that would enable China to play the role of an authentic great power.

Fourth, two catalytic events transformed perceptions of China's international standing and likely future role. First, the International Monetary Fund's (IMF) decision in 1993 to switch its method of calculating national wealth from one based on currency exchange rates to one that relied on purchasing power parity (PPP) resulted in a flurry of reports that China's GDP was actually four times larger than previously thought. The announcement ostensibly portrayed a breathtaking change in the world economic order as it was, and would be. China immediately advanced from having the tenth largest GDP in the world to having the third, putting it narrowly behind Japan and on a course to surpass the United States early in the twenty-first century.[61] Nothing had actually changed overnight, of course. Indeed, the higher figures associated with the PPP method had been put forward in less visible publications prior to the IMF announcement.[62] And for those China experts and businesspeople

---

59. For doubts about the ease of tapping this potential, see Gill, "The Impact of Economic Reform"; and Arnett, "Military Technology: The Case of China."
60. For similar influences on perceptions of Russia's power prior to World War I, see Wohlforth, "The Perception of Power," p. 374.
61. Steven Greenhouse, "New Tally of World's Economies Catapults China into Third Place," *New York Times*, May 20, 1993, p. A1, from NEXIS. "Revised Weights for the *World Economic Outlook*; Annex 4," *World Economic Outlook* (May 1993), International Monetary Fund, Information Access Company, from NEXIS.
62. See "U.S. Report Projects China's Economic Rise in 2010," *Xinhua General Overseas News Service*, January 12, 1988, from NEXIS.

familiar with the situation on the ground, the reports merely corrected what had long been understood to be the old statistics' gross understatement of the economic vitality of the large areas of China that had benefited from the reforms.[63] But for others, these reports were a wake-up call that helped crystallize the view of China as East Asia's newest economic dynamo.

The second catalytic event, actually a series of events, was the reactivation of the dispute over Taiwan in 1995 and especially 1996. Fearful of permitting Taiwan's leadership to pursue a more independent international role, Beijing responded to what it saw as dangerous U.S. complicity in this effort by abandoning the fruitful cross-straits diplomacy of the early 1990s. Instead, China tried to signal relevant audiences in both Washington and Taipei (party leaders and the voters in parliamentary and presidential elections) that it would not tolerate a drift toward, let alone an outright declaration of, independence. Between the summer of 1995 and the spring of 1996, Beijing deployed ground, air, and naval forces to the region, staged military exercises including the repeated launching of missiles that disrupted the sea-lanes around the trade-dependent island, and floated a thinly veiled threat about the risk of nuclear escalation that could touch the American homeland should the United States become directly involved in any cross-straits confrontation.[64] These measures crystallized the perception that China was prepared to use whatever capabilities it had to pursue its international interests.[65] Although sober defense analysts noted that Beijing lacked a military capability to do more than inflict punitive damage on the Taiwanese and frighten their trading

---

63. See Jim Rohwer, "Rapid Growth Could Make China World's Largest Economy by 2012," *South China Morning Post*, November 28, 1992, p. 1, from NEXIS; and William H. Overholt, *The Rise of China* (New York: W.W. Norton, 1993). For competing estimates of Chinese GDP and an attempt to evaluate their merits, see Lardy, *China in the World Economy*, pp. 14–18. Although most analysts prefer the PPP calculations to those based on exchange rates, the partial nature of price reform and the persistence of a black market in China introduce distortions in prices that weaken confidence in the figures upon which PPP calculations must rely. To the extent that economic reforms eliminate the legacy of dual-track (market-based and subsidized or state-regulated) pricing, PPP estimates should become more reliable. I thank Mark Groombridge for explaining this complication to me.

64. See Patrick E. Tyler, "Beijing Steps Up Military Pressure on Taiwan Leader," *New York Times*, March 7, 1996, pp. A1, 10; Jim Wolf, "China Aides Gave U.S. Nuclear Warning, Official Says," Reuters, March 17, 1996, clari.tw.nuclear, ClariNet Communications (hereafter Clari.nuclear); and Patrick E. Tyler, "As China Threatens Taiwan, It Makes Sure U.S. Listens," *New York Times*, January 24, 1996, p. A3.

65. See "Testimony, March 20, 1996, Floyd D. Spence, Chairman House National Security, Security Challenges: China," *Federal Document Clearing House, Congressional Testimony*, Federal Document Clearing House, from NEXIS; also David Morgan, "Gingrich Calls for U.S. Defense against Nuclear Attack," Reuters, January 27, 1996, Clari.nuclear.

partners, these actions seemed to confirm concerns about the PLA's modernization program.[66] Prior to the mid-1990s, some in the foreign policy elite had been talking about China replacing the former Soviet Union as the United States' principal great power security concern and military planning contingency. But the Taiwan Straits confrontation of 1995–96 appeared almost certain to be a watershed in shifting the perception of a wider audience.[67] Its significance lies not in capabilities displayed (if anything, the episode confirmed the relatively disadvantaged state of China's current forces[68]), but rather in catalyzing the belief that China's first steps in modernizing its military should be interpreted as foreshadowing a trajectory of growth with consequences that had not been fully appreciated.

CHINA'S SELF-PERCEPTION

How do these changes in the way the outside world views China fit with China's self-perception? Some inferences can be drawn from circumstantial evidence or official policies and statements, though it must be conceded that these may not necessarily reflect actual beliefs. With this limitation in mind, I offer the following brief sketch, because it is relevant to the theoretical arguments presented in the next section.

As China's economy has expanded and become more integrated with global trade and investment, Beijing's view of its international position has changed. At the beginning of its "opening to the outside," China played the role mainly of economic suitor, attempting to entice foreign investors with preferential tax arrangements; a large supply of relatively inexpensive, submissive labor; and the ever-present lure of a potentially huge domestic market demand for consumer goods. By the mid-1990s, Beijing appeared to be moving beyond seeing itself in the role of suitor to seeing itself as an emerging major player with the strength to negotiate more aggressively, although not to stipulate, the terms on which it will participate in the international economy. Beijing's hard bar-

---

66. See Jeffrey Parker, "China Taiwan Drills 'Proof' of PLA Modernization," Reuters, March 19, 1996, Clari.world.asia.china, ClariNet Communications (hereafter Clari.china); "China Claims Readiness for 'Future War,'" UPI, March 18, 1996, Clari.china; and Gerald Segal, "The Taiwanese Crisis: What Next?" *Jane's Intelligence Review*, June 1996, pp. 269–270.
67. Debate began to focus mainly on a choice between "containment" and "engagement." See "Containing China," *The Economist*, July 29, 1995, pp. 11, 12; David Shambaugh, "Containment or Engagement of China: Calculating Beijing's Responses," *International Security*, Vol. 21, No. 2 (Fall 1996), p. 202; and Gerald Segal, "East Asia and the 'Constrainment' of China," *International Security*, Vol. 20, No. 4 (Spring 1996), pp. 107–135.
68. See Patrick E. Tyler, "Shadow over Asia: A Special Report; China's Military Stumbles Even as Its Power Grows," *New York Times*, December 3, 1996, p. A1.

gaining to gain admission to the World Trade Organization (WTO) as a charter member, without relinquishing its demand that it be granted the favorable status of a developing country, reflects China's attempt to become a force in the councils of economic power while retaining the advantages it has enjoyed during the early stages of its economic takeoff.[69] The CCP is also using China's emerging economic strength as a diplomatic tool. Beginning in June 1989, China was threatened with economic sanctions for various policy infractions, most notably the recurrent U.S. warnings that most-favored-nation trading status would be revoked if China's domestic and international behavior did not meet certain standards. By the mid-1990s, China was not only continuing to stand fast against such economic pressure, but despite prior claims that political disagreements should not complicate mutually beneficial economic exchange, Beijing was using its own economic leverage to signal unhappiness with U.S. complaints about China's exports of arms and dual-use technologies, and more important, anger at the Clinton administration's policy in the Taiwan Straits.[70] Beijing's behavior suggests that it sees itself in a transition from "object to subject" in the international economy, a shifting self-perception already visible in its activism within the Asian Pacific Economic Cooperation forum, one that will likely inform the role China plays once it joins the WTO and be fully completed when Beijing decides the time is ripe to join the Group of Seven.

In the military realm, China's view of its international role has also been changing. During the Cold War, China saw itself, correctly, as outclassed in a system dominated by rival superpowers. The CCP regime's goal was to ensure its security through varying combinations of self-reliant military preparation (to support a strategy of dissuasion by conventional deterrence while developing a nuclear alternative) and grudging dependence on the support of one superpower against the threat posed by the other.[71] China was essentially a

---

69. Despite suggestions after the revision in IMF calculations in 1993 that China should be invited to join the Group of Seven, Beijing has not shown interest, probably to avoid discrediting its claim to being a developing country entitled to preferential trading arrangements within the WTO. See Greenhouse, "New Tally," p. A1; and "China Bucks G-7 Membership, Wants WTO," UPI, July 2, 1996, Clari.china.

70. See Rajiv Chandra, "China: European, U.S. Aircraft Producers Compete for Boom Market," Inter Press Service, July 19, 1996, from NEXIS.

71. See Avery Goldstein, "Discounting the Free Ride: Alliances and Security in the Postwar World," *International Organization*, Vol. 49, No. 1 (Winter 1995), pp. 39–73. For an analysis that highlights the importance of influences other than the strategic triangle, see Robert S. Ross, *Negotiating Cooperation: The United States and China, 1969–1989* (Stanford, Calif.: Stanford University Press, 1995).

survivalist state, husbanding its limited capabilities and adjusting to the realities of its precarious position in a dangerous environment. Since the end of the Cold War, China has become a thriving state basically secure against foreign threats, and seeks to employ its growing capabilities to shape, and not just cope with, a fluid if still potentially dangerous environment. It is pursuing this goal using a two-pronged approach—cultivating independent economic and military strength, which reduces the need for dependence on powerful allies, and trying to prevent foreseeable international roadblocks on the path to greatness that Beijing plans to follow. The first task, self-strengthening, is easy to grasp, if hard to accomplish. The second, diplomacy, requires some clarification.

China's diplomatic challenge is to prevent three undesirable outcomes. First, China needs to prevent the United States from maintaining its de facto hegemony in East Asia, although a continued U.S. presence in some respects is desirable (especially as an anchor on Japan). Second, China needs to prevent Japan from becoming a full-fledged great power rival in East Asia. Third, China needs to prevent lesser regional actors (ASEAN states, Russia, and India) from siding with a rival United States or Japan in ways that could result in China's strategic encirclement. These three challenges are complicated by their own interconnections and partial incompatibility (e.g., a reduced U.S. role may encourage others to hedge their bets against China through patterns of alignment and armament) as well as their collective incompatibility with the other prong of China's strategy for becoming a great power. It is not easy for big states to repeat the virtuoso performance of Bismarck who at least temporarily postponed the more adverse reactions to growing German power. Early indications suggest that Beijing's leaders lack the subtle diplomatic skills that are needed for them to succeed in such an effort. During the 1990s, at least, China's determined pursuit of its interests in the South China Sea and the Taiwan Straits, and insistence on continuing its nuclear weapons testing through mid-1996 while others observed a moratorium, have married concerns about future Chinese capabilities with behavior that raises doubts about its intentions.

THE FIT BETWEEN ESTIMATED POWER, PERCEPTIONS, AND REALITY

A state's estimated power and perceived power—that is, the fit between various data usually thought to reflect the influence a state can bring to bear internationally and the beliefs of policymakers about such influence—are unlikely to coincide. The degree of disparity varies for reasons discussed with reference to the Chinese case above, but in addition is also likely to vary directly with the occurrence of events that provide for the hard test of actual competition in the international arena. Crises, militarized conflicts, and wars provide the most accurate guide to real power relations; the absence of such direct tests provides the greatest leeway for faulty estimates and distorted perceptions.[72]

Power tests, enabling China and others to assess the country's ability and determination to act on its foreign policy preferences, were relatively frequent during the first three decades of China's existence. The Korean War, crises in the Taiwan Straits in 1954–55 and 1958, war with India in 1962, border clashes with the Soviets in 1969, and the brief invasion of Vietnam in 1979, each clarified China's true capabilities relative to its adversaries at different points in time. After 1979, however, seventeen years passed before anything occurred that might qualify as a clarifying event testing China's ability to wield military power. Moreover, 1979 marked the beginning of the reform program that has triggered the claims of China's growing power. Thus, although analysts can agree that the reforms are producing a militarily stronger China, they can debate but not resolve the key question, "How much stronger?"[73]

The Taiwan Straits "military exercises" in 1996 provided some information. First, they signaled that Beijing was prepared, as it had repeatedly stated, to use force if necessary to ensure Taiwan's future political reunification with the mainland. Second, they demonstrated that the PLA had the ability to rely on missiles to coerce Taiwan, either through disrupting its economic lifeline of trade or through engaging in a campaign of strategic bombardment designed for punitive purposes. Such a capability can serve to frighten the Taiwanese in order to dissuade them from moving toward independence or, if dissuasion fails, could serve as the means to compel Taiwan to reverse steps that Beijing finds intolerable. Third, the military exercises revealed the enduring limits on the PLA's ability to actually project power, even in China's backyard. Analysts observing the exercises noted that the PLA could not muster the forces to launch an invasion of Taiwan that could succeed at reasonable cost, whether or not the United States chose to assist the island in its defense.[74] And the Clinton administration's naval maneuvers, together with guarded warnings to

---

72. Wohlforth, "The Perception of Power," pp. 377–378.
73. This situation parallels that which Wohlforth observed with regard to Russia just prior to World War I. See Wohlforth, "The Perception of Power," pp. 377–378. A similar uncertainty may have characterized France's position just prior to the 1870 war with Prussia. I thank Tom Christensen for pointing this out.
74. For a May 1996 U.S. Office of Naval Intelligence assessment, see Jim Wolf, "U.S. Navy Says China Rehearsed Taiwan Invasion," Reuters, November 11, 1996, Clari.china. See also Peter Slevin,"China Could Not Easily Overwhelm Taiwan, Analysts Agree," *Philadelphia Inquirer*, February 16, 1996, p. A4.

China, indicated that despite the ambiguity of U.S. policy toward Taiwan, Beijing should anticipate some sort of American military response with forces against which China still could not match up.[75]

China's Growing Power: Theoretical Expectations

China's power is clearly on the rise, although current estimates and perceptions may well be exaggerating the speed and extent of this change. Much of the attention paid to this trend is rooted in this concern that China's rise could make international politics more dangerous. In this section, I set aside disagreements about the rate of China's ascent and briefly consider what international relations theory has to say about its likely consequences, looking for early indicators about the usefulness of its insights. Simply put, most of the well-established strands of theory provide strong support for the expectation that as China's power grows in the coming decades, potentially dangerous international conflicts involving China will be more frequent. Some, however, suggest that the expected conflicts need not be uncontrollably intense, and one offers persuasive reasons to believe that the worst-case scenario of major power war will in any event remain implausible. I examine five theoretical perspectives distinguished by their emphasis on changing power relations, the significance of regime type, the role of international institutions, the effects of economic interdependence, and the strategic consequences of the nuclear revolution.

POWER PERSPECTIVES

Theories that explicitly focus on the dynamics of changing power relations in the international system provide some of the most troubling predictions. Two such theories—"hegemonic instability theory" and balance-of-power theory—emphasize the difficulties associated with the rise and fall of the system's dominant states. "Hegemonic instability theory" asserts that incongruity between a rising power's growing capabilities and its continued subordinate status in an international political system dominated by an erstwhile hegemon

---

75. Ambiguity dates to the 1972 Shanghai communiqué that provided a framework for Sino-American relations in the years following President Nixon's visit. Continuing ambiguity may have led China to underestimate the likelihood of a forceful U.S. reaction. See "Perry Criticized on Taiwan," Associated Press, February 28, 1996, Clari.china. After the March 1996 exercises, the United States more clearly signaled that it would respond to Beijing's future use of force against Taiwan. See Paul Basken, "Clinton: U.S. Wants 'Peaceful' One-China," UPI, July 23, 1996, Clari.china.

results in conflicts that are typically resolved by the fighting of major wars.[76] Although one does not yet see the intense sort of rivalry the theory expects to precede such a hegemonic showdown, recent conflicts between an ever-more capable China and the world's leading power, the United States, are consistent with the theory's logic. In the 1990s Beijing has more vociferously than ever criticized U.S. human rights policy as an effort to impose American values on the rest of the world, and U.S. international economic policy—especially on China's accession to the WTO—as an attempt to preserve American economic dominance.[77] In Washington, growing trade deficits with China have aroused concerns about allegedly unfair economic competition, while Beijing's military modernization and regional assertiveness have contributed to China becoming a prominent planning contingency for assessing the adequacy of the U.S. armed forces, especially its strategic nuclear arsenal.[78]

Balance-of-power theory, like hegemonic-instability theory, alerts one to the potentially disruptive effects of a rising China. The theory's core argument about balancing behavior leads to the expectation that China's increasing capabilities will trigger a reaction among those most concerned about the uses to which its power can be put.[79] As Stephen Walt has emphasized, great power in and of itself may not be deemed a threat requiring a response, but geography as well as the region's experience with China's dominance prior to the arrival of Western imperialism in the nineteenth century suggest it will be hard for Beijing to allay fears about how it may wield its growing capabilities. And there have already been rumblings of the sort that balance-of-power theory would predict, including reactive arms buildups in the region and the search for allies to compensate for limits in national strength (most notably, the still-tentative consultations among ASEAN states and the April 1996 reaffirmation of the U.S.-Japan security treaty).[80]

76. See Robert Gilpin, *War and Change in World Politics* (New York: Cambridge University Press, 1981); A.F.K. Organski and Jacek Kugler, *The War Ledger* (Chicago: University of Chicago Press, 1980); and Paul Kennedy, *The Rise and Fall of the Great Powers* (New York: Vintage, 1987).
77. See "China Slams U.S. Demands for WTO Entry," UPI, July 21, 1996, Clari.china.
78. See William W. Kaufmann, *Assessing the Base Force: How Much Is Too Much?* (Washington, D.C.: Brookings Institution, 1992); and Michael O'Hanlon, *Defense Planning for the Late 1990s* (Washington, D.C.: Brookings Institution, 1995).
79. On balancing, see Kenneth N. Waltz, *Theory of International Politics* and *Man, the State, and War: A Theoretical Analysis* (New York: Columbia University Press, 1959). See also Stephen M. Walt, *The Origins of Alliances* (Ithaca, N.Y.: Cornell University Press, 1988).
80. See President Clinton's speech to the Japanese Diet in "Clinton: Japan, U.S. Must Continue to Be Partners," *Daily Yomiuri*, April 19, 1996, from NEXIS; also "United States to Retain Strong Presence in Pacific: Christopher," Agence France-Presse, July 23, 1996, from NEXIS. See also Ball,

Balance-of-power theory alone does not indicate that the dynamics it explains must result in war. Some scholars, however, have argued that the polarity of an international system may determine whether or not it will be characterized by peaceful balancing.[81] What does their work suggest about the consequences of China's rise to prominence? First, it is important to note that it remains unclear whether post–Cold War East Asia, where China's influence will first be felt, will be a bipolar or multipolar arena. Bipolarity may return, anchored this time by the United States and China, with a militarily self-limited Japan and an internally weakened Eurocentric Russia playing marginal roles. If so, China's rise might pose the dangers identified as the risks of balancing under bipolarity, especially hostile overreaction. Early in the post–Cold War era, it would certainly appear that China and the United States rather quickly have come to focus on each other as the two key players in the game and to view each other's actions as potentially threatening. Each worries about allegedly shifting balances of military power and mutual perceptions of resolve. The early signs suggest that a bipolar East Asia would be dominated by recurrent Sino-American conflict.

What expectations prevail if China emerges instead as one of several great powers in a multipolar East Asia (including not just the United States but also a less restrained Japan, a resurgent Russia, perhaps even a more widely engaged India, and a newly risen Indonesia)? Unfortunately, as Aaron Friedberg has noted, some of the influences that reduce the dangers of multipolarity in post–Cold War Europe (e.g., consensus on the lessons from past war fighting, long experience with international diplomacy, the homogeneity of

---

"Arms and Affluence"; "SE Asians Arming Up to Protect Their Resources," Reuters, January 29, 1996, Clari.defense; Shambaugh, "Growing Strong," p. 44; "Singapore's Lee Warns of Growing Power of China," Reuters, February 24, 1996, Clari.china; and "Asian Reaction Swift to China's Maritime Expansion," Reuters, May 17, 1996, Clari.china.

81. For three articles that helped trigger the polarity debate, see Karl W. Deutsch and J. David Singer, "Multipolar Power Systems and International Stability"; Richard N. Rosecrance, "Bipolarity, Multipolarity, and the Future"; and Kenneth N. Waltz, "International Structure, National Force, and the Balance of World Power," all available in James N. Rosenau, ed., *International Politics and Foreign Policy*, 2d ed. (New York: Free Press, 1969). On the dangers inherent in bipolar and multipolar systems, see Thomas J. Christensen and Jack Snyder, "Chain Gangs and Passed Bucks: Predicting Alliance Patterns in Multipolarity," *International Organization*, Vol. 44, No. 2 (Spring 1990), pp. 137–168; also, Barry R. Posen, *The Sources of Military Doctrine: France, Britain, and Germany between the World Wars* (Ithaca, N.Y.: Cornell University Press, 1984); John J. Mearsheimer, "Back to the Future: Instability in Europe after the Cold War," *International Security*, Vol. 15, No. 1 (Summer 1990), pp. 5–56; Stephen Van Evera, "Primed for Peace: Europe after the Cold War," *International Security*, Vol. 15, No. 3 (Winter 1990/91), pp. 7–57; and Thomas J. Christensen, "Perceptions and Alliances in Europe, 1865–1940," *International Organization*, Vol. 51, No. 1 (Winter 1997), pp. 65–98.

domestic political orders) are not as evident in East Asia.[82] Moreover, military-strategic considerations that can sometimes offset the dangers of balancing under multipolarity may be lacking. It is not clear, for example, that a need for allies would exert much of an inhibiting effect on China, especially given that many scenarios for its disruptive behavior in the region would not require joint efforts.[83] Instead, because some of the most important flash points entail disputes over maritime claims to largely unpopulated islands or undeveloped surface and subsurface geological formations, belief in the feasibility of offensive military actions with minimal risks of escalation could tempt adventurous behavior if it is anticipated that multiple potential adversaries will pass the buck and accept a fait accompli—one of the classic risks under multipolarity. That such seemingly safe bets sometimes turn out to be disastrously incorrect predictions is one of the reasons to worry about the consequences of China's rise in a multipolar setting.

Theoretical discussion of the security dilemma, closely related to balance-of-power theory, also suggests that China's growing power will contribute to increased international conflict. It indicates that unavoidable uncertainty about others' capabilities and intentions, combined with the difficulty of establishing binding commitments under anarchy, means that each state's effort to enhance its security poses a potential threat to which others are likely to respond.[84] Although the literature does suggest that variations in strategic beliefs and military technology may dampen this dynamic,[85] at the end of the century China's policies and the reaction to them are intensifying rather than mitigating the security dilemma. Beijing's investment in power projection capabilities, reassertions of sovereignty over waters and territory from the Diaoyu Islands to Taiwan to the Spratlys, and the limited military actions it has already undertaken all contribute to consternation in Tokyo, Taipei, the capitals of the ASEAN countries, and most openly in Washington, D.C. Seeing China's current assertiveness as a portent of things to come, all others hedge against the

---

82. Friedberg, "Ripe for Rivalry," pp. 9–10, 27–28.
83. See Van Evera's "drunk tank" analogy to explain the beneficial restraining influence of allies in a multipolar world. "Primed for Peace," p. 39.
84. See John H. Herz, "Idealist Internationalism and the Security Dilemma," *World Politics*, Vol. 2, No. 2 (January 1950); Waltz, *Theory of International Politics*, pp. 186–187; Robert Jervis, "Cooperation under the Security Dilemma," *World Politics*, Vol. 30, No. 2 (January 1978); Glenn H. Snyder, "The Security Dilemma in Alliance Politics," *World Politics*, Vol. 36, No. 4 (July 1984), pp. 461–495; and Christensen and Snyder, "Chain Gangs and Passed Bucks."
85. See Jervis, "Cooperation under the Security Dilemma"; and Christensen and Snyder, "Chain Gangs and Passed Bucks."

possibility of a more potent future China threat.[86] Beijing, in turn, deems such fears as at best groundless and at worst as disguising the interest rivals have in keeping China down.[87] Beijing sees its own relative weaknesses, not its emerging strengths, and views its policy statements and limited military efforts in the East Asian theater merely as efforts to ensure its vital interest in defending national sovereignty. Beijing considers the exaggeration of its capabilities and misinterpretation of its motives a smoke screen for revived Japanese militarism, or a U.S.-sponsored strategy of containment aimed at China that includes military assistance to regional actors and the cultivation of regional anti-China alliances.[88] In short, this is a situation in which malign mutual perceptions seem to be feeding worst-case (or at least "bad-case") planning that results in spiraling conflict.

REGIME PERSPECTIVES

Two strands of international relations theory suggest that conflict will increase, not because of China's growing capabilities, but rather because China is a flawed regime. The first is democratic peace theory, which argues that the distinctive domestic institutions and political values of liberal democracies ensure peace among them, but not between liberal democracies and non-democracies.[89] This perspective suggests that democratic great powers will feel

---

86. See "Vietnam, China in Dispute over Offshore Drilling," Reuters, March 17, 1997, Clari.china; "U.S. Forces Welcome in South China Sea," UPI, May 20, 1997, Clari.china; Nicholas D. Kristof, "Tension with Japan Rises alongside China's Star," *New York Times*, June 16, 1996, p. E3. Japan's 1996 Defense White Paper added a call to keep a cautious eye on China's buildup and activism. See Brian Williams, "Japan Sees China as Growing Military Challenge," Reuters, July 19, 1996, Clari.china.
87. See, for examples, "China Defense Minister Says Threat Theory Absurd," Reuters, June 27, 1996, Clari.china; David Shambaugh, "Growing Strong," p. 43; and Benjamin Kang Lim, "Beijing Slams West for Playing Up China Threat," Reuters, November 3, 1995, Clari.china.
88. For criticism of U.S. motives, see Jane Macartney, "China Army Wants Nuclear Arms Destruction, Test End," Reuters, June 13, 1996, Clari.nuclear; and "China Says Future U.S. Ties Hinge on Taiwan," Reuters, February 8, 1996, Clari.china. Statements of U.S. China policy are not unambiguous. See "China Building Up for Spratlys—U.S. Official," Reuters, January 23, 1996, Clari.china; also "Testimony before the House International Relations Committee Subcommittee on Asia and the Pacific, by Admiral Richard C. Macke, U.S. Navy Commander in Chief, United States Pacific Command," Federal News Service, June 27, 1995, Federal Information Systems Corporation, from NEXIS; and "'American Interests and the U.S.-China Relationship' Address by Warren Christopher." On China's suspicion of Japan's motives, see "China's Jiang Zemin Warns against Japan Militarism," Reuters, November 13, 1995, Clari.china; Thomas J. Christensen, "Chinese Realpolitik," *Foreign Affairs*, Vol. 75, No. 5 (September/October 1996), pp. 37–52; and Holly Porteous, "China's View of Strategic Weapons," *Jane's Intelligence Review*, Vol. 8, No. 2 (March 1996), pp.134–137.
89. For a small sample from the wide-ranging debate about the interdemocratic peace, see Michael W. Doyle, "Kant, Liberal Legacies, and Foreign Affairs," *Philosophy and Public Affairs*, Vol. 12 (Fall 1983), pp. 323–353; Christopher Layne, "Kant or Cant: The Myth of the Democratic Peace,"

justified in embracing confrontational policies against a Chinese regime that rejects liberal democratic values and in which the foreign policy decision-making process on crucial security matters is not much constrained by institutions, but rather monopolized by at most a handful of leaders only loosely accountable to a slightly larger elite.[90] And because China's small, authoritarian ruling group believes that the West is engaged in a campaign of "peaceful evolution" designed to subvert communist rule without a fight, hostility and intransigence will be reciprocated.[91]

The second flawed-regime approach is "democratic transition theory," which focuses on states making the shift from authoritarianism to democracy.[92] It suggests that competitors for leadership in these regimes adopt aggressive foreign policies that garner popular support by tapping into nationalist sentiments and elite support by placating the institutional remnants of authoritarian rule, especially the military. China has hardly made much of a shift toward democracy, so the relevance of this line of reasoning remains to be seen. But the strength of nationalism among the Chinese people in the 1990s, in particular among the young, raises concerns about its potential role if political participation does expand. Contemporary Chinese nationalism manifests not merely pride in the accomplishments of the reform era, but also popular resentment at alleged mistreatment by foreigners that may make it difficult for leaders in a future democratizing China to compromise in disputes with other states.[93] The likelihood that China's military will continue to be a significant political player in any transitional Chinese regime is also cause for concern. As

International Security, Vol. 19, No. 2 (Fall 1994); pp. 5–49; and Henry S. Farber and Joanne Gowa, "Polities and Peace," *International Security*, Vol. 20, No. 2 (Fall 1995), pp. 123–146.

90. On lower priority matters, the foreign policy process is less centralized, and more bureaucratized. See Michael D. Swaine, "The PLA in China's National Security Policy: Leaderships, Structures, Processes," *China Quarterly*, No. 146 (June 1996), pp. 360–393; Shambaugh, "Containment or Engagement," pp. 196–201; A. Doak Barnett, *The Making of Foreign Policy in China: Structure and Process* (Boulder, Colo.: Westview Press, 1985).

91. See David Shambaugh, "Growing Strong," p. 50; and David Shambaugh, "The United States and China: A New Cold War?" *Current History*, Vol. 94, No. 593 (September 1995), p. 244.

92. Edward D. Mansfield and Jack Snyder, "Democratization and the Danger of War," *International Security*, Vol. 20, No. 1 (Summer 1995), pp. 5–38.

93. See Gerald Segal, "China Takes on Pacific Asia," *Jane's Defence '96: The World in Conflict*, pp. 67–68; Allen S. Whiting, "Chinese Nationalism and Foreign Policy after Deng," *China Quarterly*, No. 142 (June 1995), pp. 295–316; Michel Oksenberg, "China's Confident Nationalism," *Foreign Affairs*, Special Issue, Vol. 65 (1987), pp. 501–523; Jonathan Unger, ed., *Chinese Nationalism* (Armonk, N.Y.: M.E. Sharpe, 1996); Fei-ling Wang, "Ignorance, Arrogance, and Radical Nationalism: A Review of *China Can Say No*," *Journal of Contemporary China*, Vol. 6, No. 14 (March 1997), pp. 161–165; Hongshan Li, "China Talks Back: Anti-Americanism or Nationalism? A Review of Recent 'Anti-American Books' in China," *Journal of Contemporary China*, Vol. 6, No. 14 (March 1997), pp. 153–160.

competition among the leadership's elite expands, those who hope to lead will still need to earn the support of the military,[94] and this may require a commitment to large defense budgets and a willingness to permit the military to demonstrate its credentials as a professional fighting force, rather than as a tool of domestic suppression.[95]

INSTITUTIONAL PERSPECTIVE

Theories that adopt what might loosely be termed "the institutionalist perspective" also suggest that China's greater role in international politics may increase the level of conflict. Institutionalist approaches depict formal and informal organizational practices that mitigate the effects of anarchy, dampen conflict, and enhance the prospects for cooperation.[96] Unfortunately, the conditions for successful institutionalization that have contributed to its effectiveness in post–World War II Europe are largely absent in post–Cold War Asia.[97] In contrast with Europe, organized attempts at international cooperation on economic and security affairs in East Asia have a comparatively short history; conflicting rather than common interests are salient; cultures are diverse; and an overarching transnational identity and sense of community that might undergird institution building are lacking.[98] Perhaps most troubling, China's clear preference for bilateral, rather than multilateral, approaches to resolving its international conflicts *has* diminished the prospects for effective regional institutions. Beijing *has* sometimes demonstrated a willingness to participate in international regimes and multilateral efforts at problem solving, but not when China's vital interests, especially historically sensitive issues of territorial

---

94. On the current web of military-political elite ties, see Ellis Joffe, "Party-Army Relations in China: Retrospect and Prospect," *China Quarterly*, No. 146 (June 1996), pp. 299–314; Swaine, "The PLA in China's National Security Policy"; and Baum, "China after Deng."
95. For this sort of interpretation of the Taiwan Straits military exercises of 1995 and 1996, see Shambaugh, "Containment or Engagement," pp. 190–191; also Shambaugh, "China's Commander-in-Chief: Jiang Zemin and the PLA," in Lane, Weisenbloom, and Liu, *Chinese Military Modernization*, pp. 209–245.
96. See, for example, Stephen D. Krasner, ed., *International Regimes* (Ithaca, N.Y.: Cornell University Press, 1983); and John Gerard Ruggie, ed., *Multilateralism Matters* (New York: Columbia University Press, 1993), p. 7. For a flavor of the intense debate with realists about the importance of international institutions, see John J. Mearsheimer, "The False Promise of International Institutions," *International Security*, Vol. 19, No. 3 (Winter 1994/95), pp. 5–49, and the exchange of views it provoked in *International Security*, Vol. 20, No. 1 (Summer 1995).
97. See Friedberg, "Ripe for Rivalry," pp. 22–23; John Gerard Ruggie, "Multilateralism: The Anatomy of an Institution," in Ruggie, *Multilateralism Matters*, p. 4.
98. Friedberg, "Ripe for Rivalry," p. 24. See also Charles A. Kupchan and Clifford A. Kupchan, "Concerts, Collective Security, and the Future of Europe," *International Security*, Vol. 16, No. 1 (Summer 1991), pp. 124–125.

sovereignty, are at stake.[99] China's track record during the 1990s in pressing its claims to the Spratly Islands has in fact undermined the region's most significant effort at building international institutions to dampen security conflicts, the ASEAN Regional Forum (ARF).[100] As a result, states concerned about China's maritime aspirations continue to pursue traditional realpolitik methods for coping with their insecurity.[101] Although the ongoing efforts of regional and extraregional states to nurture the ARF make it premature to write off its possible future importance,[102] weak institutional arrangements have not yet provided much of a constraint on the international behavior of an increasingly powerful China.

INTERDEPENDENCE PERSPECTIVE
Economic interdependence theory offers a comparatively sanguine outlook on the consequences of China's growing capabilities. It identifies incentives for states to contain their international disputes when the costs of conflict are great (because one alienates valued economic partners) and the benefits from the use of force are small (because the foundations of modern economic and military power depend less on assets like labor and natural resources that conquerors can seize and more on knowledge and its technological fruits).[103] China's rising power in the late twentieth century is based on rapid economic development fueled by dramatically increased levels of international trade and

99. See Johnston, "Prospects for Chinese Nuclear Force Modernization," pp. 575–576. On possible differences within China's leadership about the acceptability of multilateralism, see David Shambaugh, "China's Commander-in-Chief: Jiang Zemin and the PLA," pp. 234–235; and Shambaugh, "China's Military in Transition," p. 273.
100. See Michael Leifer, *The ASEAN Regional Forum*, Adelphi Paper, 302 (London: International Institute for Strategic Studies [IISS], July 1996), pp. 37, 43–44; and Mark J. Valencia, *China and the South China Sea Disputes*, Adelphi Paper, 298 (London: IISS, October 1995). On other "confidence- and security-building measures," see Ball, "Arms and Affluence."
101. On Indonesia's bilateral security treaty with Australia, see Leifer, *The ASEAN Regional Forum*, pp. 50–52. On the Philippines' efforts to rejuvenate its military alliance with the United States after clashing with China over Mischief Reef in 1995 and Scarborough Shoal in 1997, see "Philippines to Seek Revision of Defense Pact with U.S.," Japan Economic Newswire, May 14, 1997, from NEXIS.
102. Leifer, *The ASEAN Regional Forum*, pp. 53–60.
103. Robert O. Keohane and Joseph S. Nye Jr., *Power and Interdependence*, 2d ed. (Boston: Scott, Foresman, 1989); and John E. Mueller, *Retreat from Doomsday: The Obsolescence of Major War* (New York: Basic Books, 1989). For criticism of this line of reasoning, see Kenneth N. Waltz, "The Myth of National Interdependence," in Charles P. Kindleberger, ed., *The International Corporation* (Cambridge, Mass.: MIT Press, 1970); Robert J. Art, "To What Ends Military Power?" *International Security*, Vol. 4, No. 4 (Spring 1980), pp. 3–35; Peter Liberman, "The Spoils of Conquest," *International Security*, Vol. 18, No. 2 (Fall 1993), pp. 125–153; and Norrin M. Ripsman and Jean-Marc F. Blanchard, "Commercial Liberalism Under Fire: Evidence from 1914 and 1936," *Security Studies*, Vol. 6, No. 2 (Winter 1996/97), pp. 4–50.

investment. Sharp reductions in international economic activity would seriously damage China's ability to sustain the high rates of growth that are necessary, if not sufficient, for its emergence as a great power. Thus, because of the easily understood consequences of provoking sanctions among its most valued American, Japanese, and European economic partners, and not just because of possibly temporary limitations on the PLA's capabilities, China's leaders will continue to be constrained in their efforts to resolve international disputes. States' arms may not be tightly chained by economic concerns, but they may yet be loosely bound in ways that are conducive to international cooperation.[104]

NUCLEAR PEACE PERSPECTIVE

What might be termed "nuclear peace theory" provides the strongest reasons to expect that the dangers associated with China's arrival as a full-fledged great power will be limited. This theory asserts that the advent of nuclear weapons, especially thermonuclear weapons that can be loaded atop ballistic missiles, has revolutionized international politics by fundamentally altering the costs of conflict among the great powers. Because nuclear powers cannot confidently eliminate the risk of unacceptable retaliation by their adversaries, they cannot engage one another in military battles that have a real potential to escalate to unrestrained warfare. Thus, in its purest form, nuclear peace theory argues that among the great powers the nuclear revolution has resulted in easily established relationships of mutual deterrence that provide not only a robust buffer against general war, but also a strong constraint on both limited war and crisis behavior.[105] Limited wars and crises between nuclear states with survivable retaliatory forces may yet occur, but their outcome is more likely to be determined by the balance of political interests that underpins international resolve than by estimates of the balance of military capabilities.[106]

---

104. In the China case, the dangerous attractiveness of valued natural resources, especially oil, in disputed maritime territories must somehow be weighed against the interest in not disrupting broader patterns of trade and investment.

105. See Bernard Brodie, *War and Politics* (New York: Macmillan, 1973), especially chapter 9; Kenneth N. Waltz, "Nuclear Myths and Political Realities," *American Political Science Review*, Vol. 84, No. 3 (September 1990), pp. 731–745; Robert Jervis, *The Illogic of American Nuclear Strategy* (Ithaca, N.Y.: Cornell University Press, 1986); and Robert Jervis, *The Meaning of the Nuclear Revolution* (Ithaca, N.Y.: Cornell University Press, 1989). For an introduction to the debate about the logical and empirical validity of nuclear deterrence theory, see the special issue of *World Politics*, Vol. 41, No. 2 (January 1989).

106. See Richard K. Betts, *Nuclear Blackmail and Nuclear Balance* (Washington, D.C.: Brookings Institution, 1987). The stability/instability paradox suggests that the frequency of limited wars

Nuclear peace theory, then, suggests that the alarmist implications for international security of China's rise to power have been overstated, because many analysts fail to explain why the powerful nuclear constraints on policymaking would not apply for a Chinese decision maker and his counterpart in a rival great power.[107] Uncertainties about shifts in relative capabilities caused by China's growing strength, this theory suggests, will be overshadowed by certainty about the unacceptable damage even a small nuclear exchange could cause. In this view, China's probes against Taiwan and adventurism in the South China Sea or elsewhere in East Asia are feasible only as long as the risk of an escalating conflict with a nuclear-armed rival is virtually zero. Once such a risk-laden military engagement becomes a serious possibility, the incentives for nuclear adversaries to keep their conflicts within bounds would lead Beijing and Washington, for example, to feel the same pressures to find negotiated solutions that Washington and Moscow felt during their various Cold War crises.

Conclusion

Assuming China's political coherence is not dramatically undermined, early in the twenty-first century its military capabilities will have increased, but will continue to lag behind those of the other advanced industrial states, certainly behind those of the United States. Even if the PLA's modernization program overcomes the many challenges described above, it will field forces by the second or third decade of the next century, most of which would have been state of the art in the 1990s. And despite impressively robust economic growth, there is little likelihood that Beijing can greatly accelerate this modernization process, mainly because China has not yet established the necessary world-class scientific research and development infrastructure. Moreover, as the revolution in military affairs takes hold, and the battlefield advantage increasingly

---

involving nuclear powers may even increase, but only in situations where they feel confident that the risks of escalation are minimal and can be managed.
107. Nuclear peace theorists would dismiss the recent Chinese interest in a nuclear war-fighting capability as a futile attempt to "conventionalize" strategy, which has repeatedly emerged among those who must plan for the use of the state's armed forces. See Johnston, "China's New 'Old Thinking.'" Nuclear peace theorists see such conventionalization as at best irrelevant and at worst recklessly wasteful, but not strategically destabilizing because the dominant deterrent logic prevails when leaders are forced to make war/peace decisions. For pessimistic views of the effects of nuclear weapons in East Asia, especially under conditions of multipolarity, see Friedberg, "Ripe for Rivalry"; Christensen and Snyder, "Chain Gangs and Passed Bucks"; and Christensen, "Perceptions and Alliances in Europe, 1865–1940."

shifts to those best able to exploit the frontiers of computer science and advanced electronics, it is unlikely that the PLA can compensate for shortcomings in quality by deploying lesser forces in greater quantity. In any case, without a problematic restructuring, China's defense industry will be unable to produce and maintain quantities of modern weaponry, including selective imports, that would decisively overmatch its most potent adversaries. China's regional and global rivals have their own impressive resources that will continue to make it difficult for the PRC to dramatically increase its power in relative rather than absolute terms.

Nevertheless, although China's power will fall short of some observers' greatest expectations, in the first half of the next century the country will become an increasingly capable actor. Insights from the various strands of theory presented above can be combined to understand better the implications of this process for international security. Most of the theoretical perspectives identify reasons why a rising China, with extensive and growing international interests, will find itself in conflict with others. Concerns about power transitions, the complexities of power balancing, flawed regime type, and inadequate institutions highlight the likely sources of conflict. Although identifying the difficulties ahead, these more pessimistic theories leave open questions about the intensity of anticipated conflicts and the chance they will lead to war. Interdependence theory and (if regional organizations evolve beyond their current infancy) institutionalist arguments suggest reasons to expect the muting of conflicts in which a rising China will be involved. Nuclear peace theory reminds us that while conflict is a necessary condition for war, it is far from sufficient.

Even some of the theories that raise red flags suggest guidelines for managing if not eliminating conflict. Democratic peace theory indicates that encouraging political liberalization in China may eventually yield peace dividends, while democratic transition theory instructs that such efforts be carefully designed to discredit rather than feed the more xenophobic varieties of nationalism. The security dilemma literature alerts one to the spirals of conflict that will result if states hedge against the presumption of a more dangerous China and China interprets such behavior as an unprovoked indicator of hostile intent. Yet avoiding such spirals will be difficult. Important institutional interests in China have a stake in resisting the steps to improve transparency that might defuse exaggerated concerns about the PLA's capabilities; at the same time, important institutional interests elsewhere, especially in the United States, have a stake in highlighting the specter of a threatening China to justify the burden of large-scale military investment in a Soviet-less post–Cold War world.

If other theories provide, at best, modest hope of soft constraints on the conflicts likely to characterize a more active China's international relations, nuclear peace theory explains why such conflicts, however wisely managed, are unlikely to result in great power war. Because the lessons of the nuclear revolution are so simple to grasp, indeed hard to ignore, their effects should prevail regardless of the many complicating influences that might otherwise lead states into war with their rivals. Thus the warnings from the literature about hegemonic shifts and the security dilemma notwithstanding, even a future filled with recurrent spirals of conflict between a dominant United States and an increasingly capable China should at worst result in manageable, if undesirable, cold war.

In sum, this review supports a forecast that is less alarmist than many. It also underscores the importance for policymakers of assessing actual capabilities rather than presumed potential. Overestimating China's strength may well create a self-fulfilling prophecy of rivalry based on premature extrapolation; this could prove costly if it results in unnecessarily burdensome military budgets and unnecessarily intense international conflicts. China's rise to the ranks of the great powers will be an unsettling and frequently difficult experience. As long as the constraints of the nuclear revolution prevail, the danger that China's ascent will trigger great power war is small, but mismanaging the process may make it a more painful experience than necessary.

Legitimacy and the Limits of Nationalism

China and the Diaoyu Islands

Erica Strecker Downs and Phillip C. Saunders

Influenced by the resurgence of nationalism in the post–Cold War era, international relations scholars have produced a pessimistic evaluation of ways that nationalism increases the chances of international conflict. Three broad themes have emerged in the literature. The first focuses on the use of nationalism to divert attention from the state's inability to meet societal demands for security, economic development, and effective political institutions.[1] Illegitimate regimes may seek to bolster their grip on power by blaming foreigners for their own failures, increasing international tensions.[2] The second looks at groups within the state that have expansionist or militarist goals. By propagating nationalist or imperialist myths, they can generate broad public support for their parochial interests.[3] The third emphasizes how political elites can incite nationalism to gain an advantage in domestic political competition. Nationalism can be used both to mobilize support for threatened elites and to fend off potential challengers.[4] This function can be particularly important in democratizing or liberalizing authoritarian regimes, which lack established political institutions to channel

Erica Strecker Downs is a Ph.D. candidate in the Politics Department at Princeton University. She has worked on Chinese security issues for RAND. Phillip C. Saunders is a Ph.D. candidate at the Woodrow Wilson School of Public and International Affairs, Princeton University. He has worked on Asian issues for the United States Air Force, RAND, and the Council on Foreign Relations, and is currently completing a doctoral dissertation on priorities in U.S. China policy since Tiananmen Square.

The authors would like to thank Michael Dark, David Denoon, Herb Levin, Liu Baopu, David Reuther, Gil Rozman, James Shinn, Richard Ullman, Wang Xu, Lynn T. White III, two anonymous reviewers, and a Beijing scholar for their helpful comments on earlier drafts. The Center of International Studies and the Council on Regional Studies at Princeton University provided financial support for this research.

1. Jack Snyder, "Nationalism and the Crisis of the Post-Soviet State," in Michael E. Brown, ed., *Ethnic Conflict and International Security* (Princeton, N.J.: Princeton University Press, 1993), pp. 79–101.
2. Stephen Van Evera, "Hypotheses on Nationalism and War," *International Security*, Vol. 18, No. 4 (Spring 1994), pp. 30–33.
3. Jack Snyder, *Myths of Empire: Domestic Politics and International Ambition* (Ithaca, N.Y.: Cornell University Press, 1991).
4. V.P. Gagnon, "Ethnic Nationalism and International Conflict," *International Security*, Vol. 19, No. 3 (Winter 1994/95), pp. 130–166.

International Security, Vol. 23, No. 3 (Winter 1998/99), pp. 114–146

popular participation and reconcile contending claims.[5] All three approaches focus on nationalism's instrumental value for insecure elites seeking to gain or hold onto power. Nationalism can not only aggravate ethnic relations within the state, but it can also spill over borders and increase the likelihood of international conflict. Once the public has been mobilized through nationalistic appeals, elites can become trapped in their own rhetoric and choose to pursue risky security strategies rather than jeopardize their rule by not fulfilling popular nationalist demands. Even though nationalist myths are primarily aimed at a domestic audience, other states may misinterpret them as a serious threat and respond in kind, giving rise to a security dilemma.

Some scholars who have observed the Chinese government's increasing reliance on nationalism since the 1989 Tiananmen Square massacre have begun to apply this literature to China. Several have noted the potential for Chinese nationalism to interact with China's growing relative power in destabilizing ways.[6] If China's rapid growth continues, projections suggest that China will eventually have the world's largest economy and develop military capabilities that could support a more aggressive policy.[7] Economic development might not only improve Chinese capabilities, but also push China into aggressive efforts to control energy supplies needed for future development.[8] David Shambaugh states that "as China has grown economically more powerful in recent years, nationalism has increased exponentially," and predicts that increased Chinese strength "is likely to result in increased defensiveness and assertiveness."[9] Some Chinese chauvinists are promoting a new variety of

---

5. Edward Mansfield and Jack Snyder, "Democratization and the Danger of War," *International Security*, Vol. 20, No. 1 (Summer 1995), pp. 5–38.
6. Aaron Friedberg, "Ripe for Rivalry: Prospects for Peace in a Multipolar Asia," *International Security*, Vol. 18, No. 3 (Winter 1993/94), pp. 13–15; Allen S. Whiting, "Chinese Nationalism and Foreign Policy after Deng," *China Quarterly*, No. 141 (June 1995), p. 316; and David Shambaugh, "Containment or Engagement of China? Calculating Beijing's Responses," *International Security*, Vol. 21, No. 2 (Fall 1996), pp. 204–209.
7. Charles Wolf, Jr., K.C. Yeh, Anil Bamezai, Donald P. Henry, and Michael Kennedy, *Long-Term Economic and Military Trends, 1994–2015: The United States and Asia* (Santa Monica, Calif.: RAND, 1995). Balanced assessments of military modernization can be found in David Shambaugh, "China's Military: Real or Paper Tiger?" *Washington Quarterly*, Vol. 19, No. 2 (Spring 1996), pp. 19–23; Denny Roy, "The China Threat Issue: Major Arguments," *Asian Survey*, Vol. 36, No. 8 (August 1996), pp. 759–764; and Avery Goldstein, "Great Expectations: Interpreting China's Arrival," *International Security*, Vol. 22, No. 3 (Winter 1997/98), pp. 36–73.
8. Michael Leifer, "Chinese Economic Reform and Security Policy: The South China Sea Connection," *Survival*, Vol. 37, No. 2 (Summer 1995), pp. 44–45.
9. Shambaugh, "Containment or Engagement of China?" p. 205.

nationalism with an explicitly expansionist character.[10] Both history and international relations theory suggest that a rising power's challenge to a declining hegemon often results in war.[11] This structural concern is heightened by the popularity of a number of nationalist tracts, as well as recent aggressive Chinese military actions that have stimulated talk of a "China threat."[12] Some analysts suggest that a powerful, nationalist China is likely to come into conflict with the United States.[13]

This article argues that concerns about aggressive Chinese nationalism are overstated, or at least premature. China's leaders (President Jiang Zemin, National People's Congress Chairman Li Peng, Prime Minister Zhu Rongji, and other members of the Politburo Standing Committee) have employed both nationalism and economic performance in their efforts to restore the domestic legitimacy of the Chinese Communist Party (CCP). Domestic legitimacy and international behavior have a reciprocal relationship: efforts to enhance legitimacy not only influence China's foreign policy behavior, but foreign policy performance can also affect the regime's domestic standing. An examination of Chinese behavior in two territorial disputes with Japan over the Diaoyu (Senkaku) Islands[14] in 1990 and 1996 reveals a complex relationship between legitimacy, nationalism, and economic performance that differs from the predictions of the literature on nationalism and international conflict. Despite the

---

10. Edward Friedman, "Chinese Nationalism, Taiwan Autonomy, and the Prospects of a Larger War," *Journal of Contemporary China*, Vol. 6, No. 14 (March 1997), pp. 5–32; and Barry Sautman, "Racial Nationalism and China's External Behavior," *World Affairs*, Vol. 160, No. 2 (Fall 1997), pp. 78–95.

11. Paul M. Kennedy, *The Rise and Fall of the Great Powers: Economic Change and Military Conflict from 1500 to 2000* (New York: Random House, 1987); and Robert Gilpin, *War and Change in World Politics* (New York: Cambridge University Press, 1981).

12. Most of these books are commercial ventures intended to appeal to nationalist sentiment, not government-funded propaganda. Song Qiang, Zhang Zangyang, and Qiao Bian, eds., *Zhongguo Keyi Shuo Bu* [China can say no] (Beijing: Zhonghua Gongshan Lianhe Chubanshe, 1996); and Sai Xianwei, *Zhongguo da Zhanlüe: Lingdao Shijie de Lantu* [China's grand strategy: blueprint for world leadership] (Hainan: Hainan Publishing House, 1996). For reviews and summaries in English, see Fei-Ling Wang, "Ignorance, Arrogance, and Radical Nationalism: A Review of *China Can Say No*," *Journal of Contemporary China*, Vol. 6, No. 14 (March 1997), pp. 161–165; Hongshan Li, "China Talks Back: Anti-Americanism or Nationalism?" *Journal of Contemporary China*, Vol. 6, No. 14 (March 1997), pp. 153–160; and John W. Garver, "China as Number One," *China Journal*, No. 39 (January 1998), pp. 61–66.

13. Richard Bernstein and Ross H. Munro, *The Coming Conflict with China* (New York: Alfred A. Knopf, 1997); and John W. Garver, *Face Off: China, the United States, and Taiwan's Democratization* (Seattle: University of Washington Press, 1997), pp. 157–166.

14. Because our focus is on the calculations of Chinese leaders, we use the Chinese name "Diaoyu Islands" for the remainder of the article. This does not imply acceptance of any side's sovereignty claims.

efforts of nationalist groups on both sides to escalate the disputes, the Chinese government proved willing to incur significant damage to its nationalist credentials by following restrained policies and cooperating with the Japanese government to prevent the territorial disputes from harming bilateral relations. When forced to choose, Chinese leaders pursued economic development at the expense of nationalist goals. This article therefore seeks to document and explain the contrast between China's nationalist rhetoric and its restrained international behavior.

We begin by exploring the meaning of legitimacy, nationalism, and economic performance in the Chinese context. We then seek to explain how domestic legitimacy concerns and relative power constraints influence China's foreign policy choices. Next we examine how Chinese leaders responded when right-wing Japanese groups reasserted claims to the Diaoyu Islands in 1990 and 1996. By choosing two similar cases separated over time, we can assess the impact of rising nationalism and improvements in China's relative power position while holding other variables constant.[15] We then consider whether this pattern of restrained behavior is likely to apply to the cases of Taiwan and the Spratly Islands and assess the future effectiveness of the CCP's legitimation strategies.

Legitimacy, Nationalism, and Economics

Marxist, Leninist, and Maoist ideology has been gradually losing its ability to legitimate the CCP's continued rule. Internationally, the collapse of communism in Eastern Europe and the Soviet Union revealed communism's bankruptcy as a political ideology and as a viable economic model. Within China, market- oriented economic reforms have increasingly undercut the CCP's claim that China is a socialist country; calls for adhering to the socialist road have been largely devoid of economic content. Socialism's ideological focus on workers and state ownership of capital clashes with government policies that emphasize the importance of markets, the suppression of independent labor unions, and the dismantlement of state-owned enterprises. Rampant official corruption, periodic bouts of high inflation, and widespread unemployment

---

15. Our analysis focuses on the symbolic value of disputed territory to the regime's nationalist credentials, the economic impact of aggressive pursuit of territorial claims, and the relative power of the states involved. The first two factors measure the likely impact of the crisis on regime legitimacy; the third influences the international consequences of aggressive action. Compared with China's claims to Taiwan and the South China Sea, the Diaoyu Islands are an intermediate case along all three dimensions.

illustrate the disjuncture between socialist ideology and economic reality. This tension was an important cause of the 1989 Tiananmen Square protests. The political crisis brought on by the use of force to suppress the Tiananmen demonstrations (reflecting communism's collapse as a legitimating ideology) compelled the Chinese government to seek new sources of legitimacy. Political legitimacy is established by the compatibility of the values of the rulers and the ruled. Every political system attempts to establish and cultivate the belief in its legitimacy in order to have orders obeyed willingly rather than by the threat of force. Although China's political leaders continue to employ socialist rhetoric, the search for normative arguments that can legitimate the CCP's rule has led them in two potentially incompatible directions. The first emphasizes nationalist goals and highlights the party's success in building China into a powerful state; the second emphasizes economic goals and claims that the political stability provided by CCP rule is necessary for continued economic growth. Each legitimation strategy seeks to appeal to values and goals shared by the Chinese people. The party's claim to legitimacy now rests largely on its performance in achieving these goals, not on its adherence to ideological standards.

Chinese nationalism emerged from the shock of extensive contacts with the West in the nineteenth century, which challenged both the traditional Confucian cultural worldview and China's territorial integrity and national unity.[16] The Qing dynasty's inability to resist Western and Japanese imperialism caused Chinese intellectuals to turn to nationalism as a means of mobilizing the energies of the Chinese people to "save China." Foreign countries repeatedly compromised Chinese sovereignty by demanding trade and extraterritorial privileges, carving out economic spheres of influence, and seizing territory under Chinese control (including Hong Kong, Taiwan, Korea, and parts of Manchuria). By the 1890s foreigners appeared poised to dismantle China entirely. The development of Chinese nationalism in this context has given sovereignty and territorial integrity intense symbolic value. Although the content of Chinese nationalism has varied as successive state leaders have tried to impose definitions that served their immediate political goals, nationalist values such as territorial unity and national power provide citizens with an independent basis for evaluating the government's performance.[17] The CCP

---

16. For a useful exposition and critique of the culturalism-to-nationalism thesis, see James Townsend, "Chinese Nationalism," in Jonathan Unger, ed., *Chinese Nationalism* (Armonk, N.Y.: M.E. Sharpe, 1996), pp. 1–30.
17. John Fitzgerald, "The Nationless State: The Search for a Nation in Modern Chinese Nationalism," in ibid., pp. 56–85.

has sought to appeal to these values, claiming that where previous regimes compromised or capitulated, the communists were willing to stand up and fight. The CCP has also sought to shape the character of Chinese nationalism, drawing selectively on Chinese history to meet the political and strategic needs of the moment. We use "nationalism" to refer both to government efforts to appeal to preexisting nationalist sentiment and to deliberate attempts to stir up nationalist sentiment for political ends.

Japan has played a central role in the rise of Chinese nationalism, both as a spur for the development of Chinese state patriotism and as a target for Chinese xenophobia.[18] Japan's military victory in the 1895 Sino-Japanese War and its subsequent seizure of Taiwan and Korea were particularly humiliating because the Chinese have traditionally considered Japan to have a derivative and inferior culture. Japan's invasion of China in the 1930s and wartime atrocities such as the 1937 Nanjing massacre gave rise to popular anti-Japanese sentiment that continues to resonate widely. The CCP's initial claim to legitimacy rested largely on its role in organizing resistance to Japan.[19] Japan continues to provide a useful target that allows Chinese leaders to define China's national identity in opposition to Japanese aggression and imperialism.[20] Appeals to anti-Japanese sentiment still pay domestic political dividends; the regime has used propaganda campaigns, exhibits depicting Japanese wartime atrocities, and anniversaries of past Japanese acts of aggression to exploit these popular feelings.[21]

The CCP's economic claims to legitimacy lie in its ability both to develop China into a powerful modern economy and to raise individual living standards. China's impressive overall growth rates have not been matched by performance in improving living standards for all citizens. Economic reforms have had differential impacts in rural and urban areas, and in coastal and interior provinces, resulting in a rapid increase in economic inequality.[22] Gen-

---

18. Chih-Yu Shih, "Defining Japan: The Nationalist Assumption in China's Foreign Policy," *International Journal*, Vol. 50, No. 3 (Summer 1995), pp. 543–544.

19. Chalmers Johnson, *Peasant Nationalism and Communist Power: The Emergence of Revolutionary China, 1937–1945* (Stanford, Calif.: Stanford University Press, 1962).

20. Shih, "Defining Japan," p. 545.

21. Since the CCP's patriotic education campaign began in 1992, the Nanjing massacre exhibit at the Museum of the Revolution in Beijing has expanded dramatically, and attendance at the Nanjing museum, which features a large exhibit on the massacre, has doubled. Visits by Phillip Saunders; and Patrick Tyler, "China's Campus Model for the 90's: Earnest Patriot," *New York Times*, April 23, 1996, p. A4.

22. World Bank, *Sharing Rising Incomes: Disparities in China* (Washington, D.C.: World Bank, 1997); and Azizur Rahman Khan and Carl Riskin, "Income and Inequality in China: Composition, Distribution, and Growth of Household Income, 1988 to 1995," *China Quarterly*, No. 154 (June 1998), pp. 221–253.

eral improvements in the economic situation can substitute for improvements in personal economic circumstances for a while, but tolerance of inequality does not last indefinitely. Survey data indicate that Chinese citizens view growth in economic inequality and "pocketbook issues" such as inflation, job security, and social services as important measures of government performance.[23] Since Tiananmen, China's leaders have tried to forge a new ideological connection between economic performance and legitimacy by arguing that political stability is an essential precondition for economic development. The CCP has emphasized a development-oriented neo-authoritarianism that claims that authoritarian rule is necessary during the early stages of economic development.[24] The argument that the CCP is the only force capable of holding China together and guiding economic development has proved persuasive to many Chinese.[25]

Domestic Legitimacy and International Behavior

China's top political leaders have sought to restore the regime's legitimacy following the Tiananmen massacre by appealing to nationalism and by raising living standards.[26] Both are potentially important sources of legitimacy, but economic performance matters to a wider segment of the population.[27] Ideally, the CCP would like to maximize its legitimacy by making strong appeals to nationalism while simultaneously raising living standards, but power constraints and the contradictions between domestic appeals to nationalism and

23. Guoming Yu and Xiayang Liu, *Zhongguo Minyi Yanjiu* [Research on public opinion in China] (Beijing: People's University Press, 1994), pp. 85–87; and Jie Chen, Yang Zhong, Jan Hillard, and John Scheb, "Assessing Political Support in China: Citizen's Evaluations of Government Effectiveness and Legitimacy," *Journal of Contemporary China*, Vol. 6, No. 16 (November 1997), p. 558.

24. See Barry Sautman, "Sirens of the Strongman: Neo-Authoritarianism in Recent Chinese Political Theory," *China Quarterly*, No. 129 (March 1992), pp. 72–102; and Stanley Rosen, ed., "Nationalism and Neoconservatism in China in the 1990s," special issue of *Chinese Law and Government*, Vol. 30, No. 6 (November–December 1997).

25. Yang Zhong, "Legitimacy Crisis and Legitimation in China," *Journal of Contemporary Asia*, Vol. 26, No. 2 (1996), pp. 212–218.

26. Although top Chinese leaders compete for power and sometimes have different policy preferences, our analysis focuses on their common interest in regime survival. In the interest of parsimony and given the lack of reliable information on individual leadership preferences, we treat CCP civilian leaders as a collective, unitary actor. Our argument could be extended to analyze other relationships in which legitimacy matters, such as civil-military relations or the relationship of competing top CCP leaders to medium-level officials.

27. Legitimacy claims based on nationalism and economic performance can be conceptualized either as appealing to both sentiments in a single individual or as separate appeals to groups with different preferences. In reality, the two formulations overlap considerably.

a development strategy that relies heavily on foreigners mean trade-offs exist between nationalism and economic performance. The CCP's challenge is to pursue both sources of legitimacy in a complementary manner, seeking to manipulate foreign and domestic perceptions so that the contradictions between a legitimation strategy based on nationalism and one based on economic performance do not become unmanageable.

Three sets of constraints prevent Chinese leaders from leaning too heavily on either nationalism or economic performance. The first (and firmest) constraint is China's international power position, which limits its ability to attain nationalist objectives. Excessive nationalism can stir up demands for assertive international policies that Chinese leaders cannot presently satisfy. Conversely, maximizing economic growth to create new jobs requires China to make economic concessions and to accept a politically uncomfortable degree of economic dependence on foreigners. The second constraint is international reactions to Chinese behavior and rhetoric. Excessive nationalism may affect the willingness of other states to trade with and invest in China or even stimulate military reactions. Conversely, Chinese efforts to maximize international economic cooperation will likely require accepting foreign demands for restraint in China's military buildup.[28] The third constraint is domestic reactions. If Chinese leaders push nationalism so far that it interferes with economic growth, they are likely to increase unemployment and popular discontent.[29] For that matter, any severe external shock that affects the Chinese economy could hurt the government's legitimacy. Conversely, if Chinese leaders pursue economic development at the expense of nationalism, the government will be vulnerable to criticism from economic nationalists on the grounds that they are selling out China's interests to foreigners, especially if citizens believe corruption among CCP leaders influences economic decisionmaking.[30]

These constraints severely limit China's options. In the short run, Chinese leaders make tactical shifts between the two sources of legitimacy, stressing nationalism and blaming foreigners when the economy is doing poorly, and emphasizing the party's successful economic management when the economy

---

28. Japan's suspension of some developmental aid after China conducted nuclear tests in May and August 1995 is one example.
29. There is an additional domestic constraint against excessive nationalism: appeals based on Han superiority would likely fuel separatism among non-Han minorities in Xinjiang and Tibet.
30. See Allen S. Whiting and Xin Jianfei, "Sino-Japanese Relations: Pragmatism and Passion," World Policy Journal, Vol. 8, No. 1 (Spring 1991), pp. 109–112, 116, 129; and Kuang-Sheng Liao, Antiforeignism and Modernization in China (Hong Kong: Chinese University Press, 1990).

is doing well.[31] In order to exploit both sources of legitimacy in a complementary manner, the government seeks to shore up its nationalistic credentials through propaganda aimed at a domestic audience while simultaneously sending reassuring messages about China's desire for international cooperation to foreign audiences. If foreigners challenge China's nationalistic claims, however, the contradictions between the two legitimation strategies can become evident, and the government may be forced to choose between satisfying popular nationalist demands and pursuing economic performance. This dilemma is especially acute because China's territorial claims reflect dissatisfaction with the status quo and historical grievances that resonate deeply with nationalist sentiment. Even if diplomatic agreements to shelve disputes do not prejudice China's future negotiating position, failure to pursue Chinese claims aggressively when nationalistic issues arise damages the regime's nationalist credentials.

The Chinese leadership's strategy also has a longer-term international focus. China's weak power position and economic dependence restrict the government's international bargaining power. In negotiations with the United States over the status of Taiwan from 1969 to 1989, for example, Chinese leaders consistently refused to accept unsatisfactory agreements that reflected China's weak bargaining position, preferring instead to defer the resolution of critical issues until China's position improved.[32] The Chinese government is confident that economic growth and improvements in China's technological and military capabilities will eventually increase its relative power and reduce its economic dependence. By deferring the resolution of territorial and border conflicts until China's position improves, the leadership hopes to eventually be able to dictate settlements on Chinese terms. Chinese political leaders make tactical shifts between the two sources of legitimacy to maintain their rule, waiting until the country becomes powerful enough to achieve their nationalist objectives. Although China's leaders share nationalist goals such as reunifying Taiwan with

---

31. This interpretation differs from those that see shifts between economic reform and political orthodoxy as the product of conflicts between conservatives and reformers in the CCP leadership. Carol Lee Hamrin argues that economic difficulties strengthened conservative influence and shifted policy toward orthodoxy. See Hamrin, "Elite Politics and the Development of China's Foreign Relations," in Thomas W. Robinson and David Shambaugh, eds., *Chinese Foreign Policy: Theory and Practice* (New York: Oxford University Press, 1994), pp. 105–106. We agree that elite conflicts matter, but feel our analysis parsimoniously captures this dynamic by focusing on the common goal of maintaining CCP legitimacy.
32. Robert S. Ross, *Negotiating Cooperation: The United States and China, 1969–1989* (Stanford, Calif.: Stanford University Press, 1995).

the mainland, asserting Chinese claims over the Diaoyu and Spratly Islands, and increasing China's power and international prestige, we argue that their use of nationalist rhetoric is aimed primarily at a domestic audience and is intended to shore up the regime's legitimacy. Specifically, the recent rise in Chinese nationalism is partly the product of the regime's conscious efforts to craft a new ideology that can justify continued CCP rule.[33] Chinese political leaders are rational actors who balance the need to maintain domestic legitimacy with the pursuit of longer-term international objectives. Although pressure from the military or factions within the CCP that favor a more aggressive pursuit of nationalist goals has sometimes affected Chinese foreign policy, we argue that civilian control and cautious behavior that balances economic and strategic objectives are the norm.[34]

The Chinese leadership's delicate balancing act depends on the ability to manage the contradictions between its domestic legitimation strategies while maintaining access to the international economy. China's economic partners tolerate the CCP's efforts to stir up nationalism and antiforeign sentiment because they benefit economically and therefore have been willing to make allowances for the Chinese leadership's domestic need to cloak capitalist economic reforms in socialist and nationalist rhetoric. In the case of Sino-Japanese relations, fears that an unstable Chinese regime would damage regional stability have led Japan to employ economic diplomacy to help maintain political stability; they have also prompted low-key responses to confrontational Chinese statements and anti-Japanese polemics in official media.[35] Aided by provocative statements and actions of Japanese nationalists, however, Chinese

---

33. For details on recent efforts to craft nationalism into an ideology that might replace socialism, see Joseph Fewsmith, "Neoconservatism and the End of the Dengist Era," *Asian Survey*, Vol. 35, No. 2 (July 1995), pp. 635–651; and Zhao Shuisheng, "China's Intellectuals' Quest for National Greatness and Nationalistic Writings in the 1990s," *China Quarterly*, No. 152 (December 1997), pp. 730–738.

34. Jiang Zemin's political weakness in early 1996 likely permitted the military a greater voice in policy, but since Deng Xiaoping's death Jiang's authority has become clear. Jiang has reasserted CCP control over the military through retirement of People's Liberation Army (PLA) elders, appointment of new senior officers, and moves to reduce PLA policy influence and prerogatives. These measures include defense cuts of an additional 500,000 men, the lack of a PLA representative on the Politburo Standing Committee, and Jiang's July 1998 order for the PLA to divest its vast business holdings. For views that emphasize military influence, see Whiting, "Chinese Nationalism and Foreign Policy after Deng"; and Garver, *Face Off*. For a more skeptical view, see Michael Swaine, "The PLA and Chinese National Security Policy: Leadership, Structures, Processes," *China Quarterly*, No. 146 (June 1996), pp. 360–393.

35. For an analysis of Japanese motives for stable relations and how they have affected economic relations, see Qingxin Ken Wang, "Recent Japanese Diplomacy in China: Political Alignment in a Changing World Order," *Asian Survey*, Vol. 33, No. 6 (June 1993), pp. 625–641.

leaders have also been able to use the issue of Japan's wartime behavior to portray China as a victim and keep Japan on the defensive. Although these tactics have been effective, growing concerns about aggressive Chinese behavior and structural changes in the Japanese political system may be diminishing Japan's tolerance for Chinese nationalism.[36]

Competing Claims to the Diaoyu Islands

The Diaoyu Islands are a set of five uninhabited islets and three barren rocks claimed by China, Taiwan, and Japan. The islands lie in the East China Sea about 125 miles northeast of Taiwan and 185 miles southeast of Okinawa, adjacent to a continental shelf believed to contain 10–100 billion barrels of oil. This estimate is based on geological surveys; no test wells have actually been drilled in the disputed area.[37] According to oil industry sources, there is no firm evidence that commercially exploitable oil reserves exist.[38] China, Japan, and Taiwan have overlapping claims to large parts of the East China Sea continental shelf near the Diaoyu Islands.[39] Resolution of these competing claims is complicated by the sovereignty dispute over the Diaoyu Islands, Taiwan's status, and the existence of competing principles for fair division of the continental shelf.[40] Possession of the Diaoyu Islands could convey sovereignty over about 11,700 square nautical miles of the continental shelf perceived to have good petroleum potential.[41] Although the 1982 United Nations

---

36. Michael J. Green and Benjamin L. Self, "Japan's Changing China Policy: From Commercial Liberalism to Reluctant Realism," *Survival*, Vol. 38, No. 2 (Summer 1996), pp. 35–58; and Gerald Segal, "The Coming Confrontation between China and Japan?" *World Policy Journal*, Vol. 10, No. 2 (Summer 1993), pp. 27–32.
37. For a geological analysis of the area's oil and gas potential and review of competing claims (with maps), see Mark J. Valencia, *Offshore North-East Asia: Oil, Gas, and International Relations* (London: Economist Intelligence Unit, 1988).
38. Multinational oil companies currently have little interest in drilling near the Diaoyus because of difficult terrain, political uncertainty, existence of unexploded ordnance from the use of the islands as a target range, and doubts about whether any reserves that might exist can be exploited on commercially viable terms. Western oil companies spent $5 billion drilling in geologically similar areas in the northern part of the South China Sea without discovering any significant commercial finds. See Sanqiang Jian, "Multinational Oil Companies and the Spratly Dispute," *Journal of Contemporary China*, Vol. 6, No. 16 (January 1997), pp. 596–597.
39. For a detailed legal analysis of the claims, see Jeanette Greenfield, *China's Practice in the Law of the Sea* (New York: Oxford University Press, 1992), pp. 127–149.
40. Japan argues that the continental shelf should be divided along the median line between the two countries; China advocates use of natural prolongation of the continental shelf, which would give it most of the territory.
41. Mark J. Valencia, "Energy and Insecurity in Asia," *Survival*, Vol. 39, No. 3 (Autumn 1998), pp. 97–98. This estimate assumes that the Diaoyu Islands are islets or rocks that "cannot sustain human habitation or economic life of their own" and therefore do not generate a 200–nautical mile

Convention on the Law of the Sea includes extensive dispute resolution procedures, the convention does not address conflicting sovereignty claims over islands.

China's claims to the Diaoyu Islands rest partly on historical records dating back to the Ming dynasty (1368–1644), which include scattered references to the islands.[42] Japan contends that it acquired the islands upon gaining control of Okinawa in 1879, although they were not formally annexed until 1895.[43] After China's defeat in the 1895 Sino-Japanese War, the Qing dynasty (1644–1911) formally ceded Taiwan "and its surrounding islands" to Japan under the Treaty of Shimonoseki. China claims that this transfer included the Diaoyu Islands. The United States gained control of the Diaoyus following Japan's defeat in World War II.[44] In 1972 the United States returned "administrative rights" over the islands to Japan along with Okinawa, but refused to take a position on the sovereignty dispute.[45] The U.S. decision was based on a desire to avoid offending either China or Japan and on the recognition that both sides had some basis for their claims. The Chinese government argues that the reversion of the Diaoyu Islands to Japanese rule violated the 1943 Cairo Declaration and the 1945 Potsdam Proclamation. The Cairo Declaration stipulated that Japan must return all the Chinese territories it had annexed, while the Potsdam Proclamation, which Japan accepted upon its surrender, called for the execution of the terms of the Cairo Declaration. Thus China claims that the Diaoyu Islands should have reverted to Chinese rule.[46] Japan argues that the islands were not specifically mentioned in any of the treaties except the 1972 Okinawa reversion treaty.

---

exclusive economic zone or separate continental shelf claim. Article 121.3 of the Convention on the Law of the Sea, which concerns rocks, contains ambiguities that make it possible for Japan to argue that the Diaoyus are islands that convey rights to a much broader area of the continental shelf. See Greenfield, *China's Practice in the Law of the Sea*, pp. 134–135.

42. For a detailed statement of the historical basis of China's sovereignty claim, see Zhong Yan, "China's Claim to Diaoyu Island Chain Indisputable," *Beijing Review*, November 4–10, 1996, pp. 14–19.

43. Bruce Gilley, Sebastian Moffet, Julian Baum, and Matt Forney, "Rocks of Contention," *Far Eastern Economic Review*, September 19, 1996, p. 15.

44. Zhong, "China's Claim to Diaoyu Island Chain Indisputable," pp. 17–18. The islands were not explicitly mentioned in the treaty and were first defined as part of the Okinawa archipelago by a 1953 U.S. administrative order. See Jean-Marc F. Blanchard, "The Contemporary Origins of the Sino-Japanese Dispute over the Diaoyu (Senkaku) Islands: The U.S. Role," paper presented at the annual meeting of the American Political Science Association, Boston, Massachusetts, September 3–6, 1998.

45. For an analysis of the Diaoyu dispute and U.S. policy during this period, see Selig S. Harrison, *China, Oil, and Asia: Conflict Ahead?* (New York: Columbia University Press, 1977). Details of the U.S. diplomatic position on the status of the Diaoyus are in *Okinawa Reversion Treaty*, Hearings before the Committee on Foreign Relations, U.S. Senate, October 27–29, 1971, pp. 88–93, 144–154.

46. Zhong, "China's Claim to Diaoyu Island Chain Indisputable," p. 14.

Although China, Taiwan, and Japan did not pay much attention to the Diaoyu Islands prior to the announcement in 1969 that the East China Sea might contain oil, the dispute quickly became linked to nationalism. A September 1970 incident, in which reporters raising a Taiwanese flag were evicted from the Diaoyu Islands, sparked anti-Japanese protests and inspired a "Protect the Diaoyu Islands" movement in North America. The inclusion of the Diaoyus in the Okinawa reversion treaty led to a second round of diplomatic and popular protests, which ended with a 1972 agreement between Beijing and Tokyo to shelve the dispute indefinitely. In March and April 1978, right-wing Japanese Diet members opposed to a Peace and Friendship Treaty with China raised the issue of the Diaoyus in an effort to block the treaty, and the right-wing Japanese Youth Federation erected a lighthouse on the largest of the islands to symbolize Japan's claims. China responded by sending a flotilla of more than eighty armed fishing boats that repeatedly circled the islands.[47] The People's Liberation Army (PLA) Navy commander reportedly planned a major naval exercise as a show of force, but was overruled by Deng Xiaoping.[48] Because attaining an antihegemony clause in the Sino-Japanese treaty was a higher priority, China again agreed to shelve the dispute for future consideration.

The Chinese government's responses to Japanese challenges over the Diaoyu Islands in 1990 and 1996 offer an excellent opportunity to examine the relationship between the domestic search for legitimacy and foreign policy behavior. Both cases demonstrate the efforts of Chinese leaders to balance nationalism and economic performance. During the months prior to each crisis, the CCP promoted patriotism and anti-Japanese sentiment. When Japanese right-wing groups reasserted Japan's claim to the islands, there was popular pressure inside China for a strong response, forcing the leadership to choose between their nationalist and economic legitimation strategies. In each case the leadership chose to abandon its strident rhetoric in order to avoid damage to Sino-Japanese economic ties and to maintain domestic stability. The perceived failure of the CCP to defend China's territorial claims vigorously led to public criticism and had a negative impact on the regime's legitimacy.[49] These cases

47. Daniel Tretiak, "The Sino-Japanese Treaty of 1978: The Senkaku Incident Prelude," *Asian Survey*, Vol. 18, No. 12 (December 1978), pp. 1235–1249.
48. David Bachman, "Structure and Process in the Making of Chinese Foreign Policy," in Samuel S. Kim, ed., *China and the World*, 4th ed. (Boulder, Colo.: Westview Press, 1998), pp. 40–41.
49. It is fair to ask how much the average Chinese knows or cares about the Diaoyu Islands. A 1992 poll of over 1,000 Beijing college students found that 98.6 percent supported the overseas

suggest that economic development goals may be an effective restraint on nationalism, at least in the short term.

THE 1990 DISPUTE

The 1990 dispute over the Diaoyu Islands occurred when China's leaders were under extreme pressure from internal and external forces. Domestically, the 1989 Tiananmen massacre revealed the government's lack of legitimacy, and the subsequent political crackdown undermined efforts to address socioeconomic problems. The government's austerity program drove the economy into a severe downturn during the first two quarters of 1990. Real gross national product grew at a rate of only 1.8 percent during the first half of the year, state enterprises posted losses of $3.2 billion (twice the 1989 total), and rural unemployment soared.[50] China's leaders mounted a major propaganda campaign to appeal to nationalism and to shore up their legitimacy. On June 3, 1990, CCP General Secretary Jiang Zemin warned 3,000 youths about the threat of "peaceful evolution" from hostile forces at home and abroad and urged them to "carry forward" China's tradition of patriotism.[51] A month later the 150th anniversary of the Opium War provided another opportunity to play to Chinese nationalism.[52] Although most propaganda focused on the threat of "peaceful evolution" from the West, the Anti-Japanese War Museum in Beijing hosted an exhibition and film commemorating Chinese resistance to Japanese aggression between 1937 and 1945.[53] The strong performance of Chinese athletes at the 1990 Asian Games, held in Beijing, provided another vehicle for stirring up nationalism.

Following the Tiananmen crackdown the United States, Japan, and Western European countries suspended high-level contacts with the Chinese leader-

---

movements to protect the Diaoyu Islands. "Beijing Campuses Are Permeated with Anti-Japanese Feelings," *China Times Weekly,* October 18–24, 1992, pp. 22–23. A December 1995 poll conducted for the *China Youth Daily* found that 91.5 percent agreed that Japanese militarists had issued a strong challenge to China by erecting a lighthouse on the Diaoyus. Xinhua, "Youth Polled on Japan's Invasion of China," February 16, 1997, in World News Connection (WNC). WNC is the electronic version of the Foreign Broadcast Information Service (FBIS). The authors also encountered a number of Chinese analysts and students in Beijing in 1996 and 1997 who expressed nationalistic and anti-Japanese views and were both informed and concerned about the Diaoyus.
50. David Shambaugh, "China in 1990," *Asian Survey,* Vol. 31, No. 1 (January 1991), pp. 36–49.
51. "Patriotism and the Mission of Chinese Intellectuals—Speech by Jiang Zemin at a Report Meeting Held by Youth in the Capital to Commemorate 'May 4th,'" Xinhua, May 3, 1990, in FBIS, *Daily Report: China* (hereafter FBIS-CHI), May 4, 1990, pp. 8–13.
52. Xinhua, June 3, 1990, in FBIS-CHI, June 4, 1990, p. 44.
53. Xinhua, "Anti-Japanese War Exhibition Opens in Beijing," July 7, 1990, in FBIS-CHI, July 10, 1990, p. 6.

ship. In addition, the World Bank, the Asian Development Bank, and the Japanese government each froze billions of dollars of loans to China.[54] Although Japan initially cooperated with diplomatic and economic sanctions, it also stressed the importance of not isolating China. Accordingly, Japan supported the resumption of small-scale World Bank loans to China in October 1989, and announced its unilateral decision to resume official development loans to China (including a $5.6 billion loan package that had been frozen after Tiananmen) at the July 1990 Group of Seven summit.[55] These actions not only helped break China's diplomatic isolation, but also placed Japan in a position to influence the flow of foreign capital and development assistance crucial for Chinese efforts to restore economic growth. The announcement that development assistance would resume triggered a series of visits to Beijing by Japanese officials and businessmen, but the loan agreement was not formally signed until November 3, a delay that gave Japan diplomatic leverage during the 1990 Diaoyu Islands crisis.[56]

The dispute began when the Japanese press reported on September 29, 1990, that Japan's Maritime Safety Agency was preparing to recognize the lighthouse built on the main Diaoyu island in 1978 as an "official navigation mark."[57] The Japan Youth Federation, an extreme right-wing political group with about 3,000 members, had repaired the lighthouse in 1988 and 1989 to meet the safety agency's technical standards and applied for official recognition.[58] Although Taiwan immediately delivered a written protest to Japanese officials, China did not comment on the reports until October 18, when a Ministry of Foreign Affairs spokesperson responded to a press conference question by condemning the recognition of the lighthouse as a violation of China's sovereignty and demanding that the Japanese government curtail the activities of nationalistic

54. According to Walter Fauntroy, chairman of the U.S. House Subcommittee on International Development, Institutions, and Finance, loans pending or in the pipeline to China in 1989 included $4.7 billion at the World Bank, $1.1 billion at the Asian Development Bank, and $5.6 billion in bilateral development loans from Japan. "Congressmen Urge Block on World Bank Lending to China," *Journal of Commerce*, June 21, 1989, p. 7A.
55. Quansheng Zhao, *Interpreting Chinese Foreign Policy* (New York: Oxford University Press, 1996), pp. 163–168.
56. Whiting and Xin, "Sino-Japanese Relations," pp. 108–115; and Fan Cheuk-wan, *Hong Kong Standard*, November 3, 1990, p.1.
57. Kyodo, September 29, 1990, in FBIS, Daily Report: East Asia (hereafter FBIS-EAS), October 2, 1990, pp. 11–12. According to a former U.S. diplomat who questioned Japanese officials directly, the safety agency's intention to recognize the lighthouse was based on its utility as a navigational aid and was not intended to press Japanese sovereignty claims.
58. Kyodo, October 23, 1990, in FBIS-EAS, October 23, 1990, p. 5; and Sebastian Moffet, "The Right and Its Wrongs," *Far Eastern Economic Review*, November 21, 1996, p. 30.

right-wing organizations.[59] The Japanese Foreign Ministry responded with a statement reaffirming Japan's claim to the islands.

Three days later tensions rose when the Maritime Safety Agency repelled two boats of Taiwanese activists who were attempting to place a torch on the Diaoyu archipelago as a symbol of Taiwan's sovereignty. China's foreign ministry spokesperson responded to a Taiwanese reporter's question by denouncing the safety agency's actions and demanding that Japan "immediately stop all violations of China's sovereignty over the islands and in neighboring waters."[60] In Hong Kong the incident inspired anti-Japanese demonstrations and newspaper articles condemning Japanese militarism.[61] Taiwan held an emergency cabinet meeting and issued a statement protesting the Japanese action, reaffirming Taiwan's sovereignty claim, and calling for the issue to be handled through diplomatic means.[62] At the same time, the government stressed that it was "inopportune and infeasible to use force" and quietly took steps to prevent Taiwanese boats from approaching the Diaoyus.[63]

On October 22 Japan's chief cabinet secretary, Misoji Sakamoto, reaffirmed Japan's sovereignty claim but also cited Deng Xiaoping's 1978 statement that ownership of the Diaoyus should be settled by a later generation.[64] China's news agency criticized the Japanese claim as arrogant. The next day Japanese Prime Minister Toshiki Kaifu promised that Japan would adopt a "cautious attitude" in dealing with the lighthouse application, and the Japanese Foreign Ministry stated there were no plans to dispatch military ships to patrol the islands.[65] Kaifu's statement demonstrated Japan's desire to prevent the issue from escalating and sought to reassure China that the pending Diet bill authorizing deployment of Japanese forces for United Nations peacekeeping missions did not represent a resurgence of Japanese militarism.[66] When Chinese

---

59. Taipei Central News Agency (CNA), October 19, 1990, in FBIS-CHI, October 22, 1990, pp. 55–56; and Japanese broadcast from Beijing, October 19, 1990, in FBIS-CHI, October 22, 1990, p. 7.
60. "Both Sides of the Straits Unite in Dealing with the Foreign Country and Safeguarding China's Sovereignty over Diaoyu Island," *Wen Wei Po*, October 23, 1990, p. 2, in FBIS-CHI, October 23, 1990, p. 11; and Gan Cheng, "The Storm over Diaoyu Island," Zhongguo Tongxun She [China News Agency], October 24, 1990, in FBIS-CHI, October 24, 1990, p. 3.
61. "Japan Casts Greedy Eyes on Diaoyutai," *Wen Wei Po*, October 20, 1990, p. 2, in FBIS-CHI, October 22, 1990, pp. 8–9; and Hsieh Ying, "Diaoyu Island Is China's Sacred Territory," *Wen Wei Po*, October 22, 1990, p. 2, in FBIS-CHI, October 25, 1990, pp. 3–4.
62. Taipei Domestic Service, October 21, 1990, in FBIS-CHI, October 24, 1990, p. 68.
63. Taipei Domestic Service, October 22, 1990, in ibid., p. 69; and Willy Wo-lap Lam, *South China Morning Post*, October 30, 1990, p. 9.
64. Kyodo, October 23, 1990, in FBIS-EAS, October 23, 1990, p.3.
65. Kyodo, October 24, 1990, in FBIS-EAS, October 24, 1990, p.2.
66. Tai Ming Cheung and Charles Smith, "Rocks of Contention," *Far Eastern Economic Review*, November 1, 1990, p. 19.

Vice Foreign Minister Qi Huaiyuan finally met with the Japanese ambassador on October 27, he reaffirmed China's claim of "indisputable sovereignty" while urging Japan to agree to joint development of the area's resources. Qi's mildly worded statement criticized the safety agency's interception of the Taiwanese boats and Tokyo's "attitude of noninterference" toward the group that built the lighthouse, and requested that Japan "immediately cease unilateral action related to the Diaoyu Islands and the surrounding waters."[67] Three days later, diplomats in Beijing and Tokyo reported that both countries had agreed to quietly drop the dispute and avoid further provocative actions.[68]

Although the governments of China, Taiwan, and Japan adopted restrained policies that reaffirmed their sovereignty claims while preventing the dispute from escalating, a return to the status quo that left the lighthouse standing and Japan in control of the Diaoyu Islands was unsatisfactory to Chinese nationalists. In Hong Kong about 10,000 people demonstrated against Japan's claims to the islands.[69] In Taiwan protesters rallied outside Japan's unofficial embassy and Huang Hsin-chieh, chairman of the opposition Democratic Progressive Party, announced plans to lead 300 fishing boats to surround the islands to protest Japan's control.[70] Chinese students in Macao demanded that China lodge an official protest against Japanese actions, while Chinese protesters in the United States staged demonstrations in front of the Japanese embassy and consulates.[71]

The Hong Kong press criticized the Chinese government's response as "weak and inadequate," noting that China had not invoked the aggressive rhetoric or military threats it normally used in response to sovereignty violations, that senior CCP leaders had not spoken out on the Diaoyu issue, and that Beijing's joint development proposals amounted to concessions.[72] A *South*

---

67. "Qi Huaiyuan Makes an Urgent Appointment with the Japanese Ambassador to China to Discuss Issues of Territorial Rights and Military Policy," *Renmin Ribao Overseas Edition,* October 29, 1990, p. 1, in FBIS-CHI, October 29, 1990, pp. 8–9.
68. Lam, October 30, 1990, p. 9.
69. Bellette Lee and Shirley Yam, "Protests Continue," *South China Morning Post,* October 29, 1990, pp. 1–2.
70. "Addressing the Tiaoyutai Issue," *China Post,* October 24, 1990, p. 4, in FBIS-CHI, October 30, 1990, p. 56. The announcement was probably intended to score political points by taking a tougher line on nationalist issues than the ruling Nationalist Party; the Taiwanese government prevented the fishing-boat flotilla from sailing.
71. Catherine Beck and Daniel Kwan, "Diaoyu Islands Campaign Called 'Ruse,'" *South China Morning Post,* October 26, 1990, p. 2; and Taipei CNA, November 12, 1990, in FBIS-CHI, November 15, 1990, p. 73.
72. Lin Pao-hua, "New Trends in Beijing's Relations toward Japan," *Ming Pao,* October 30, 1990, p. 9, in FBIS-CHI, October 30, 1990, p. 9; Chao Han-ching, "We Want Diaoyu Islands; We Do Not Want Japanese Yen" *Cheng Ming,* November 1, 1990, pp. 8–9, in FBIS-CHI, November 2, 1990, p. 7.

China Morning Post columnist criticized Vice Foreign Minister Qi's mild condemnation of Japanese actions as "a classic piece of appeasement posing as protest."[73] The perceived linkage between the CCP's accommodating posture toward the Diaoyu dispute and the resumption of Japanese loans highlighted the contradictions between the Chinese leadership's nationalist claims and its passive actions during the dispute. One writer scoffed at the claim that the National People's Congress Standing Committee had not received a telegram from Hong Kong deputies calling for urgent discussion of the Diaoyu Islands prior to its October 25 meeting, and criticized Prime Minister Li Peng for "begging for Japanese loans" at the same time that the CCP was banning anti-Japanese demonstrations.[74] A Chinese-controlled Hong Kong newspaper that had taken a hard-line position earlier in the dispute now responded by defending China's "firm stand and prudent attitude."[75]

China's restrained diplomacy was coupled with domestic efforts to minimize the significance of the Diaoyu dispute and to prevent anti-Japanese demonstrations. Following the landing attempt by Taiwanese activists, the CCP issued a circular to local party committees stressing that tensions over "these economically and strategically insignificant islands should not affect friendly relations between China and Japan."[76] The Chinese leadership sought to quell expressions of anti-Japanese sentiment by imposing a blackout on coverage of the protests occurring overseas, while the Beijing municipal government refused permission for rallies on university campuses and increased security in the university district.[77] The CCP's guidance to public security officials banned student demonstrations, called for intensified ideological education, and warned that people with ulterior motives might exploit anti-Japanese sentiment among students.[78]

Despite the media blackout, students in Beijing learned about the initial incident and the protests abroad through the British Broadcasting Corporation and Voice of America, and sought to express their anger toward the Japanese. They expected that the government would grant permission to stage anti-Japa-

73. Willy Wo-lap Lam, "China: Beijing Turns a Blind Eye," *South China Morning Post*, October 31, 1990, p. 15.
74. Lin, "New Trends in Beijing's Relations toward Japan," p. 7, in FBIS-CHI, October 30, 1990, p. 9.
75. "Firm Stand, Prudent Attitude," *Wen Wei Po*, November 1, 1990, in FBIS-CHI, November 1, 1990, p. 7.
76. Lo Ping, "Bowing to Japanese Yen Has Angered the Masses," *Cheng Ming*, November 1, 1990, pp. 6–7, in FBIS-CHI, November 5, 1990, p. 7.
77. Lam, "China: Beijing Turns a Blind Eye," p. 15; Chao, "We Want Diaoyu Islands," p. 7; and Lo, "Bowing to Japanese Yen," p. 7.
78. Document cited in Lo, "Bowing to Japanese Yen," p. 7.

nese protests because the demonstrations would be based on "patriotic senti-ment" and "national dignity."[79] Although the government clampdown pre-vented large-scale protests, many Beijing students felt the government had been too soft on Japan.[80] The demonstration ban angered students, who ac-cused China's leaders of failing to live up to their nationalistic rhetoric: "'Is there any patriotism to speak of when they don't even want the territory?' 'Diplomacy is diplomacy and public opinion is public opinion. Why can't the public express its opinion?' 'This only proves that this country is not the people's country.'"[81] By banning anti-Japanese demonstrations, the CCP itself became the target of public complaints. In Beijing students hung posters criticizing the CCP, and citizens distributed handbills entitled "We Want the Diaoyu Islands, Not Yen," censuring the CCP for sacrificing Chinese territory for Japanese loans.[82]

The conflicting demands of efforts to rebuild legitimacy through economic performance and nationalist appeals put the CCP in a difficult position. The aggressive defense of Chinese territorial claims that nationalists were demand-ing would threaten economic ties with Japan and Japanese diplomatic support, which was critical in persuading the Group of Seven to support the resumption of multilateral lending to China. A passive defense of China's territorial claims, however, made the regime vulnerable to domestic criticism and created the appearance that Taipei was more willing to defend China's sovereignty than was Beijing. Given the regime's shaky hold on power after Tiananmen, fear of what might happen once students took to the streets was also a major concern. A senior cadre in Beijing indicated that China's leaders were afraid that dem-onstrations might not only jeopardize the resumption of Japanese lending but also turn into antigovernment protests.[83] Although the Chinese leadership's pragmatic diplomacy improved China's international position and preserved its economic ties with Japan, the failure to back up nationalistic rhetoric with action angered many Chinese, who regarded Beijing's reactive posture as evidence that Chinese leaders did not actually support the patriotic sentiments they promoted.

---

79. Fan Cheuk-Lam and Alan Nip, "Intellectuals Criticize Government," *Hong Kong Standard,* October 31, 1990, p. 10; and Cheung Po-ling, "Request for Anti-Japanese Rally Probe," *Hong Kong Standard,* December 19, 1990, p. 6.
80. Fan and Nip, *Hong Kong Standard,* p. 10.
81. Lo, "Bowing to Japanese Yen," p. 7.
82. Chao, "We Want Diaoyu Islands," p. 7; and Lo, "Bowing to Japanese Yen," p. 7.
83. Chao, "We Want Diaoyu Islands," p. 7.

THE 1996 DISPUTE

The Chinese government's international and domestic position had improved considerably by 1996; however, another dispute over the Diaoyu Islands was still unwelcome. The U.S. decision to allow Taiwan's president, Lee Teng-hui, to make a private visit to the United States in June 1995 infuriated China. The U.S. policy reversal discredited President Jiang Zemin and Foreign Minister Qian Qichen's Taiwan policy and may have strengthened the hand of military hard-liners who favored a confrontational policy.[84] The PLA conducted extensive military exercises from late June to August 1995 that included live missile firings near Taiwan. A second round of exercises prior to the March 1996 Taiwanese elections included the launch of ballistic missiles that landed within 25 miles of Taiwanese ports, leading the United States to deploy two carrier battle groups to the area and prompting quiet discussion of the "China threat" throughout Asia. Chinese officials were aware of negative international reactions and sought to downplay China's military capabilities for fear of driving Japan closer to the United States.[85] China's desire for a lower military profile and an opportunity to repair relations with Japan influenced its policy toward the Diaoyu Islands. When China ratified the Convention on the Law of the Sea in May 1996, the legislation refrained from specifying China's territorial baseline around Taiwan to avoid triggering a dispute with Japan over the Diaoyu Islands.[86]

As in 1990, renewed claims to the islands by right-wing Japanese groups brought the Chinese leadership's legitimation strategies into conflict. Domestically, Jiang Zemin and the CCP had launched major "patriotic education" and "spiritual civilization" campaigns in 1995–96 that stressed nationalism and played to anti-Japanese sentiment. The one-hundredth anniversary of the Treaty of Shimonoseki and the fiftieth anniversary of World War II prompted numerous government-sponsored patriotic activities—including a film re-creating the Nanjing massacre and public exhibits documenting Japanese acts

---

84. Shambaugh, "Containment or Engagement of China?" pp. 190–191; Garver, *Face Off*, pp. 60–62; and Robert G. Sutter, "China Policy: Crisis over Taiwan, 1995—A Post-Mortem," Congressional Research Service Report 95-1173 F, December 5, 1995, pp. 5–6.
85. Phillip Saunders's interviews with Chinese analysts in Beijing and Shanghai, August–September 1996 and June–July 1997.
86. "State Adopts UN's Maritime Law," *Beijing Review*, June 3–9, 1996, p. 5; and "News Briefing by Chinese Foreign Ministry," ibid., p. 10. In 1992 China's inclusion of the Diaoyu Islands in its domestic territorial waters law (reportedly at the behest of the PLA) had triggered Japanese protests. By not specifying baselines around Taiwan, China avoided provoking Japan without weakening its sovereignty claim.

of aggression.[87] The draft revision of U.S.-Japan security guidelines to give Japan a larger regional security role also provoked strong nationalistic feelings in China. Successful efforts to promote nationalism raised the political stakes in the territorial dispute. At the same time, the Chinese leadership also sought to enhance its legitimacy by improving economic relations with Japan. Japan had become an increasingly important market for Chinese goods, with exports to Japan reaching $30.9 billion in 1996.[88] China's economic position had improved considerably, but Chinese leaders were still eager to attract Japanese investment, to obtain new concessional loans, and to have Tokyo reinstate the grant aid it froze to protest China's nuclear tests in August 1995.[89] The suspended grant aid and delays in finalizing the loan package gave Japan diplomatic leverage throughout the crisis.

The 1996 dispute over the Diaoyu Islands began when the right-wing Japan Youth Federation erected a second makeshift lighthouse on July 14 to buttress Japan's sovereignty claim. On July 20 Japan ratified the Convention on the Law of the Sea, declaring a 200–nautical mile exclusive economic zone that included the Diaoyu Islands. Five days later, the Japan Youth Federation applied to the Maritime Safety Agency to have the lighthouse recognized as an official beacon. Japanese Prime Minister Ryutaro Hashimoto's visit to the Yasukuni shrine (which honors Japan's war dead) on July 29 further heightened Sino-Japanese tensions. On August 18 the Senkaku Islands Defense Association, a small right-wing group, placed a wooden Japanese flag next to one of the lighthouses.[90] In discussions with Hong Kong officials on August 28, Japanese Foreign Minister Yukihiko Ikeda reaffirmed Japan's claim to the islands. A Hong Kong newspaper quoted Ikeda as saying, "The Diaoyu Islands have always been Japan's territory; Japan already effectively governs the islands, so the territorial issue does not exist."[91]

Ikeda's statement prompted the stern warnings from China that had been absent during the 1990 dispute, reflecting improvements in China's relative

---

87. Maggie Farley, "China Enlists WWII Fervor to Foster National Strength," *Los Angeles Times,* August 12, 1995, p. A1; and Sheila Tefft, "China Remembers a Cruel Japan," *Christian Science Monitor,* August 14, 1995, p. 1.
88. Japan imported 20 percent of China's total exports in 1996. International Monetary Fund, *Direction of Trade Statistics Yearbook, 1997* (Washington, D.C.: International Monetary Fund, 1997), p. 157.
89. Christopher B. Johnstone, "East Asian Dispute Sparks Regional Jitters," JEI (Japan Economic Institute of America) Report No. 37, October 4, 1996, in LEXIS/NEXIS.
90. Taipei CNA, August 22, 1996, in BBC Summary of World Broadcasts, August 24, 1996, in LEXIS/NEXIS.
91. "No Japanese Challenge against Chinese Sovereignty Allowed," *Wen Wei Po,* September 2, 1996, in WNC.

power position. Foreign ministry spokesperson Shen Guofang condemned Ikeda's remarks as irresponsible, and stressed that the actions of right-wing Japanese groups were related to the Japanese government's attitude.[92] The *People's Daily* published a front-page editorial declaring that "whoever expects the 1.2 billion Chinese people to give up even one inch of their territory is only daydreaming."[93] A petition by a Chinese activist calling upon Jiang Zemin and China's top military leaders to send warships to dismantle the lighthouse garnered 257 signatures.[94] At a press conference on September 3, Shen denied that Japanese loans would alter China's sovereignty claims: "Japanese yen loans are helpful for promoting Sino-Japanese economic cooperation and trade, but as far as the issue of sovereignty is concerned, the Chinese government cannot make any compromise." Shen repeated China's offer to shelve the dispute in favor of joint development and cautioned against unilateral actions by either side that might intensify the conflict.[95]

On September 9 members of the Japan Youth Federation returned to repair the new lighthouse, which had been damaged by a typhoon. The next day they reapplied for official recognition of the lighthouse. China's foreign ministry lodged a strong protest with the Japanese government, and Shen stated that if the Japanese government did not take measures to prevent right-wing groups from infringing on China's sovereignty, "the situation will become more serious and the issue more complicated."[96] On September 13–14 the PLA practiced blockades and landings on islands off Liaoning Province that may have been intended to warn Tokyo against further incursions on the Diaoyu Islands.[97] Chinese in Hong Kong, Macao, and Taiwan staged anti-Japanese demonstrations, while Hong Kong activists presented the Chinese government with 15,000 signatures urging a tougher stand against the Japanese.[98]

On September 24 Chinese Foreign Minister Qian met with Japanese Foreign Minister Ikeda at the United Nations General Assembly in New York. Both governments were determined to prevent nationalist groups from escalating the dispute. Qian affirmed the importance of Sino-Japanese relations, but also

92. Kyodo, "China Blasts Ikeda's Remarks on Senkaku Islands," August 29, 1996, in LEXIS/NEXIS.
93. "Japan, Do Not Do Foolish Things," Xinhua, August 30, 1996, in WNC.
94. Kyodo, September 2, 1996, in WNC.
95. Zhongguo Tongxun She, September 3, 1996, in WNC.
96. Xinhua, September 11 and 12, 1996, in WNC.
97. "Party Leaders, Generals to Discuss Diaoyu Islands at Plenum," *Hong Kong Standard,* September 23, 1996, p. 1.
98. Nicholas D. Kristof, "An Asian Mini-Tempest over Mini-Island Group," *New York Times,* September 16, 1996, p. A8.

called upon the Japanese government to take effective measures to control the actions of right-wing groups. He urged Japan to remove the lighthouse, but made no threats. Ikeda stated that Tokyo had no plans to officially recognize the lighthouse, but made no commitment to remove the structure. Each foreign minister reaffirmed his country's claim to the islands, but both agreed that the dispute should not overshadow good bilateral ties.[99]

Despite the conciliatory tone of the Qian-Ikeda meeting, anti-Japanese sentiment surged two days later following the death of David Chan, a pro-China activist from Hong Kong who drowned after jumping in the water when Japan's Maritime Safety Agency prevented his boat from landing on one of the Diaoyu Islands. Chan's death inspired large anti-Japanese protests and boycotts in Hong Kong and Taiwan, and prompted a second and more successful attempt by Hong Kong and Taiwanese activists to plant their national flags on the Diaoyu Islands on October 9.[100] Within China seventeen members of a small newly formed anti-Japanese group wore black armbands to protest Chan's death.[101] As demonstrations in Hong Kong and Taiwan escalated, the Chinese leadership became increasingly eager to end the controversy over the islands. A foreign ministry spokesperson refused to answer a question about whether China would take measures to protect protesters.[102] Premier Li Peng blamed the incident on "a tiny handful of right-wingers and militarists in Japan" and called upon the Japanese government to safeguard the relationship.[103] In an interview with Japan's NHK TV, Chinese Vice Foreign Minister Tang Jiaxuan pressed for a resolution of the dispute in light of the upcoming twenty-fifth anniversary of the normalization of Sino-Japanese diplomatic relations.[104] Foreign Minister Qian expressed similar sentiments to a group of Japanese reporters visiting China and repeated Beijing's long-standing proposal for joint exploration of the area's resources.[105] On October 29 Tang

---

99. Kyodo, September 25, 1996, in LEXIS/NEXIS; and Xinhua, September 25, 1996, in LEXIS/NEXIS.

100. "Democrats Start Week of Action over Diaoyu Islands," *Hong Kong Standard*, October 1, 1996, p. 3; and "Diaoyu Activists Storm Japanese Consulate," *South China Morning Post*, October 10, 1996, p. 1.

101. "Tong Zeng Reveals That Protect Diaoyu Activities Are Still Being Carried Out on the Mainland," *Hsin Pao*, October 1, 1996, p. 10, in WNC.

102. Vivien Pik-Kwan Chan, "China Reluctant to Help," *South China Morning Post*, September 27, 1996, p. 2.

103. Kyodo, "Premier Li Slams Japan on Chinese National Day, "September 30, 1996, in LEXIS/NEXIS.

104. "Vice Foreign Minister Interviewed on Island Dispute with Japan," NHK TV, October 9, 1996, in BBC Summary of World Broadcasts, October 11, 1996, in LEXIS/NEXIS.

105. "China's Qian Calls for Joint Exploration of Senkakus," Kyodo, October 13, 1996, in LEXIS/NEXIS; and "Qian Urges Tokyo to Keep Pledge on Senkakus," Jiji Press Ticker Service, October 14, 1996, in LEXIS/NEXIS.

traveled to Tokyo and used an informal meeting to press Prime Minister Hashimoto to remove the new lighthouse. Hashimoto refused, claiming that because the lighthouse was on private property, the government could not legally remove it.[106] Tang was forced to settle for a vague commitment from Deputy Foreign Minister Shunji Yanai that Japan would "properly" handle outstanding issues in Sino-Japanese relations, including the Diaoyu Islands.[107] This brought the issue to a close.

Throughout the dispute over the Diaoyu Islands, China's leaders sought to quash expressions of anti-Japanese sentiment for fear that they would damage Sino-Japanese economic relations and might turn into antigovernment protests. Chinese newspapers ignored the demonstrations in Hong Kong and Taiwan. When government authorities became aware that more than 200 messages calling for anti-Japanese protests were circulating on campus electronic bulletin boards, they deleted the messages and tightened control over university computer systems.[108] Jiang Zemin banned student demonstrations, and the State Education Commission instructed university officials in mid-September to channel students' feelings properly and prevent "too drastic words and deeds" that might hurt national stability and economic growth. Schools were ordered to inform students that the CCP was capable of safeguarding national sovereignty, and that social stability was a prerequisite for a powerful and prosperous country. In some cities, government authorities warned influential professors and writers not to express their opinions on the Diaoyu Islands dispute.[109] As the September 18 anniversary of Japan's invasion of Manchuria approached, the government sent leading anti-Japanese activists out of the capital to preempt plans for a rally in front of the Japanese embassy.[110] The central government also ordered local officials throughout China to contain

---

106. In fact, the Japanese owner had not given permission for construction of either lighthouse and regarded landings on the islands as illegal entry. "Islands of Extremism," *South China Morning Post*, September 22, 1996, p. 16.
107. Kyodo, October 30, 1996 in LEXIS/NEXIS; and Kwan Weng Kin, "No Legal Power to Remove Lighthouse: Hashimoto," *Straits Times*, October 31, 1996, p. 3, in LEXIS/NEXIS.
108. Willy Wo-lap Lam, "Keeping Western Influence at Bay," *South China Morning Post*, October 2, 1996, p. 17; and Steven Munson, "Chinese Protest Finds a Path on the Internet," *Washington Post*, September 17, 1996, p. A9.
109. Marylois Chan, "Jiang Issues Campus Gag Order on Diaoyu Incident," *Hong Kong Standard*, September 17, 1996, p. 1; and Lin Chin-yi, "State Education Commission Sends a Message to Institutions of Higher Education Nationwide Warning Them Against Too-Drastic Words and Deeds," *Ming Pao*, September 17, 1996, p. A4, in WNC.
110. "Diaoyu Protesters Told to Stop Their Activities," *Hong Kong Standard*, September 13, 1996, p. 1; and "Activist: 'Military Confrontation' with Japan 'Possible,'" *Hong Kong Standard*, October 1, 1996, p. 3.

pro-Diaoyu activities because of fears that migrant workers and the unemployed might use the demonstrations as a pretext for criticizing the government.[111] Despite the claim that Japanese loans would not influence Beijing's policy toward the islands, instructions issued by the central government in early October ordered provincial governments to place top priority on domestic economic development and to prevent anti-Japanese protests. The instructions stated that "the central government is determined to prevent elements of the Hong Kong public from destroying relations between Japan and China by intensifying their criticisms of Japan."[112]

The Chinese leadership's efforts to quell domestic unrest and downplay the dispute again hurt the regime's nationalist credentials. Hong Kong commentators drew unflattering parallels between China's willingness to fire missiles near Taiwan and its reluctance to defend Chinese protesters in Chinese waters. The CCP's pragmatic diplomacy clashed with its earlier anti-Japanese propaganda campaigns. Although the government crackdown prevented large anti-Japanese demonstrations like those in Hong Kong and Taiwan, it also prompted accusations that the Chinese leadership was illegitimate and unpatriotic. During the dispute, Chinese citizens sent over 37,000 letters and petitions with more than 150,000 signatures to the *People's Daily* and the *People's Liberation Daily*, demanding that the central government aggressively defend China's claim to the Diaoyu Islands.[113] Students in Beijing universities told reporters that the Chinese leadership's policy toward Japan was not firm enough and that they supported the Hong Kong demonstrations. Some declined to stage protests out of fear of punishment; others explicitly blamed the communist system for the leadership's insufficiently nationalist response.[114] In Shanghai, Fudan University students who had been prevented from demonstrating created a leaflet criticizing the *People's Daily* (and by implication the CCP) for its weak stance toward Japan.[115] Other Shanghai residents hung posters and distributed handbills directly censuring the CCP. District party

---

111. "Beijing Said Ordering Cities to Curb Diaoyu Protests," *South China Morning Post*, October 18, 1996, p. 12.
112. "Beijing Moves to Keep Lid on Protests," *Daily Yomiuri*, October 7, 1996, p. 1, in LEXIS/NEXIS.
113. Lo Ping, "Army, Civilians Call Jiang Zemin to Account," *Cheng Ming*, October 1, 1996, pp. 6–8, in WNC.
114. Jasper Becker, "Students in Beijing 'Too Scared' to Protest," *South China Morning Post*, September 26, 1996, p. 8; and authors' interview with a participant in the protests, Princeton, New Jersey, March 1998.
115. Huang Ling, "Leaflets Spread on Fudan Campus Calling for 'Breaking the Ice' on Diaoyu Islands," *Ming Pao*, September 17, 1996, p. A4, in WNC.

committees received leaflets entitled "What should be the punishment for suppressing the patriotic campaign of protecting the Diaoyu Islands?" and "A true Communist Party should stand by the people who are determined to protect the Diaoyu Islands!" Hu Sheng, president of the Chinese Academy of Social Sciences, warned that if the Chinese leadership continued to suppress anti-Japanese sentiment and ignore popular desires for a firm stance on the Diaoyu Islands, nationwide unrest could bring about "greater trouble than the political turbulence of 1989."[116]

The Chinese leadership's "unpatriotic" management of the Diaoyu Islands dispute also invited criticism from the military. A "well-informed source in Beijing" noted that China's conciliatory posture toward Japan was under fire.[117] Party officials and generals criticized Foreign Minister Qian for his soft stance on territorial issues. A Chinese military expert claimed that air force and naval exercises conducted off the coast of Liaoning Province were intended to send a message not only to Japan, but also to "government officials preoccupied with economic ties to Japan who apparently ignore the nationalist sentiments among soldiers."[118] A group of thirty-five army generals reportedly submitted a joint letter to the Chinese leadership demanding stronger efforts to "resist Japanese militarism and recapture the Diaoyu Islands," and criticizing the government's relaxed stand on the issue.[119] Despite both military and popular demands for a tougher policy toward Japan, the CCP leadership again proved willing to undermine its nationalist credentials in pursuit of economic development.

The Limits of Nationalism: Findings and Challenges

The Chinese leadership's actions in the 1990 and 1996 Diaoyu Islands disputes reveal a very different relationship between nationalism and international behavior than the international relations literature predicts. Before each crisis, Chinese leaders had promoted nationalist and anti-Japanese sentiment to increase their domestic legitimacy, while simultaneously trying to maintain good

116. Lo, "Army, Civilians Call Jiang Zemin to Account."
117. Jen Hui-wen, "Zhongnanhai Points Out Three Aspects Which Should Not Be Ignored in Dealing with Japan and the United States," Hsin Pao, September 13, 1996, p. 14, in WNC.
118. "Party Leaders, Generals to Discuss Diaoyu Issue at Plenum," Hong Kong Standard, September 23, 1996, p. 1.
119. Lo Ping, "Jiang Zemin Seen Facing Crisis over Diaoyutai Issue," Cheng Ming, October 1, 1996, pp. 6–8, in WNC.

economic relations with Japan to encourage economic growth. Renewed Japanese claims to the Diaoyu Islands created a conflict between these two goals. In each case the Chinese government chose to pursue economic growth at the expense of its nationalist credentials, adopting a conciliatory policy that maintained economic ties with Japan. China's improved power position in 1996 permitted a more assertive initial diplomatic response, but the Chinese government again acted firmly to contain nationalism when anti-Japanese sentiment started to escalate to a level that might have harmed bilateral relations. The government was willing to bear the domestic costs of reduced legitimacy caused by suppressing nationalist sentiment, and even proved willing to tolerate military criticism. An analysis of nationalism that neglects economic factors cannot explain this pattern of Chinese restraint. We argue that the relationship between legitimacy, nationalism, and economic performance presented above is a useful model for understanding Chinese behavior that can also be applied to other cases.

Some might contend that we have misinterpreted the significance of the protests and overstated their impact on the CCP's legitimacy. This interpretation views the Diaoyu Islands issue as a pretext: Chinese students used it as a safe means of expressing resentment against the CCP, Hong Kong democrats used it to demonstrate their patriotism, and Taiwanese opposition parties used it to criticize the ruling Nationalist Party. Although some protesters undoubtedly had ulterior motives, the majority appear to have been genuinely concerned about Japan's actions and the status of the Diaoyu Islands. The alternative interpretation ignores the dynamic of the incidents, in which initial opposition to Japan later turned into criticism of the CCP's actions. It also neglects the depth of the protests (including many participants without plausible ulterior motives), their breadth (including protests in North America), and their context as part of a rising nationalist trend. Because the Chinese government suppressed demonstrations and many critics were afraid to speak out, it is difficult to judge the strength of the protest movement inside China and the degree to which the government's legitimacy was affected. We have presented evidence that suggests a significant number of Chinese were concerned about the Diaoyu Islands and that some students and military officers were disappointed enough by their government's performance to express their dissatisfaction despite fears of punishment. Criticism of the CCP's performance was much stronger in the 1996 case, reflecting heightened nationalist sentiment. Collectively, our evidence suggests that some Chinese did draw a connection between the CCP's handling of the Diaoyu incidents and the regime's legitimacy.

Others might question whether our model can be extended to other cases. The argument presented above can also be applied to Taiwan and the Spratly Islands, but because the relationship between legitimacy, nationalism, and economic impact differs in each case, the pattern of Chinese behavior also differs. Taiwan's status is directly linked to the CCP's legitimacy, giving Chinese leaders less room to maneuver. At the same time, the economic and military costs of aggressive action are much higher (given the possibility of U.S. economic sanctions and military intervention). The stakes in terms of legitimacy are therefore very high, but Chinese options are constrained. The 1996 missile firings were an extreme response to perceived Taiwanese provocations and suspicion that the United States supported Taiwanese moves toward independence. They may have also reflected Jiang Zemin's political weakness during the leadership transition and the belief that the United States would not intervene. As the economic and strategic costs of China's March 1996 actions have become clear, however, China has adopted a restrained policy intended to maintain economic ties and to reassure the United States and Japan that it is not a military threat.[120] China's actions slowed Taiwan's movement toward independence and enhanced the regime's nationalist credentials, permitting CCP leaders to return to a strategy of balancing between sources of legitimacy while waiting for China's power position to improve. A formal declaration of Taiwanese independence would directly challenge the legitimacy of China's leaders, and economic considerations would be unlikely to moderate their response. In the absence of a direct challenge, however, Chinese leaders will likely continue to find ways to reconcile their sovereignty claims with Taiwan's de facto independence, as they have since rapprochement with the United States in 1971.

The Spratly Islands are a group of small islands and coral reefs that sit above potentially large but unproven oil reserves in the South China Sea; six countries claim sovereignty over all or some of the islands. China's claim to the Spratlys is less strongly linked to nationalism, so the Chinese leadership has more room to maneuver without endangering its nationalist credentials. At the same time, the other parties to the dispute (Taiwan, Vietnam, Brunei, the Philippines, and Malaysia) have less economic leverage over China, and China is by far the most powerful actor. The result has been a pattern of opportunistic

---

120. This restrained policy may be correlated with Jiang Zemin replacing Li Peng as head of the Foreign Affairs Leading Small Group, China's top foreign policy coordinating group, in late 1996. Bachman, "Structure and Process in the Making of Chinese Foreign Policy," pp. 37–39.

and sometimes aggressive Chinese behavior. When the Association of Southeast Asian Nations has presented China with a common front and outside actors such as Japan and the United States have been focused on Chinese expansionism, the economic (and potential military) costs of aggressive Chinese actions have been higher, and Chinese behavior has been more restrained. This restraint has been evident since the 1995 Mischief Reef incident focused attention on Chinese actions in the South China Sea.[121] Although the outcomes of these cases differ somewhat from the Diaoyu Islands cases, we argue that they are broadly consistent with our model.

Legitimacy and Regime Survival: Seven Scenarios

The Chinese government's search for new sources of legitimacy must be considered at least partially successful. China's leaders have skillfully handled the reversion of Hong Kong to Chinese sovereignty, ended China's post-Tiananmen international isolation, won diplomatic recognition from South Korea and South Africa, and slowed, at least temporarily, movement toward Taiwanese independence. Economically, their policies have sustained a high growth rate, lifted hundreds of millions of people out of poverty, and weathered the East Asian economic crisis. Per capita incomes have quadrupled since reforms began in 1978, although social and economic inequality is also increasing rapidly.[122] These accomplishments, combined with the "negative legitimacy" provided by the lack of viable alternatives to party rule, have helped the regime stay in power.[123] One survey of Chinese political opinion concluded that "the CCP leadership as the prevailing regime in China continues to enjoy political legitimacy, and hence is able to maintain the 'stability of society.'"[124] Another concluded that "there is an increasing level of acceptance of [the] CCP's new legitimation claims by the general public in the PRC."[125]

Despite these successes, the Communist Party's position remains fragile. Its legitimacy claims now rest on performance and emphasize the achievement of nationalist and economic objectives. The government has only a limited ability

---

121. The incident occurred when China erected territorial markers and structures on a reef also claimed by the Philippines; the Philippine government protested the Chinese action and later sent warships to demolish the structures.
122. World Bank, *China 2020: Development Challenges in the New Century* (Washington, D.C.: World Bank, 1997), pp. 1–4, 43–59; and Khan and Riskin, "Income and Inequality in China."
123. Zhong, "Legitimacy Crisis and Legitimation in China," pp. 214–215.
124. Chen et al., "Assessing Political Support in China," p. 565.
125. Zhong, "Legitimacy Crisis and Legitimation in China," p. 215.

to deliver on these goals, and will have difficulty satisfying the rising expectations created by its own claims. Achieving nationalist goals such as reunification with Taiwan, control over the Diaoyu and Spratly Islands, greater influence in Asia, and increased international prestige depends largely upon China's relative power, which is currently insufficient. Aggressive efforts to achieve these goals would interfere with economic performance, which requires expanded access to the international economy. Moreover, wrenching economic reforms with high social costs lie ahead, as the government moves from a planned economy to dismantling state-owned enterprises (creating a massive increase in urban unemployment) and constructing a new social welfare network. China will continue to suffer from the dislocations of modernization and remain dependent on international loans, foreign investment, technology transfers, and access to foreign markets. Chinese leaders will have difficulty delivering the level of performance necessary to maintain legitimacy.

Our analysis of the constraints and incentives that influence the Chinese leadership's behavior implies the need for a careful balance between nationalism and economic performance, between short-term regime survival and long-term nationalist goals. Seven potential developments could alter the leadership strategy described above.

First, major economic failure could remove economic performance as a source of legitimacy. Nationalism might not be a sufficient substitute, especially if corruption among party leaders or economic mismanagement were to be blamed for economic collapse. Given the economic challenges China faces as it tackles state enterprise reform in the midst of the Asian economic crisis, this scenario must trouble Chinese leaders, even if the alternatives to reform are equally unattractive.

Second, new political actors could challenge the leadership for not defending China's interests with sufficient vigor. The obvious source of a challenge is the PLA, but factions within the CCP could also use nationalism to attack the current leadership. Even an unsuccessful challenge could force leaders to adopt more aggressive international policies to shore up their domestic position. Leaders might push nationalism too far, despite recognition of potential negative consequences.

Third, nationalist rhetoric could frighten Japan and the United States into seeking to contain China. China might not only weaken its relative power position but also create enemies, which would decrease its security. The strategy outlined above depends on the ability to tailor nationalist messages for domestic purposes without adverse international consequences. Chinese leaders have managed this successfully in the past, but China's rising power means that nationalist statements now attract increased foreign scrutiny. Recent efforts to counter the Western perception of a China threat suggest that the leadership is aware of this danger.

Fourth, we describe contradictions between nationalism and economic performance, but Chinese leaders could redefine the relationship between these goals. China became a net oil importer in 1993, and the PLA Navy has argued that oil reserves under the Spratly and Diaoyu Islands are crucial to China's future economic development.[126] These geostrategic arguments weaken the conflict between nationalist and economic sources of legitimacy by suggesting that an aggressive foreign policy would serve both goals. We believe that Chinese leaders are unlikely to accept this argument because access to international markets will continue to be more important to China's development than control of energy supplies. Energy is not currently a binding constraint, and the time required to move these reserves into production—if they exist—makes this a long-term argument unlikely to appeal to a leadership focused on more immediate challenges.

Fifth, the expected Diaoyu (and South China Sea) oil reserves might not exist, or might not be commercially exploitable. The absence of significant oil reserves would remove the economic dimension of the conflict and reduce the issue to a sovereignty dispute over uninhabited rocks, diminishing the importance of the issue and making a settlement easier to achieve. Chinese and Japanese fisherman peacefully shared fishing grounds near the Diaoyus for centuries; the two governments signed an agreement in September 1997 allowing reciprocal fishing privileges.[127]

Sixth, China's economic dependence might not decrease, keeping the economic costs of military action high and preventing China from using force to achieve nationalist goals. Despite the negative side effects, Chinese leaders have recognized the necessity of keeping the door to the outside world open. Interdependence has continued to grow despite the efforts of Chinese leaders to control its costs.[128] China's integration into the world economy may not only improve China's power position, but it may also channel how China can use

---

126. Garver, "China's Push through the South China Sea," pp. 1018–1020.
127. "Calmer Waters," *South China Morning Post,* September 18, 1997, p. 22.
128. Thomas W. Robinson, "Interdependence in China's Foreign Relations," in Samuel S. Kim, ed., *China and the World: Chinese Foreign Relations in the Post–Cold War Era* (Boulder, Colo.: Westview Press, 1994), pp. 187–201.

its power. This is a fundamental premise of liberal international relations theory and the basis of the U.S. engagement strategy.[129]

Seventh, our focus on nationalism and economic performance as sources of legitimacy assumes that Chinese leaders are committed to the survival of the current Chinese political system. Political reforms are back on the government's agenda, however, and might help the government develop new sources of legitimacy. The widespread use of local elections as a means of disciplining corrupt local officials is one example of how political reforms have the potential to increase the government's legitimacy and improve state capacity.[130] Political reforms could reduce the government's reliance on nationalism as a source of legitimacy.[131] Restoration of Chinese sovereignty over uninhabited islands might be less important to a Chinese government that had other bases of popular support.

Conclusion

Are the pessimists right to worry about Chinese nationalism? We argue that fears that nationalism will interact with rising Chinese power to produce aggressive behavior are overstated, or at least premature.[132] China's behavior in the Diaoyu Islands disputes demonstrates that Chinese leaders sought to maintain good relations with Japan and pursue economic sources of legitimacy even at heavy cost to their nationalist credentials. Nationalism did not drive China into irrational actions. Although circumstances exactly comparable to the Diaoyu disputes are relatively rare, many authoritarian or liberalizing countries face similar trade-offs between appealing to nationalist sentiment on territorial issues and adopting restrained policies that maximize access to the

129. See Robert O. Keohane and Joseph S. Nye, *Power and Interdependence* (Boston: Little, Brown, 1977); Richard Rosecrance, *The Rise of the Trading State: Commerce and Conquest in the Modern World* (New York: Basic Books, 1986); John R. Oneal and Bruce M. Russett, "The Classical Liberals Were Right: Democracy, Interdependence, and Conflict, 1950–1985," *International Studies Quarterly,* Vol. 41, No. 2 (June 1997), pp. 267–294; and Andrew Moravcsik, "Taking Preferences Seriously: A Liberal Theory of International Politics," *International Organization,* Vol. 51, No. 4 (Autumn 1997), p. 522.
130. Wang Xu, "Mutual Empowerment of State and Peasantry: Grassroots Democracy in Rural China," *World Development,* Vol. 25, No. 9 (September 1997), pp. 1431–1442.
131. A more responsive Chinese government might be pressured even harder by popular nationalist demands, but this would be less worrying than current deliberate government efforts to maintain legitimacy by stirring up nationalism.
132. For a similar argument that emphasizes China's current international weakness, see Andrew J. Nathan and Robert S. Ross, *The Great Wall and the Empty Fortress: China's Search for Security* (New York: W.W. Norton, 1997).

international economy and promote economic development. The evidence from these case studies suggests that the literature on nationalism and international conflict may be too pessimistic. We agree that relative power and economic dependence are the main forces currently restraining Chinese leaders, and that they intend to achieve nationalist goals once China's power position improves. One official reportedly stated after the 1996 Diaoyu crisis that China could afford to be patient, because China would catch up to Japan's economy in the next few decades. "When that happens, Japan will review its position on the Diaoyus and find that China has been right all along."[133] However, conclusions about China's future international behavior based solely on today's nationalist rhetoric are premature. Nationalism is currently an important source of government legitimacy, but economic performance also matters. The seven scenarios outlined above suggest that domestic and international conditions could change dramatically before China is in a position to achieve its goals. Chinese nationalism is cause for concern, but not yet cause for alarm.

---

133. "Beijing Takes the Long View," *Asia Times,* October 31, 1996, p. 8.

China's Search for a Modern Air Force

John Wilson Lewis
and Xue Litai

$\mathbf{F}$or more than forty-eight years, the People's Republic of China (PRC) has sought to build a combat-ready air force.[1] First in the Korean War (1950–53) and then again in 1979, Beijing's leaders gave precedence to this quest, but it was the Gulf War in 1991 coupled with growing concern over Taiwan that most alerted them to the global revolution in air warfare and prompted an accelerated buildup.

This study briefly reviews the history of China's recurrent efforts to create a modern air force and addresses two principal questions. Why did those efforts, which repeatedly enjoyed a high priority, fail? What have the Chinese learned from these failures and how do they define and justify their current air force programs? The answers to the first question highlight changing defense concerns in China's national planning. Those to the second provide a more nuanced understanding of current security goals, interservice relations, and the evolution of national defense strategies.

With respect to the first question, newly available Chinese military writings and interviews with People's Liberation Army (PLA) officers on the history of the air force suggest that the reasons for the recurrent failure varied markedly from period to period. That variation itself has prevented the military and political leaderships from forming a consensus about the lessons of the past and the policies that could work.

In seeking to answer the second question, the article examines emerging air force and national defense policies and doctrines and sets forth Beijing's rationale for the air force programs in light of new security challenges, particularly those in the Taiwan Strait and the South China Sea. In the 1990s, the air force has fashioned both a more realistic R&D (research and development) and procurement policy and a more comprehensive strategy for the PLA Air Force (PLAAF) in future warfare. We conclude that this strategy is recasting time-

John Wilson Lewis and Xue Litai are members of the Stanford University Center for International Security and Cooperation and have coauthored a number of studies on Chinese military programs.

The authors acknowledge with thanks the contributions made by two anonymous reviewers and by Kenneth Allen, William J. Perry, and Dean Wilkening.

Unless otherwise stated, all Chinese-language publications are published in Beijing.
1. Two English-language studies, though now dated, provide the foundation for any understanding of this subject: Kenneth W. Allen, Glenn Krumel, and Jonathan D. Pollack, _China's Air Force Enters the Twenty-first Century_ (Santa Monica, Calif.: RAND, 1995); and Duan Zijun, chief ed., _China Today: Aviation Industry_ (Beijing: China Aviation Industry Press, 1989).

International Security, Vol. 24, No. 1 (Summer 1999), pp. 64–94
© 1999 by the President and Fellows of Harvard College and the Massachusetts Institute of Technology.

honored Chinese dogma concerning "active defense" and no first strike, and that PLA theorists have inched closer to Western concepts on the role of air power in warfare.[2]

We begin with an overview of Beijing's response to heavy losses from U.S. air strikes against Chinese forces in the Korean War, and the PLA's abortive three-decade effort to build a modern air force. With the ending of the chaotic Cultural Revolution and the Mao Zedong era in 1976, China's new leader, Deng Xiaoping, and his military commanders once more gave priority to air force modernization. Here we analyze the Chinese inability to achieve the objectives of the 1980s and provide the background for the PLA's urgent reevaluation of air power that followed the 1991 Gulf War. We then examine the conclusions reached in that reevaluation and show how these conclusions have changed PLAAF strategy and procurement policies. The final sections of the article discuss how Beijing's concerns about a future conflict in the Taiwan Strait intensified internal PLA debates on air force missions and further transformed its modernization programs. We end with an assessment of the Chinese case for continuing the search for a modern air force in light of the decades of repeated setbacks and the overwhelming air superiority of its potential adversaries.

Marching in Place

Chinese leader Mao Zedong first elevated the importance of his fledgling air force in the early stages of the Korean War. In 1951, faced with mounting Chinese casualties from U.S. air strikes, he called for the formation of a national aviation industry, and in October, his diplomats inked an accord in Moscow on technical support for that industry. Although Moscow long resisted a serious commitment to providing air support during the Korean War, within weeks after the October agreement, Soviet experts began heading to China to help construct assembly plants for planes and jet engines.[3]

---

2. Zheng Shenxia and Zhang Changzhi, "On the Development of the Modern Air Force and the Change in Military Strategy," *Zhongguo Junshi Kexue* [China military science], No. 2 (1996), pp. 82–89.

3. Duan Zijun, chief ed., *Dangdai Zhongguo de Hangkong Gongye* [Contemporary China's aviation industry] (Beijing: Chinese Social Science Press [hereafter CSS Press], 1988), pp. 18–19. We review the Sino-Soviet controversy over air support in Sergei N. Goncharov, John W. Lewis, and Xue Litai, *Uncertain Partners: Stalin, Mao, and the Korean War* (Stanford, Calif.: Stanford University Press, 1993), chap. 6.

Paying for these factories did not pose an initial insurmountable obstacle. Mao had negotiated a pledge of $300 million in credits during his journey to Moscow in the winter of 1949–50. The Chinese at first resolved to devote the bulk of this sum to buying Soviet naval equipment for an invasion of Taiwan planned for the summer of 1950. Chinese losses to U.S. air raids in Korea changed Mao's mind, however, and in February 1952, he redirected half of the credits to the air force. Over time, virtually all these credits flowed to the purchase of planes and aviation ordnance from Moscow.[4] Thereafter China manufactured Soviet-designed jet fighters and then bombers under license.

The record of accomplishment from this investment is unimpressive.[5] Poor planning, lack of financial and human resources and the requisite industrial base, misguided bureaucratic meddling, Nikita Khrushchev's denigration of air power at a time of Soviet influence within the PLA, and the rising importance attached to building the strategic forces interrupted progress toward a combat-ready air force for the next quarter century. Chief of the General Staff Luo Ruiqing, reflecting deepening PLA concerns about the mounting conflict in Indochina, did try again to accelerate the aircraft program in 1964,[6] and by 1966, China had begun making light and medium bombers as well as fighters based on leftover Soviet blueprints. In 1966 Mao also approved construction of an assembly center and other pioneering facilities in Shaanxi Province for manufacturing parts for the Soviet-designed bombers, and gave precedence to the production of bombers over all other aircraft. Still, the results did not match the mandated effort or commitment of scarce resources.

The mistakes and missteps extended well beyond the pace of production. Dictated by the PLA's traditional strategy of "active defense," including the protection of its big cities and industrial bases, China should have assigned a comparable priority to R&D programs on fighters, radar systems, surface-to-air missiles, and electronic countermeasures for strengthening air defense. That decision, too, was not forthcoming. Decades later PLA historians would blame Beijing's senior leaders for their failure to grasp the need for such protection.

Mao was also mired in outmoded concepts about the nature of warfare. Even as he was expressing his fears of imminent global conflict in the 1960s and

---

4. Yang Guoyu, chief ed., *Dangdai Zhongguo Haijun* [Contemporary China's navy] (Beijing: CSS Press, 1987), p. 687.
5. Unless otherwise cited, the information in this paragraph and the next is from Song Yichang, "The Startup of China's Modern Aviation Industry and Reflections on It," *Zhanlüe yu Guanli* [Strategy and management], No. 4 (1996), pp. 102–106.
6. Huang Yao and Zhang Mingzhe, *Luo Ruiqing Zhuan* [Biography of Luo Ruiqing] (Beijing: Contemporary China Press, 1996), pp. 398–399.

pushing the quest for nuclear weapons and long-range missiles, he impeded all weapons procurement programs by launching massive industrial construction in China's interior or "Third Line." In these remote bastions, primitive factories would manufacture the tools of war for the survivors of the predicted nuclear holocaust. Just at the moment violent clashes broke out on the Sino-Soviet frontier in March 1969, Mao remained so committed to this Third Line construction that most of the money for the aviation industry was poured into Third Line projects that were doomed from the outset.[7]

The fault lay with form as well as substance. To succeed, any R&D program on advanced aircraft and their armaments must be minutely planned and take into account technological uncertainties, long lead times, and the vagaries of political commitment. However, the Central Military Commission (CMC)—the PLA's small but powerful senior command and policymaking body—in a near frenzy caused by the mounting border tensions and the general crisis mood of the times, ruined any possibility for such success. In 1971 it ordered the aviation ministry to commence R&D programs on 27 new types of aircraft.[8] By starting everything at once, nothing truly started.

During the Cultural Revolution (1966–76), moreover, the onslaught of Mao-inspired radicalism exacted a wrenching toll on the cohesion of the air force command system and its fighting capacity. Factional pressures and simplistic slogans paralyzed the PLAAF, causing it to slight pilot training and flight operations. For example, in 1964 every fighter pilot had 122 flying hours, but each pilot averaged only 24 and 55 flying hours in 1968 and 1970, respectively. Many pilots had only 30–40 flying hours a year, some even fewer than 20 hours, and plane crashes came with tragic regularity. By 1972 only 6.2 percent of PLAAF pilots could fly safely at night in good weather, and a mere 1 percent could do so under marginal night conditions.[9]

For a while, nothing seemed to go well. In 1973, for example, Zhou Enlai called on the air force to heighten its fighting skills within two and a half years.[10] However, the lack of well-trained pilots was so consequential that the

7. Peng Min, chief ed., *Dangdai Zhongguo de Jiben Jianshe* [Contemporary China's capital construction] (Beijing: CSS Press, 1989), vol. 1, pp. 159–160; Duan, *Dangdai Zhongguo de Hangkong Gongye*, p. 73; and Yan Fangming, "A Review of Third Line Construction," *Dangshi Yanjiu* [Studies on the party's history], No. 4 (1987), p. 73.
8. Lin Hu, "The Development of Air Force Equipment in the Seventh Five-Year Plan Period (1986–90)," in Wang Runsheng, chief ed., *Kongjun Huiyi Shiliao* [The air force: historical materials on recollections] (Beijing: Liberation Army Press [hereafter PLA Press], 1992), p. 784; and Duan, *Dangdai Zhongguo de Hangkong Gongye*, pp. 95–96, 100, 136, 145.
9. Lin Hu, chief ed., *Kongjun Shi* [The history of the air force] (Beijing: PLA Press, 1989), p. 197.
10. Zhang Tingfa and Gao Houliang, "The Construction of the Air Force Has Entered a New Historical Stage after Bringing Order out of Chaos," in Wang, *Kongjun Huiyi Shiliao*, p. 620.

air force could not assign a single organic squadron to provide air cover during the Sino-South Vietnamese armed conflict, January 15–20, 1974.[11] As an emergency measure, the air force had to transfer qualified commanders from different squadrons on an ad hoc basis to fly these missions.

During these same years of upheaval, Mao's radical bannermen launched a large-scale persecution of aircraft designers and engineers, one of the ideologically targeted groups of "intellectuals." Moreover, technical and logistics bugs, the result of "politics in command," continued to plague airplane production. A typical case was the J-6 fighter, a version of the MiG-19. In 1971, 7 of the 40 J-6s built for foreign sale proved defective.[12] Hundreds of the J-6c's (the most advanced version of this plane) were built before the design was finalized, and millions of yuan had to be budgeted to have them dismantled and rebuilt. In this and similar ways, the aviation ministry wasted 65.8 percent of its R&D funds. In 1972 Marshal Ye Jianying, who had replaced Lin Biao to oversee CMC operations, told the ministry never to "give birth to a child before giving birth to its father," but to no avail. Throughout the decade, the ministry, without doing the necessary planning, launched a series of "unsuccessful efforts to finalize aircraft designs."[13]

What is more, the institutes under the Aviation Research Academy (or Sixth Academy) made sorry headway in their quest for new designs. For example, Chinese engineers could not finish the designs for the J-7 and J-8, two fighters then under development, until more than ten years after the inaugural test flights of their prototypes. Not until 1979, thirteen years after the test flights of a prototype J-7, did the ministry approve the J-7 to replace the J-6.[14] Program after program fell far short of minimal requirements and firm deadlines.

By the end of the Cultural Revolution in 1976, the aviation industry was reeling from the decade of neglect and strife.[15] Quality problems occurred

11. The information in the rest of this paragraph is from Lin, *Kongjun Shi*, p. 197.
12. Zhao Dexin, chief ed., *Zhonghua Renmin Gongheguo Jingji Zhuanti Dashiji (1967–1984)* [A specialized chronology on the economy of the People's Republic of China (1967–1984)] (Zhengzhou: Henan People's Press, 1989), p. 110.
13. Yao Jun, "The Scientific Research Works of the Air Force," in Wang, *Kongjun Huiyi Shiliao*, p. 710; Lin, *Kongjun Shi*, p. 200; and Duan, *Dangdai Zhongguo de Hangkong Gongye*, pp. 95–96, 100, 136, 145. The quotes are from Duan, *Dangdai Zhongguo de Hangkong Gongye*, pp. 83, 100.
14. Duan, *Dangdai Zhongguo de Hangkong Gongye*, pp. 82–84; and Xie Guang, chief ed., *Dangdai Zhongguo de Guofang Keji Shiye* [Contemporary China's defense science and technology cause] (Beijing: Contemporary China Press, 1992), vol. 2, p. 191.
15. The information in this paragraph and the next is from Wang Dinglie, chief ed., *Dangdai Zhongguo Kongjun* [Contemporary China's air force] (Beijing: PLA Press, 1989), pp. 545–546; Lin, *Kongjun Shi*, pp. 236–237; and Zhang and Gao, "Construction of the Air Force," pp. 621–622, 625, 628–629. The quote is from Wang, *Dangdai Zhongguo Kongjun*, p. 546.

on the vanes of the J-6c turbojet engines. Rivets on the Q-5 attacker (fighter-bomber) were found loosened. Rotary wings dropped from Z-5 helicopters. Engineers found flaws endemic in the J-6c fighter and the Q-5 attacker as well as the Z-5, and shipped 1,050 of these aircraft back to the factories where technicians hunted down thousands of defects. The air force summarized these faults as "backward equipment, poor-quality products, and inadequate components." Moreover, it could not break free from its reliance on the Soviet aircraft and R&D methods introduced in the 1950s and 1960s, and PLAAF leaders concluded that the revolutionary advancements in foreign aviation technologies had increased the inequality between China and other military powers.

After years of fruitless striving, official examinations exposed unresolved training issues and leadership failures. Fifty percent of pilots could not accurately land by instrument. Most fighter pilots had failed to master the art of hitting targets from a wide angle of attack. Some fighter squadrons had a percentage of hits in mock dogfights as low as 1.7 percent, and most attacker and bomber pilots had equally dismal records on the target ranges. Many pilots had few, if any, opportunities to fire a gun or make a bombing run. To make matters worse, a third of their commanders were deemed incompetent. The results of near nonstop investigations confirmed the extent of the problems but failed to come up with agreed solutions.

By 1977 senior air force commanders faced the costs of these failures and drafted a Three-Year Plan for Constructing the Air Force (1978–80) for the CMC's approval.[16] The plan focused on pilot training and new weapons systems and called for a fresh attempt to end the confusion and the stalemate. The favored remedies dealt with command and discipline at the regimental level and above. The key, the CMC proclaimed, lay in organizational and leadership reforms, the time-honored Maoist panaceas for programmatic shortcomings.

What happened after Deng Xiaoping took charge of the CMC in 1977 interests us most, because of his emphasis on air force modernization. In August he ordered the air force to shape up, saying, "the frequent and recent plane accidents were the result of inadequate training and aircraft quality." By

---

16. This and the next paragraph are based on Zhang and Gao, "Construction of the Air Force," pp. 621–623, 628; Wang Hai and Zhu Guang, "Consolidate the Air Force Pilots' Training with Combat Capabilities as a Criterion," in Wang, *Kongjun Huiyi Shiliao*, p. 778; and Wang, *Dangdai Zhongguo Kongjun*, p. 515. Deng's quote is from Zhang and Gao, "Construction of the Air Force," p. 621.

then, the air force had begun assigning pilots many more flying hours, and compared with 1974, the serious aircraft accident rate dropped sharply from 0.62 percent to 0.3 percent per 10,000 flying hours by 1978.

At about the same time, Deng began by pressing the bureaucratic aviation ministry to finalize the J-7b as a replacement for the J-6.[17] Early in 1978, the CMC had announced a new guiding principle: "The air force must enhance domestic air defense capability with air defense of strategic points as a center and strengthen its capability to provide support in land and naval battles." In response, the ministry called a meeting in July 1978 to rethink its R&D programs. This session ended with an order to concentrate on the J-7b and to begin planning for follow-on generations to replace it.

Convinced that the air force would play a much greater part in any future large conflict, Deng publicized his general conclusions about its role. He wrote: "The army and navy both need air cover. Otherwise, the enemy air force will run rampant. . . . We must possess a powerful air force to ensure air domination [in a future war]." He told the CMC to "attach primary importance" to the pursuit of air superiority. On January 18, 1979, Deng, who by then had become China's "paramount leader," elevated his perspective on air power to official CMC dogma:[18] "Without the air force and air domination, winning a future war is out of the question. The army needs air support and air cover. Without air cover, winning a naval battle is also out of the question. . . . Give priority to the future development of the air force. . . . Stress investment in the development of the aviation industry and the air force to ensure air domination."

Deng's secondary, though unstated, purpose in concentrating on the air force was to assert his authority over what he and other senior officials regarded as a potentially dangerous service. The new leadership attached special political weight to the air force because Lin Biao had wrested control of the PLAAF at the onset of his abortive coup against Mao in 1971. As a result of these and other power struggles in the Cultural Revolution that involved the air force, party leaders thereafter sought to keep a much tighter rein over the air force

---

17. The aviation ministry did not finalize the J-7b's designs until 1979 and later put the J-7b into series production to replace the J-6s. The information in this paragraph is from Duan, *Dangdai Zhongguo de Hangkong Gongye*, pp. 83, 95–96, 99–101, 136, 145. The quote is from pp. 99–100.
18. Shao Zhenting, Zhang Zhengping, and Hu Jianping, "Theoretical Thinking on Deng Xiaoping's Views on the Buildup of the Air Force and the Reform of Operational Arts," *Zhongguo Junshi Kexue*, No. 4 (1996), pp. 43, 44, 45; and Wang, *Dangdai Zhongguo Kongjun*, pp. 550–551. Deng's quotes are from Shao, Zhang, and Hu, "Theoretical Thinking," pp. 43, 44, 45.

than the other service arms. Later, PLA officers credited Deng's action to "removing a sword of Damocles" over his head,[19] but quietly acknowledged that some political leaders continue to distrust the air force.

So the question is: With so much emphasis given to the air force after 1977, what happened next? Herein lies an enigma coming at a mandated turning point in the history of the PLAAF.

Choosing Priorities: The Air Force in the 1980s

What we see here is a case of "small politics" operating in the context of "large politics," as the Chinese say. While Deng at one level was elevating the air force in his security equation, his overriding and competing "larger" goal was to consolidate his power base as the nation's supreme leader. From late 1977 on, Beijing became enmeshed in a grand leadership realignment, and Deng sought time for his supporters to regain the powers wrested from them during the Cultural Revolution. The rivals expanded their arena of engagement to encompass all areas of the political and socioeconomic system. In need of "soldiers" who would man their coalition, Deng and his associates assigned top priority to reversing "unjust verdicts" on loyalists brought down by the Cultural Revolution radicals. It was a matter of numbers. He had to rehabilitate the more than 6,000 senior officials who would become his main foot soldiers.[20] From 1979 to 1981, power politics placed on hold his programs to revitalize the air force.

Only in 1981 did the air force begin trying to implement its second and third three-year plans for training and combat readiness. Fundamental changes to be carried out by the air force were announced, and Deng as CMC chairman singled out his air force commanders, praising them for "strict enforcement of orders and prohibitions." "The air force has a good style of work," he said, and "has made great achievements in training, style of work, and discipline."[21] Blessed by Deng, PLAAF headquarters once more urged the aviation industry to gear up for high production and performance.

What happened in the air force programs, however, could not have been more disappointing to the military high command. For public consumption, air force units and the aviation industry put on a face of intense activity while

---

19. Information from a PLA senior colonel, July 1997.
20. Quan Yanchi and Huang Lina, *Tiandao Zhou Hui yu Lushan Huiyi* [Heavenly principle: Zhou Hui and the Lushan conference] (Guangzhou: Guangdong Tourism Press, 1997), pp. 1–3.
21. Zhang and Gao, "Construction of the Air Force," pp. 622–624, 631, 637–638.

resorting to traditional delaying tactics: meetings, platitudes, studies, and reports recommending more meetings and more studies. The air force, for example, sponsored a series of theoretical studies and became masters of the obvious: "Air domination is playing a more and more important role under modern conditions. Although air domination cannot determine the outcome of a war, it does produce a great impact on the course and outcome of a war."[22] In appearance, the air force was on track. In practice, it was standing still.

For their part, the leaders in the defense industry echoed Deng's edict giving high priority to the air force. Still, in 1981 the director of the National Defense Science and Technology Commission (NDSTC), Zhang Aiping, conceded that the air force was one of the two weak links in the Chinese military and again prodded the aviation industry to produce advanced weaponry.[23] And once more, actions did not match the official word.

In March 1983, presumably in a mood of frustration but technically with orders and organizations in place, the Commission of Science, Technology, and Industry for National Defense (COSTIND), which had replaced the NDSTC the year before, convoked a national defense-industry conference.[24] At this gathering, the CMC demanded that the aviation ministry clarify its approach to "renewing a generation, developing a generation, and conducting pre-study on a generation [of new weapons and aircraft]." Yang Shangkun, the CMC's executive vice chairman, directed COSTIND to "revitalize the aviation industry," and Zhang Aiping, now minister of defense, for good measure added that the ministry should "ensure success in essential systems, attach greater importance to scientific research, and replace obsolete weapons."

By the mid-1980s, the CMC had to face facts: it revisited its policy priorities and finally revamped its weapons procurement policy. First, holding that local conventional wars under nuclear deterrence were the most likely to occur in the future, the CMC determined that the R&D programs on conventional weapons should take precedence over those on strategic weapons. Second, the

---

22. Hua Renjie, Cao Yifeng, and Chen Huixie, chief eds., *Kongjun Xueshu Sixiang Shi* [The history of the academic thinking of the air force] (Beijing: PLA Press, 1992), p. 316. Hua quotes "leading air force comrades" but does not identify them.
23. According to Zhang Aiping, the other weak link was the Second Artillery Corps. Zhang Aiping, "Speech at a Conference Attended by Leading Cadres from Aviation Industrial Enterprises (March 6, 1981)," in Zhang, *Zhang Aiping Junshi Wenxuan* [Selected military writings of Zhang Aiping] (Beijing: Yangtze River Press, 1994), pp. 371–374.
24. Unless otherwise cited, the information in this and the next paragraph is based on Yao, "Scientific Research Works," pp. 712, 715; and Duan, *Dangdai Zhongguo de Hangkong Gongye*, pp. 100–104. The quote is from Duan, *Dangdai Zhongguo de Hangkong Gongye*, p. 100.

military was enjoined to strengthen the existing conventional forces and to fashion new weapons. Third, whereas ground weapons originally dominated these forces, the navy and the air force now were given pride of place. Of all the services, the air force was awarded highest priority, though, as we shall see, this was not to last.[25] The immediate result of this policy edict was to bring the high-profile SLBM (submarine-launched ballistic missile) and nuclear-powered submarine programs to a halt.

In the meantime, the CMC prescribed these future wartime tasks for the air force: defend strategic points and provide air cover for strategic deployment of mass troops; maintain air domination in the main theaters of operations in support of the army and the navy; launch surprise attacks on high-value targets of the enemy; participate in nuclear counterattack; and conduct strategic aerial reconnaissance. The CMC further directed the PLAAF to prepare defenses against air raids and to support the other services opposing a ground invasion or launching counteroffensives.[26] The effect of this directive, almost unnoticed at the time, was to give the air force license to fashion its own strategy, a strategy that was to become full-blown in the 1990s.

One reason for the failure to notice the change was the rush of activity on the production front. In line with its newly defined strategic missions and weapons priorities, the air force began drafting a series of procurement directives and multiyear plans. These plans emphasized domestic air defense and listed a number of high-priority projects: surface-to-air missiles, medium/long-range all-weather interceptors, early-warning systems, electronic countermeasure equipment, and automatic command-and-control systems. The air force was supposed to undertake research on space defense weapons and long-range bombers that could launch cruise missiles. Yet most R&D programs centered on fighters and fighter-bombers, the HQ-7 surface-to-air missile, a navigation system for the H-6 medium bomber, new-type radar systems, unmanned reconnaissance aircraft, and avionics for fighters.[27]

Moreover, during the 1980s, the PLAAF air fleet had begun to grow, although obsolete aircraft, weapons systems, and training protocols dramatically

---

25. Liao Guoliang, Li Shishun, and Xu Yan, *Mao Zedong Junshi Sixiang Fazhan Shi* [The development of Mao Zedong's military thinking] (Beijing: PLA Press, 1991), p. 600.
26. "The Cross-Country Trends of the Chinese Air Force: Interview with Air Force Commander Liu Shunyao," *Xizang Wenxue* [Tibet literature] (Lhasa), supplement to No. 4 (1998), pp. 42–43. See also Gao Rui, *Zhanlüe Xue* [Strategy] (Beijing: Military Science Press, 1987), pp. 113–114.
27. Zhang and Gao, "Construction of the Air Force," pp. 628–629; Gao, *Zhanlüe Xue*, p. 114; Lin, *Kongjun Shi*, pp. 239–241; and Yao, "Scientific Research Works," p. 715.

weakened its combat readiness. In attempting to respond to revolutionary changes in Western military aviation, the PLAAF found itself caught between the leadership's demand for near-term improvements and the Maoist-era insistence on self-reliance. The ensuing compromise restricted the definition of self-reliance to the outright purchase of aircraft, while extending the meaning of Deng Xiaoping's Open Door policy to permit the acquisition of foreign air-launched weapons and avionics. The most dramatic evidence of the compromise came in 1986, when a consortium of U.S. companies led by Grumman signed a deal to install avionics on 55 J-8b fighters. Other Western countries also signed contracts for upgrading both avionics and weapons.[28]

At about the same time, Deng made what was to be his last real attempt to adhere to self-reliance in building the air force. His initial solution: the air force must clean house. "The total number of our air personnel is perhaps the largest in the world," he said, and only after deep reductions in personnel and outdated planes could the air force "significantly raise its efficiency." Deng blasted those officers who sought remedies in foreign purchases: "How many advanced airplanes can you afford to purchase? . . . We will become poor soon after we have bought a few airplanes."[29] The emphasis on efficiency simply masked the more basic compromise. Self-reliance was still the mandated policy, but it merely precluded the purchase of foreign aircraft.

Yet this limitation was to have a short half-life. Rapid obsolescence was moving faster than paced acquisitions and rendering the modified self-reliance policy unworkable.[30] By 1988, 48.8 percent of aircraft, 53.9 percent of aircraft engines, 42 percent of radar systems, 50 percent of HQ-2 surface-to-air missiles, and 42 percent of HQ-2 missile guidance sites were not operational. This state of disrepair restricted pilot training and further degraded combat readiness.

For these and other reasons, the CMC, while attempting to heed Deng's instructions, finally was forced to face these failures, but it could not directly blame the policy or its assumption that the PLAAF could modernize quickly on its own. As it had done so often in the past, the high command first

---

28. "China's F-8II Upgrade to Include Litton Navigation System," *Jane's Defence Weekly*, March 19, 1988, p. 529; "Grumman in Chinese Fighter Deal," *Jane's Defence Weekly*, November 19, 1988, p. 1261; and "Asia Watch: Military A-5M Fantan," *Asian Aviation*, November 1988, p. 11. This Grumman deal was put on hold in the summer of 1989 as a result of the Tiananmen incident and then canceled in 1990.
29. Deng's quotes are from Shao, Zhang, and Hu, "Theoretical Thinking," pp. 45, 47.
30. Unless otherwise cited, the information in this paragraph and the next two is from Lin, "Development of Air Force Equipment," pp. 789–791. The quote in the next paragraph is from ibid., pp. 789–790.

concluded that management and budget deficiencies were at fault. Obediently, the PLAAF called for "reducing equipment, readjusting flying hours, differentiating the first-line combat units from others, and abolishing obsolete equipment," and for a time, carrying out these changes seemed to make a difference. Compared with 1989, readiness in 1990 increased in most main sectors: aircraft, engines, radar systems, surface-to-air missiles, and missile guidance sites.

Following suit, COSTIND pushed the aviation ministry to expand aircraft acquisitions. The revised wish list was defensible but overly ambitious: five types of replacement fighters, three new fighter-bombers, five fighters under development or under study, and new types of ground attack aircraft. The aviation ministry directed work to proceed on the next-generation surface-to-air and air-to-air missiles.[31] By the early 1990s, initial replacement systems had begun to enter the inventory, and the high command seemed to relax.

By this time, PLA strategists and intelligence specialists had begun recalculating the strategic balance. They weighed the future threat of a superpower surprise attack against China's coastal areas and proposed a coordinated response with the air force playing the pivotal role. Decades hence, the United States or another military power, even Japan or India, might pose such a threat, they argued, and the danger of a lightning or surgical strike against strategic Chinese targets would be particularly acute during escalating crises. They further warned their commanders about the transfer of advanced airborne weapons from the West and Russia to China's neighbors and potential adversaries. They believed that these weapons outclassed China's, and cited India as an example of a military power making the transition from a defensive to an offensive air capability. The PLA, they maintained, had only a defensive air force, and a weak one at that.[32] New aviation technologies were further widening the technology gap to China's disadvantage.

In May 1990, at the high tide of assessments focusing on the air force, CMC Executive Vice Chairman Yang Shangkun convened a conference to discuss air combat systems and once more issued bureaucratic directives echoing those of the past to "accelerate the development of the air force equipment."[33] For all

---

31. For information on the R&D on the HQ, PL, and other missile series, see Xie, *Dangdai Zhongguo de Guofang Keji Shiye*, vol. 2, pp. 14–39, 47–61; and Michael Mecham, "China Displays Export Air Defense Missile," *Aviation Week & Space Technology*, December 2, 1996, p. 61.
32. Teng Lianfu and Jiang Fusheng, *Kongjun Zuozhan Yanjiu* [Studies on air force operations] (Beijing: National Defense University Press, 1990), pp. 148, 250, 266–267; and Yu Guantang, chief ed., *Kongjun Zhanlüe Yanjiu* [On air strategy] (Beijing: Military Translation Press, 1991), pp. 181, 195, 196.
33. Lin, "Development of Air Force Equipment," p. 784.

practical purposes, Yang's call and the resultant CMC directive duplicated Deng's directives of a decade earlier. Despite the flurry of activity in the 1980s, the result, in short, was an air force weaker in comparative terms than the one that began the decade. The questions are why, and what led to a turning point for the PLAAF?

The Turning Point and the Emergence of an Air Force Strategy

The search for an answer takes us back to the mid-1950s, an era of forced social change and constrained resources. From then to the 1980s, Mao Zedong and his heirs were embarked on a crusade to create a nuclear and missile arsenal, and, as we have noted, that goal blunted any sustained quest for PLAAF modernization. Even in the Cultural Revolution, Mao attempted to protect his strategic weapons programs from the turmoil,[34] but R&D on conventional weapons was mostly shut down. There was no national commitment to the air force or other conventional programs comparable to the one that built the bomb and its missile delivery systems.

For a quarter century, the defense industry received mixed messages. Despite ritual calls to build up the conventional forces, the industry's main target remained the development of nuclear weapons and their delivery systems, and everyone knew that this goal took primacy over all others. Money, expertise, and political backing told the real story, and promotions went to those who made their mark in the strategic programs. Where it mattered, few truly cared about the aviation industry, and everyone, especially those in the oft-criticized aviation ministry, knew it.

When they did worry about conventional arms in the 1960s and 1970s, Mao and his lieutenants in practice favored the ground forces with which they were most familiar. Confining the navy and the air force to subordinate status, they echoed the PLA mission statement that stressed "domestic air defense and support for operations of the army and the navy." When conventional weapons did rise to priority status in the latter half of the 1980s, the conflict with Vietnam and other Southeast Asian states over ownership of the Spratly Islands in the South China Sea cast a shadow on all planning, and contravening the stated priority given to the air force, naval equipment for a time went to

---

34. John W. Lewis and Xue Litai, *China Builds the Bomb* (Stanford, Calif.: Stanford University Press, 1988), chap. 3; and Lewis and Xue, *China's Strategic Seapower: The Politics of Force Modernization in the Nuclear Age* (Stanford, Calif.: Stanford University Press, 1994), chaps. 3, 6.

the head of the list.[35] Such repeated contradictions, it should be noted, plagued all conventional weapons programs and count among the main causes in the chain of air force program failures.

In addition to a lack of focus on the air force because of strategic and naval priorities, the Chinese military had to cope with the overriding change of policy in the early 1980s that turned the nation's economy to civilian production. After his return to power, Deng dismissed the likelihood of near-term conflicts and ordered the near-total shift to activating the economy.[36] Sharp reductions in the defense budget followed, and the PLA's share of the annual state budget dropped from a high of 18.5 percent in 1979 to about 8 percent in 1989.[37] The downward spiral of defense orders in turn undermined morale in a labor force feeling insecure in increasingly idle defense factories. The most qualified workers and staff began scouring the nonstate sector for higher pay and better career opportunities. For an industry based on self-sacrifice and high purpose, the new money culture and accelerated defense conversion further diluted any concerted attempt to strengthen the air force. Some Chinese officers compared the increased priority for the air force in a declining military to filling a bathtub on a sinking ship. For the PLA, potential external threats might become real overnight. For Deng, "overnight" was decades away, but so was his dream of self-reliance.

The revolution in air-delivered weapons dramatized by the United States in the 1991 Gulf War shattered Beijing's complacency. Time was no longer an ally. The danger ahead was total, perhaps permanent, obsolescence with the result that China's air defenses could not prevent surprise attacks deep into the nation's heartland.[38] Neither offense nor defense was a viable option given the

---

35. Luo Ping and Shi Keru, "For Enhancing Air Offensive Capabilities," *Zhongguo Kongjun* [Chinese air force], No. 3 (1997), p. 11; Liao, Li, and Xu, *Mao Zedong Junshi Sixiang Fazhan Shi*, pp. 600–601; and Chen Weijun, "Jiang Zemin and Li Peng Support Generals' Request for a Large Increase in the Military Budget in Preparation for Any Contingency," *Guangjiaojing* [Wide-angle Lens] (Hong Kong), No. 2 (1991), p. 12. The quote is from Luo and Shi, "For Enhancing Air Offensive Capabilities," p. 11.
36. In 1985 Deng Xiaoping predicted that China could focus on economic construction in a peaceful environment for the next fifty years. "Deng Xiaoping's Informal Talks on the Situation at Home and Abroad," *Liaowang* [Outlook], September 16, 1985, p. 10.
37. Qi Miyun, "The Shift of the Guiding Principle for Army Construction Judged by [the Decrease in] Military Funds," *Junshi Shilin* [Military history circles], No. 4 (1987), p. 20; and Yuan Jiaxin, "Pondering the Strategic Shift of the Guiding Ideology for Our Army's Construction," *Junshi Shilin*, No. 4 (1987), p. 10.
38. For a Chinese estimate of the penetrability of modern bomber weapons capable of launching deep surprise attacks, see Chen Hongyou, chief ed., *Xiandai Fangkong Lun* [On modern air defense] (Beijing: PLA Press, 1991), pp. 54–56; and Hua, Cao, and Chen, *Kongjun Xueshu Sixiang Shi*, p. 273.

state of the force. Some strategists analyzed the possibility of such attacks in the context of a future confrontation between the PRC and Taiwan, and assigned a greater probability to future hostilities with the United States should cross-strait tensions increase.[39] As reports of Iraq's defeat poured into his office, CMC Executive Vice Chairman Yang Shangkun attempted to blunt the psychological impact produced on his army by the U.S.-led victory: "The model [of the Gulf War] is not universal. It cannot, at least, be applied in a country like China, which has a lot of mountains, forests, valleys, and rivers. Another characteristic of this war is that the multinational forces faced a very weak enemy."[40]

For the air force, air operations in the Gulf War came as an especially rude wake-up call. For decades, the PLAAF had been given only operational and tactical assignments to provide air cover and fire support for the other two services in combined operations. It had no identifiable strategy of its own, though it did sponsor strategic studies and seminars on implementing Mao's concept of People's War "under modern conditions." In the latter half of the 1980s, the CMC had begun to give the air force additional defensive assignments, but these assignments served to further highlight the technological chasm between the advanced countries and China and forced the PLAAF planners to extend their research to encompass foreign air strategies. They resolved that their service would have to establish its own strategic direction and that the central condition for its successful implementation lay in technology, meaning advanced knowledge, not just new hardware.[41]

From the late 1970s on, Deng Xiaoping had issued a series of directives defining the PLAAF's combat tasks. He said: "Active defense itself is not necessarily limited to a defensive concept. . . . Active defense also contains an offensive element. If we are attacked, we will certainly counterattack. . . . The bombers of the air force are defensive weapons. . . . We [must] have what others have, and anyone who wants to destroy us will be subject to retaliation." His recurring message called for the air force to shift from a purely defensive to a combined defensive-offensive posture. Freed from the shackles of the more traditional interpretation of People's War, PLA strategists began a systematic refinement of "China's concept" of deterrence. They pored over the West's

---

39. Hua, Cao, and Chen, *Kongjun Xueshu Sixiang Shi*, pp. 357–358.
40. Quoted in "The United States Also Sells Weapons," *U.S. News & World Report*, May 27, 1991, p. 44.
41. Gao, *Zhanlüe Xue*, p. 114; Teng and Jiang, *Kongjun Zuozhan Yanjiu*, pp. 147, 150, 151; and Yu, *Kongjun Zhanlüe Yanjiu*, pp. 25, 30.

writings on high-technology warfare and concluded that in order to move toward a combined-forces posture, the PLAAF must add more offensive forces.[42]

This conclusion in turn spurred further research. Air force strategists assumed that China would continue to face regional military threats. Operating within the prescribed military strategy of "active defense," they began elaborating the nation's first air strategy to meet those threats. They reviewed global politics and military relations, potential combat scenarios, current missions and assignments, China's economic and industrial capacity, and existing PLAAF capabilities.[43] These strategists further assumed that the most likely wars would be limited and held that air domination was a prerequisite for victory. Such wars would always begin with air strikes, they declared, and air power would decide "the destiny of the state."[44]

The emerging air strategy emphasized both the requirements and tactics of air power and deemed the two interrelated and interactive. Echoing the strategists, the CMC declared that by the end of the twentieth century the air force must be able to "cope with local wars and contingencies of various types and make preparations for rapid expansion in case of a full-scale war."[45] Heralding this declaration, the air force issued its own slogan calling for "quick reaction, integrated coordination, and combat in depth (*kuaisu fanying, zhengti xietiao, zongshen zuozhan*)." "Quick reaction," "integrated coordination," and "combat in depth" sounded like textbook phrases from a U.S. defense paper, but when taken together and compared with previous policy statements, they infused the new PLAAF strategies with greater substance and provided cover for even bolder thinking. The air force had begun to claim its coveted lead position in grand strategy and now turned to its operationalization.

That position, when more fully elaborated, modified the prevailing interpretations of active defense, although translating that position into significant results proved elusive throughout the 1990s. The PLA still ruled out preemptive air strikes, especially against more powerful opponents, and held to the

42. Deng's quotes are from Shao, Zhang, and Hu, "Theoretical Thinking," pp. 44, 46–47.
43. Yu, *Kongjun Zhanlüe Yanjiu*, pp. 49, 55–56, 196.
44. Liu Yichang, chief ed., *Gao Jishu Zhanzheng Lun* [On high-tech war] (Beijing: Military Science Press, 1993), p. 225; Teng and Jiang, *Kongjun Zuozhan Yanjiu*, pp. 81, 98, 142; and Yu, *Kongjun Zhanlüe Yanjiu*, p. 98. The quote is from Yu, *Kongjun Zhanlüe Yanjiu*, p. 98.
45. In 1986 the CMC approved the fifteen-year strategic goal for the air force. Wang, *Dangdai Zhongguo Kongjun*, pp. 649–650. The quote is from ibid., p. 650. Unless otherwise cited, the information in this paragraph and the next is from Teng and Jiang, *Kongjun Zuozhan Yanjiu*, pp. 126–151; and Yu, *Kongjun Zhanlüe Yanjiu*, pp. 39, 43, 163.

declaratory policy of retaliation only. Yet the air force recognized its fate if required to remain totally passive in a first strike.[46] Once hit, there would be little left for a second-strike response, and herein began the modification.

"Quick reaction" would provide part of the mandate to launch the instant second blow as a prerequisite for deterrence, even survival. Moreover, "integrated coordination" would begin at first warning, and give the air force access to and even control over various high-tech arms in conventional war. This "coordination" would continue throughout the entire course of the conflict and include collecting and analyzing intelligence information; conducting command, control, and communications; organizing combat units of various arms in combined operations; and guaranteeing sustained logistical support.

By calling for "integrated coordination," the CMC gave the air force the authority to manage the long-range bomber air groups and oversee the initial stages of joint operations with the other services and between air combat units stationed in different military regions.[47] The CMC itself would issue orders through a dual command-and-control system for employing all air combat units; that is, all corps- and division-level air units would come under the joint administration of PLAAF headquarters and the seven greater military region commands. Strategic or theater combat units in large operations would report directly to air force headquarters, while tactical combat units in local operations would be directed by air force commanders in the greater military regions.

At the same time, the presumed requirement to conduct operations over a wide geographical area was leading the PLAAF to embrace the concept of "combat in depth," and it was the thinking underlying this concept that most tested the operational limits of the hallowed no-first-strike inhibition. (It should be noted at the outset that the PLAAF has not adopted nor is it considering a forward strategy and that many of the elements of the traditional "active defense" policy remain untouched. Rather, it adheres to the principle of "light deployment in the frontier and massive deployment in the rear.") According to the early formulations of this combat-in-depth principle, the military still would not be allowed to retaliate until the enemy had inflicted

---

46. According to PLA strategists, the "gap" in aviation technologies between China and its rivals and the strategy of "active defense" predetermine "quick reaction" as the essence of air strategy. Teng and Jiang, *Kongjun Zuozhan Yanjiu*, p. 260.
47. The information in this and the next paragraph is from Yu, *Kongjun Zhanlüe Yanjiu*, pp. 25, 79, 86, 163; Hua, Cao, and Chen, *Kongjun Xueshu Sixiang Shi*, pp. 324–325; and Teng and Jiang, *Kongjun Zuozhan Yanjiu*, pp. 186–187. The quote is from Teng and Jiang, *Kongjun Zuozhan Yanjiu*, p. 186.

the initial blow, and the emerging strategy implied that in that first engagement the frontier forces would be sacrificed. The air force would have deployed all its bombers, transport planes, and most attackers to the rear, and only the frontier-based fighters would probably be lost.

Yet even these fighters were to be deployed for maximum survivability. Fighter air groups would be dispersed throughout the nation, while bombers and attackers would be concentrated in the rear as a second-strike deterrent.[48] To facilitate this deployment policy, air combat units were divided into three types: quick reaction air groups (*kuaisu fanying budui*), alert air groups (*zhanbei zhiban budui*), and strategic reserves (*zhanlüe yubeidui*).[49]

PLAAF commanders knew, of course, that a discontinuity existed between these policy pronouncements and combat reality. As a stopgap measure, the frontier air groups were ordered to camouflage their aircraft and move them to semi-hardened shelters even though their commanders realized the futility of such measures in surviving a sustained attack by advanced precision-guided munitions. Other measures quickly followed to increase survivability and readiness. The air force selected highways and other alternative sites as emergency runways for the dispersion of frontier planes, and began to develop equipment for the refueling of fighters on freeways in emergencies. It is unclear how many of these measures have actually been tested or could be implemented under combat conditions.

The CMC also approved the establishment of a national air defense network. Plans called for military and civilian cooperation to minimize and recover from the destructive effect of air raids, and preparations began for the drafting of a new national air defense law adopted some years later.[50] Like the combat units, air defense systems were deployed "lightly" at the frontier and "massively" in designated rear areas. The CMC more recently has called for further strengthening the air defense network at strategic points and airfields in theater and multitheater zones.[51]

As a result of the transition to a combined offensive-defensive posture, the balance has steadily tilted toward the offense. This ongoing shift was quick-

---

48. Teng and Jiang, *Kongjun Zuozhan Yanjiu*, pp. 186–187, 258.
49. The information in this sentence and the next paragraph is from Yu, *Kongjun Zhanlüe Yanjiu*, pp. 75, 81, 82, 86, 228; and "A Support System Set Up in China Ensuring Military Aircraft to Land on Freeways," *Qiao Bao* [The China press] (New York), May 31, 1996, p. 2.
50. The People's Air Defense Law of the People's Republic of China was adopted on October 29, 1996.
51. Hua, Cao, and Chen, *Kongjun Xueshu Sixiang Shi*, pp. 320–322; Yu, *Kongjun Zhanlüe Yanjiu*, pp. 102, 112–113, 115; and Teng and Jiang, *Kongjun Zuozhan Yanjiu*, pp. 158–159, 187.

ened by tactics to defend against attacks on theater targets and by the reassignment of air groups as shock units against the enemy's rear areas.[52] Step-by-step but without fanfare, significant changes were occurring in Chinese military doctrine, and the clarity between an actual strike and a warning of an attack as the cause for launching the rear-based bombers and attackers was lost.

Moreover, the changes and the debate at the highest levels continue. Some strategists still doubt the soundness of the current strategy in a limited war involving the use of high-tech weapons. They belittle the wisdom of a mere partial shift toward an active offensive strategy. Precision-guided bomber weapons and cruise missiles, they argue, could inflict surprise attacks deep inside China, and despite the latitude implied by combat in depth, these attacks could well wipe out any retaliatory forces and countermeasures and leave the leadership without workable options in an escalating crisis.[53] The argument about the impact of high-tech weapons remains unsettled and has become a focal point in the strategic studies of the late 1990s.

Impact on Procurement

To close the gap between plans and performance, PLA analysts have concluded from their studies and debates that the force structure must be revamped. The total number of aircraft and air force personnel within the PLA must be reduced, and the composition and size of the main PLAAF combat units and their arming must be reviewed. Along with its preoccupation with enhanced air defenses, the air force has fretted about its puny ground attack capability. For decades, more than 70 percent of the PLA's military aircraft were fighters, while bombers, attackers (fighter-bombers), helicopters, and transport planes made up the balance.[54] In line with the new strategy, the air force began to adjust the mix of its order of battle and to retire large numbers of obsolete

---

52. In the Chinese military lexicon, theater coordination (*zhanyi xietong*) and tactical coordination (*zhanshu xietong*) mean coordination carried out between services in a campaign and a battle, respectively. Hua, Cao, and Chen, *Kongjun Xueshu Sixiang Shi,* p. 319. This interpretation is suitable for the difference between theater and tactical operations. The information in this paragraph is from ibid., pp. 312–313, 318–319, 323.

53. Zheng and Zhang, "On the Development of the Modern Air Force," pp. 84–85; Teng and Jiang, *Kongjun Zuozhan Yanjiu,* pp. 101–102; and Liu, *Gao Jishu,* pp. 226–235.

54. Hu Guangzheng, "Drawing Lessons from the Development of the Military Establishments in the Twentieth Century," *Zhongguo Junshi Kexue,* No. 1 (1997), p. 124; Yu, *Kongjun Zhanlüe Yanjiu,* pp. 28, 68, 220; and Hua, Cao, and Chen, *Kongjun Xueshu Sixiang Shi,* pp. 311, 312.

aircraft. Although fighters still far outnumber attackers and bombers, the ratio is shifting, and increasing numbers of reconnaissance planes, electronic countermeasures aircraft, early-warning aircraft, air refueling aircraft, and transport planes are entering the force.[55]

The strategists have particularly applauded the greater attention given to attackers. They maintain that all leading military powers have mandated such a priority. They argue that attackers, air refuelable and equipped with precision-guided cruise missiles, match bombers in range and destructiveness. With greater maneuverability, attackers could help repulse an aggressor. While a certain number of strategic bombers could reinforce deterrence and complicate an enemy's strategic calculus, attackers could do both and in the future should far outnumber deployed bombers. This planned reversal in plane ratios also had a political rationale. Any marked growth of China's strategic bomber fleet might aggravate the suspicions of its neighbors and fuel an arms race.[56] The nuclear-capable attacker was considered the near-perfect plane to obscure the boundary between offense and defense and between retaliation and first strike.

Thus changes in strategy increasingly interacted with shifts in weapons procurement. The air force earlier had worked out short-term (five years), medium-term (ten years), and long-term (twenty years) procurement programs,[57] but almost before they were ready for promulgation, they had to be redrafted. Finally, in 1992 a new procurement policy was adopted: *duo yanzhi, shao shengchan, zhongdian zhuangbei* (literally, more R&D, less production, and focus on key equipment). In an attempt to upgrade air weapons systems, the air force stressed surface-to-air missiles; long-range, all-weather fighters; command, control, and information systems; early-warning aircraft and air refueling aircraft; and ground attack capabilities with a focus on airborne precision-guided cruise missiles. Simultaneously, the air force also began upgrading its technical and strategic knowledge base.[58] Chinese commanders had absorbed the lesson from the West: create the technical and industrial infrastructure first.

In early 1993, following a prolonged review of the Gulf War's "lessons," the CMC called for two cardinal changes by the year 2000: change the military

---

55. Unless otherwise cited, the information in this sentence and the next paragraph is from Yu, *Kongjun Zhanlüe Yanjiu*, pp. 211–212, 220; Hu, "Drawing Lessons," p. 124; and Teng and Jiang, *Kongjun Zuozhan Yanjiu*, pp. 296–298.
56. Information from a senior Chinese security specialist, 1997.
57. Yu, *Kongjun Zhanlüe Yanjiu*, p. 193.
58. Gao, *Zhanlüe Xue*, p. 114; Teng and Jiang, *Kongjun Zuozhan Yanjiu*, p. 151; and Yu, *Kongjun Zhanlüe Yanjiu*, pp. 25, 30.

from dependence on manpower and People's War to greater reliance on science and technology; and switch plans for military preparedness from winning a conventional local war to winning a high-tech local war.[59] PLA strategists further downgraded the likelihood of regional or global wars and acknowledged that the two changes highlighted the gap between Chinese and Western air forces.

This was a sobering finding because in earlier decades they had consistently belittled the idea that a decisive inequality even existed. In self-defense, the strategists claimed that the gap was of recent origin and had not always existed between China and the West. They held that J-6 fighters of the 1960s were comparable then to fighters anywhere in the world, but that the development of avionics in Western countries had created what they called "short legs" (*duantui*). PLA aircraft, they said, were short on avionics and had short ranges.[60]

The shadow of a possible conflict in the Taiwan Strait made these short legs especially dangerous. Should that conflict occur, the PLAAF would now expect to be defeated. Any domestic program to correct this weakness, moreover, would require the creation of a much more sophisticated industrial base and a huge investment, and would face long lead times. Even before the 1993 decision, the choice had become clear: total self-reliance would have to be abandoned.[61] The best planes for the next decade would have to come from foreign countries. Although PLA strategists rationalized such purchases as being "mutually complementary" to the dogma of self-reliance,[62] everyone in the high command had come to recognize that Mao's dictum for military modernization again must be set aside in practice. Once more the supplier would have to be Russia, where many senior Chinese leaders had been trained in the 1950s and whose arsenals were becoming available for a price.

In November 1992, shortly before the "two changes" decision, senior Russian and Chinese military officials began annual meetings on military-technical cooperation and signed a so-called Protocol I to formalize their commitment to long-term ties.[63] During his visit to Beijing that December, Russian President

59. Hu Changfa, "Some Theoretical Issues on Operational Command under High-Tech Conditions," *Guofang Daxue Xuebao* [National Defense University gazette], No. 4 (1997), p. 30; "The Communist Army Is Pursuing Two Fundamental Changes by the Beginning of the Next Century," *Shijie Ribao* [World journal] (New York), September 15, 1996, p. A13; and "Strategic Changes in the Guiding Principle for Building Up China's Army in the 1990s," *Qiao Bao*, July 31, 1997, p. A4.
60. Song, "Startup of China's Modern Aviation Industry," pp. 103, 104.
61. Teng and Jiang, *Kongjun Zuozhan Yanjiu*, p. 300.
62. See, for example, Yu, *Kongjun Zhanlüe Yanjiu*, p. 226.
63. Unless otherwise cited, the information in this paragraph and the next is from interviews with a knowledgeable Russian official in 1993 and 1994.

Boris Yeltsin signed the "Memorandum of Understanding on Sino-Russian Military Equipment and Technology Cooperation," the origins of which could be traced to a similar, though largely unfulfilled, agreement dated December 28, 1990. Protocol I included provisions for the sale of 26 Su-27 fighters and jet engines as well as the training of Chinese pilots. The second annual meeting, which took place in Moscow in June 1993, led to the conclusion of Protocol II in May 1994. Inter alia, this document simplified the approval procedures endorsed in 1990.

Even before the signing of Protocol I, the PLAAF had concluded its own agreement with the Russians, signed on August 3, 1992, for delivery of an advanced air defense system, and the contract for its delivery was finalized in July 1993. Protocol II added to the list of air defense systems and itemized areas for further defense industrial and technology cooperation, especially the areas of communications and electronic countermeasures. Consistent with the protocol, the CMC told the PLAAF to reinforce its "shield" while sharpening its "spear" and to purchase Russian air defense systems, including S-300 and TOR-M1 surface-to-air missile systems.[64]

China has so far purchased 72 Su-27s from Russia, and of these, 48 have already been shipped to bases in Wuhu, Anhui Province, and Suixi, Guangdong Province. In the first phase of what was to become a quite complex deal, China signed a contract to pay Russia a $2.5 billion license fee for manufacturing 200 Su-27s (J-11s) over fifteen years. The 72 Su-27s purchased from Russia are the basic model Su-27S, while the planes to be built in China are the higher-performance Su-27SKs. At the same time, China's aviation industry has been cooperating with Russia and other nations such as Israel, Iran, Great Britain, and Pakistan in developing advanced fighters for the PLAAF and for export.[65] Negotiations on other planes and aviation systems continue with these countries but are seldom fully reported.

The concentration on hardware attracted the most publicity, of course, but personnel requirements carried equal weight as the procurements progressed. The existing pilot training programs, which were written between 1987 and 1994, mainly dictate how to fight conventional local wars. They do not meet

---

64. "Communist China Is Reportedly Negotiating for the Purchase of Russian High-Performance Weapons," *Shijie Ribao*, September 3, 1996, p. A12; and "Communist China Is Reportedly Purchasing Antiaircraft Missile Systems from Russia," *Shijie Ribao*, January 16, 1996, p. A2.
65. Ma Zhijun and Qiu Minghui, "Exclusive Interview with Chief Commander of the [Taiwanese] Air Force Huang Xianrong," *Xin Xinwen* [The journalist] (Taipei), May 31–June 6, 1998, p. 47; Zeng Huiyan, "The Chinese Military Will Enhance Its Fighting Capacity in an All-Round Way," *Shijie Ribao*, January 5, 1997, p. A2; and Xie and Sun, "New Fighter," p. 8.

the terms set forth by the new guiding principle for the Chinese military to wage a high-tech local war. In 1997 the PLAAF finished drafting training programs for such wars, but in carrying them out, it has encountered a fundamental problem because only 20.7 percent of air officers are college graduates. Quick fixes or short-term training classes cannot solve the lack of qualified technical personnel to operate high-tech air weapons in an environment that attracts the best to civilian occupation.[66] Senior officers are coming to recognize that the real costs may be the price tag to attract and hold skilled men and women.

Taiwan as the Focal Point: Making Conventional Deterrence Credible

China's planned introduction of advanced air weapons and improved training understandably carry weight in assessments of the PLAAF's capabilities in the Asia Pacific region. Significant in these calculations are estimates of China's crisis behavior, and how it reflects traditional Chinese perspectives on deterrence.[67] Mao's revolutionary doctrine, if not ancient strategies, long ago dictated the threatened use of force in manipulating an adversary's responses, and China's leaders have consistently demanded the military's acquiescence to political authority when calibrating the magnitude and timing of the pain, if any, to be inflicted. In these circumstances, recourse to force always remains subordinate to political stipulations that can violate standard military principles.

The Taiwan crisis in 1996 is a typical example of current Chinese views on deterrence. By the mid-1990s, PLA planners had concluded that the momentum of the independence movement in Taiwan and its increasing recognition by the international community had become an ever more grave challenge. "Danger from without" was coinciding, they believed, with "trouble from within." The needed preparations for a possible conflict across the Taiwan Strait then prompted additional changes in China's force posture and defense strategy. By the fall of 1995, the CMC had formulated the *wen nan bao bei* policy, which, loosely translated, meant that the PLA would shift its planning priorities from the South China Sea to Taiwan and its "foreign supporters." The

---

66. "It Is Hard to Give Full Play to Advanced Fighters," *Shijie Ribao*, August 22, 1997, p. A12.
67. Allen S. Whiting, *The Chinese Calculus of Deterrence: India and Indochina* (Ann Arbor: University of Michigan Press, 1975), pp. 202–203, 233; and Alastair Iain Johnston, "China's Militarized Interstate Dispute Behaviour, 1949–1992: A First Cut at the Data," *China Quarterly*, No. 153 (March 1998), pp. 1–30.

fundamental challenge, Beijing declared, was the threat to the nation's territorial integrity and national sovereignty.

By late 1995, China's leaders believed the time had come to draw a line that separatists in Taiwan must not cross.[68] The question was: How could Beijing signal threats and inducements that would influence the Taiwanese population and their leaders without leading to unwanted or uncontrolled conflict? Taipei would have to be forced to choose between the status quo and escalating violence, and the Taiwanese would be put in a position of having to decide for themselves. According to one military official: "They will think twice before making a radical push." The Taiwanese presidential election of 1996 would constitute the decision point, but what kind of force, he asked, would change the election outcome in Beijing's favor and not create a backlash?

Chinese policymakers, including those in the PLA, argued most about the threats to be used. What short of war would influence Taiwan? In the end, they singled out the missile option as the most effective way to deliver the signal. Accurately controlled and easily escalated or suspended on a step-by-step basis, missile "flight tests" in international waters near Taiwan, they believed, could help convey the appropriate deterrent warning but allow Beijing to avert a head-on collision with Taipei and direct foreign intervention. The logic of controlled coercion, it would seem, was consonant with Robert McNamara's in the early stages of U.S. intervention in Vietnam.

In fact, Beijing's leaders did not have feasible alternatives, and in any event, they believed the missile would carry the most convincing message. The use of air power was clearly not an option, for the PLAAF could convey only a weak threat, its planes had no targets outside Taiwan itself, and the CMC could not be sure how the superior Taiwanese air force would react. The PLAAF was unprepared to deliver a clear and controllable threat.[69]

The stark reality was that the PLAAF was not ready for combat. Poor logistics, an inadequate budget, and a string of Su-27 accidents were still plaguing air force command. According to an American specialist, Chinese Su-27 pilots lacked adequate training and "were unable to perform anything other than navigation flights." All PLAAF interceptors relied principally on

---

68. For an informed treatment of the 1996 Taiwan crisis in retrospect, see Chas. W. Freeman, Jr., "Preventing War in the Taiwan Strait: Restraining Taiwan–and Beijing," *Foreign Affairs*, Vol. 77, No. 4 (July/August 1998), pp. 6–11. The quote is from an interview with a senior PLA officer, December 1995.
69. "Su-27 Pilots Conduct Navigation Training in Night Flights," *Shijie Ribao*, January 17, 1997, p. A10.

land-based centers to conduct command and control in air battles.[70] The actual deployment of its combat units was still on a defensive (not an offensive) basis, and Beijing's intelligence knew that the Taiwanese military had little fear of the mainland's aircraft.

The March 1996 missile "tests" thus constituted the only real option China had to threaten Taiwan with actions intended to serve as a lasting omen. Beijing hoped that this high-risk undertaking, even when it provoked the deployment of U.S. aircraft carriers, would not permanently impair U.S.-China relations. With the restoration of military-to-military ties in late 1997 and subsequent security exchanges and agreements, this hope appeared to have been well founded until late 1998, when allegations arose concerning Chinese espionage in the U.S. nuclear and missile programs. The tests themselves did alert Taiwan to what one Taiwanese scholar called "the most vulnerable part of our defense network."[71] Moreover, the "test firings" produced a deep impression on Taiwan's population, forcing many Taiwanese to reevaluate their long-term economic interests and dreams of independence.

The missile firings and the ensuing crisis with the United States, of course, did not come without some near-term repercussions for Beijing, including the activation of U.S. congressional interest in theater missile defense for Taiwan. Steadily deteriorating U.S.-China relations quickly drove the Chinese military to understand the limits of U.S. restraint and its latent sympathies in any future Taiwan-PRC conflict. The CMC also could not dodge the truth of the PLA's lack of readiness for war, large or small, and it ordered the PLAAF to work on contingency planning with the Taiwanese air force and the U.S. Air Force as imaginary enemies. The PLAAF also responded by revising its prescribed tactics for a high-tech local war. The PLAAF commander defined such tactics in general as "air deterrence, air blockade, and air strikes," but added little detail.[72]

In the winter of 1996–97, the CMC followed up on these developments and convened a high-level symposium on command and control in future battles. Commanders from all services and military regions attended and listened to

70. Barbara Opall and Michael J. Witt, "China Pits U.K. vs. Israel in AEW Quest," *Defense News*, August 5–11, 1996, p. 19; "Su-27 Pilots Conduct Navigation Training," p. A10; "Many Su-27s Damaged by the Chinese Air Force," *Shijie Ribao*, April 15, 1997, p. A12; and "The PLA Has Purchased Production Lines for Building Su-27s," *Shijie Ribao*, August 12, 1997, p. A2.
71. This and the next paragraph are based on Barbara Opall, "PLA Missiles Diminish Value of Taiwan's Islands," *Defense News*, August 26–September 1, 1996, p. 8; and Li Suolin, "Notes of the Commander of a 'Blue Squadron,'" *Zhongguo Kongjun*, No. 1 (1995), pp. 4–6.
72. Sun Maoqing, "Air Force Commander Liu Shunyao in an Interview with Journalists Says That China Will Build a Modern Air Force," *Renmin Ribao* [People's daily] (overseas edition), April 16, 1997, p. 4.

panels on how to fight a high-tech local war. Given the country's technological shortcomings, the main presenters stressed the importance of innovative force deployments and tactical operations—what they called "software"—in mitigating shortcomings in military hardware. A common theme in the presentations was the urgency of planning for contingencies in the Taiwan Strait.[73]

In line with China's deterrence criteria, senior commanders at the meeting told their subordinates how to coordinate combined-services landing operations against Taiwan in case deterrence should fail. They stressed the salience of air force operations throughout a possible Taiwan campaign and assigned the PLAAF the special mission of coordination. Meanwhile, the navy would operate according to a new strategy: "Block ports to surround the enemy and intercept its reinforcements, seize opportunities to annihilate the enemy at sea, enforce a blockade of the strait, and prevent the enemy from launching a surprise attack (*fenggang weijie, haishang xunjian, fengbi haixia, fangdi tuxi*)." The navy also adopted a policy for conducting possible future landing operations, while the army advanced a strategy for breaking Taiwan's coastal defenses after such initial landings. Although these formulas appeared simplistic as promulgated, they spurred the services to prepare detailed operational plans for potential landing operations against Taiwan. By discussing and justifying offensive contingencies at such a senior-level and well-publicized symposium, PLA generals and their political leaders intended to demonstrate China's resolve to check Taiwan's drift toward independence—as a last resort by force.

Woven into the new operational dicta were lessons from the Gulf War. General Liu Jingsong (then commander of the Lanzhou Greater Military Region and now president of the Academy of Military Science) stressed that the very assembly and deployment of coalition forces constituted the "first firing" and justified preemptive military action. Such preemptive action might "postpone or even deter the outbreak of a war,"[74] reflecting the revised no-first-strike and deterrence policies. Liu ended by commenting on a hypothetical confrontation over Taiwan between China and the United States.

Thus, by 1997, a strategic calculus had begun to take shape. The CMC had switched priorities from nuclear to conventional weapons and slowed down the deployment of strategic forces. The air force had claimed precedence over

---

73. The information in this and the next paragraph is from Hu Changfa, "Some Issues on Operational Theory in a High-Tech Local War," *Guofang Daxue Xuebao*, No. 1 (1997), pp. 32–38.
74. Liu Jingsong, "Key Principles for Waging Combined Operations against Invading Enemies in a Theater," *Guofang Daxue Xuebao*, No. 5 (1997), p. 41. On Liu's views as perceived by the Pentagon, see Barbara Opall, "Study Pits PLA Nukes against U.S., Taiwan," *Defense News*, September 23–29, 1996, p. 10.

the other service arms, and the People's War as a unifying dogma had given way to service-specific strategies. As Taiwan became the focal point of Chinese military planning, the procurement of Russian aircraft, presumably a stopgap measure, had qualified Deng Xiaoping's call for self-reliance. With the shadow of a threatened U.S.-Chinese confrontation over Taiwan looming larger, some PLA senior generals advocated scrapping the no-first-strike policy in favor of "retaliation" on warning. Interpretations of "combat in depth" also signaled a fundamental change in the Chinese military strategy of "active defense" toward a more proactive strategy to fight high-tech local wars. The reassessment of China's security interests had spawned an ongoing process of constant debate and reformulation within the military and political hierarchies.

In that process, the die is already cast concerning the future of the air force. The CMC knows that it must rely on the country's conventional forces should deterrence fail. In any military showdown across the strait, air power and defense against air strikes would hold the key to victory or defeat.[75]

The Case for the Quest

Our examination of the shift away from the antiquated thinking of People's War and of the strategic reasoning underpinning the search for a modern air force leaves a central question unanswered: Is that quest realistic? All of China's potential adversaries have the advantage of long experience in producing or importing ever more advanced fighters and bombers, and several have employed those aircraft in combat and repeated combat exercises. There is no near- to medium-term likelihood that China's air force could match those of its possible foes.

Beijing's leaders do not dispute this. Rather, they advocate the development of the nation's air arm as a condition for China to become a major military power and a technological competitor in defense and commercial aerospace. The dominant position of the air force in contingency plans for combat in the Taiwan Strait helps focus on and mobilize resources to meet that condition, but the priority would remain even if Taiwan were not in the calculus. Four principal arguments provide the core of the Chinese rationale for the priority and the policies sustaining the quest. We focus on the fourth of these arguments, which relates to Taiwan, because it has the overriding impact on current

---

75. Pan Shiying, *Xiandai Zhanlüe Sikao* [Considerations of modern strategies] (Beijing: World Knowledge Press, 1993), pp. 128–129.

military discussions in China. At this writing, it remains to be seen whether the security crisis after the Indian and Pakistani nuclear tests in May 1998 will lead to a further refinement of those arguments, although the elements of the current "Taiwan case" could readily be extended to an unwanted showdown with India.[76]

The first argument simply echoes the Chinese belief that all nations, regardless of size, must prepare for war and that recent large-scale wars have demonstrated the deadly destructiveness of air power. To the Chinese, the proposition is self-evident: the contemporary state requires a combat-ready air force. One PLA officer in typical fashion states, "India, Iran, Iraq, and even North Korea have attached great importance to the buildup of air power even though their air forces could never match the U.S. Air Force."[77] Speaking as the CMC's chairman, Jiang Zemin told his commanders that the nation would "bitterly suffer" if it did not strive to create a powerful air force.[78]

The Chinese military makes a second argument that the most likely non-nuclear threats to its security will come first from the air, especially from Taiwan or the United States. From the Korean War to the Gulf War, China has drawn the lesson that conceding control of the air to an adversary can lead to political intimidation and humiliation, not to mention huge losses. China's national security and diplomatic influence require that it demonstrate the will and commitment to challenge any would-be attacker from the air even as its leaders acknowledge the PLAAF's current weaknesses.

The third argument links the deterrent force of advanced aircraft to nuclear deterrence. PLA strategists, not just those from the PLAAF, hold that the revolution in conventional weapons has increased the need for air power in reinforcing nuclear deterrence. A deputy commander of the PLAAF has said, "Nuclear deterrence might not work without a high-tech air force, especially in the post-nuclear era," and many of his colleagues have expressed doubts about whether nuclear weapons alone could deter a devastating conventional attack. Because the essence of the revised PLA strategic guidelines is to "prevent the outbreak of a war and prevail after its outbreak," a powerful air force has become an indispensable component of nuclear deterrence and all steps

---

76. For an authoritative study of China's response to the May tests, see Zou Yunhua, *Chinese Perspectives on the South Asian Nuclear Tests* (Stanford, Calif.: Center for International Security and Cooperation, Stanford University, 1999).
77. Interview with a PLA senior colonel, 1996.
78. Quoted in Liu Taihang, "Strengthen Studies on Air Force Military Theory to Guide the Quality Construction of the People's Air Force," *Zhongguo Junshi Kexue*, No. 4 (1997), p. 46.

on the escalation ladder.[79] Although it would be easy to dismiss these statements as special pleading on the part of a deputy air force commander, the PLA does appear to be taking steps to link air and missile command systems in the new strategy.

The PLA's conclusions on the likelihood of future wars being local and high-tech supports a fourth argument: a nation cannot plan to fight a high-tech war without having an effective air arm. This fourth argument follows from the third one above and applies with special force to any future military showdown over the Taiwan Strait caused by a Taiwanese declaration of independence. As in the past, the CMC would prefer to threaten or "blockade" Taiwan with the use of missiles fired in measured numbers close to, but not against, the island itself. PLA generals hold that for such a calculated demonstration of force to work, the missile bases would have to be protected. That military requirement in turn would make the PLAAF Taipei's first target. If Taiwan's planes could easily destroy the air bases protecting China's missile bases, the missile forces would face the classic use-it-or-lose-it dilemma, and not surprisingly, Taipei's public statements concerning its war plans appear consistent with this PLA assessment.[80] Thus the anticipated outcome of the battle for air dominance would determine the ultimate political and military effectiveness of the missiles as a weapon of choice to threaten or blockade the island.

The Chinese analysis of such a conflict with Taiwan does not end there, however. Beijing knows that halting Taiwan's move toward independence could spark a U.S. military response in an escalating cross-strait crisis. In the worst case, which neither side wants, the United States might be faced with the choice of intervention or a Taiwanese defeat. A critical element in the fourth argument is the assumption that formidable Chinese air power could cause Washington to pause. The very possibility of that hesitation could inhibit Taipei's move toward independence in the first place, because Taiwan would not be sure it could prevail in the air. A PLA officer puts it this way, "The Taiwan issue involves the territorial integrity and national sovereignty of China. It is our vital security interest to prevent Taiwan from drifting toward independence. In contrast, the future of Taiwan does not involve U.S. vital

---

79. Quoted in Zhang Changzhi, "Air Deterrence and National Resolve," *Zhongguo Kongjun*, No. 1 (1997), p. 14.
80. One Taiwan military officer has asserted, "As a last resort, we can carry out air raids against strategic targets in sixteen provinces of the Chinese mainland including coastal areas and interior provinces." Conversation with a Taiwan army officer in Taipei, 1996.

interests. If Beijing copes with the Taiwan issue properly and demonstrates resolve at the crucial moment, Washington will probably keep its hands off the issue."[81]

Operationally, the ability to execute a policy of missile intimidation and air defense has necessitated carrying out carefully planned exercises. The purpose of these exercises is both to enhance and to publicize the PLA's readiness for conflict in the strait. At the end of 1996, following the well-advertised issuance of CMC directives, a group of specialists from the PLAAF, the Second Artillery Corps (the Strategic Missile Force), and other services completed the operational rules for coordinating combined-services campaigns across the strait and carrying out exercises to validate them.[82]

Although the literature on the fourth argument deals primarily with Taiwan, the policy imperative is much more profound. The future of the island is only one element in the defining principle that underlies Chinese policy: restoring and preserving the nation's territorial integrity and sovereignty. The issue is how to prevent any foreign intervention that could threaten that principle. Preserving its sovereignty lies at the heart of China's national security policy, and that sovereignty is assumed to be indivisible.

Taiwan is the domino most vulnerable to a foreign "push," but its toppling could lead to the loss of control in other border areas such as Tibet, Xinjiang, and Inner Mongolia. Should fear of foreign intervention lead to Beijing's compromise on the Taiwan issue, so the argument goes, other separatists might become more defiant in a chain reaction. The modern-day CMC officers have read the history of the last centuries and seen how foreigners splintered the nation and showed contempt for its sovereignty. They have concluded that only ready military forces can discourage separatists and their foreign champions. The logic of that conclusion has led them to foresee a sequence of action and reaction in which the air force would play a decisive part, and it is that sequence that leads us back to the first argument: a modern state must have a modern air force.

Arguments based on national stature, threat assessments, deterrence, and sovereign independence, of course, are neither new nor unique to China. What

---

81. Interview with a PLA senior colonel, 1997.
82. See, for example, Liu Shunyao, "Follow the Direction Given by Our Party's Third-Generation Collective Leadership to Build a Powerful Modern People's Air Force," *Zhongguo Junshi Kexue*, No. 3 (1997), p. 90; and Zheng Shengxia, "Importance Shall Be Attached to Certain Issues Concerning the Employment of the Air Force in Combined-Services Campaigns," *Guofang Daxue Xuebao*, No. 1 (1997), p. 46.

is relatively new is the centrality given to the air force in Beijing's formulation of those arguments, particularly as they apply to Taiwan and the United States. China's search for an effective air force also reaches back to the foundations of the PRC and the Korean War. Although the recent formulations giving saliency to the air force make military and political "sense" at least to senior PLA commanders, the question remains: Can China actually build the credible air power that will deter foreign aggressors and minority separatists alike?

Embedded in the policy are assumptions concerning the directions of technology, the nature of future conflicts, the behavior of foreign states, and the sustainability of current defense programs. After examining the security implications of the PLAAF's buildup in the decade ahead, we conclude that the answer to that question is far from clear even to the Chinese who have placed their bets on the air force. More than three decades have passed since then Chief of the General Staff Luo Ruiqing called for a shift in priorities from strategic to conventional weapons, with the emphasis on the air force. A victim of the Cultural Revolution, Luo's call vanished with him. The challenge of an emerging independent Taiwan appears to have resurrected Luo's dream of a world-class air force. Standing in the way are competing demands and policies beyond the military's, even beyond China's, control. After decades of failed plans, the realists know that the dream could fade once again.

China's Military Views the World | *David Shambaugh*

Ambivalent Security

Most observers of Asian international politics agree that the strategic orientation and military posture of the People's Republic of China (PRC) will be a key variable determining regional stability and security in the twenty-first century. Indeed, the PRC's strategic profile will influence global politics as well, as China increases its national power and becomes more engaged in world affairs. How China behaves will depend, of course, on a host of factors and actors—but certainly the People's Liberation Army (PLA) is a central one.

Domestically, the PLA has long sustained the Chinese Communist Party in power and enforced internal security.[1] In internal policy debates, the PLA is the hypernationalistic guardian of claimed Chinese territorial sovereignty and is the institution charged with enforcing these claims. Economically, until the recent divestiture of most of its financial assets, the PLA operated a far-flung commercial empire. Regionally and internationally, the modernization of China's military affects the balance of power, serves as a source of concern to many nations, and stimulates defense development in neighboring countries. As others have argued, China's assertive territorial claims, bellicose nationalistic rhetoric, *parabellum* strategic culture, and accelerating military modernization program have created an intense "security dilemma" in East Asia.[2] If

David Shambaugh is Professor of Political Science and International Affairs and Director of the China Policy Program in the Elliott School of International Affairs at George Washington University, and is a nonresident Senior Fellow in the Foreign Policy Studies Program at the Brookings Institution in Washington, D.C. He is the author of many studies on contemporary China and East Asian affairs.

This article draws on parts of my forthcoming book *Reforming China's Military* (Berkeley: University of California Press, 2000), particularly chapters 4 and 7. A related version will appear as "China's National Security Environment: Perceptions of the Intelligence Community," in David M. Lampton, ed., *The Making of Chinese Foreign and Security Policy in the Era of Reform* (Stanford, Calif.: Stanford University Press, forthcoming 2000). I have benefited particularly from comments by Thomas Christensen, Harry Harding, Iain Johnston, and Allen Whiting on earlier drafts.

1. This is discussed in David Shambaugh, "The PLA and PRC at Fifty: Reform at Last," *China Quarterly*, No. 159 (September 1999), pp. 660–672.
2. See Thomas J. Christensen, "China, the U.S.-Japan Alliance, and the Security Dilemma in East Asia," *International Security*, Vol. 23, No. 4 (Spring 1999), pp. 49–80. The classic statement of the *parabellum* strategic culture is Alastair Iain Johnston, *Cultural Realism: Strategic Culture and Grand Strategy in Chinese History* (Princeton, N.J.: Princeton University Press, 1995).

International Security, Vol. 24, No. 3 (Winter 1999/2000), pp. 52–79
© 1999 by the President and Fellows of Harvard College and the Massachusetts Institute of Technology.

these elements combine to produce an assertive and aggressive China, as some hypothesize, the PLA will likely be both a principal catalyst and the institution required to project Chinese power.

The evidence of PLA perceptions presented in this article suggests that the military's views of the regional and international security environment reveal a considerable amount of ambivalence. While China enjoys an unprecedented period of peace and absence of direct external military pressure, Chinese military commentators nonetheless identify numerous uncertainties and latent security threats. In many instances PLA perceptions also diverge from—and are usually tougher than—those of civilian officials and security specialists, who tend to see a more benign world.[3] The PLA's view of the world is by no means relaxed. Rather, a deep angst exists about the structure of the international system and disposition of power with which China must contend—particularly the global predominance of the United States.

The article begins with a discussion of the socialization of the current Chinese military leadership, the difficulties of gaining insights into their worldview, and the sources available to illuminate their perceptions. This is followed by a brief discussion of the prominent sense of angst and ambivalence apparent in the PLA's views of its national security. The heart of the article then assesses the Chinese military's perceptions of the Yugoslav war of 1999, the United States and its global posture, Northeast Asia, Russia and Central Asia, Southeast Asia and multilateral security, and South Asia. It concludes with a discussion of the implications of the PLA's ambivalent sense of security, and particularly the policy implications for the United States of managing a long-term "strategic competition" with China.

Shedding Light on Opaque Perceptions

Given the importance of the PLA to China's strategic orientation and the security calculations of other nations, the military's perceptions of international politics and China's national security environment are a critical variable. Gaining insights into the *Weltanschauung* and strategic thinking of China's high command is, however, extremely difficult. Surprisingly little is known about

---

3. Therefore foreign analysts should not assume close correlation between the more-accessible civilian and less-accessible military perceptions. For a comparison, see David Shambaugh, "China's National Security Environment: Perceptions of the Intelligence Community," in David M. Lampton, ed., *The Making of Chinese Foreign and Security Policy in the Era of Reform* (Stanford, Calif.: Stanford University Press, forthcoming 2000).

how China's military leaders and intelligence analysts see the world and the PLA's role in it. Direct interactions with the PLA elite remain rare and are tightly scripted, while an extremely low level of transparency further obscures the perspectives and capabilities of the PLA. Although they occasionally travel abroad, the seven military members of the Central Military Commission (CMC) and their principal deputies in the four "general headquarters" (*zong siling bu*) rarely meet with foreign visitors in China, and when they do it is almost always with their military counterparts in carefully controlled meetings or visits to military installations.[4] In these sessions PLA generals rarely depart from their "talking points," often reading them verbatim, and they are known to be uncomfortable in freewheeling strategic dialogue with foreign military leaders. Their lack of assuredness in such dialogue is commensurate with their socialization and professional backgrounds.[5]

The PLA high command today largely comprises elder officers in their late sixties and seventies who possess battlefield, command, and lengthy service experience. Many of them commanded forces in the 1979 Sino-Vietnamese border war, and some fought in the 1962 Sino-Indian conflict and the Korean War. In a departure from past practice, most did not come up through the ranks as political commissars.[6] Relatedly, the current high command no longer comprises soldier-politicians, who are active in the rough-and-tumble world of Chinese elite politics (CMC Vice-Chairman Chi Haotian being the exception). This change signals a potentially very significant development in Chinese politics—the breaking of the "interlocking directorate" and long-standing symbiotic relationship between the Communist Party and the PLA. For the first time since the Red Army was created in 1927 and the Chinese Communist Party rode it to power in 1949, a growing bifurcation of the two institutions is now evident. Corporatism and a more autonomous identity are taking root in

---

4. The military members of the CMC today are Generals Zhang Wannian and Chi Haotian (vice-chairmen), and Generals Fu Quanyou, Wang Ke, Yu Yongbo, Wang Ruilin, and Cao Gang-chuan (members). Since 1993, and the removal of General Yang Baibing, the CMC has not had a secretary-general and has been comprised of a civilian chairman (President Jiang Zemin), two vice-chairmen (usually one of whom is the minister of defense), and the heads of the four "general headquarters" (General Staff Department, General Political Department, General Logistics Department, and General Armaments Department).
5. See David Shambaugh, "China's Post-Deng Military Leadership," in James R. Lilley and David Shambaugh, eds., *China's Military Faces the Future* (Armonk, N.Y. and Washington, D.C.: M.E. Sharpe and AEI Press, 1999), pp. 11–35.
6. There are only three political commissars among the top thirty or so members of the PLA elite: Defense Minister Chi Haotian, General Political Department Director Yu Yongbo, and CMC member General Wang Ruilin. Even General Chi is a decorated veteran who saw extensive battlefield experience in Korea.

the armed forces. The PLA today is much more prepared to resist party encroachment into military affairs, including attempts to pull the PLA into domestic politics or domestic security.[7]

With few exceptions, members of the PLA leadership today have spent their careers largely in regional field commands deep in the interior of China, cut off from interaction with the outside world. They have not traveled extensively or studied abroad, and do not speak foreign languages. Most have a shallow understanding of modernity, much less modern warfare. Their backgrounds as ground-force field commanders make them more comfortable discussing battlefield tactics than global security or political-military issues. Accordingly, they display a distinctly insular worldview. Their nationalism is fierce, sometimes bordering on xenophobia. Many senior PLA officers evince a deep suspicion of the United States and Japan in particular. They have also been socialized in a military institution and political culture that prizes discipline and secrecy—thus they do not appreciate the importance of defense transparency as a security-enhancing measure, and view foreign requests to improve it with suspicion. They refuse to join alliances or participate in joint military exercises with other nations, are reticent to institutionalize military cooperation beyond a superficial level, and are leery of multilateral security cooperation.[8] Although they covet high-technology weapons, they have no direct exposure to them on the battlefield, nor do they truly appreciate the complexities of producing and maintaining them.[9] Given PLA doctrine and needs—trying to become a high-tech military capable of peripheral defense that emphasizes air and naval power projection, nuclear force modernization, ballistic and cruise missiles, electronic countermeasures, information warfare, antisatellite weapons, laser- and precision-guided munitions, and so on—one is struck by the fact that the PLA today is a military led by senior officers with minimal exposure to these kinds of weapons, technologies, and doctrine.

---

7. For discussion of recent party-army relations, see Ellis Joffe, "The Military and China's New Politics: Trends and Counter-Trends," in James Mulvenon and Richard H. Yang, eds., *The People's Liberation Army in the Information Age* (Santa Monica, Calif.: RAND, 1999), pp. 22–47.
8. Interviews with U.S., European, and Asian military officers who have interacted with these individuals confirm these impressions. See also David Shambaugh, *Enhancing Sino-American Military Ties* (Washington, D.C.: Sigur Center for Asian Studies, George Washington University, 1998).
9. In the case of the PLA Air Force, see John Wilson Lewis and Xue Litai, "China's Search for a Modern Air Force," *International Security*, Vol. 24, No. 1 (Summer 1999), pp. 64–94; and Kenneth W. Allen, Glenn Krumel, and Jonathan D. Pollack, *China's Air Force Enters the Twenty-first Century* (Santa Monica, Calif.: RAND, 1995).

Beneath the current PLA leadership, however, is a large tier of major generals and senior colonels in their forties and fifties who are better educated and trained. A number of these younger officers have spent time abroad, speak foreign languages, and do not evince the same insular tendencies. They display a far better grasp of at least the theoretical practice of modern warfare (although no PLA officer has had *any* actual combat experience for twenty years). It is this generation who will command the PLA in the early twenty-first century, as the current high command retires within five years.

Opportunities for foreign interaction with the next generation of PLA leaders are increasing, although they remain limited. Constrained by lack of direct access to field commanders and those officers outside of a handful of select PLA institutions in Beijing, as well as the PLA's broader efforts to limit transparency, foreign analysts and researchers are thus forced to rely on an eclectic assembly of sources. Perhaps the most enticing source is also the least reliable: the Hong Kong media. While one or two magazines, such as *Guang Jiao Jing* [Wide angle], have demonstrated a more reliable track record and are known to have established ties to the PLA, the majority of articles published by the Hong Kong press, which are often based on purported special access to high-level military deliberations and debates with Communist Party leaders, are often unreliable exaggerations. Given the dearth of direct access to PLA officers, reading PLA publications is vital to understanding the military's view. Several hundred books are published by PLA publishers every year, although they are never translated by foreign governments. PLA journals are also numerous (more than two hundred[10]), but with the exception of a handful, the vast majority are classified and restricted in their circulation, and thus are not available to foreigners. Interviews with officers in the PLA General Staff's Second Department (intelligence) and its affiliated think tanks,[11] military attachés posted abroad, and personnel at the Academy of Military Sciences and the National Defense University provide important supplementary views to the documentary database.

An Ambivalent Sense of Security

A combination of these sources forms the evidentiary basis of the PLA's worldview presented below. The sampling indicates a deep ambivalence in

---

10. This estimate is based on a survey of the periodical section of the Academy of Military Sciences Library.
11. The two think tanks are the China Institute of International Strategic Studies and the Foundation for International Strategic Studies.

PLA perceptions of the world. At an objective level, at the beginning of the twenty-first century, China seemingly faces no immediate external military threat to its national security. Its borders are peaceful, the Soviet threat has disappeared (relations with Russia are the best they have been in nearly half a century), and China has forged normal diplomatic relations with all of its neighbors for the first time in its modern history. China's impressive economic growth and steady military modernization should contribute to a sense of assurance and security.

Yet potential problems remain, and China's military is concerned. North Korea continues to be unstable and unpredictable, impinging directly on Chinese security. Beijing's former influence over Pyongyang has been greatly reduced. India's military capabilities and acquisition of nuclear weapons has increased the specter of a new potential threat on China's southern flank. China's maritime claims in the East and South China Seas remain as potential conflict zones. Political tensions with Taiwan constantly have the potential to escalate to a military level, as long as China steadfastly refuses to renounce the use of force against the island. Most of all, strained relations with Japan and the United States (and the strengthening of defense ties between them), combined with deep anxieties about American military deployments and willingness to use force around the world, further complicate China's and the PLA's security calculus. This essential ambivalence in assessments of China's security environment is evident in the writings of, and discussions with, Chinese military personnel.

The 1999 war in Yugoslavia further fueled these anxieties. The Chinese government and the PLA were deeply disturbed by the display of military might by the North Atlantic Treaty Organization (NATO). Like the impact of the 1990–91 Gulf War, one demonstrable effect was to further remind PLA leaders and analysts of how poorly equipped and trained the Chinese military was to defend against modern militaries and fight modern wars.

The PLA's Lessons from Kosovo

PLA analysts paid close attention to the military dimensions of the Yugoslav war, and in particular NATO's strategy, tactics, and weapons. They also noted that the tactics and firepower used against Yugoslavia were similar to those employed in the Gulf War. These included initial attacks against Yugoslavia's command and control infrastructure; extensive electronic jamming of both military and public communications; remote targeting by long-range cruise missiles, launched from sea and air; achievement of "information dominance," making extensive use of space-based sensors and satellites;[12] and air strikes launched from as far away as North America, utilizing in-flight refueling.

PLA analysts were surprised, however, by new features evident in the Yugoslav conflict—for example, the use of several new weapons systems such as improved laser-guided precision munitions that employ a variety of new active homing and direction-finding devices. One of these was the GBU-28/B laser-guided "smart" gravity bomb—five of which were launched from B-2 strategic bombers, mistakenly striking the Chinese embassy in Belgrade. Also on display were an array of satellite-guided bombs, delivering 1,000–2,500 pound warheads with accuracy of a few meters. PLA analysts also noted the use, for the first time, of microwave bombs that could sabotage electronic equipment, missile target seekers, computer networks, and data transmission lines.[13]

The extensive use of cruise missiles and other precision-guided munitions from ranges outside Yugoslav point defenses had a major impact on PLA planners (although they had witnessed similar displays of power during the Gulf War); they were particularly impressed by the increased accuracy of such weapons.[14] This prominence of "smart weapons" impressed upon the PLA the fact that wars can be prosecuted from great distances, far over the horizon, without visual range targeting or encountering antiair and ballistic missile defenses, and without even being able to engage enemy forces directly. Even the Gulf War involved ground forces and force-on-force engagements—but not in Yugoslavia. This was a stark realization for PLA commanders whose whole orientation and doctrine to date had been one of fighting adversaries in land battles on China's soil or in contiguous territory. PLA analysts were profoundly disturbed by the very idea that, in modern warfare, an enemy could penetrate defenses and devastate one's forces without the defender's ability to see or hear, much less counterattack, the adversary.[15]

This perceived vulnerability reportedly prompted a review of the PLA's strategic air defenses and defensive capabilities for jamming and confusing incoming smart weapons.[16] Leaving little to the imagination about potential

12. See, in particular, Wang Baocun, "Information Warfare in the Kosovo Conflict," *Jiefangjun Bao*, May 25, 1999, in Foreign Broadcast Information Service Daily Reports—China Daily Report (hereafter FBIS-CHI), June 23, 1999.
13. Wang Zudian, "The Offense and Defense of High-Technology Armaments," *Liaowang*, May 24, 1999, in FBIS-CHI, May 27, 1999.
14. Interview with Academy of Military Sciences officer, Beijing, May 16, 1999.
15. Interviews with PLA attachés and visiting scholars, Washington, D.C., July 1999.
16. James Kinge, "Chinese Army Calls for Strategic Review," *Financial Times*, May 5, 1999.

Chinese adversaries, one PLA analyst pointedly noted, "In the future, we will be faced mostly with an enemy who uses advanced smart weapons and long-range precision-guided weapons."[17] According to Academy of Military Sciences Senior Colonel Wang Baocun, a leading PLA expert on electronic and information warfare, NATO "decapitated" more than 60 Serbian command and control targets on the first day of the war with attacks from more than 100 Tomahawk missiles and 80 air-launched precision-guided missiles.[18]

PLA analysts were also surprised by NATO's sustained strategic bombing campaign. After destroying Serbian C^4I nodes (command, control, communications, computers, and intelligence), NATO bombers waged a prolonged strategic campaign against a wide range of other targets. In seventy days of sustained bombing, more than 33,000 sorties were flown, including 12,575 strike sorties, targeting approximately 14,000 bombs and cruise-missile ordnance.[19] Many involved planes based far away and utilizing more than 300 in-flight refueling tankers (more than 30 were deployed in Italy alone). The B-2 Stealth strategic bomber, for example, traveled 20,000 kilometers round-trip from the United States on each sortie. Many planes flew 2,500 kilometers from bases in England and northern Europe. The operational tempo of these sorties also impressed PLA analysts; most aircraft would fly daily missions, and some attack fighters flew several sorties per day.[20]

Some PLA analysts applied the lessons from the Kosovo conflict to China's own defenses. They particularly noted the importance of air defenses to protect against aerial bombing. Two analysts from the Academy of Military Sciences, the PLA's top doctrine and operations research center, noted that Yugoslavia had been successful in protecting its antiaircraft defenses by scattering them in mountain caves and along highways and by not activating their radars. This made it difficult, Senior Colonels Yao Yunzhu and Wang Baocun concluded, for NATO planes to quickly attack the surface-to-air missile (SAM) sites with precision-guided munitions.[21] The Chinese media and PLA analysts seemed to relish the loss of planes lost by NATO—particularly the one F-117 Stealth

17. Jia Weidong, "Asymmetrical Warfare and Our Defense," *Jiefangjun Bao*, April 17, 1999, in FBIS-CHI, May 24, 1999.
18. Wang, "Information Warfare in the Kosovo Conflict."
19. "NATO Campaign Showcased Use of Air Power," *Wall Street Journal*, June 2, 1999.
20. Interview with Academy of Military Sciences officer, Beijing, May 16, 1999.
21. Yao Yunzhu, "Federal Republic of Yugoslavia Crisis Shows Need to Strengthen PLA: Discussion of the Kosovo Crisis among Experts and Scholars," *Jiefangjun Bao*, April 13, 1999, in FBIS-CHI, April 28, 1999; and Wang, "Information Warfare in the Kosovo Conflict." Conversely, Wang and Yao did not mention that it allowed NATO bombers to attack virtually with impunity.

fighter downed by a SAM (apparently when the plane's bomb doors opened and were silhouetted against a white cloud background). Some PLA analysts noted China's need to harden and better defend its C[4]I facilities.[22] Senior Colonel Yao also noted the difficulty that NATO attackers had in locating Yugoslav forces—as they were scattered; made good use of mountains, forests, and villages; moved at night; and camouflaged their equipment well. Attacks on ground forces, moreover, required low ground- attack aircraft and helicopters—which were more vulnerable to interdiction. Senior Colonel Wang noted that Yugoslav forces concealed their tanks, armored personnel carriers, artillery, and other equipment in forests, caves, and other locations difficult to identify from the air. He also pointed out that forces used corrugated iron and other methods to deceive heat-seeking missiles and smart weapons.

In general, PLA analysts took consolation in Yugoslavia's fortitude against NATO's overwhelming firepower, and they pointed out in interviews that it would be much easier for China to absorb such punishment. China's geographic expanse was cited as a particular asset against sustained aerial bombing and over-the-horizon cruise missile attacks, because Chinese strategic targets are far more dispersed, hidden, and hardened. China's antiaircraft, antistealth, and electronic countermeasure capabilities are probably also better than Yugoslavia's. In a potential conflict against the United States or Japan, given the necessary staging-area needs of the U.S. and Japanese navies in northeast Asia and the western Pacific, the PLA Navy could disrupt—but not defeat—operations as far as 200 nautical miles offshore. Also, in a conflict contingency over Taiwan, the most likely contingency to bring the PLA into combat, China would not likely face a broad coalition of countries, much less an integrated and experienced military command structure like NATO's. These factors are not lost on PLA strategic planners.

When contemplating China's own potential coercive military action against Taiwan, PLA planners must have drawn little comfort from the Yugoslav conflict. At current force levels, the PLA Air Force could not gain control of the skies over the Strait or Taiwan island, much less carry out a sustained bombing or ground-attack campaign. Given that the PLA would have to rely heavily on ballistic and naval cruise missile attacks to "soften up" the island for a follow-on amphibious invasion force,[23] the example of Yugoslavia having absorbed

22. Interviews with PLA attachés, Washington, D.C., July 1999.
23. Western analysts estimate that this would require at least a 3:1 advantage in landing forces (approximately 750,000 troops). Today, and for the foreseeable future, the PLA has nowhere near the necessary sea or airlift capabilities to mount such an assault.

an enormous pounding from the air without capitulating does not auger well for PLA planners, given a determined Taiwanese population.[24] For its part, the Yugoslav conflict taught Taiwan to harden its C^4I nodes and other potential strategic targets, such as airfields.[25]

Worried about the Hegemon

Judging from publications and interviews, the United States is by far the greatest security concern for PLA leaders and analysts—both generally and in the particular contexts of Taiwan, Korea, and Japan. PLA assessments are in general highly critical of U.S. strategic posture, global behavior, and military deployments. Numerous Chinese military analyses portray the United States as hegemonic, expansionist, and bent on global and regional domination. This predominant view is shared by civilian Chinese officials and international relations specialists. It has its origins in the Cold War,[26] but has become a singular theme since the Soviet Union's collapse and the Gulf War. The view of the United States as an expansionist hegemon has been evident in civilian and PLA journals throughout the 1990s, but the published attacks on the United States gained an unusual intensity and bellicosity in the wake of the 1999 Yugoslav conflict.[27] Some Hong Kong media even asserted that incensed senior PLA generals sought a military confrontation with the United States.[28] One cited Central Military Commission Vice-Chairman General Zhang Wan-nian as being prepared to wage nuclear war.[29] According to this report, the CMC ordered the Second Artillery to expand its stockpile of tactical nuclear weapons and neutron bombs.[30]

---

24. The stigma of bombing civilian population centers would be a major consequence of ballistic missile strikes.
25. Interviews with Taiwanese military and intelligence officials, Taipei, May 10–15, 1999.
26. See David Shambaugh, *Beautiful Imperialist: China Perceives America, 1972–1990* (Princeton, N.J.: Princeton University Press, 1991), chap. 6.
27. Among many, see, for example, Pan Shunrui, "War Is Not Far From Us," *Jiefangjun Bao,* June 8, 1999, in FBIS-CHI, July 6, 1999.
28. See, for example, Lo Ping, "The Military Is Heating Up Its Anti-Americanism Again"; and Li Tzu-ching, "The Chinese Military Clamors for War: Vowing to Have a Fight with the United States," *Zhengming,* June 1, 1999, in FBIS-CHI, June 28, 1999.
29. Li, "The Chinese Military Clamors for War."
30. In refuting the Cox Committee report, China officially admitted in July 1999 that it possessed neutron weapons. See "Facts Speak Louder Than Words and Lies Will Collapse by Themselves—Further Refutation of the Cox Report," Information Office of the State Council, July 19, 1999. The Cox Committee was formally constituted as the Select Committee on U.S. National Security and

PLA analysts have identified the following manifestations of the U.S. quest for global hegemony:[31]

- the domination of international trading and financial systems;
- an ideological crusade to "enlarge" democracies and subvert states that oppose U.S. foreign policy;
- an increase in "humanitarian intervention" and dispatch of U.S. military "peacekeeping" forces overseas;
- the strengthening of old and building of new military alliances and defense partnerships;
- an increased willingness to use military coercion in pursuit of political and economic goals;
- direct military intervention in regional conflicts;
- the pressing of arms control regimes on weaker states; and
- the domination and manipulation of regional multilateral security organizations.

While PLA and civilian analysts in China are critical of U.S. hegemonic behavior, they see it has having long-standing roots in American history. One PLA scholar noted that "the United States has been expansionist since its birth."[32] But, as another colonel in PLA intelligence put it, "Just because America's hegemonic behavior is understandable from a historical perspective does not mean it is acceptable."[33]

Although alarmed by perceived U.S. aggression worldwide and potentially against China itself, PLA analysts continue to voice the standard Chinese optimism that hegemonic nations are constrained by countervailing power and that the era (*shidai*) of "peace and development" will prevail over "power politics." They have an innate belief that the history of international relations consists of repetitive cycles of rising and falling hegemons, all of which eventually collapse because of the unjust nature of their aggression and the countervailing balance of power. Opposition to hegemony has been the explicit sine qua non of Chinese Communist foreign policy since the 1950s, but has its origins in traditional Chinese thought dating to the Spring and Autumn Period

Military/Commercial Concerns with the People's Republic of China, chaired by Rep. Christopher Cox (R-Calif.). It submitted its full report to Congress on January 3, 1999; a declassified partial version was released to the public on May 25, 1999.
31. These views are expressed in a wide range of PLA articles.
32. Interview with Academy of Military Sciences officer, Washington, D.C., May 14, 1998.
33. Interview with General Staff Department Second Department officer, Beijing, May 4, 1998.

(722–481 B.C.).[34] The philosopher Mencius (c. 372–289 B.C.), a disciple of Confucius, is credited with distinguishing the illegitimate rule through force (*badao*) from legitimate benevolent rule (*wangdao*). Ever since, those who employed coercive power to maintain their rule domestically or internationally were considered illegitimate hegemons that needed to be opposed.

Today, most military and civilian analysts in China see the rise of multipolarity (*duojihua*) as the greatest check on the perceived U.S. quest for global hegemony (*baquanzhuyi*). They argue that the post–Cold War balance of power has become "one superpower, many strong powers" (*yi chao duo qiang*) or "one pole, many powers" (*yi ji duo qiang*), with the latter able to check the former.[35] Like other analysts, Colonel Li Qinggong, director of the Comprehensive Security Research Division of the Second Department of the PLA's General Staff Department (intelligence), identifies U.S. "hegemonism and power politics" as the major security problem in Asia and the world. In addition, Li predicts that multipolarity will check U.S. hegemony, a confrontation will emerge between Japan and the United States (beginning with economic conflict and then extending into other spheres), and Russo-Japanese animosity will deepen.[36] The view that the United States and its allies will inevitably come into conflict, given the perceived overbearing nature of U.S. hegemony, is a frequent theme in Chinese writings. Like the theory of multipolarity, however, it is much more wishful thinking than objective analysis. Many in the PLA mistakenly believe that the United States had to force all the NATO allies (which, after the outbreak of the 1999 Yugoslav conflict, was regularly referred to in the Chinese media as the "U.S.-led NATO") to go along with the attacks on Serbia during the conflict, and that the war strained the alliance to the breaking point.[37] Ding Shichuan of the PLA Institute of International Relations similarly argues that unspecified "contradictions" (*maodun*) between the United States and other powers are accelerating and that a new form of "big power relations" will emerge in which American power is weakened.[38]

34. For further discussion of the philosophical origins and history of the concept of hegemony in Chinese thought, see Shambaugh, *Beautiful Imperialist*, pp. 78–83.

35. See the discussion in Pan Xiangting, ed., *Shijie Junshi Xingshi, 1997–98* [The world military situation] (Beijing: National Defense University Press, 1998), pp. 1–7.

36. Li Qinggong, "Wulun Leng Zhan hou shijie junshi geju de bianhua" [An examination of changes in the post–cold war global military structure], *Zhongguo Junshi Kexue*, No. 1 (1997), pp. 112–119.

37. Interview with National Defense University personnel, April 8, 1999, and PLA attaché, Washington, D.C., July 7, 1999.

38. Ding Shichuan, "Readjustments in Big Power Relations towards the New Century," *International Strategic Studies*, No. 2 (1999), pp. 6–14.

It is in the context of assessing the United States' perceived quest for global domination that PLA analysts perceive U.S. policies toward China. They are unequivocal about the alleged desire of the United States to contain the PRC both strategically and militarily, a position they have held throughout the 1990s. This perspective is apparent in numerous articles and interviews. In 1996 and 1997, however, some analysts interpreted the new Clinton administration policy of "engagement" as evidence of the failure of the policy of containment.[39] The majority, though, perceived "engagement" to be but a tactical adjustment—one that still amounts to "soft containment."[40] According to one PLA analyst, commenting in the aftermath of the Clinton administration's announcement of the "engagement" policy, "The United States will still try to exert maximum influence on China."[41] "The U.S. desire to 'shape' China, as is clear [in the Defense Department's 1998 *East Asia Strategy Report*]," said one PLA general, "is doomed to futility."[42]

In addition to seeing a U.S. policy of strategic containment, many PLA officers argue privately that the United States seeks the permanent separation of Taiwan from Chinese sovereignty.[43] A PLA general stated bluntly: "The U.S. is opposed to China's reunification and seeks to keep separation permanent."[44] In the wake of Taiwanese President Lee Teng-hui's July 1999 statement that the island and the mainland should negotiate with each other on a state-to-state basis (*guojia yu guojia*), the Hong Kong media were filled with articles alleging that Chinese leaders believed that Lee was emboldened to make such a "separatist" statement only because of U.S. support and military supplies, and that the PLA was actively arguing the need to teach Lee and Washington another "lesson" (as Beijing believed it had done with the missile "tests" in 1995 and 1996).

Given the central importance of Taiwan in PLA calculations, it is interesting to note that little discussion of Taiwan is evident in those Chinese military journals and books available to foreigners (no doubt this is a subject that the PLA wishes to keep secret). One exception is the journal *Junshi Wenzhai* (Mili-

---

39. See, for example, Col. Guo Xinning, "Qianyi Kelindun zhengfu de Ya Tai zhanlue" [The Clinton government's basic Asia strategy] *Guofang Daxue Xuebao: Zhanlue Yanjiu*, No. 1 (March 1997), pp. 18–24; and Xie Wenqing, "Adjustment and Trend of Development of U.S. Policy toward China," *International Strategic Studies*, No. 3 (1996), pp. 14–20.
40. For further analysis, see David Shambaugh, "Containment or Engagement of China? Calculating Beijing's Responses," *International Security*, Vol. 21, No. 2 (Fall 1996), pp. 180–209.
41. Guo, "Qianyi Kelindun zhengfu de Ya Tai zhanlue," p. 23.
42. Interview, Beijing, December 8, 1998.
43. A good example is Xu Yimin and Xie Wenqing, "U.S. Hegemonism on the Question of Taiwan," *International Strategic Studies*, No. 3 (1995), pp. 10–16.
44. Interview, Beijing, December 8, 1998.

tary digest),[45] which carries a regular feature assessing Taiwan's military and defenses. These articles offer valuable insights into PLA thinking and planning about how to penetrate Taiwan's air and naval defenses. One special issue devoted to Taiwan's defenses provided surprisingly detailed assessments of how to electronically "blind" Taiwan's command and intelligence systems, how to sink its surface ships with submarines, how to neutralize Taiwan's superiority in fighters, and how to utilize ballistic missile strikes, as well as other potential offensive actions that could be employed in a conflict with Taiwan.[46] Another issue analyzed the capabilities of new weapons the United States sold to Taiwan.[47] Although discussion of the Taiwan military is limited in PLA journals available to foreigners, it certainly is a subject of study in PLA institutions.[48] Not surprisingly, a considerable amount of war gaming for potential conflict with Taiwan takes place at the war-game centers of the National Defense University, the Academy of Military Sciences, Nanjing Military Region Headquarters, and other PLA units.[49]

PLA analysts also pay particular attention to U.S. alliances and deployments overseas.[50] Some analysts argue that U.S. military forces are overextended and undersupported logistically and financially to achieve dominance in the Asia-Pacific, Middle East and Persian Gulf, European, and Latin American theaters simultaneously.[51] Further, they do not believe that the United States will be able to wage and win two wars at the same time. Other analysts, such as Academy of Military Sciences strategist General Wang Zhenxi, argue that the U.S. alliance structure and nonalliance defense relationships give the United States greater flexibility and strategic reach, and have significantly extended U.S. "global dominance."[52]

45. *Junshi Wenzhai* is published by the Second Research Institute of China Aerospace and the Chinese Military Scientists Association. While the journal is available in some Chinese libraries, foreigners must acquire this restricted-circulation publication from street vendors in China.
46. See the nine articles published in the section "Taiwan Teji" [Taiwan Special Focus], *Junshi Wenzhai*, Nos. 16–17 (August 1993), pp. 3–45.
47. Ai Hongren, "Taiwan de Junshi fangxiang" [The direction of Taiwan's military], *Junshi Wenzhai* No. 50 (December 1998), pp. 10–12.
48. For example, a visit to the National Defense University in December 1998 revealed a course being taught to the current class of commanding officers on "Taiwan's Weaponry and Military."
49. Interviews with knowledgeable PLA officers, Beijing, May 1998 and April 1999.
50. See, for example, Lu Xinmei, "New Characteristics of the Plan for Arms Buildup of the New U.S. Administration," *International Strategic Studies*, No. 2 (1993), pp. 18–21.
51. See, for example, Fu Chengli, "The Post–Cold War Adjustment of U.S. Military Strategy," *International Strategic Studies*, No. 1 (1994), pp. 27–33; and Fu, "Xin Meiguo de Ya Tai zhanlue" [The new American Asia strategy], *Guofang*, No. 5 (1996), pp. 30–31.
52. Wang Zhenxi and Zhang Qinglei, "Post–Cold War U.S. Alliance Strategy," *International Strategic Studies*, No. 3 (1998), pp. 1–9.

Most PLA analysts still voice opposition to U.S. alliances, even if they have moderated their critical tone since 1997 (when they explicitly called for their abrogation). PLA analysts have certainly taken note of the strengthening and expansion of American alliances and security partnerships worldwide since the end of the Cold War and argue that these moves are part of a master plan to achieve global dominance. They believe that the United States is seeking to create an "international security order" under its control, in which NATO will assume a "global mission" and other U.S. allies will be junior partners in this quest for "security dominance."[53] PLA writers believe that the extension of NATO into Central Europe, the precedent set for "humanitarian intervention" by NATO in the 1999 Yugoslav crisis, which they describe as "Clintonism," and the use of the alliance for "out-of-area crisis response" all foreshadow a dangerous escalation in military alliances and U.S. attempts to dominate the world.[54] Other analysts argue that U.S. aggression constitutes a new style of "gunboat diplomacy" that will aggravate international tensions and lead to a global arms race.[55]

PLA and civilian Chinese analysts tend to take a zero-sum view of alliances, in which such mutual security pacts must have an explicitly identified enemy—or they should have no reason to exist. The positive-sum notion that alliances can exist to preserve stability and deter aggression, without singling out specific enemies, is alien to Chinese realpolitik security thinking. Moreover, Chinese analysts strongly suspect that these alliances (at least those in the Asia-Pacific region) are aimed at China. This is certainly true of Chinese perceptions of the U.S.-Japan alliance and the extension of Partnership for Peace to Central Asia, the reactivation of the Five-Power Defense Pact, as well as the recently enhanced U.S. security ties with Australia, Thailand, the Philippines, and Singapore.

Although I have never read of or heard of a PLA officer endorse U.S. alliances overseas as conducive to stability, peace, security, and economic development, some do take a slightly more sanguine and less-threatened view. One analysis of the 1998 U.S. Defense Department *East Asia Strategy Report*[56]

53. Dong Guozheng, "Security Globalization Is Not Tantamount to Americanization," *Jiefangjun Bao*, May 24, 1999, in FBIS-CHI, June 3, 1999.
54. See, in particular, Wang Naicheng and Jun Xiu, "Whither NATO?" *International Strategic Studies*, No. 2 (1999), pp. 27–32; and Xie Wenqing, "Observing U.S. Strategy of Global Hegemony from NATO's Use of Force against the FRY," *International Strategic Studies*, No. 3 (1999), pp. 1–9.
55. Luo Renshi, "New U.S. Gunboat Diplomacy and Its Strategic Impact," *International Strategic Studies*, No. 3 (1999), pp. 10–14.
56. Secretary of Defense, *The United States Security Strategy for the East Asia-Pacific Region* (Washington, D.C.: Department of Defense, 1998).

offered a straightforward and uncritical report on the strengthening of U.S. alliances and security partnerships.[57] A senior colonel at the National Defense University observed that "we do not mind U.S. alliances per se, [but] only if they are used to destabilize the region. We understand that they are 'left over from history' and that the United States has security interests in the region. But they should not be used to interfere in others' internal affairs, such as China's Taiwan."[58] Another colonel affiliated with the General Staff's Second Department observed, "In the long-term the U.S. [military] presence in East Asia should decrease step by step; a rapid pullout would cause concerns. U.S. alliances [in the region] are not opposed to China ipso facto, but they should not be used to interfere in our internal affairs—Taiwan."[59]

Of course, Chinese officials and PLA leaders have, in recent years, put forward an alternative vision for international relations devoid of alliances, which they consider to be "remnants of the Cold War and power politics." The new Chinese vision is known as the "new security concept."[60] First put forward by former Foreign Minister Qian Qichen at the Association of Southeast Asian Nations (ASEAN) Regional Forum (ARF) in 1997, it was echoed by Chinese Defense Minister Chi Haotian in speeches in Japan, Australia, and Singapore in 1998 and 1999. The new security concept was formulated in direct response to the expansion of NATO and efforts by the United States to strengthen its alliances and security ties worldwide. Despite its Pollyannaish prescription for peace and harmony among nations, the new security concept does represent the most systematic and official exposition of China's *prescriptive* view, to date, of how international relations should be conducted and security maintained.

PLA perceptions of U.S. alliances often parallel views of U.S. force deployments abroad. Many PLA writers are skeptical that the United States is committed to maintaining 100,000 troops in both the European and Asian theaters. Further, they argue that U.S. forces will increasingly face small and limited conflicts—such as Bosnia and Haiti—that are not conducive to using the U.S. military's overwhelming firepower and technological prowess.

---

57. Xu Xiaogang, "U.S. Asia-Pacific Security Strategy towards the Twenty-first Century," *International Strategic Studies*, No. 2 (1999), pp. 47–52.
58. Interview, National Defense University Institute of Strategic Studies, Beijing, April 7, 1999.
59. Interview, China Institute of International Strategic Studies, Beijing, May 4, 1998.
60. For an excellent assessment of the new security concept, see David M. Finkelstein, "China's New Security Concept: Reading between the Lines," *Washington Journal of Modern China*, Vol. 5, No. 1 (Spring 1999), pp. 37–50.

Northeast Asia

PLA analysts uniformly express deep suspicions about Japan's "militarist" tendencies, potential for an expanded regional security role, possible intervention in Korean and Taiwan contingencies, and strengthened defense ties with the United States.[61] They see Japanese defense policy as shifting from being locally to regionally oriented, and changing from passive to active defense.[62] Japan's new geographic strategic thrust is said to have shifted from the north (Russia and Korea) to the west (China) and south (ASEAN).[63] Some articles are very alarmist about Japan's military capabilities, including its latent nuclear capabilities.[64] They view the redefined U.S.-Japan Mutual Security Treaty (1996) and Defense Guidelines (1997), and the Four-Year National Defense Buildup Program (1995), as key manifestations of Japan's new assertiveness and strategic ambitions.[65] Most PLA analysts consider these initiatives as part and parcel of Japan playing the junior partner in the United States' attempt to contain China.[66] Said one PLA National Defense University specialist, "The common strategic goal of the U.S.-Japan relationship is to contain the 'China threat'—the newly strengthened alliance allows the United States to use Japan to restrain the growth of China."[67] Another analyst, however, cautioned that while Japan did indeed have ambitions to become a symmetrical (economic, political, military) great power, serious constraints (domestic and international) would limit its ability to realize these ambitions.[68] PLA analyses concentrate

---

61. See Christensen, "China, the U.S.-Japan Alliance, and the Security Dilemma in East Asia"; and Banning Garrett and Bonnie Glaser, *China and the U.S.-Japan Alliance at a Time of Strategic Change and Shifts in the Balance of Power,* Asia/Pacific Research Center Discussion Paper (Stanford, Calif.: Asia/Pacific Research Center, Stanford University 1997). Garrett and Glaser's analysis suggests a debate, rather than unanimity, among Chinese security specialists.
62. Liang Yang, "Riben fangwei zhengce tiaozheng jichi dui Ya Tai anquan xingshi de yingxiang" [Adjustment of the scope of Japan's defense policy and its influence on the structure of Asian security], *Guofang,* No. 9 (1996), pp. 13–14.
63. Ibid.
64. Ji Yu, "Riben junguozhuyi miewang fure" [Vigilance against the revival of Japanese militarism], *Guofang,* No. 9 (1996), pp. 15–16.
65. Zhang Taishan, "New Developments in the U.S.-Japan Military Relationship," *International Strategic Studies,* No. 4 (1997), pp. 28–33.
66. See, for example, Lu Guangye, "The Impact of Reinforcement of the Japan-U.S. Military Alliance on Asia-Pacific Security and World Peace," *International Strategic Studies,* No. 3 (1999), pp. 21–24.
67. Jiang Lingfei, "Yingxiang Ya-Tai anquan xingshi de sange zhongda wenti" [Three big factors influencing the East Asian security situation], *Guofang Daxue Xuebao,* No. 3 (March 1997), p. 46.
68. Tang Yongsheng, "Riben duiwai zhanlue de tiaozheng jichi zhiji yinsu" [Revisions to Japan's foreign strategy and its limiting factors], *Guofang Daxue Xuebao,* No. 3 (1997), pp. 44–49.

on changes in Japanese defense doctrine from "exclusive defense" of the home islands to enlarged "surrounding areas";[69] redeployment of forces from Hokkaido to western Japan (opposite China and Korea) and streamlining of the Japanese Self-Defense Forces; procurement of new force projection air and naval weapons platforms; and increasingly close integration of intelligence, training, and planning with U.S. forces.[70] Japan's participation in the U.S. theater missile defense (TMD) research and development program is particularly alarming to PLA strategists and Chinese officials, and they are vigorous in their criticisms of it.[71] However, they seem more disturbed by the political and strategic implications of U.S.-Japan cooperation in this area, than by the purely military dimensions of TMD.

The anti-Japanese sentiment one encounters among the PLA at all levels is palpable. Distrust of Japan runs deep, transcends generations, and is virulent among the generation of PLA officers in their forties and fifties. Japan stimulates an emotional reaction not even evident in anti-American diatribes. In conversations with PLA personnel, Americans are regularly subjected to the view that the United States is naïve to consider Japan as an ally or a partner, and they often counsel the United States to be wary of Japanese intentions and military modernization. One leading specialist at the National Defense University's Institute of Strategic Studies argues that instead of cooperating with Japan, the United States should join forces with China "to keep Japan down!"[72]

In contrast to their concerns about Japan, PLA analysts seem strangely relaxed about, if sometimes frustrated with, North Korea. They often reflect a view of the security and humanitarian situation in North Korea profoundly different from that found in Washington or Tokyo. While many PLA interlocutors generally support U.S. goals of a nonnuclear North Korea, the Four-Party Talks, and peace and stability on the peninsula, they privately voice frustration with Pyongyang and emphasize Beijing's limited influence over North Korea. They advocate marketization and international opening of North Korea's economy, and caution against the potentially dangerous effects of pressuring Pyongyang. For China and the PLA, the maintenance of North Korea as a

69. Zhang Jinfang, "Serious Threat to China's Security: Experts Comment on the Strengthening of the Japanese-U.S. Military Alliance," *Jiefangjun Bao*, June 4, 1999, in FBIS-CHI, June 17, 1999.
70. Zhang Taishan, "Japan's Military Strategy in the New Era," *International Strategic Studies*, No. 3 (1998), pp. 17–20.
71. Numerous interviews, Beijing, October and December 1998.
72. Interview, National Defense University Institute of Strategic Studies, Beijing, April 6, 1999.

sovereign state and security buffer is the highest priority.[73] Several military writings and interviews have criticized South Korea and the United States for exacerbating tensions and continuing the Cold War on the Korean peninsula.[74] One PLA general attacked joint exercises and the presence of U.S. forces on the peninsula as "provocative," calling for their eventual removal.[75] Chinese officials and analysts, civilian and military alike, are strongly critical of what they describe as U.S. "pressure tactics" against Pyongyang. One PLA general asks, "What is the purpose of U.S. pressure? To force North Korea into collapse or into changing and developing?"[76] "The tougher the U.S. response and pressure, the closer to the brink [North] Korean leaders will be willing to go," another general opined.[77] PLA interlocutors argue that China does not wish to see weapons of mass destruction on the Korean peninsula (including potential U.S. weapons in South Korea), and that the PRC seeks stability on the peninsula. Yet, bizarrely, they do not believe that the humanitarian situation in the North is dire, denying evidence of famine, starvation, and malnutrition. ("The North Koreans have a great capacity to endure hardship," they often argue.) Nor do they express deep concern about North Korean ballistic missile tests, possible nuclear weapon development sites, or the likelihood that the country and the Kim Jung Il regime may implode.[78] Some PLA analysts are even optimistic about North Korea's prospects.[79] Most PLA officers, however, would likely be opposed to the presence of U.S. forces on the peninsula in the event of Korean reunification. One member of the Institute of Strategic Studies at the PLA National Defense University did concede, however, that such a presence would be a matter to be resolved by the U.S. and reunified Korean governments, and that China would not in principle oppose such forces—*if* they remained south of the 38th parallel and had no offensive mission other than protection of Korean national security.[80]

---

73. For an excellent assessment of Chinese views, see Banning Garrett and Bonnie Glaser, "China's Pragmatic Posture toward the Korean Peninsula," *Korean Journal of Defense Analysis* (Winter 1997), pp. 63–91.
74. Pan Junfeng, "Zhanlue geju, daguo guanxi, Ya-Tai huanjing" [Strategic areas, great power relations, and the Asia-Pacific environment], *Guofang*, No. 1 (1997), pp. 10–11.
75. Interview, China Institute of International Strategic Studies, Beijing, December 6, 1998.
76. Ibid.
77. Ibid.
78. PLA interlocutors have conveyed these views in numerous conversations over the last two years. See Eric McVadon, "Chinese Military Strategy for the Korean Peninsula," in Lilley and Shambaugh, *China's Military Faces the Future*, pp. 271–294.
79. Wang Dahui, "The Post–Cold War Situation on the Korean Peninsula," *International Strategic Studies*, No. 3 (1997), pp. 31–36.
80. Interview, National Defense University, Beijing, April 6, 1999. For a more diverse range of PLA views, see McVadon, "Chinese Military Strategy for the Korean Peninsula"; and Taeho Kim,

Uncertainty about the Neighbors to the North

Over the past decade, China's security calculations with Russia and the Central Asian republics to the north have fundamentally transformed. Moscow and Beijing have moved from the brink of nuclear war to a "strategic partnership."[81] Although it would be an exaggeration to claim that Russia has turned from China's adversary to its ally (as both countries profess that this is not their goal), this new strategic partnership has substantially enhanced their mutual and regional security and has given them common cause in opposing "hegemonism and power politics" (Beijing's code words for the United States).[82] The 1999 Kosovo crisis and Yugoslav war helped to cement the newfound Sino-Russian strategic solidarity, but even before Kosovo the two governments had increasingly begun to side together against the United States in the United Nations Security Council and other international forums. Since Kosovo, the anti-U.S. rhetoric has become more explicit and frequent—as was evident at the August 1999 summit of Presidents Jiang Zemin, Boris Yeltsin, and their counterparts from Kyrgystan, Kazakhstan, and Tajikistan.[83] There is little doubt that Chinese leaders and strategists view the United States as the greatest threat to world peace, as well as to China's own national security and foreign policy goals. China's 1998 Defense White Paper is only thinly veiled on this point: "Hegemonism and power politics remain the main source of threats to world peace and stability; the cold war mentality and its influence still have a certain currency, and the enlargement of military blocs and strengthening of military alliances have added factors of instability to international security. Some countries, by relying on their military advantages, pose military threats to other countries, even resorting to armed intervention."[84] Thus far, Sino-Russian opposition to the United States and its allies has remained largely rhetorical, although stepped-up arms sales from Moscow to

"Strategic Relations between Beijing and Pyongyang: Growing Strains and Lingering Ties," in Lilley and Shambaugh, China's Military Faces the Future, pp. 295–321.
81. See Jennifer Anderson, The Limits of Sino-Russian Strategic Partnership, Adelphi Paper No. 315 (London: International Institute for Strategic Studies, 1997); and Sherman W. Garnett, ed., Limited Partnership: Russia-China Relations in a Changing Asia (Washington, D.C.: Carnegie Endowment for International Peace, 1998).
82. See, for example, "China-Russia Relations at the Turn of the Century," joint statement of Presidents Jiang Zemin and Boris Yeltsin, November 23, 1998. Text is carried in Beijing Review, December 14–20, 1998.
83. See, for example, "Anti-Western Edge to Russian-Chinese Summit," Jamestown Foundation Monitor, August 26, 1999, available at www.jamestown.org/htm/pub-monitor/htm..
84. China's National Defense (Beijing: Information Office of the State Council of the People's Republic of China, 1998), p. 5.

Beijing and joint diplomatic initiatives on Kosovo, Iraq, and TMD suggest that their "strategic partnership" is becoming more tangible.

The relaxation of tensions between China and Russia has been evident in several spheres. The two former enemies have completely demarcated their long-disputed 4,340-mile border and have demilitarized the border region. Both sides have placed limits on ground forces, short-range attack aircraft, and antiair defenses within 100 kilometers of the frontier. As part of two landmark treaties—the Agreement on Confidence Building in the Military Field along the Border Areas and the Agreement on Mutual Reduction of Military Forces in the Border Areas—signed together with Russia, Tajikistan, Kazakhstan, and Kyrgyzstan in April 1996 and April 1997, respectively, China and the other signatories agreed to force reductions that will limit each to maintain a maximum of 130,400 troops, 3,900 tanks, and 4,500 armored vehicles within this 100-kilometer zone. Other provisions of the agreements prohibit military exercises exceeding 40,000 personnel, prior notification of exercises and mandatory observers for any involving more than 35,000 personnel, and a limit of one exercise each year of 25,000 personnel or more. China and Russia have also signed several other bilateral agreements to stabilize and enhance their mutual security—including a nuclear nontargeting agreement (1994) and an agreement to prevent accidental military incidents (1994).

The Chinese and Russian heads of state and government have held annual reciprocal summit meetings, while ministerial-level officials shuttle regularly between the two capitals. The two military establishments have forged particularly close relations—including the transfers of substantial numbers of Russian weapons and defense technologies (including training) to China. Russian arms exports to China in 1996 were an estimated $2.1 billion, comprising nearly one-third of their total bilateral trade. Overall, China bought approximately $8 billion in Russian weapons between 1991 and 1999. During the 1990s, these sales included a wide range of weapons, among them: 15 Ilyushin-72 transport aircraft; 100 RD-33 turbofan engines for China's J-10 fighter; 72 Sukhoi-27 fighters, with a license to coproduce 200 more; 24 Mi-17 transport helicopters; the SA-10 "Grumble" air-defense missile system, with 100 missiles; 4 Kilo-class diesel submarines; 2 Sovremennyi-class guided missile destroyers (currently undergoing sea trials in Russia); 50 T-72 main battle tanks; and 70 armored personnel carriers.[85] More recently (August 1999), after four years of negotiation, Moscow and Beijing concluded a deal for 60 Sukhoi-30 fighters.

---

85. See Bates Gill and Taeho Kim, *China's Arms Acquisitions from Abroad: A Quest for "Superb and Secret Weapons,"* Stockholm International Peace Research Report No. 11 (Oxford: Oxford University Press, 1995).

Overall, two-way trade remains relatively minuscule ($5.5 billion in 1998, representing only 2 percent of total PRC trade volume and less than 5 percent of Russia's). It is largely limited to compensation trade and some exchange in the spheres of machine building, electronics, power generation, petrochemicals, aviation, space, and military technology and weapons. China and Russia have set a target of $20 billion for two-way trade by 2000, although this seems far too ambitious as the two actually have few economic complementarities. Indeed bilateral trade declined from $6.8 billion in 1997 to $5.5 billion in 1998. In an ironic historical reversal, Beijing even pledged a $5 billion concessionary loan to Moscow in 1998, in an effort to help alleviate its basket-case economy.

Improved Sino-Russian relations are not necessarily mirrored on the perceptual level. In contrast to many Chinese civilian analysts who portray Russia as a passive and weak power in decline that no longer threatens China,[86] some military analysts express reservations about Russia's long-term strategic ambitions and current defense policies. They argue that Russia seeks to rebuild and reassert itself as a great power,[87] particularly across Eurasia and in East Asia.[88] In both cases, Russia is seen as trying to use collective security mechanisms as a wedge to reassert its strategic presence in lieu of its former military presence in the region.[89] While PLA analysts recognize the problems affecting Russia's military forces,[90] not all assess the Russian military as atrophied. They point to the Russian armed forces' increased emphasis on developing large-scale mobile assault forces, while maintaining a robust nuclear deterrent.[91] This is a strategy of necessity, some National Defense University analysts believe, as the Russian navy has collapsed and rusts in port.[92] Although articles in some PLA journals discuss the deteriorating domestic situation in Russia[93] and the im-

---

86. See Shambaugh, "China's National Security Environment," in Lampton, *The Making of Chinese Foreign and Security Policy in the Era of Reform.*
87. Wang Rui and Zhang Wei, "A Preliminary Analysis of Russian Military Strategy," *International Strategic Studies,* No. 3 (1997), p. 42.
88. Xue Gang, "The Present Security Policy Framework of Russia," *International Strategic Studies,* No. 1 (1995), pp. 22–27; and Xue and Xu Jun, "Russia's Asia-Pacific Strategy," *International Strategic Studies,* No. 4 (1995), pp. 14–20.
89. Xue, "The Present Security Policy Framework of Russia."
90. Xue Gang, "Retrospect and Prospect of Russia's Economic and Political Transformation," *International Strategic Studies,* No. 3 (1998), p. 13.
91. Wang and Zhang, "A Preliminary Analysis of Russian Military Strategy."
92. Chen Youyi and Yu Gang, "Eluosi zhanlue xingshi de tedian ji duiwai zhengce zouxiang" [Special characteristics of Russian strategy and trends in foreign policy], *Guofang Daxue Xuebao,* No. 3 (1997), p. 42.
93. See Yin Weiguo and Gu Yu, "Review and Prospect of the Situation in Russia," *International Strategic Studies,* No. 2 (1999), pp. 53–59.

proved Sino-Russian relationship,[94] there is no commentary in these open-source journals on the extensive military-to-military relationship or on what Russia is doing to assist PLA force modernization.[95]

China's ties with the Central Asian states have also improved. Following the collapse of the Soviet Union, China moved quickly to establish diplomatic relations with the newly independent Central Asian republics and has subsequently built sound ties with its new neighbors to the north. Central Asian oil reserves are estimated at about 200 billion barrels, and this has become strategically important to China, which became a net importer of crude oil in 1996 and relied on the Middle East for 53 percent of its total imports in the same year. The PRC has paid particular attention to Kazakhstan, with which it has signed several accords for joint energy exploitation. Accordingly, an oil pipeline has been built between the two countries, which began to carry crude to China in 1997.

Another principal motivation for Beijing to solidify ties with the Central Asian states is its own fears of ethnic unrest among its Muslim and minority populations in Xinjiang Province. Small arms and other support have flowed to insurgents in China's northwest from Iran, Afghanistan's Taliban, and sympathetic brethren in the former Soviet Union.

ASEAN and Multilateral Regional Security

While China's relations with Southeast Asia are correct, a wariness in the region exists toward China and the PLA.[96] For their part, PLA analysts tend not to write about Southeast Asia and subregional security issues. Because China considers its maritime claim to the South China Sea to be a "domestic issue," a position similar to China's claim on Taiwan, the *Liberation Army Daily* and other PLA publications do not write about them. One senior PLA intelligence official defined the South China Sea issue as both a "sovereignty matter" (*zhuquan yinsu*) and a dispute over territory and resources (*lingtu yu ziran chongtu*).[97]

---

94. See, for example, Xue Gang, "Sino-Russian Relations in the Post–Cold War International Structure," *International Strategic Studies*, No. 2 (1996), pp. 12–16.
95. One of the few even to discuss exchanges in the military realm was the National Defense University's 1997–98 strategic survey. See Pan, *Shijie Junshi Xingshi, 1997–98*, pp. 277–279.
96. See, for example, Koong Pai-ching, *Southeast Asian Perceptions of China's Military Modernization*, Asia Paper No. 5 (Washington, D.C.: Sigur Center for Asian Studies, George Washington University, 1999); and Allen S. Whiting, "ASEAN Eyes China: The Security Dimension," *Asian Survey*, Vol. 37, No. 4 (April 1997), pp. 299–322.
97. Interview with General Staff Department Second Department official, Beijing, December 8, 1998.

To the extent that PLA interlocutors are positive about the potential for regional cooperative security mechanisms (and they generally are not), they tend to view these regimes as means to constrain U.S. hegemony and to break through the perceived U.S.-Japan containment policy toward China.[98] Few, if any, PLA analysts assess the ARF and the idea of cooperative security in their own right; Luo Renshi of the PLA General Staff Department's China Institute of International Strategic Studies is an exception.[99] A retired PLA officer and former Chinese delegate to the Conference on Disarmament in Geneva, Luo is one of China's most knowledgeable experts on cooperative security institutions. His writings show an appreciation of the underlying norms—including transparency—of such regimes, rather than viewing them as mere tactical instruments to pursue realpolitik. Some, such as Colonel Wu Baiyi of the Foundation for International Strategic Studies (another General Staff Department–affiliated think tank), are more explicit in promoting multilateral security and the new security concept as a means of countering U.S. hegemony and alliances.[100] Other PLA interlocutors argue that a new East Asia security architecture should have three overlapping strands: common security, cooperative security, and comprehensive security.[101] Most PLA analysts remain wed to traditional geometric and balance-of-power approaches to Asian security, and pay little heed to multilateral institutional mechanisms;[102] some, however, see the ARF as evidence of the rising regional role of ASEAN as a "new power."[103]

---

98. Jiang Linfei, "Yingxiang Ya Tai anquan xingshi de sange zhong da wenti" (Three major issues influencing the Asian security situation), *Guofang Daxue Xuebao*, No. 3 (1997), pp. 13–17; and Wu Guifu, "The U.S. Asia-Pacific Strategy in Adjustment," *International Strategic Studies*, No. 3 (1992), pp. 1–8.

99. See Luo Renshi, "Post–Cold War Strategic Trends in the Asia-Pacific Region," *International Strategic Studies*, No. 3 (1994), pp. 5–13; Luo, "Progress and Further Efforts to Be Made in Establishing Confidence Building," *International Strategic Studies*, No. 2 (1995), pp. 18–24; and "New Progress and Trend in the Establishment of Confidence and Security Building Measures in the Asia-Pacific Region," *International Strategic Studies*, No. 4 (1996), pp. 6–12.

100. Wu Baiyi, "Dong Ya guojia anquan zhengce de tedian yu yitong" [Similarities and differences in East Asian countries' security policies], unpublished paper (May 1998).

101. Ronald Monteperto and Hans Binnendijk, "PLA Views on Asia-Pacific Security in the Twenty-first Century," *Strategic Forum* (Washington, D.C.: National Defense University Institute for National Strategic Studies, No. 114, June 1997).

102. See, for example, Xu Yimin, "The Strategic Situation in East Asia and China's Place and Role," *International Strategic Studies*, No. 1 (1996), pp. 16–24; Zhu Chun, "A Discussion about the Situation and Security Problems in the Asia-Pacific Region, *International Strategic Studies*, No. 1 (1993), pp. 18–22; and Zhang Changtai, "Some Views on the Current Situation in the Asia-Pacific Region," *International Strategic Studies*, No. 1 (1997), pp. 27–32.

103. Sr. Col. Luo Yuan, "Dongmeng de chuqi yu Ya Tai anquan hezuo" [The rise of ASEAN and Asian security cooperation], *Guofang*, No. 7 (1996), pp. 23–24.

Worries over South Asia

PLA analysts have not published much on South Asia. Unlike their civilian counterparts, prior to 1998, they were even silent about Indian "regional hegemony." India's May 1998 nuclear tests, however, sounded an alarm to the Chinese military. "India's Attempt to Seek Regional Hegemony Has Been Longstanding!" roared a headline in the *Liberation Army Daily* within days of the blasts.[104] Another article in the armed forces newspaper elaborated in unprecedented detail the composition and order of battle of India's conventional military forces (one wonders how analysts felt describing how much more advanced these forces are compared with the PLA in virtually all conventional categories). "Through fifty years of efforts, India now boasts a mighty army," the authors observed. To what end is the Indian buildup to be put? The article was clear: "The military strategic targets of India are to seek hegemony in South Asia, contain China, control the Indian Ocean, and strive to become a military power in the contemporary world. To attain these targets, since independence India has always pursued its military strategy of hegemonist characteristics." The authors continued by chastising the Indian policy of "occupying Chinese territory in the eastern sector of the border region" (saying nothing, of course, about the western sector where Chinese forces occupy 14,500 square kilometers of Indian-claimed territory), targeting its missiles on southern and southwestern China, and "maintaining its military superiority in the Sino-Indian boundary region to consolidate its vested interests and effectively contain China." India, the authors concluded, "is waiting for the opportune moment for further expansion to continue to maintain its control over weak and small countries in South Asia, advance further southward, and defend its hegemonist status in the region."[105]

While PLA vitriol increased, so did its deployments opposite India.[106] Other PLA commentators expressed fear of an accidental nuclear exchange between India and Pakistan, citing the situation on the subcontinent as "far more serious than the Cuban missile crisis of 1962."[107] The PLA has seemingly found a new adversary in India.

104. Liu Wenguo, "India's Attempt to Seek Hegemony Has Been Longstanding," *Liberation Army Daily*, May 26, 1998, in FBIS-CHI, June 3, 1998.
105. Liu Yang and Guo Feng, "What Is the Intention of Wantonly Engaging in Military Ventures?—India's Military Development Should Be Watched Out For," *Liberation Army Daily*, May 19, 1998, in FBIS-CHI, May 21, 1998.
106. "India Reports China Reinforces Troops on the Border," Agence France-Presse, October 23, 1998, in FBIS-CHI, November 8, 1998.
107. Yang Haisheng, "Harmful Effects of India's Nuclear Tests on the World Strategic Situation," *International Strategic Studies*, No. 4 (1998), p. 17.

Policy Implications and Conclusions

This article has surveyed the PLA's perceptions of China's security environment after the Cold War. It has argued that although China enjoys its most peaceful and least threatening environment since 1949, the PLA nonetheless perceives a variety of sources of instability, uncertainty, and potential threat. Perhaps it is the nature of military analysts and planners worldwide to find (and hence exaggerate) potential threats, even when they do not objectively exist, but the PLA perceptions presented above are notable for their angst. After half a century of feeling encircled by hostile powers, the PLA finds it difficult to break this mind-set.

As perceptions underlie and precede policy decisions and actions, the PLA's sense of uncertainty about its security environment has implications for the United States and nations near China. The most evident implication is the need to continue to engage the PLA at many levels, officially and unofficially, in security-related dialogues. The United States and other nations must better understand the PLA's view of the world and the underlying reasons for its perceptions. Interlocutors must also realize that although many of these perceptions are at variance with their own (often times extremely so), and the PLA often seems stubbornly rigid, at the same time these perceptions are not necessarily immutable. Although China's Leninist political culture and PLA discipline contribute to a remarkable uniformity of articulated perceptions, it is also evident that a range of perspectives exist among PLA officers and between the military and civilian leaders and analysts. These need to be constantly probed and better understood.

The PLA's views of the United States and its security posture outlined in this article should be of considerable concern for U.S. policymakers, and suggest that the United States should be on guard against Chinese attempts to undermine core U.S. security interests in Asia and elsewhere. Dialogue may increase clarity and understanding—even if it does not narrow differences—but those Americans who interact with the PLA, officially or unofficially, should be under no illusion about the depth of China's suspicion and animosity toward the United States. This has long been apparent, but it has worsened since the 1999 Yugoslav war and mistaken bombing of the Chinese embassy in Belgrade, after which popular images of the United States turned from cautiously critical to overtly hostile overnight. The attacks by thousands of Chinese demonstrators on the U.S. embassy in Beijing and consulates elsewhere expressed the depth of public hostility, which was also evident in elite attitudes and commentary. A torrent of anti-American invective was unleashed in the Chinese media the likes of which had not been seen since the Cultural Revolution. The official *People's Daily*, the mouthpiece of the Communist Party, published a series of authoritative "Observer" and "Commentator" articles lambasting U.S. "hegemonism," "imperialism," "arrogance," "aggression," and "expansionism."[108] One article accused the United States of seeking to become "Lord of the Earth" and compared contemporary U.S. hegemony to the aggression of Nazi Germany.[109]

The political fallout from the embassy bombing and the Yugoslav war will be felt for some time in Sino-American relations, and it has introduced new instability to an inherently fragile relationship. It has also enhanced the element of strategic competition between China and the United States. Despite China's lack of global political influence and military power projection capabilities, there exists a new strategic competition between the two countries today. Thus far, it has largely been a war of words, despite the mistaken bombing of the Chinese embassy in Belgrade and Chinese "missile diplomacy" near Taiwan in 1995–96. Increasingly, though, the two nations' hard national security interests rub up against each other in the Asia-Pacific region, the Persian Gulf region, and South Asia, while differences over the Kosovo crisis momentarily brought the strategic competition to Europe. Institutionally, the Sino-American strategic competition is increasingly apparent in the United Nations Security Council and other international forums. Although not yet a new Cold War of geopolitical competition or a "clash of civilizations" in the Huntingtonian sense,[110] the essence of the competition is very much a clash of worldviews about the structure, nature, and norms of international relations and security.

---

108. See, for example, Zhang Yuqing, "Irrefutable Proof of the Swelling of U.S. Hegemonism," *Renmin Ribao*, May 19, 1999, in FBIS-CHI, May 19, 1999; Observer, "On the New Development of U.S. Hegemonism," *Renmin Ribao*, May 27, 1999, in FBIS-CHI, May 28, 1999; and Huang Hong and Ji Ming, "United under the Great Banner of Patriotism—Thoughts on the Strong Condemnations against U.S.-Led Atrocities," *Renmin Ribao*, May 27, 1999, in FBIS-CHI, June 6, 1999.
109. "China Says U.S. Wants to Become 'Lord of the Earth,'" Reuters, June 22, 1999.
110. Samuel Huntington's *The Clash of Civilizations* makes much of the potential for Sino-American rivalry—in ideological, cultural, and geopolitical senses—although he portrays China's quest for regional hegemony as the fundamental characteristic of the rivalry to come. Oddly, he also sees the achievement of Chinese hegemony as "reducing instability and conflict in East Asia." See Huntington, *The Clash of Civilizations and the Remaking of World Order* (New York: Simon and Schuster, 1996), especially pp. 229–238, quotation at p. 237. For a counterargument of why China cannot achieve hegemony, see David Shambaugh, "Chinese Hegemony over East Asia by 2015?" *Korean Journal of Defense Analysis*, Vol. 9, No. 1 (Summer 1997), pp. 7–28.

Geography and long-term national interests suggest, however, that the United States and China must coexist in the world and in the Asia-Pacific region.[111] Increasingly, too, the United States and other nations must live with a more capable and modern Chinese military. A valuable opportunity remains to influence how the PLA views the world and the region, how it understands its—and others'—national interests, and the uses to which it will put its new military capabilities.[112] To have a chance to sensitize the PLA to other nations' perceptions and interests requires, however, that the PLA increase its travel abroad and interact much more extensively with Americans and other foreigners in China.

Given the PLA's perceptions and suspicions outlined above, it will be an uphill battle working and coexisting with the Chinese military. But coexistence is one sibling of strategic competition, as competitors need not become adversaries. The other—confrontation—is to be avoided if possible. An opportunity remains for the United States and its allies and security partners to establish a strategic relationship of competitive coexistence with elements of cooperation with the PRC. Given the clash of national interests and divisive perceptions outlined in this article, competitive coexistence is probably the most realistic relationship that can be achieved. Even this kind of relationship will require constant high-level attention to policy and hard work by both sides, if an adversarial relationship is to be avoided.

---

111. See Robert S. Ross, "The Geography of the Peace: East Asia in the Twenty-first Century," *International Security*, Vol. 23, No. 4 (Spring 1999), pp. 81–118.
112. See Ashton B. Carter and William J. Perry, *Preventive Defense* (Washington, D.C.: Brookings, 1999), pp. 92–122; and Perry and Carter, *The Content of U.S. Engagement with China* (Stanford, Calif. and Cambridge, Mass.: Center for International Security and Cooperation, Stanford University, and Belfer Center for Science and International Affairs, Harvard University, 1998).

Part II:
China and Asia-Pacific Security

China, the U.S.-Japan Alliance, and the Security Dilemma in East Asia

Thomas J. Christensen

Many scholars and analysts argue that in the twenty-first century international instability is more likely in East Asia than in Western Europe. Whether one looks at variables favored by realists or liberals, East Asia appears more dangerous. The region is characterized by major shifts in the balance of power, skewed distributions of economic and political power within and between countries, political and cultural heterogeneity, growing but still relatively low levels of intraregional economic interdependence, anemic security institutionalization, and widespread territorial disputes that combine natural resource issues with postcolonial nationalism.[1]

If security dilemma theory is applied to East Asia, the chance for spirals of tension in the area seems great, particularly in the absence of a U.S. military presence in the region. The theory states that, in an uncertain and anarchic international system, mistrust between two or more potential adversaries can

Thomas J. Christensen is Associate Professor of Political Science and a member of the Security Studies Program at the Massachusetts Institute of Technology. He is author of Useful Adversaries: Grand Strategy, Domestic Mobilization, and Sino-American Conflict, 1947–1958 *(Princeton, N.J.: Princeton University Press, 1996).*

A version of this article was presented to the 1998 University of Pennsylvania and Dartmouth College conferences on "The Emerging International Relations of the Asia Pacific Region" and will appear in a forthcoming volume edited by G. John Ikenberry and Michael Mastanduno. For helpful comments I am grateful to Robert Art, David Asher, Paul Giarra, Bonnie Glaser, Paul Godwin, Avery Goldstein, John Ikenberry, Iain Johnston, Peter Katzenstein, Jonathan Kirshner, George Lewis, Li Hong, Michael Mastanduno, Thomas McNaugher, Robert Pape, Barry Posen, Theodore Postol, Edward Rios, Richard Samuels, Harvey Sapolsky, Stephen Van Evera, Cindy Williams, Xu Xin, four anonymous reviewers, and the members of the Brandeis University International Relations Seminar, the China Study Group at the Foreign Policy Research Institute in Philadelphia, the National Security Group Seminar at Harvard University's John M. Olin Institute, the Security Studies Program and MISTI China seminars at MIT, and the Penn-Dartmouth project mentioned above. I would like to thank the Olin Institute's East Asia Security Project for its generous research funding. I am also grateful to Kristen Cashin for administrative assistance.

1. Aaron L. Friedberg, "Ripe for Rivalry: Prospects for Peace in a Multipolar Asia," *International Security*, Vol. 18, No. 3 (Winter 1993/94), pp. 5–33; Richard K. Betts, "Wealth, Power, and Instability," *International Security*, Vol. 18, No. 3 (Winter 1993/94), pp. 34–77; Stephen Van Evera, "Primed for Peace: Europe after the Cold War," *International Security*, Vol. 15, No. 3 (Winter 1990/91), pp. 7–57; and James Goldgeier and Michael McFaul, "A Tale of Two Worlds," *International Organization*, Vol. 46, No. 2 (Spring 1992), pp. 467–492.

lead each side to take precautionary and defensively motivated measures that are perceived as offensive threats. This can lead to countermeasures in kind, thus ratcheting up regional tensions, reducing security, and creating self-fulfilling prophecies about the danger of one's security environment.[2] If we look at the variables that might fuel security dilemma dynamics, East Asia appears quite dangerous. From a standard realist perspective, not only could dramatic and unpredictable changes in the distribution of capabilities in East Asia increase uncertainty and mistrust, but the importance of sea-lanes and secure energy supplies to almost all regional actors could encourage a destabilizing competition to develop power-projection capabilities on the seas and in the skies. Because they are perceived as offensive threats, power-projection forces are more likely to spark spirals of tension than weapons that can defend only a nation's homeland.[3] Perhaps even more important in East Asia than these more commonly considered variables are psychological factors (such as the historically based mistrust and animosity among regional actors) and political geography issues relating to the Taiwan question, which make even defensive weapons in the region appear threatening to Chinese security.[4]

One way to ameliorate security dilemmas and prevent spirals of tension is to have an outside arbiter play a policing role, lessening the perceived need for regional actors to begin destabilizing security competitions. For this reason, most scholars, regardless of theoretical persuasion, seem to agree with U.S. officials and local leaders that a major factor in containing potential tensions in East Asia is the continuing presence of the U.S. military, particularly in Japan.[5] The historically based mistrust among the actors in Northeast Asia is

---

2. For the original security dilemma and spiral models, see Robert Jervis, "Cooperation under the Security Dilemma," *World Politics*, Vol. 30, No. 2 (January 1978), pp. 167–174; and Jervis, *Perception and Misperception in International Politics* (Princeton, N.J.: Princeton University Press, 1976), chap. 3.
3. For writings on the destabilizing influence of offensive weapons and doctrines, see Stephen Van Evera, "The Cult of the Offensive and the Origins of the First World War," *International Security*, Vol. 9, No. 1 (Summer 1984), pp. 58–107; Van Evera, "Offense, Defense, and the Causes of War," *International Security*, Vol. 22, No. 4 (Spring 1998), pp. 5–43; and Sean M. Lynn-Jones, "Offense-Defense Theory and Its Critics," *Security Studies*, Vol. 4, No. 4 (Summer 1995), pp. 660–691.
4. My understanding of the Chinese perspectives reflects more than seventy interviews, often with multiple interlocutors, that I conducted during four month-long trips to Beijing in 1993, 1994, 1995, and 1996, and two shorter trips to Beijing and Shanghai in 1998. My interlocutors were a mix of military and civilian analysts in government think tanks as well as academics at leading Chinese institutions. The government think-tank analysts are not decisionmakers, but they advise their superiors in the following key governmental organizations: the People's Liberation Army (PLA), the Foreign Ministry, the State Council, and the Chinese intelligence agencies. For obvious reasons, the individual identities of particular interviewees cannot be revealed.
5. In fact, even optimistic projections for the region are predicated on a long-term U.S. military presence. See, for example, Robert S. Ross, "The Geography of the Peace: East Asia in the Twenty-first Century," *International Security*, Vol. 23, No. 4 (Spring 1999), pp. 81–118.

so intense that not only is the maintenance of a U.S. presence in Japan critical, but the form the U.S.-Japan alliance takes also has potentially important implications for regional stability. In particular, the sensitivity in China to almost all changes in the Cold War version of the U.S.-Japan alliance poses major challenges for leaders in Washington who want to shore up the alliance for the long haul by encouraging greater Japanese burden sharing, but still want the U.S. presence in Japan to be a force for reassurance in the region. To meet these somewhat contradictory goals, for the most part the United States wisely has encouraged Japan to adopt nonoffensive roles that should be relatively unthreatening to Japan's neighbors.

Certain aspects of U.S. policies, however, including joint research of theater missile defenses (TMD) with Japan, are still potentially problematic. According to security dilemma theory, defensive systems and missions, such as TMD, should not provoke arms races and spirals of tension. In contemporary East Asia, however, this logic is less applicable. Many in the region, particularly in Beijing, fear that new defensive roles for Japan could break important norms of self-restraint, leading to more comprehensive Japanese military buildups later. Moreover, Beijing's focus on preventing Taiwan's permanent separation from China means that even defensive weapons in the hands of Taiwan or its potential supporters are provocative to China. Given the bitter history of Japanese imperialism in China and Taiwan's status as a Japanese colony fom 1895 to 1945, this certainly holds true for Japan.

In the first section of this article I describe why historical legacies and ethnic hatred exacerbate the security dilemma in Sino-Japanese relations. In the second section I examine Chinese assessments of Japan's actual and potential military power. In the third section I address how changes in the U.S.-Japan relationship in the post–Cold War era affect Chinese security analysts' views of the likely timing and intensity of future Japanese military buildups. I argue that, for a combination of domestic and international reasons, the United States faces tough challenges in maintaining the U.S.-Japan alliance in a form that reassures both Japan and its neighbors. In the fourth section I discuss why certain aspects of recent efforts to bolster the alliance through Japanese commitments to new, nonoffensive burden-sharing roles are potentially more provocative than they may appear on the surface. In the fifth section I detail how China's attitudes about Japan affect the prospects for creating confidence-building measures and security regimes that might ameliorate the security dilemma over the longer term. In the sixth section I discuss the relevance of my analysis for U.S. foreign policy in the region and why, despite the problems outlined above, there are reasons for optimism if trilateral relations between the United States, China, and Japan are handled carefully in the next two decades.

Why China Would Fear a Stronger Japan

Chinese security analysts, particularly military officers, fear that Japan could again become a great military great power in the first quarter of the twenty-first century. Such a Japan, they believe, would likely be more independent of U.S. control and generally more assertive in international affairs. If one considers threats posed only by military power and not who is wielding that power, one might expect Beijing to welcome the reduction or even elimination of U.S. influence in Japan, even if this meant China would have a more powerful neighbor. After all, the United States is still by far the most powerful military actor in the Western Pacific.[6] However, given China's historically rooted and visceral distrust of Japan, Beijing would fear either a breakdown of the U.S.-Japan alliance or a significant upgrading of Japan's role within that alliance.[7] This sentiment is shared outside China as well, particularly in Korea. Although Chinese analysts presently fear U.S. power much more than Japanese power, in terms of national intentions, Chinese analysts view Japan with much less trust and, in many cases, with a loathing rarely found in their attitudes about the United States.

THE HISTORICAL LEGACY

The natural aversion to Japan that sprang from its brutal occupation of China has been preserved in part by Tokyo's refusal to respond satisfactorily to Chinese requests that Tokyo recognize and apologize for its imperial past—for example, by revising history textbooks in the public schools.[8] Chinese sensibilities are also rankled by specific incidents—for example, Prime Minister

---

6. One might argue that the geographical proximity of Japan alone would make a new regional power a greater threat to China than the more distant United States. In any case, the decision over what poses a larger threat—a distant superpower or a local great power—cannot be reached by analyzing the international balance of power alone. As in the Chinese case, the assessment of which country poses the greater threat will be based on historical legacies and national perceptions. I am grateful to Stephen Walt for helpful comments on this point.
7. For the classic study, see Allen S. Whiting, *China Eyes Japan* (Berkeley: University of California Press, 1989).
8. It is possible that the concerns expressed by Chinese analysts discussed below about Japan and the United States are purely cynical tactics designed to prevent the rise of a new regional power by affecting the debate in the United States and Japan. Such a "spin" strategy could also help justify at home and to regional actors more aggressive Chinese weapons development and diplo-

Ryutaro Hashimoto's 1996 visit to the Yasukuni Shrine, which commemorates Japan's war dead, including war criminals like Tojo.[9] Although some fear that Japan's apparent amnesia or lack of contrition about the past means that Japan could return to the "militarism" (*junguozhuyi*) of the 1930s, such simple historical analogies are relatively rare, at least in Chinese elite foreign policy circles.[10] Chinese analysts' concerns regarding Japanese historical legacies, although not entirely devoid of emotion, are usually more subtle. Many argue that, by downplaying atrocities like the Nanjing massacre and underscoring events like the atomic bombing of Hiroshima and Nagasaki, Japanese elites portray Japan falsely as the victim, rather than the victimizer, in World War II. Because of this, some Chinese analysts fear that younger generations of Japanese citizens may not understand Japan's history and will therefore be insensitive to the intense fears of other regional actors regarding Japanese military power. This lack of understanding will make them less resistant to relatively hawkish elites' plans to increase Japanese military power than their older compatriots, who, because they remember World War II, resisted military buildups during the Cold War.[11]

Chinese analysts often compare Japan's failure to accept responsibility for World War II to the more liberal postwar record of Germany, which has franker discussions of the war in its textbooks, has apologized for its wartime aggres-

---

macy. Although I believe this probably was the intention of some of my interlocutors, given the large number of interlocutors, the diversity of opinions expressed on various issues over the five years of my discussions, and the controversial positions I sometimes heard expressed on issues such as the Tiananmen massacre or the Chinese missile exercises near Taiwan, I find it difficult to believe that Beijing, or any other government, could manufacture such complex theater over such an extended period of time.

9. Also in that year Japanese rightists built structures on the Diaoyu/Senkaku Islands, which are contested by both Japan and China. Many Chinese analysts saw Tokyo's complicity in their activities, especially after the dispatch of Japanese Coast Guard vessels to prevent protestors from Hong Kong and Taiwan from landing on the Japanese-controlled islands.

10. See Yinan He, "The Effect of Historical Memory on China's Strategic Perception of Japan," paper prepared for the Ninety-forth Annual Meeting of the American Political Science Association," Boston, Massachusetts, September 3–6, 1998. For example, my interlocutors generally did not believe that a militarily stronger Japan would try to occupy sections of the Asian mainland as it did in the 1930s and 1940s.

11. The problem of Japan's lack of contrition was raised in nearly every interview I conducted. See Zhang Dalin, "Qianshi Bu Wang, Houshi Zhi Shi" [Past experience, if not forgotten, is a guide for the future], *Guoji Wenti Yanjiu* [International studies], No. 3 (1995), pp. 6–11. For a critical Japanese perspective on the textbook issue, see Saburo Ienaga, "The Glorification of War in Japanese Education," *International Security*, Vol. 18, No. 3 (Winter 1993/94), pp. 113–133. The Chinese view on the generational issue in Japan is similar to the Japanese pacifist view. See Kunihiro Masao, "The Decline and Fall of Pacifism," *Bulletin of the Atomic Scientists*, Vol. 53, No. 1 (January/February 1997), pp. 35–39.

sion, and has even offered financial payments to Israel.[12] Now a new unflattering comparison is sure to arise. During their November 1998 summit in Tokyo, Prime Minister Keizo Obuchi refused to offer an apology to China's President Jiang Zemin that used the same contrite wording as the rather forthright apology Japan offered to South Korea earlier in the year. This divergence in apologies will probably only complicate the history issue between Tokyo and Beijing.[13]

It may seem odd to the outside observer, but the intensity of anti-Japanese sentiment in China has not decreased markedly as World War II becomes a more distant memory. There are several reasons in addition to those cited above. Nationalism has always been a strong element of the legitimacy of the Chinese Communist Party (CCP), and opposing Japanese imperialism is at the core of this nationalist story. As a result, Chinese citizens have been fed a steady diet of patriotic, anti-Japanese media programming designed to glorify the CCP's role in World War II. Although far removed from that era, most Chinese young people hold an intense and unapologetically negative view of both Japan and, in many cases, its people.[14] As economic competition has replaced military concerns in the minds of many Chinese, China's basic distrust of Japan has been transferred to the economic realm. Japanese businesspeople are often described as unreliable, selfish, and slimy (youhua). As a result, despite five decades of peace and a great deal of economic interaction, chances are small that new Japanese military development will be viewed with anything but the utmost suspicion in China.

Elite analysts are certainly not immune to these intense anti-Japanese feelings in Chinese society. These emotions, however, have not yet affected the practical, day-to-day management of Sino-Japanese relations. On the contrary, since the 1980s the Chinese government has acted to contain anti-Japanese sentiment in the society at large to avoid damaging bilateral relations and to prevent protestors from using anti-Japanese sentiment as a pretext for criticiz-

---

12. For published Chinese comparisons of postwar Germany and Japan, see Su Huimin, "Yi Shi Wei Jian, Mian Dao Fuzhe: Deguo dui Erci Dazhan de Fansi" [Take lessons from history and avoid the recurrence of mistakes: Germany's introspection about World War II], Guoji Wenti Yanjiu [International studies], No. 3 (1995), pp. 12–16; and Sun Lixiang, "Zhanhou Ri De Liang Guo You Yi Shili zhi Bijiao" [A comparison of the postwar right-wing forces in the two nations of Japan and Germany], Waiguo Wenti Yanjiu [Research on foreign problems], No. 2 (1988), pp. 1–10.
13. Nicholas D. Kristof, "Burying the Past: War Guilt Haunts Japan," New York Times, November 30, 1998, pp. A1, A10.
14. In 1993 government scholars pointed out that, in many ways, China's youth is more actively anti-Japanese than the government. They pointed to student protests against Japanese "economic imperialism" in 1986 as an example.

ing the Chinese government, as occurred several times in Chinese history.[15] But Chinese analysts' statements about the dangers that increased Japanese military power would pose in the future suggest that anti-Japanese sentiment does color their long-term threat assessments, even if it does not always alter their immediate policy prescriptions. Because they can influence procurement and strategy, such longer-term assessments may be more important in fueling the security dilemma than particular diplomatic policies in the present.

Chinese Assessments of Japanese Military Power and Potential

In assessing Japan's current military strength, Chinese analysts emphasize the advanced equipment that Japan has acquired, particularly since the late 1970s, when it began developing a navy and air force designed to help the United States contain the Soviet Union's growing Pacific Fleet. Chinese military writings highlight Japanese antisubmarine capabilities (such as the P-3C aircraft), advanced fighters (such as the F-15), the E-2 advanced warning aircraft, Patriot air defense batteries, and Aegis technology on surface ships.[16] Chinese analysts correctly point out that, excluding U.S. deployments in the region, these weapons systems constitute the most technologically advanced arsenal of any East Asian power. They also cite the Japanese defense budget, which, although small as a percentage of gross national product (GNP), is second only to U.S. military spending in absolute size.[17]

Despite their highlighting of Japan's current defense budget and high levels of military sophistication, Chinese analysts understand that Japan can easily do much more militarily than it does. While they generally do not believe that Japan has the requisite combination of material capabilities, political will, and ideological mission to become a Soviet-style superpower, they do believe that Japan could easily become a great military power (such as France or Great Britain) in the next twenty-five years. For example, although these analysts often argue that it is in Japan's economic interest to continue to rely on U.S. military protection in the near future, they do not think that significantly increased military spending would strongly damage the Japanese

---

15. Interviews, 1996. See also Hafumi Arai, "Angry at China? Slam Japan," *Far Eastern Economic Review*, October 3, 1996, p. 21. It is clear that compared to students and other members of the public, the Chinese government was a voice of calm during the 1996 Diaoyu/Senkaku affair.
16. Pan Sifeng, ed., *Riben Junshi Sixiang Yanjiu* [Research on Japanese military thought] (Beijing: Academy of Military Sciences Press, October 1992), pp. 388–392 (internally circulated).
17. Multiple interviews, 1993–98.

economy.[18] They have also been quite suspicious about the massive stockpiles of high-grade nuclear fuel that was reprocessed in France and shipped back to Japan in the early 1990s. Many in China view Japan's acquisition of this plutonium as part of a strategy for the eventual development of nuclear weapons, something, they point out, Japanese scientists would have little difficulty producing.[19] Chinese security analysts also have stated that Japan can become a great military power even if it forgoes the domestically sensitive nuclear option. Chinese military and civilian experts emphasize that nuclear weapons may not be as useful in the future as high-tech conventional weapons, and that Japan is already a leader in dual-use high technology.[20]

In particular, Chinese experts recognize that Japan has practiced a great deal of self-restraint in eschewing weapons designed to project power far from the home islands. For example, in 1996 one military officer stated that despite the long list of current Japanese capabilities mentioned above, Japan certainly is not yet a normal great power because it lacks the required trappings of such a power (e.g., aircraft carriers, nuclear submarines, nuclear weapons, and long-range missile systems).[21] For this officer and many of his compatriots, the question is simply if and when Japan will decide to adopt these systems. For this reason, Chinese analysts often view Japan's adoption of even new defensive military roles as dangerous because it may begin to erode the constitutional (Article 9) and nonconstitutional norms of self-restraint (e.g., 1,000-nautical-mile limit on power-projection capability, prohibitions on the military use of space, and tight arms export controls) that have prevented Japan from realizing its military potential.

Interestingly, many Chinese analysts do not consider economic hard times in Japan to be particularly reassuring. On the contrary, in terms of intentions, some fear that economic recession and financial crises could improve the fortunes of relatively hawkish Japanese elites by creating a general sense of uncertainty and threat in Japanese society, by fueling Japanese nationalism

---

18. In 1992 an internally circulated analysis of Japan's military affairs points out that Japan could easily spend 4 percent of GNP on its military without doing fundamental harm to its long-term economic growth. The examples of much higher levels of spending in healthy economies in the United States and Europe during the Cold War are cited as evidence. Ibid., p. 499. Similar positions were taken by active and retired military officers in 1996 and 1998.

19. This was a particularly sensitive issue in 1993 and 1994, and remains so today.

20. Multiple interviews, 1996. For written materials, see Gao Heng, "Shijie Junshi Xingshi" [The world military scene], *Shijie Jingji yu Zhengzhi* [World economy and politics], No. 2 (February 1995), pp. 14–18. For a similar Western view on Japanese "technonationalism," see Richard J. Samuels, *Rich Nation, Strong Army: National Security and the Technological Transformation of Japan* (Ithaca, N.Y.: Cornell University Press, 1994).

21. Interview, 1996.

more generally, and by harming relations with the United States (Japan's main provider of security). In terms of capabilities, some Chinese analysts argue that Japan's technological infrastructure, which would be critical to a modern military buildup, does not seem affected by Japan's recent economic woes.[22]

Factors That Would Encourage or Prevent Japanese Military Buildups

Although almost all Chinese analysts would fear the result, they have differed in their assessment of the likelihood that Japan will attempt to realize its military potential in the next few decades. The more pessimistic analysts have argued that this outcome is extremely likely or even inevitable. Their views are consistent with the predictions of balance-of-power theories, but they do not agree with the analysis of some Western experts on Japan who believe that cultural pacifism after World War II, domestic political constraints, and economic interests will steer Japan away from pursuing such a strategy.[23] Even the more pessimistic Chinese analysts are aware of these arguments about Japanese restraint and do not dismiss them out of hand, but some view such obstacles to Japanese military buildups merely as delaying factors in a long-term and inevitable process. Other more conditionally pessimistic and cautiously optimistic analysts place greater faith in the hypothetical possibility of preventing significant Japanese buildups over the longer run, but have expressed concern over the hardiness of the delaying factors that could theoretically prevent such buildups. The most optimistic analysts have argued that these factors should remain sturdy and will prevent Japan from injuring its regional relations by pursuing a more assertive military role.[24]

The vast majority of these optimists and pessimists believe that, along with the domestic political and economic stability of Japan, the most important

22. This was a consistent theme in interviews from 1993 to 1998, and was repeated in 1998 during the financial crisis.

23. For the realist view, see Christopher Layne, "The Unipolar Illusion: Why New Great Powers Will Rise," *International Security*, Vol. 17, No. 4 (Spring 1993), pp. 5–51. For the argument that Japan will likely not remilitarize, see Thomas U. Berger, "From Sword to Chrysanthemum: Japan's Culture of Anti-Militarism," *International Security*, Vol. 17, No. 4 (Spring 1993), pp. 119–150; and Peter J. Katzenstein, *Cultural Norms and National Security: Police and Military in Postwar Japan* (Ithaca, N.Y.: Cornell University Press, 1996).

24. The simplest versions of the most optimistic and most pessimistic forecasts about Japan's future were offered most frequently during my first three research trips from 1993 to 1995. After the Taiwan Strait crisis of 1995–96, one hears less often the most optimistic liberal argument that economic interests will trump security interests in the post–Cold War world. Following the 1995 Nye report, one hears the simplest versions of the pessimists' scenarios less often because they were often predicated on fragility in the post–Cold War U.S.-Japan alliance.

factor that might delay or prevent Japanese military buildups is the status of the U.S.-Japan relationship, particularly the security alliance.[25] The common belief in Beijing security circles is that, by reassuring Japan and providing for Japanese security on the cheap, the United States fosters a political climate in which the Japanese public remains opposed to military buildups and the more hawkish elements of the Japanese elite are kept at bay. If, however, the U.S.-Japan security alliance either becomes strained or undergoes a transformation that gives Japan a much more prominent military role, Chinese experts believe that those ever-present hawks might find a more fertile field in which to plant the seeds of militarization.[26]

THE CHINA-JAPAN SECURITY DILEMMA AND U.S. POLICY CHALLENGES
For the reasons offered above, most Chinese analysts fear almost any change in the U.S.-Japan alliance. A breakdown of U.S.-Japan ties would worry pessimists and optimists alike. On the other hand, Chinese analysts of all stripes also worry to varying degrees when Japan adopts greater defense burden-sharing roles as part of a bilateral effort to revitalize the alliance. These dual and almost contradictory fears pose major problems for U.S. elites who are concerned that the alliance is dangerously vague and out of date and is therefore unsustainable, but who still want the United States to maintain the reassurance role outlined in documents such as the 1998 East Asia-Pacific Strategy Report.[27] Especially before the recent guidelines review, the U.S.-Japan alliance had often been viewed in the United States as lopsided and unfair because the United States guarantees Japanese security without clear guaran-

---

25. Interviews, 1993–98. See also Pan, *Riben Junshi Sixiang Yanjiu*, p. 501. This book states in typical fashion, "Of all the factors that could compel Japan's military policy to change, U.S.-Japan relations will be the deciding factor." See also Wang Yanyu, ed., *Riben Junshi Zhanlüe Yanjiu* [Research on Japanese military strategy] (Beijing: Academy of Military Sciences Press, 1992), pp. 308–310 (internally circulated); and Liu Shilong, "Dangqian Rimei Anbao Tizhi de San Ge Tedian" [Three special characteristics of the current U.S.-Japan security structure], *Riben Yanjiu* [Japan studies], No. 4 (1996), pp. 18–30, at p. 27. One article bases its optimism largely on the author's belief that, despite economic frictions, the U.S.-Japan alliance is stable. See He Fang, "Lengzhan Hou de Riben Duiwai Zhanlüe" [Japan's post–cold war international strategy], *Waiguo Wenti Yanjiu* [Research on foreign problems], No. 2 (1993), pp. 1–4.
26. For an early discussion of the two very different potential paths to Japanese buildups, see Cai Zuming, ed., *Meiguo Junshi Zhanlüe Yanjiu* [Studies of American military strategy] (Beijing: Academy of Military Sciences Press, 1993), pp. 218–233 (internally circulated).
27. For the logic of reassurance in official U.S. defense policy, see the Pentagon's *United States Security Strategy for the East Asia-Pacific Region 1998*, which states: "In addition to its deterrent function, U.S. military presence in Asia serves to shape the security environment to prevent challenges from developing at all. U.S. force presence mitigates the impact of historical regional tensions and allows the United States to anticipate problems, manage potential threats, and encourage peaceful resolution of disputes."

tees of even rudimentary assistance from Japan if U.S. forces were to become embroiled in a regional armed conflict.[28]

Before 1995 some U.S. elites argued that the alliance was overrated and that it had prevented the United States from pursuing its economic interests in the U.S.-Japan relationship. Some even argued that the United States should use the security relationship as leverage against Japan in an attempt to open Japanese trade and financial markets to American firms.[29] In this view Japan had been able to ride free for too long on the U.S. economy because of Washington's concern over preserving an apparently unfair alliance relationship.

Since the publication of the critically important February 1995 East Asia Strategy Report (also known as the Nye report), U.S. leaders have been expressing very different concerns about the U.S.-Japan relationship. The Nye report, and the broader Nye initiative of which it is a part, placed new emphasis on maintaining and strengthening the security alliance and on keeping economic disputes from poisoning it. The report reaffirms the centrality of U.S. security alliances in Asia, places a floor on U.S. troop strength in East Asia at 100,000, and calls for increased security cooperation between Japan and the United States, including greater Japanese logistics support for U.S. forces operating in the region and consideration of joint research on TMD.[30]

Despite the Clinton administration's decision to insulate the U.S.-Japan security relationship from economic disputes, there has been a widely held concern that, purely on security grounds, the alliance could be dangerously weakened if Japanese roles are not clarified and expanded and if the two militaries are not better integrated in preparation for joint operations.[31] Japan's checkbook diplomacy in the Gulf War was considered insufficient support for U.S.-led efforts to protect a region that supplies Japan, not the United States,

---

28. This common view often ignores the clear benefits to the United States of the Cold War version of the alliance. The United States was guaranteed basing in Japan, and 70–80 percent of those basing costs were covered by the Japanese. Without this basing, the United States would have great difficulty maintaining its presence in the region. For a cost analysis, see Michael O'Hanlon, "Restructuring U.S. Forces and Bases in Japan," in Mike M. Mochizuki, ed., *Toward a True Alliance: Restructuring U.S.-Japan Security Relations* (Washington, D.C.: Brookings, 1997), pp. 149–178.
29. See Eric Heginbotham and Richard J. Samuels, "Mercantile Realism and Japanese Foreign Policy," *International Security*, Vol. 22, No. 4 (Spring 1998), pp. 171–203, at p. 179.
30. The Nye report, named for former Assistant Secretary of Defense Joseph S. Nye, Jr., is *United States Security Strategy for the East Asia-Pacific Region*, Office of International Security Affairs, Department of Defense, February 1995. For an insider's look at concerns about how acrimonious economic disputes were harming the alliance, see David L. Asher, "A U.S.-Japan Alliance for the Next Century," *Orbis*, Vol. 41, No. 3 (Summer 1997), pp. 343–375, at pp. 346–348.
31. For discussion of these issues, see Mike M. Mochizuki, "A New Bargain for a New Alliance" and "American and Japanese Strategic Debates," in Mochizuki, *Toward a True Alliance*, pp. 5–40, 43–82, especially pp. 35, 69–70.

with the bulk of its oil. It also became clear during the 1994 crisis with Pyongyang over North Korea's nuclear weapons development that, under the existing defense guidelines, in a Korean conflict scenario Japan was not even obliged to allow the U.S. military use of its civilian airstrips or ports. In fact, if the crisis had escalated, Japan might not have provided overt, tangible support of any kind. Even U.S. access to its bases in Japan for combat operations not directly tied to the defense of the Japanese home islands was questionable.[32] Aside from the obvious military dangers inherent in such Japanese passivity, Japanese obstructionism and foot-dragging could undermine elite and popular support in the United States for the most important security relationship in East Asia. It appeared to many American elites that the Cold War version of the U.S.-Japan alliance could be one regional crisis away from its demise. Such concerns were a major driver behind the Nye initiative, which was designed to clarify and strengthen Japan's commitment to support U.S.-led military operations. Fearing instability in Japanese elite and popular attitudes on defense issues, Washington also wanted to increase the number of functional links between the two militaries to tie Japan more firmly into the U.S. defense network for the long run.[33]

Chinese security analysts followed these trends in U.S.-Japan relations with great interest and concern. Before 1995 most pessimistic Chinese analysts predicted and feared Japanese military buildups largely because they sensed the potential for trouble, not strengthening, in the post–Cold War U.S.-Japan alliance. Those analysts posited that, given the lack of a common enemy and the natural clash of economic interests between Japan and the United States, political conflict between the two allies was very likely. This conflict could eventually infect and destroy the U.S.-Japan security relationship, which in turn could lead to the withdrawal of U.S. forces and eventually Japanese military buildups. In this period some Chinese analysts also discussed how domestic factors such as U.S. neo-isolationism, rising Japanese nationalism, the inexperience and lack of security focus in the newly elected Clinton adminis-

32. For the importance of the 1994 Korean crisis in officials' calculations, see Kurt M. Campbell, "The Official U.S. View," in Michael J. Green and Mike M. Mochizuki, *The U.S.-Japan Security Alliance in the Twenty-first Century* (New York: Council on Foreign Relations Study Group Papers, 1998), pp. 85–87.
33. For discussion of these issues, see Bruce Stokes and James Shinn, *The Tests of War and the Strains of Peace: The U.S.-Japan Security Relationship* (New York: Council on Foreign Relations Study Group Report, January 1998). For the fear among U.S. officials that the Japanese public was moving away from support for the alliance in the 1990s, see Campbell, "The Official U.S. View."

tration, and domestic instability in Japan could combine with worsening U.S.-Japan trade conflicts to speed the alliance's demise.[34]

By mid-1995 it seemed to an increasingly large group of Chinese analysts that U.S.-Japan trade conflict was being contained and that the Clinton administration was paying more attention to international security affairs and to Asia in particular.[35] Key contributors to this growing confidence in U.S. staying power were the Nye report and the failure of the automobile parts dispute between Tokyo and Washington to escalate.

The news for China was not all good, however. By spring 1996 the Nye initiative had led to harsh reactions in China, exposing the subtle challenges facing the United States in managing the U.S.-China-Japan triangle. China's cautious optimism about trends in the U.S.-Japan alliance turned to pessimism, as concerns about future Japanese military assertiveness grew rapidly. But the new reasons for pessimism were quite different than in the period before 1995. The fear was no longer potential discord in the U.S.-Japan relationship, but concern that the United States would encourage Japan to adopt new military roles and develop new military capabilities as part of a revitalized alliance in which Japan carried a greater share of the burden and risk.[36]

On April 17, 1996, President Clinton and Prime Minister Hashimoto issued a joint communiqué that called for revitalization of the alliance to better guarantee the "Asia-Pacific region." In the communiqué and in the guarantees

---

34. In particular, three military officers whom I interviewed in 1994 stressed these themes. For fears about Democrats and neo-isolationism, see Cai, *Meiguo Junshi Zhanlüe Yanjiu*, p. 223; and Liu Liping, "Jilie Zhendanzhong de Meiguo Duiwai Zhengce Sichao" [The storm over contending positions on U.S. foreign policy], *Xiandai Guoji Guanxi* [Contemporary international relations], No. 6 (1992), pp. 15–18. For a similar argument made before Bill Clinton was elected president of the United States, see Li Shusheng, "Sulian de Jieti yu MeiRi zai Yatai Diqu de Zhengduo" [The disintegration of the Soviet Union and U.S.-Japan rivalry in the Asia Pacific], *Shijie Jingji yu Zhengzhi* [World economy and politics], No. 7 (July 1992), pp. 56–58. For an article about the emphasis on trade and the lack of strategic focus in Washington, see Lu Zhongwei, "Yazhou Anquanzhong de ZhongRi Guanxi" [Sino-Japanese relations in the Asian security environment], *Shijie Jingji yu Zhengzhi* [World economy and politics], No. 3 (March 1993), pp. 23–35, 42.
35. Multiple interviews, 1995. For a published work arguing along these lines, see Yang Yunzhong, "Meiguo Zhengfu Jinyibu Tiaozheng dui Ri Zhengce" [Further adjustments in America's Japan policy], *Shijie Jingji yu Zhengzhi* [World economy and politics], No. 7 (July 1995), pp. 61–65.
36. For elaborations of these arguments, see Thomas J. Christensen, "Chinese Realpolitik," *Foreign Affairs*, Vol. 75, No. 5 (September/October 1996), pp. 37–52; and an excellent article by Banning Garrett and Bonnie Glaser, "Chinese Apprehensions about Revitalization of the U.S.-Japan Alliance," *Asian Survey*, Vol. 37, No. 4 (April 1997), pp. 383–402. From various conversations it is still my strong impression that Beijing would be more fearful of a U.S. pullout if it were to occur. But this is no longer viewed as an imaginable outcome for the foreseeable future in Chinese foreign policy circles, so most analysts seem unwilling to discuss at length their views on such a hypothetical scenario.

reached in the days preceding it, Japan guaranteed base access for U.S. forces and committed itself to increased logistics and rear-area support roles. The two sides also agreed to cooperate in the "ongoing study" of ballistic missile defense.

The joint communiqué was issued one month after the most intense phase of the 1995–96 Taiwan Strait crisis, during which the United States deployed two aircraft carrier battle groups, including one based in Japan, off of Taiwan. The crisis and the joint communiqué triggered fears among Chinese experts about U.S. use of Japanese bases in future Taiwan scenarios. It also suggested that Japan might soon begin scrapping various norms of self-restraint and begin expanding its military operations into the Taiwan area and the South China Sea. In addition to focusing on new logistics roles for Japan and the potential for future joint development of missile defenses, Chinese observers believed that the joint communiqué expanded the geographic scope of the alliance from the area immediately around Japan to a vaguely defined, but clearly much larger, "Asia Pacific."[37] As one leading Chinese expert on Japan recently argued, the U.S. presence in Japan can be seen either as a "bottle cap," keeping the Japanese military genie in the bottle, or as an "egg shell," fostering the growth of Japanese military power under U.S. protection until it one day hatches onto the regional scene. Since 1996, this analyst argues, fears about the "egg shell" function of the U.S.-Japan alliance have increased markedly, while faith in the "bottle cap" function has declined.[38]

In September 1997 Chinese analysts' concerns turned to the announcement of revised defense guidelines for the U.S.-Japan alliance. These guidelines put in writing many of the changes suggested in the joint communiqué. New and clarified Japanese roles in the alliance included those logistics and rear-area support roles mentioned in the joint communiqué and added "operational cooperation" missions for Japan's Self-Defense Forces in time of regional conflict, including intelligence gathering, surveillance, and minesweeping missions. Although Washington and Tokyo quickly abandoned the provocative term "Asia Pacific" following the issuance of the joint communiqué, the 1997

37. Interviews, 1996. See also Liu, "Dangqian Rimei Anbao Tizhi de San Ge Tedian," pp. 20–22; and Yang Bojiang, "Why [a] U.S.-Japan Joint Declaration on [the] Security Alliance," *Contemporary International Relations*, Vol. 6, No. 5 (May 1996), pp. 1–12.
38. Liu Jiangyong, "New Trends in Sino-U.S.-Japan Relations," *Contemporary International Relations*, Vol. 8, No. 7 (July 1998), pp. 1–13.

guidelines are not entirely reassuring on this score either. They state that the scope of the alliance covers "situations in the areas surrounding Japan," but that the definition of those areas would be determined by "situational" rather than "geographic" imperatives. This only confirmed conspiracy theories among Beijing elites regarding the potential inclusion of Taiwan and the South China Sea in the alliance's scope.[39] Following the issuance of the revised guidelines, Jiang Zemin announced that China is on "high alert" about changes in the alliance.[40]

Chinese analysts view aspects of both the joint communiqué and the revised guidelines as troubling in the near term, mainly because they can facilitate U.S. intervention in a Taiwan contingency. They believe that the United States is currently largely in control of the U.S.-Japan alliance's military policy. But they view Japan as having both stronger emotional and practical reasons than the United States for opposing Taiwan's reintegration with the mainland and a greater stake than the United States in issues such as sea-lane protection far from the Japanese home islands.[41] More pessimistic Chinese analysts often state that Japan's material interests have not changed much from the 1930s to the present. They believe that, because Japan is still heavily dependent on foreign trade and investment, it could again choose to develop power-projection capabilities designed to protect its economic interests in the distant abroad. Vigilant about this possibility, Chinese analysts have reacted negatively to even mild new Japanese initiatives away from the home islands (such as

---

39. See "The Guidelines for U.S.-Japan Defense Cooperation," in Green and Mochizuki, *The U.S.-Japan Security Alliance in the Twenty-first Century,* pp. 55–72, at p. 65.
40. Interviews, 1996 and 1998. The Jiang quotation comes from a Reuters news service report on October 18, 1997.
41. Interviews, 1996 and 1998. Taiwan is a former Japanese colony (1895–1945). It is near international sea-lanes that are important to Japan. In addition, Chinese analysts argue that, for straight-forward reasons relating to relative national power, Japan has a strategic interest in preventing Taiwan's high-technology and capital-rich economy from linking politically with the mainland. Moreover, some Chinese analysts view Taiwan as having geostrategic significance for Japan as a potential ally because of its location near the Chinese mainland. Another issue fueling mistrust of Japan is the feeling that Taiwan's president, Lee Teng-hui, who attended college in Japan and who speaks Japanese fluently, may be more pro-Japan than pro-China. For a particularly alarmist argument along these lines, see Li Yaqiang, "What Is Japan Doing Southward?" *Beijing Jianchuan Zhishi* [Naval and merchant ships], No. 6 (June 6, 1997), pp. 7–8, in Foreign Broadcast Information Service Daily Report China, September 4, 1997. For a more sober analysis, see Yang Xuejun and Li Hanmei, "Yingxiang Weilai Riben Dui Wai Zhanlüe he Xingwei de Zhongyao Yinsu" [Important factors influencing future Japanese foreign strategy and conduct], *Zhanlüe yu Guanli* [Strategy and management], No. 1 (1998), pp. 17–22, at p. 21.

sending peacekeepers to Cambodia or minesweepers to the Persian Gulf after the Gulf War).[42]

In 1998 Chinese concerns focused on Japan's September agreement to research theater missile defense jointly with the United States. The initial proposal for joint development of TMD was made by Washington in 1993, long before the Nye initiative had been launched. It was later folded into the initiative, but Japan still seemed reluctant to commit itself to the project.[43] After five years of U.S. coaxing and Japanese foot-dragging, Tokyo finally agreed to joint TMD research after the launch of a North Korean rocket across Japanese territory on August 31, 1998. Although Chinese analysts do recognize the threat to Japan from North Korea, they still believe that development of U.S.-Japan TMD is also designed to counter China's missile capabilities, which the People's Liberation Army (PLA) and civilian analysts recognize as China's most effective military asset, especially in relations with Taiwan.[44]

Taiwan, the U.S.-Japan Alliance, and the Offense-Defense Factor

The importance of the Taiwan issue in Chinese calculations about TMD and the revised guidelines cannot be overstated and, along with the brutal legacy of World War II, is perhaps the most critical exacerbating factor in the China-Japan security dilemma. The nature of the cross-strait conflict is such that the usual argument about the offense-defense balance and the security dilemma applies poorly. That argument, simply stated, is that the buildup of defensive weapons and the adoption of defensive doctrines should not fuel the security dilemma and spirals of tension because such capabilities and methods are not useful for aggression.[45] Defensive weapons are stabilizing because they shore up the territorial status quo by deterring or physically preventing aggressors

---

42. This argument was made particularly forcefully in my interviews with three military officers in 1994. See also Pan, *Riben Junshi Sixiang Yanjiu*, pp. 502–503; and Wu Peng, "Riben Wei he Jianchi Xiang Haiwai Paibing" [Why Japan insisted on sending forces abroad], *Shijie Jingji yu Zhengzhi* [World economy and politics], No. 12 (December 1992), pp. 46–50.
43. For the earliest discussions of joint U.S.-Japan development of TMD and Tokyo's resistance to the plan, see David E. Sanger, "New Missile Defense in Japan under Discussion with U.S.," *New York Times*, September 18, 1993, p. A1. A year and a half later, the language on TMD in the 1995 Nye report belies Japan's reluctance to agree to joint research, stating that the United States "is exploring with Japan cooperative efforts" in TMD.
44. Interviews, 1998. See also Wu Chunsi, "Tactical Missile Defense, Sino-U.S.-Japanese Relationship, and East Asian Security," *Inesap Information Bulletin*, No. 16 (November 1998), pp. 20–23.
45. Jervis, "Cooperation under the Security Dilemma."

from achieving revisionist goals, whereas offensive weapons are destabilizing because they threaten that status quo.[46]

What makes offense-defense theories less applicable in the China case is that Beijing's main security goal is to prevent Taiwan from declaring permanent independence from the Chinese nation, a de facto territorial condition that Taiwan already enjoys. In other words, the main threat to China is a political change in cross-strait relations that would legalize and freeze the territorial status quo. China's main method of countering that threat is a combination of military and economic coercion. In cross-strait relations Beijing considers traditionally defensive weapons in the hands of Taiwan and any of its potential allies to be dangerous, because they may give Taiwan officials additional confidence in their efforts to legitimate the territorial status quo. In fact, given that China seems willing to risk extreme costs to deter Taiwanese independence, and, if necessary, to compel a reversal of any such decision by the Taipei authorities, and that Taiwan has fully abandoned Chiang Kai-shek's irredentist designs on the mainland, Taiwan's ability to attack the mainland, strangely, may be no more worrisome to China than Taiwan's ability to fend off the mainland's attacks on Taiwan.[47]

Given the Chinese concerns over Taiwan, future U.S. and Japanese TMD, if effective, and if transferred in peacetime or put at the service of Taiwan in a crisis, could reduce China's ability to threaten the island with ballistic missile attack, the PLA's main means of coercing Taiwan. Particularly relevant here are the ship-based systems that Japan and the United States agreed to research jointly in September 1998. China worries for the same reason that most Americans support the choice of a ship-based TMD system.[48] As one U.S. commentator applauds, ship-based systems "can be moved quickly to other regions to support out-of-area conflicts."[49] The "upper-tier" navy theater-wide system,

---

46. Although scholars differ on specific definitions of what constitutes a destabilizing offense and a stabilizing defense, all definitions in the current literature focus on states' capacity for fighting across borders and seizing enemy-held territory as the measure of the offense-defense balance. See, for example, Van Evera, "Offense, Defense, and the Causes of War"; and Charles L. Glaser and Chaim Kaufmann, "What Is the Offense-Defense Balance and Can We Measure It?" *International Security*, Vol. 22, No. 4 (Spring 1998), pp. 44–82.
47. For the various reasons why I believe China would risk war, perhaps even with the United States, to prevent Taiwan's independence, see Christensen, "Chinese Realpolitik."
48. See "U.S., Japan Agree to Study Missile Defense," *Washington Times*, September 21, 1998, p. 1; and "Japan Makes Missile-Defense Plan High Priority," *Washington Times*, November 6, 1998, p. 12.
49. Richard Fisher, quoted in Rob Holzer and Barbara Opall-Rome, "U.S. Anticipates Approval from Tokyo on Joint TMD," *Defense News*, September 21–27, 1998, p. 34. See also Peter Landers, Susan Lawrence, and Julian Baum, "Hard Target," *Far Eastern Economic Review*, September 24, 1998,

which the United States has proposed for the future, would not only be highly mobile, but because it was originally conceived to provide wide area defense for geographically large U.S. military deployments, it would, if effective, have a "footprint" that could cover the island of Taiwan. Chinese arms control and missile experts note this possibility with some concern.[50] Like their U.S. and Japanese counterparts, Chinese analysts have serious doubts about the likely effectiveness of such a system, particularly given the proximity of Taiwan to the mainland and the ability of China to launch a large number and variety of missiles. Nevertheless, they still worry about the psychological and political impact the system could have on Taipei's attitudes about seeking more diplomatic space and on U.S. and Japanese attitudes about cross-strait relations.[51]

When complaining about how specific aspects of recent changes in the U.S.-Japan alliance might influence cross-strait relations, Chinese analysts tend to focus on the potential problems of a future U.S.-Japan TMD system rather than on the less dramatic operational support roles specified for existing Japanese Self-Defense Forces in the revised guidelines (i.e., intelligence gathering, surveillance, and minesweeping). Chinese analysts' concerns about the joint communiqué and the revised guidelines tend to be more abstract, focusing on the fuzzy "situational" scope of the alliance or the possible erosion of Japanese norms of self-restraint in military affairs. However, although it appears unlikely that they would be deployed near Taiwan in a crisis, the systems of the Japanese Self-Defense Forces mentioned in the revised guidelines also could prove helpful to Taiwan. In particular, if Japan ever decided to deploy minesweepers there, this would have the potential to reduce the PLA's ability to coerce Taiwan in a cross-strait crisis or conflict by playing the purely defensive role of helping to break a real or threatened PLA blockade on shipping. For these reasons, the apparently mild operational support roles Japan agreed to in the revised guidelines may also contribute to Beijing's hostile reaction to recent trends in the U.S.-Japan alliance.[52]

---

pp. 20–21. For a discussion of China's more general concerns about TMD, see Benjamin Valentino, "Small Nuclear Powers and Opponents of Ballistic Missile Defenses in the Post–Cold War Era," *Security Studies*, Vol. 7, No. 2 (Winter 1997/98), pp. 229–232.

50. Statements by Chinese arms control and missile experts in the United States in August 1998, and discussions with one active and one retired military officer in China in November 1998.

51. Interviews with civilian analysts, November 1998.

52. Demonstrating that they are much less sensitive than TMD or other aspects of the Nye initiative, minesweepers would usually only be discussed by my interlocutors after I raised the issue.

U.S.-JAPAN ALLIANCE TRENDS AND POTENTIAL CRISIS-MANAGEMENT PROBLEMS
If the United States and Japan eventually decide to move from joint research and development to deployment of ship-based U.S. and Japanese TMD systems (at least several years from now), Japan would have the capability to involve itself in a cross-strait crisis in a meaningful way, even if it did not have any intention to do so when acquiring the system. Under such circumstances, in a future Taiwan Strait crisis involving the United States (short of a shooting war), U.S. leaders would be tempted to ask for Japanese assistance in missile defense near Taiwan in preparation for potential PLA attacks. The United States then might place Japan in the difficult position of choosing whether to help the United States in a Taiwan crisis. Such a decision by U.S. leaders would be most likely to occur if they believed that defensive Japanese roles would not be overly provocative to China.

There may be no positive outcome from such a request. If Japan chose not to help the United States in such a purely defensive role, especially if that refusal placed U.S. forces at added risk, this would have severely negative implications for the U.S.-Japan alliance. But, if Japan chose to help, the results could be worse still. Given the anti-Japanese sentiments in Chinese elite circles and popular culture, Japan's direct involvement in any form in a cross-strait crisis short of a shooting war could have a particularly detrimental impact on crisis management. Although U.S. intervention in such a crisis would be quite provocative to China in and of itself, it is safe to assume that Japanese intervention would be even more likely to lead to escalation.[53] Even if the crisis did not escalate, any hope of building a stable, long-term China-Japan security relationship could be lost. The ability of the United States and China to recover from such a standoff would likely be greater than the ability of China and Japan to do so.[54]

Although missiles are the PLA's likely weapons of choice in a cross-strait conflict or coercion campaign, it is at least imaginable that Beijing could choose less aggressive tactics than missile attacks (such as real or threatened mining

---

53. I base my conclusions about the particularly provocative nature of Japanese intervention more on a general understanding of Chinese attitudes toward Japan than on extensive interview data. In the relatively few interviews in 1998 in which I raised this issue, responses were mixed, and included the following arguments: Japanese intervention would be particularly provocative and likely to lead to crisis escalation; Japanese intervention would be only somewhat more provocative than U.S. intervention alone; and U.S. intervention alone would be sufficient to spark escalation, with or without the Japanese.
54. Of course, in a shooting war across the Taiwan Strait, calculations may be quite different because presumably such an event would severely harm Sino-Japanese relations in any case.

of ports or shipping lanes in and around Taiwan) to deter or reverse Taiwan's diplomatic adventurism.[55] A lower-level coercive strategy may be more attractive in certain instances, particularly if Taiwan's alleged violation of Beijing's prohibitions were much less clear-cut than an outright declaration of independence.[56]

The new plans for operational cooperation in the revised guidelines were almost certainly created with Korean scenarios, not Taiwan, in mind. And for several reasons, they seem much less likely to play into a Taiwan Strait crisis scenario than would a future Japanese ship-based TMD capability. But, for theoretical purposes, it is worth considering how such Japanese missions could affect a future Taiwan crisis to demonstrate how misapplied logic about offensive and defensive weapons could lead to avoidable escalation in the Taiwan Strait context.

From Taiwan's perspective, the mere threat of mine-laying would require extensive sweeping to reassure both shipping interests and military commanders.[57] In such circumstances, if for military or political reasons the United States decided that Taiwan's own minesweeping equipment should be supplemented with ships from the U.S.-Japan alliance, future U.S. decisionmakers might be tempted for either military or political reasons to ask Japan to send minesweepers to assist in such an operation. On the military side, current U.S. minesweeping capabilities, particularly those in the theater, are weak, which might make Japanese assistance look attractive (the Seventh Fleet usually has only two minesweepers at the ready in the Pacific).[58] On the political side, if

---

55. For an interesting discussion of a scenario involving a PLA blockade of Taiwan, see Paul H.B. Godwin, "The Use of Military Force against Taiwan: Potential PRC Scenarios," in Parris H. Chang and Martin L. Lasater, eds., *If China Crosses the Taiwan Straits: The International Response* (New York: University Press of America, 1993), pp. 15–34. In 1998 a Chinese military officer said that missiles are a much more likely PLA strategy than mine-laying, but the blockade possibility cannot be ruled out entirely.

56. In fact, for our purposes we can assume such a low-level Taiwanese provocation because, under current U.S. policy (President Clinton's "three no's"), a greater provocation would likely preclude a U.S. response. The "three no's" pronounced by President Clinton in Shanghai, are no [U.S.] support for Taiwan independence; no support for two China's, or one China, one Taiwan; and no support for Taiwanese entrance into international organizations for which statehood is a prerequisite.

57. According to one study, about 90 percent of minesweeping operations have been in areas with no discernible mines. See Captain Buzz Broughton and Commander Jay Burton, "The (R)evolution of Mine Countermeasures," *Proceedings of the Naval Institute*, May 1998, pp. 55–58.

58. The United States' general weakness in minesweeping is widely recognized. Although the United States recently has developed new minesweeping and mine-hunting equipment, much of it is based in the United States and would require a significant amount of time to be sent to the theater. A new naval plan, "the fleet engagement strategy," backed by Secretary of Defense

the potentially provocative nature of defensive missions, especially Japanese ones, is not fully appreciated, then U.S. leaders might request Japanese support as a high-profile demonstration of burden sharing. As in the TMD scenario, Japan would then be put into the difficult position of either sending Japanese ships to the front lines of a Taiwan crisis, thus greatly increasing the risk of escalation (less likely), or risking severe damage to the U.S.-Japan alliance by refusing to play an even purely defensive role (more likely).[59]

Chinese Attitudes and the Prospects for Regional Confidence Building

An important prerequisite for resolving a security dilemma is for the actors involved to recognize that one exists. A core factor that underpins the security dilemma is the general lack of empathy among the actors participating in a security competition. Beijing elites may be no better or worse than their counterparts in most other nations on this score. Although they may not use the technical term "security dilemma," Chinese analysts recognize the potential for arms racing and spirals of tension in the region. They even recognize that Japan might build its military out of fear, rather than aggression. China actually supported Japanese buildups in the 1970s and early 1980s in response to the development of the Soviet navy.[60] In 1994 several analysts argued that China did not want North Korea to have nuclear weapons because this might cause Japan to develop them.[61]

Beijing also has demonstrated an ability to understand that others might see China as a threat.[62] But, while many Chinese analysts can imagine some states

---

William S. Cohen, calls for increased "organic" mine-hunting and minesweeping capabilities within battle groups that would involve airborne (helicopters), surface, and submarine-based capabilities. It is unclear how effective these initiatives have been in providing U.S. forces in East Asia with readily available capability in a crisis. See ibid.; "Cohen Expected to Respond This Week to Navy Brief on Mine Warfare," *Inside the Navy*, August 17, 1998, p. 3; and "Cohen Directs Navy to Add $53 Million to Develop Minehunting System," *Inside the Navy*, August 31, 1998, p. 1.

59. Although it demonstrates the potential problems of even Japanese defensive cooperation in the U.S.-Japan alliance, fortunately there are a lot of rather large "ifs" in the above blockade scenario. Even if most of these came to pass, one would hope that U.S. leaders would be wise enough to recognize the above dangers and would not put Japan into such a difficult dilemma.

60. For example, an internally circulated analysis of those Japanese buildups does not suggest opportunism or aggressive intent. See Pan, *Riben Junshi Sixiang Yanjiu*, chap. 14, and pp. 414–415.

61. Interviews, 1994.

62. For example, Beijing at times has tried to reassure Southeast Asian nations about its desire to settle the Spratly Islands disputes peacefully. Even if these are merely cynical tactics designed to buy time for China to concentrate on the Taiwan problem or develop force projection to handle the Spratlys dispute later, they demonstrate Beijing's ability to conceive of Southeast Asian fears about China.

as legitimately worried about China and can picture Japan legitimately worried about other states, it is harder to find those who believe that Japan's military security policy could be driven by fears about specific security policies in China.[63] Chinese analysts, especially in the past two years, seem to agree that China's overall rise (*jueqi*) is a general source of concern for Japan. They tend not to recognize, however, that particular Chinese actions or weapons developments might be reason for Japan to reconsider aspects of its defense policy. For example, when asked about concerns expressed by Japanese officials about Chinese weapons developments (such as the increased numbers and improved accuracy of Chinese missiles) or provocative Chinese international behavior (such as missile firings near Taiwan or bullying of the Philippines over the Mischief Reef), Chinese analysts generally dismiss these expressions as "excuses" (*jiekou*) designed to facilitate Japanese hawks' predetermined plans for military buildups. As the work of Western experts on Japanese security policy demonstrates, these Chinese analysts are very wrong to hold this belief.[64] If such views continue to prevail in Beijing, China is unlikely to take actions to reassure Japan in either bilateral or multilateral agreements.

A different and even more troubling Chinese perspective on China's potential influence on Japanese defense policy has also gained frequency in the past two years. Perhaps because of the relatively high economic growth rates in China compared to Japan in the 1990s, some Chinese experts have expressed more confidence that China would be able to defend its security interests against Japan, even in the absence of a U.S. presence in the region. Although they hardly dismiss the potential threat of a Japan made more assertive by a U.S. withdrawal, they seem relatively confident that China's strength and deterrent capabilities could influence Japan's strategy by dissuading Tokyo from significant Japanese buildups or, at least, later military adventurism.[65] From the security dilemma perspective this attitude may be even more dangerous than the view that China can pose little threat to Japan. If increasing Chinese coercive capacity is seen as the best way to prevent or manage

---

63. For example, one book takes seriously Japan's fear of the Soviets during the Cold War, but places Japan's concern about China under the heading "Japan's Imagined Enemies," see Pan, *Riben Junshi Sixiang Yanjiu*, pp. 413–416. For another example, see Zhan Shiliang, "Yatai Diqu Xingshi he Zhongguo Mulin Youhao Zhengce" [The Asia-Pacific situation and China's good neighbor policy], *Guoji Wenti Yanjiu* [International studies], No. 4 (1993), pp. 1–3, 7.
64. See Michael J. Green and Benjamin L. Self, "Japan's Changing China Policy: From Commercial Liberalism to Reluctant Realism," *Survival*, Vol. 38, No. 2 (Summer 1996), pp. 34–58.
65. The increased frequency of such statements over time may be one effect of China's relatively high rates of economic growth in the 1990s in comparison to Japan.

anticipated Japanese buildups, then the danger of China taking the critical first step in an action-reaction cycle seems very high.

There are some more hopeful signs, however. Some Chinese analysts, usually younger experts (appearing to be in their forties or younger) with extensive experience abroad, do recognize that Chinese military strengthening and provocative actions could be seen as legitimate reasons for Japan to launch a military buildup of its own. Given the age of these analysts and the increasing number of Chinese elites with considerable experience abroad, the trends seem to be heading in a positive direction on this score. On a sober note, more than one of these empathetic experts has pointed out that Chinese experts who take Japanese concerns about China seriously are often viewed with suspicion in government circles and sometimes have difficulty when presenting their views to their older and more influential colleagues, particularly in the military.[66]

CHINA'S VIEWS ON MULTILATERAL SECURITY REGIMES

One possible way to ameliorate the security dilemma is through multilateral regimes and forums designed to increase transparency and build confidence. For various reasons, Beijing has viewed multilateral confidence building with some suspicion. Many Chinese analysts emphasize that the increased transparency called for by such institutions can make China's enemies more confident and thereby reduce China's deterrent capabilities, particularly its ability to deter Taiwan independence or foreign intervention in cross-strait relations.[67] Especially in the early 1990s they worried that multilateral forums and organizations might be fronts for great powers, and that confidence-building measures might be aspects of a containment strategy designed to keep China from achieving great power status in the military sector.[68]

---

66. In separate interviews in 1994 a military officer and a civilian analyst lamented that the vast majority of Chinese are incapable of thinking in ways empathetic to Japanese concerns about China. In 1996 a civilian analyst complained that too many Chinese leaders and security analysts are unable to separate their analyses of 1930s' Japan and 1990s' Japan.
67. Multiple interviews, 1993–98. In fact, one military officer was even quite critical of China's last round of military exercises in March 1996 because he was afraid that China revealed too much about its military to a vigilant and highly capable U.S. defense intelligence network.
68. China has worked in the past to block the creation of formal multilateral reassurance regimes in East Asia, such as the Organization for Security and Cooperation in Europe, that might lead to condemnation of China's development and/or deployment of its force-projection capabilities. As Jianwei Wang argues, China has been more open to multilateralism in the economic realm than it has been in the security realm. Jianwei Wang, "Chinese Views of Multilateralism," in Yong Deng and Feiling Wang, *In the Eyes of the Dragon: China Views the World and Sino-American Relations* (Boulder, Colo.: Rowman and Littlefield, forthcoming).

That said, China has not shunned multilateral forums. China has partici-
pated in the ASEAN Regional Forum (ARF) since its first meeting in 1994, and
in 1997 Beijing hosted an ARF intersessional conference on confidence-building
measures. Although Beijing has prevented any dramatic accomplishments at
ARF meetings on important questions such as the territorial disputes in the
South China Sea, the precedent of such Chinese participation seems potentially
important.[69] As Iain Johnston and Paul Evans argue, although still in their
nascent phases, these developments should not be dismissed as mere rhetoric
or showmanship. China is capable of participating in meaningful multilateral
accords, as is demonstrated by its recent agreements on border demarcation
and confidence-building measures struck with Russia and the former Soviet
republics in Turkish Central Asia. Moreover, there is a small but growing
community of true believers in Beijing in the benefits of arms control,
confidence-building measures, and multilateralism more generally.[70]

The reduced fear of U.S. domination of the Association of Southeast Asian
Nations (ASEAN) and of ASEAN collusion against China, combined with the
increased fear of developments in U.S. bilateral diplomacy in the Asia Pacific
since 1996, have convinced many formerly skeptical analysts that some form
of multilateralism may be the best alternative for China given the risks posed
by U.S. bilateral business as usual.[71] Given that China both fears and has little
influence over various aspects of current U.S. bilateral diplomacy (such as
strengthening the U.S.-Japan alliance or the U.S.-Australia alliance), accepting
a bigger role for multilateral dialogue, if not the creation of formal multilateral
security institutions, may be the least unpleasant method of reducing the threat

69. For example, at the July 1994 ARF conference and in earlier multilateral meetings with
Southeast Asian representatives, China blocked any meaningful discussion of territorial disputes
involving Chinese claims. See Allen S. Whiting, "ASEAN Eyes China," *Asian Survey*, Vol. 37, No.
4 (April 1997), pp. 299–322.
70. See Alastair Iain Johnston and Paul Evans, "China's Engagement of Multilateral Institutions,"
in Johnston and Robert S. Ross, eds., *Engaging China: The Management of an Emerging Power*
(London: Routledge, forthcoming); Johnston, "Learning versus Adaptation: Explaining Change in
Chinese Arms Control Policy in the 1980s and 1990s," *China Journal* 35 (January 1996), pp. 27–61;
Johnston, "Socialization in International Institutions: The ASEAN Regional Forum and IR Theory,"
paper prepared for the conference on "The Emerging International Relations of the Asia Pacific
Region," University of Pennsylvania, May 8–9, 1998. See also Rosemary Foot, "China in the ASEAN
Regional Forum: Organizational Processes and Domestic Modes of Thought," *Asian Survey*, Vol.
38, No. 5 (May 1998), pp. 425–440.
71. Interviews, 1996 and 1998. See also Wang, "Chinese Views on Multilateralism," in Deng and
Wang, *In the Eyes of the Dragon*; and Wu Xinbo, "Integration on the Basis of Strength: China's Impact
on East Asian Security," Asia/Pacific Research Center working paper, February 1998.

that U.S. bilateralism poses.[72] So, in this one sense, the revitalization of the U.S.-Japan alliance may have had some unintended positive results by encouraging China to consider more seriously the benefits of multilateral forums that might reduce mutual mistrust in the region.[73] This phenomenon runs counter to psychological and social constructivist theories on the security dilemma that emphasize how accommodation, not pressure, is the best way to make states adopt more cooperative postures.[74]

The acceptance of formal multilateral dialogue has not spread from Southeast Asia to Northeast Asia because of mistrust between China and Japan, and between the two Koreas. But there are some fledgling signs of hope. In January 1998 Beijing agreed to trilateral track-II security talks with the United States and Japan. However, Chinese analysts have argued that the time is not yet right for a formal trilateral security forum given the tensions over the revised U.S.-Japan defense guidelines and the TMD issue, the lack of basic trust between China and Japan, and the fear that China would be isolated in a two-against-one format in which it engaged the U.S.-Japan alliance as a corporate entity.[75] One should not rule out the possibility of official trilateral talks over the longer term, however. If Beijing is sufficiently concerned about U.S. transfer or codevelopment of TMD with regional actors, it might agree to

---

72. Interviews, 1996 and 1998. For an excellent analysis of ASEAN concerns and hopes about China, see Whiting, "ASEAN Eyes China." For Chinese reactions to changes in the U.S.-Japan alliance along these lines, see Zhou Jihua, "RiMei Anbao Tizhi de Qianghua yu Dongya de Anquan" [The strengthening of the U.S.-Japan security structure and the security of East Asia], *Riben Xuekan* [Japan studies], No. 4 (1996), pp. 41–42; and Zhou, "Military Accords Create Suspicions," *China Daily*, October 7, 1996.
73. Interviews, 1996 and 1998. I was impressed that multilateral options, previously often discounted by my interlocutors, were now raised as legitimate alternatives to U.S. bilateralism without my prompting.
74. In the psychological literature on the security dilemma, one is not supposed to try to solve security dilemmas by applying pressure but by reassuring distrustful states. See Jervis, *Perception and Misperception*, chap. 3. In Alexander Wendt's constructivist approach, not only do tough policies merely reproduce realist fear and cynicism, but gentle persuasion and appeasement are prescribed even for truly predatory regimes, such as Hitler's Germany or Stalin's Russia. See Wendt, "Anarchy Is What States Make of It," *International Organization*, Vol. 46, No. 2 (Spring 1992), pp. 391–425, at 409. In fact, recent work on Chinese foreign policy since Tiananmen suggests that the fear of material sanctions and social stigmatization helps explain a broad range of cooperative Chinese foreign policies from a general, more constructive regional strategy to accession to important international arms control institutions, such as the Nuclear Nonproliferation Treaty and the Comprehensive Test Ban Treaty. See Yu Bin, "China's Regional Views and Policies—Implications for the United States," and Hu Weixing, "China and Nuclear Nonproliferation," both in Deng and Wang, *In the Eyes of the Dragon*. See also Johnston and Evans, "China's Engagement in Multilateral Institutions."
75. These themes were still emphasized by my interlocutors in November 1998.

official trilateral dialogue with the United States and Japan to try to head off such an outcome.

U.S. Policy Options in the U.S.-China-Japan Security Triangle

Given the central role that the status of the U.S.-Japan alliance plays in both pessimistic and optimistic Chinese scenarios for Japan's future, there is little doubt that maintaining the U.S. presence in Japan is critical to countering the security dilemma in East Asia. If a Japanese commitment to a more active role in the alliance is essential to the survival of the alliance over the long haul, then some adjustments are necessary, regardless of Chinese reaction. In fact, given how pessimistic Chinese analysts would likely be if the alliance were to dissolve fully, they should understand that the Nye initiative is much better for China than U.S. policies before 1995 that encouraged drift in the alliance and lack of confidence in the U.S. security commitment in East Asia.

Certain new Japanese responsibilities in the alliance seem to have high payoffs in terms of U.S.-Japan alliance stability with few costs in terms of sharpening the China-Japan security dilemma. Increased Japanese logistics roles and guaranteed base access in time of conflict, both relatively nonprovocative measures for Japan's neighbors, should remedy some of the disasters U.S. officials predicted when they evaluated the alliance during the 1994 North Korean nuclear crisis. Japan's general commitment to participate in certain military support functions, such as minesweeping and surveillance, also seems like a good idea, as long as the United States does not become overly reliant on Japanese assistance in this area. For political reasons, it would seem wise for the United States to establish and maintain sufficient capabilities of its own so that it could pick and choose when to request Japanese assistance. In a cross-strait crisis, the United States would likely want to minimize Japanese participation and forgo it entirely at the front. In addition to the reasons offered above, if China's actions inadvertently brought about Japanese intervention, given Japan's reputation throughout the region, Tokyo's involvement could be exploited domestically and internationally by Beijing elites in ways that Saddam Hussein might have capitalized on an Israeli intervention during the 1990–91 Gulf crisis and Gulf War. Washington was able to forgo Israeli assistance because the United States and its allies could secure military dominance without Israeli help.

One unwise way for Japan and the United States to try to reassure China would be to exclude Taiwan explicitly from the scope of the U.S.-Japan alliance. China has pressed Japan and the United States to do this. Both have refused because neither wants to encourage irredentism by the People's Republic against Taiwan by excluding in advance the possibility that they would come to Taiwan's defense if the mainland attacked Taiwan without provocation. This is almost certainly a major reason why the scope of the alliance in the revised defense guidelines refers to "situational" rather than "geographic" conditions. Despite considerable Chinese pressure, Japan has not even agreed to parrot President Clinton's "three no's" policy, declaring only that Tokyo does not support Taiwan's legal independence. But, even if Tokyo did state the other two "no's," this would not be the same as excluding Taiwan from the scope of the U.S.-Japan alliance, which would be a radical, and I believe, potentially destabilizing policy position.[76]

A better way to reassure China without totally abandoning Taiwan or the notion of missile defenses in Japan would be for the United States to consider developing TMD without Japanese assistance. In 1998 Chinese analysts consistently pointed out that U.S.-Japan coproduction of TMD carries a fundamentally different and more provocative political meaning for China than if the United States produced such systems without Japanese help as part of its global strategy to protect U.S. troops deployed abroad. Despite the North Korean threat to Japan, U.S.-Japan codevelopment of TMD in Asia still seems primarily designed to counter China. Codevelopment with Japan also triggers many fears in Beijing about the fostering of future Japanese power that U.S. development of TMD without Japanese assistance would not.[77] For example, following the North Korean missile launch across Japan, which solidified Tokyo's decision to pursue TMD research, Tokyo announced plans to develop an independent spy satellite capability to observe foreign missile activity. If implemented this plan will weaken the effectiveness of, and may even contravene, Diet resolutions prohibiting the use of space for military purposes, an important restraint on future Japanese military power. Like TMD development, the satellite decision suggests the possibility of a more independent and unfettered Japanese military establishment for the future.[78] Chinese analysts

76. On the importance of Taiwan in the calculations regarding the scope of the U.S.-Japan alliance in the 1997 defense guidelines, see Michael Green, "The U.S. View," in Green and Mochizuki, *The U.S.-Japan Security Alliance*, p. 75. For more elaboration on my preferred position on U.S. strategy across the strait, see Christensen, "Chinese Realpolitik." For elaboration on the three no's, see footnote 56 above.
77. Multiple interviews, November 1998. Of course, Chinese analysts are concerned about U.S. development of TMD as well.
78. Many Chinese experts believe that the United States' encouragement of Japanese military development and foreign policy assertiveness will unwittingly fuel Japanese confidence and nationalism (a process that has already begun according to Chinese analysts), and that eventually U.S.-Japan security relations could still deteriorate. See, for example, Liu, "Dangqian Rimei Anbao

also point out that mobile Japanese TMD could provide a "shield" for the "sword" of more offensive Japanese forces and, if extremely effective, it may also be able to protect the Japanese home islands from Chinese missile retaliation, thus reducing Chinese defensive and deterrent capabilities and blurring the political distinction between offensive and defensive weapons.[79] Finally, agreeing with the literature on the technical indistinguishability of offensive and defensive systems, some Chinese analysts argue that some of the technology involved in TMD can itself be adapted by Japan for offensive purposes.[80]

American TMD development is part of a global strategy designed to protect U.S. forces and U.S. bases, which are threatened by the increasing quantity and accuracy of missiles in the hands of potential adversaries around the world.[81] As such, American TMD should not be bargained away in negotiations with any particular state or group of states. Decisions on American TMD should be based solely on difficult questions related to the potential effectiveness of the system against enemy missiles, the relative cost to potential adversaries of

Tizhi de San Ge Tedian," p. 30. In 1998 several Chinese analysts argued that Tokyo agreed to codevelopment of TMD in part to prepare a more independent Japanese defense capability for the future. I am grateful to David Asher, Bonnie Glaser, and Iain Johnston for helpful discussion on Japanese plans for satellites. For a Chinese statement linking the Japanese plans for satellites with the plans for U.S.-Japan joint development of TMD, see "China Concerned about Japanese Satellite Plan," Beijing (Associated Press), December 30, 1998. On the connection to the North Korean missile launch, see "Support Growing for Spy Satellite System," *Mainichi Shimbun*, September 8, 1998, Politics and Business Section, p. 2.

79. Another possible way to reduce some Chinese concerns about joint U.S.-Japan development of TMD would be to pursue a land-based theater high-altitude air defense (THAAD) system instead of a ship-based navy theater-wide system. If effective, a THAAD system could provide the Japanese home islands with missile defense, but because THAAD is immobile it could not travel to the Taiwan area or other regions, and therefore would be less likely to exacerbate Chinese concerns about real or perceived Japanese support for Taiwan independence. China still would be concerned about its deterrent capabilities against Japan and about general advancement in Japanese military technologies and assertiveness, but at least the fears about Taiwan would be somewhat reduced. But possibly because of high-profile test failures of THAAD in the United States, the United States and Japan have chosen to pursue the more provocative ship-based systems.

80. The Japanese sword and shield argument was made in China by a retired Chinese military officer and a civilian analyst in November 1998. The offense-defense indistinguishability issue and the ability to protect Japan from Chinese retaliation was raised by Chinese arms control and missile experts in the United States in August 1998. In 1998 an active military officer argued that U.S. transfer of TMD technology to Japan would likely violate the missile technology control regime. For critiques of offense-defense theory on the issue of distinguishability and responses to them, see Jack S. Levy, "The Offense-Defense Balance of Military Technology: A Theoretical and Historical Analysis," *International Studies Quarterly*, Vol. 38, No. 2 (June 1984), pp. 219–238; John J. Mearsheimer, *Conventional Deterrence* (Ithaca, N.Y.: Cornell University Press, 1983), pp. 25–26; Lynn-Jones, "Offense-Defense Theory and Its Critics"; Van Evera, "Offense, Defense, and the Causes of War"; and Glaser and Kaufmann, "What Is the Offense-Defense Balance?"

81. See Paul Bracken, "America's Maginot Line," *Atlantic Monthly*, December 1998, pp. 85–93.

developing methods that can defeat the system, and the opportunity costs of developing TMD systems in the defense budget.

But decisions about whether the United States should develop and eventually deploy the system alone or with other countries (and with whom) should be left open for consideration and perhaps for negotiation. This should hold true especially in areas like Northeast Asia, where geography and technology might allow potential adversaries to develop cheap and potentially provocative countermeasures against such systems. If the United States and Japan were willing to reconsider joint development of TMD, they might be able to exploit Chinese concerns to encourage Beijing to participate in a formal trilateral security dialogue and to begin to consider a bit more transparency in its murky military sector. Moreover, Japan and the United States may be able to gain more active participation from Beijing in discouraging further North Korean development of missiles and weapons of mass destruction. Given that Tokyo seemed at best only vaguely committed to joint development of TMD until the August 1998 North Korean rocket launch, such a security payoff, if deliverable by Beijing, might be sufficient to convince Japan to rely on U.S. advancements in TMD technology and to wait for eventual deployment of the systems to U.S. bases in Japan.[82] Such an outcome, arguably, would also have a positive effect on U.S.-Japan alliance longevity, because Japan would have added incentive to allow the U.S. navy to remain in Japanese ports for the long run.

In addition to lowering China's more general concerns about Japan, the United States could benefit in other ways from developing TMD without Japanese collaboration and from developing more organic capabilities for the Seventh Fleet. The United States would be better able to avoid scenarios in which it might be tempted to request Japanese support in these areas in time of crisis or war. Japanese agreement to supply such support in many instances cannot be assumed. Moreover, by maintaining a minimum dependence on Japanese capabilities, the United States would be better able to pick and choose when Japan's participation in a conflict would do more political harm than military good.

Of course, my prescriptions about TMD and other U.S. naval capabilities carry costs. If the United States develops TMD without Japan, for example, it will have to forgo Japanese technology and Japanese money. I am not in a position to analyze the importance of the former, but on the latter score,

---

82. For Japanese reticence on TMD, see Asher, "A U.S.-Japan Alliance for the Next Century," pp. 364–366.

speculation about Japan's expected contribution places it somewhere between several hundred million and several billion dollars over the next several years. This hardly seems irreplaceable.[83] Mine-clearing equipment is not among the navy's most expensive items. For hundreds of millions of dollars, the United States could greatly enhance its organic capabilities in the Seventh Fleet. The United States, enjoying a long period of uninterrupted economic growth, federal budget surpluses for the first time in decades, and the lowest percentage of GNP going to the military since Pearl Harbor (less than 3 percent), should be able to afford to pick up this added bill. The main problem is the leadership challenge involved in selling policies based on abstract threats, such as future regional spirals of tension in East Asia, to the American public and Congress.[84]

Even if sustainable only for the next ten to fifteen years, the U.S. strategy of carefully calibrating increased Japanese activities in the alliance should have high payoffs. If the United States can avoid an escalation of Sino-Japanese security tensions in this time frame, several objectives could be achieved. First, the very nascent efforts to create regional confidence-building measures and regimes that encourage transparency will have time to bear fruit, as will Tokyo's and Beijing's recent efforts to improve bilateral ties and high-level contacts.[85] Second, more cosmopolitan government officials and advisers should rise through the ranks in China as a generation of Chinese experts with extensive experience abroad comes of age. Third, China more generally will have time to undergo the next political transition as the "fourth generation" leadership replaces Jiang Zemin's generation, perhaps carrying with it significant political reform. Given the strong popular sentiments in China about Japan and Taiwan and the dangers of hypernationalism in the democratization process, it would be best for the region and the world if China transited political reform without the distractions and jingoism that would likely flow

---

83. There are no official published estimates of Japanese contributions to TMD. For some speculation, see Holzer and Opall-Rome, "U.S. Anticipates Approval from Tokyo on Joint TMD." The article states that Japan might pay up to 20 percent of the cost for developing a TMD system covering Japan. According to Landers, Lawrence, and Baum, in "Hard Target," such a system could cost about $17 billion over the next several years. I am grateful to Cindy Williams and Eric Labs for their help in analyzing the costs of additional mine-clearing equipment.
84. For a discussion of problems in marketing strategies, see Thomas J. Christensen, *Useful Adversaries: Grand Strategy, Domestic Mobilization, and Sino-American Conflict, 1947–1958* (Princeton, N.J.: Princeton University Press, 1996), chap. 2.
85. China and Japan exchanged visits by their defense ministers in 1998. In late 1997 there was a meeting between Premier Li Peng and Prime Minister Hashimoto, and in November 1998 there was a summit between President Zemin and Prime Minister Obuchi.

from a Sino-Japanese security competition.[86] Fourth, the process of Korean unification would be significantly simplified if it were not accompanied by a Sino-Japanese military rivalry. Fifth, the region, including both Japan and China, will have time to recover from the current economic crisis without simultaneously worrying about intensifying security competition. As the inter-war period showed, a combination of domestic instability and international tensions can lead to extremely unfortunate political changes within countries and in the relations among them. Moreover, if security relations are less tense, the financial crisis might provide an excellent opportunity to increase overall regional cooperation. Sixth, Tokyo will have more time to reconsider and rectify its treatment of the legacies of World War II.[87] Seventh, it would be best for long-term regional stability if Japan's own strands of hypernationalism were kept in check during Japan's post–Cold War political transition following the demise of the Liberal Democratic Party's monopoly on power.

We can be fairly certain that new Japanese military roles will exacerbate the atmosphere of distrust between Japan and China. It is more difficult, however, to speculate about what exactly China might do differently if Japan adopts certain new roles. For example, if Japan appears headed toward eventual deployment of ship-based theater missile defenses, China might try to develop ballistic, cruise, and antiship missiles, and perhaps antisatellite weapons faster and more extensively than it otherwise would to acquire the ability to destroy, saturate, or elude the capability of these defensive weapons.[88] Moreover, one could speculate that, if China felt it necessary to diversify and improve its nuclear deterrent in the face of proposed U.S.-Japan TMD, Beijing might abandon its commitment to the Comprehensive Test Ban Treaty in order to test warheads for new delivery systems. China might also be less cooperative with the United States on weapons technology transfers, with implications for security in South Asia and the Middle East. On the most pessimistic end of the spectrum, China might try to speed reunification with Taiwan or press its case

---

86. Even if China does not reform politically, a perceived "Japan threat" could still prove danger-ous, because it could affect negatively the nature of Chinese authoritarianism. On the dangers of democratization, see Edward Mansfield and Jack L. Snyder, "Democratization and the Danger of War," *International Security*, Vol. 20, No. 1 (Summer 1995), pp. 5–38.
87. As Nicholas Kristof argues perceptively, the worst outcome would be if Japan became more militarily active before it reached a higher degree of understanding with its neighbors. See Kristof, "The Problem of Memory," *Foreign Affairs*, Vol. 77, No. 6 (November/December 1998), pp. 37–49, at pp. 47–48.
88. China has been building up these capabilities at a relatively fast pace in recent years, but in 1998 my interlocutors, however genuinely, said that joint U.S.-Japan TMD would lead China to increase the pace of this development.

in the Diaoyu/Senkaku Islands dispute with Japan in potentially destabilizing ways, fearing that U.S.-Japan TMD or direct Taiwanese participation in a regional TMD system might make it more difficult to tackle those issues after the systems become deployed.

These possible scenarios are based on counterfactual arguments that would be difficult to prove even if one or more of the policies above were actually adopted by China. For example, given the Taiwan problem and the vast superiority of the United States in military power, China is likely to develop its missile capability to a significant degree regardless of the details of U.S.-Japan TMD cooperation. It will be difficult to discern the relative impact of specific policies on the trajectory of that development. But U.S. security policy in East Asia and much of the post–Cold War security studies literature on the region have been built on counterfactual arguments that, although impossible to prove, are almost certainly correct. If one is willing to entertain the notion that a continued U.S. presence in East Asia, especially in Japan, is the single biggest factor preventing the occurrence of destabilizing spirals of tension in the region, one should also be willing to entertain the notion that the form this presence takes will also have important implications for Japan and its neighbors.

Conclusion

Given China's intense historically based mistrust of Japan, Beijing's concern about eroding norms of Japanese self-restraint, and the political geography of the Taiwan issue, even certain new defensive roles for Japan can be provocative to China. The United States should therefore continue to be cautious about what new roles Japan is asked to play in the alliance. This is particularly true in cases where the United States may be able to play the same roles without triggering the same degree of concern in Beijing.

By maintaining and, where necessary, increasing somewhat U.S. capabilities in Japan and East Asia more generally, not only will the United States better be able to manage and cap future regional crises, it ideally may be able to prevent them from ever occurring. By reassuring both Japan and its potential rivals, the United States reduces the likelihood of divisive security dilemma scenarios and spiral model dynamics in the region. In so doing, the United States can contribute mightily to long-term peace and stability in a region that promises to be the most important arena for U.S. foreign policy in the twenty-first century.

The Geography of the Peace

Robert S. Ross

East Asia in the Twenty-first Century

The discussion of post–Cold War East Asia has focused on the prospects for regional tension and heightened great power conflict. Some scholars believe that tension will increase because of the relative absence of the three liberal/Kantian sources of peace: liberal democracies, economic interdependence, and multilateral institutions. Realists argue that the rise of China and the resulting power transition will create great power conflict over the restructuring of the regional order. Neorealists point to the emergence of multipolarity and resulting challenges to the peaceful management of the balance of power.[1]

East Asia has the world's largest and most dynamic economies as well as great power competition. This combination of economic and strategic importance ensures great power preoccupation with the East Asian balance of power. But great power rivalry is not necessarily characterized by heightened tension, wars, and crises. This article agrees that realist and neorealist variables will contribute to the character of regional conflict, but it stresses that geography can influence structural effects. Although many factors contribute to great power status, including economic development and levels of technology and education, geography determines whether a country has the prerequisites of great power status; it determines which states *can* be great powers and, thus,

Robert S. Ross is Professor of Political Science, Boston College, and Associate of the John King Fairbank Center for East Asian Research, Harvard University. His most recent books are Great Wall and Empty Fortress: China's Search for Security *(coauthor) (New York: W.W. Norton, 1997) and* Negotiating Cooperation: U.S.-China Relations, 1969–1989 *(Stanford, Calif.: Stanford University Press, 1995).*

I am grateful to Robert Art, Richard Betts, Thomas Christensen, Paul Godwin, Avery Goldstein, Robert Kaufman, Seung-young Kim, Donald Klein, Phillip Saunders, and an anonymous reviewer for their helpful comments on an earlier draft of this article.

1. For pessimistic analyses, see Aaron L. Friedberg, "Ripe for Rivalry: Prospects for Peace in a Multipolar Asia," *International Security*, Vol. 18, No. 3 (Winter 1993/94), pp. 5–33; Richard K. Betts, "Wealth, Power, and Instability: East Asia and the United States after the Cold War," ibid., pp. 34–77; and Charles A. Kupchan, "After Pax Americana: Benign Power, Regional Integration, and the Sources of Stable Multipolarity," *International Security*, Vol. 23, No. 2 (Fall 1998), pp. 62–66. See also Gerald Segal, "East Asia and the Constrainment of China," *International Security*, Vol. 20, No. 4 (Spring 1996), pp. 107–135; and Douglas T. Stuart and William Tow, *A U.S. Strategy for the Asia-Pacific: Building a Multipolar Balance-of-Power System in Asia*, Adelphi Paper No. 229 (London: International Institute for Strategic Studies [IISS], 1995). Samuel Huntington argues that Chinese hegemony is all but inevitable, so that the United States must accommodate China. Huntington, *The Clash of Civilizations and the Remaking of World Order* (New York: Simon and Schuster, 1996).

International Security, Vol. 23, No. 4 (Spring 1999), pp. 81–118
© 1999 by the President and Fellows of Harvard College and the Massachusetts Institute of Technology.

whether East Asia will be bipolar or multipolar in the twenty-first century. Geography also has two effects on the management of the balance of power. First, it affects the interests of the powers, thus influencing conflict over vital interests. Second, it affects whether a great power relationship is offense dominant or defense dominant, thus determining the severity of conflict from the security dilemma. Geographic and structural incentives can often reinforce each other. But when geography and polarity create countervailing pressures, geography trumps structure.

Nuclear weapons have transformed international politics, not least as deterrents to general war. But the Cold War revealed that in the shadow of nuclear war great power conflict continues over allies, spheres of influence, and natural resources. It also revealed that great powers continue to participate in crises, arms races, and local wars, and to threaten general war. Similarly, nuclear weapons have not eliminated the effect of geography on state behavior.

This article stresses that just as political scientists tried to understand the geography of the future balance of power and the conditions of peace as World War II was drawing to a close, in the aftermath of the Cold War it is important to examine the geography of the twenty-first-century balance of power.[2] The first section of this article argues that despite the prevailing global unipolarity, contemporary East Asia is bipolar, divided into continental and maritime regions. The second section contends that bipolarity is stable because the region's lesser great powers—Russia and Japan—lack the geopolitical prerequisites to be poles. The third section holds that both China and the United States have the geographic assets to potentially challenge each other and that they are destined to be great power competitors. The fourth section argues that U.S.-China bipolarity is likely to be stable and relatively peaceful; it does so by examining balancing trends in East Asia, the geography-conditioned interests of China and the United States, and the mitigating role of geography on the security dilemma. The final two sections consider the implications for regional order of the conflict over the Spratly Islands, the Korean Peninsula, and Taiwan, and of the potential for a reduced U.S. presence.

---

2. The classic geopolitical treatment of the emerging postwar order and from which the title of this article is taken is Nicholas John Spykman, *The Geography of the Peace* (New York: Harcourt Brace, 1944). See also Walter Lippmann's contribution, *U.S. War Aims* (Boston: Little, Brown, 1944).

The Great Power Structure of Contemporary East Asia

The post–Cold War global structure is characterized by American unipolarity. With the collapse of the Soviet Union and Russia's preoccupation with domestic political and economic turmoil and the impoverishment of its military forces, the United States is the world's sole superpower. But global supremacy does not mean that the United States possesses hegemony in regional politics. Regional structures can diverge from the pattern of the global structure. The analytical distinction between a superpower and a regional power makes this clear. As William Fox noted fifty-five years ago, a superpower is a traditional great power in regions outside its home region, while regional powers "enjoy . . . great-power status," but its "interests and influence are great in only a single theater of power conflict."[3] As Kenneth Boulding explained, the "loss of strength gradient" erodes capabilities in distant regions, thus contributing to great power parity.[4] These factors reveal how bipolar or multipolar regional balances of power can coexist in a unipolar global structure. They explain why nineteenth-century Great Britain was a superpower. Britain did not possess hegemony over Europe, but it had great power status in regions other than Europe, earning it the status of a superpower. They also explain why nineteenth-century Britain had superpower status but simultaneously contested for security in multipolar regions outside Europe, such as in East Asia, where Japan and Russia challenged British interests.

East Asia is bipolar because China is not a rising power but an established regional power. The United States is not a regional hegemon, but shares with China great power status in the balance of power. From the early 1970s to the end of the Cold War there were elements of a "strategic triangle" in East Asia composed of the United States, Russia, and China.[5] The collapse of Soviet

---

3. William T.R. Fox, *The Superpowers: The United States, Britain, and the Soviet Union—Their Responsibility for Peace* (New York: Harcourt Brace, 1944), pp. 20–21. See also Colin S. Gray, *The Geopolitics of Super Power* (Lexington: University Press of Kentucky), p. 45.

4. Kenneth E. Boulding, *Conflict and Defense: A General Theory* (New York: Harper and Row, 1963), pp. 230–232. For analyses of interplay between global and regional orders, see David A. Lake and Patrick M. Morgan, *Regional Orders: Building Security in a New World* (University Park: Pennsylvania State University Press, 1997); and Barry Buzan, "A Framework for Regional Security Analysis," in Buzan and Gowher Rizvi, *South Asian Insecurity and the Great Powers* (London: Macmillan, 1986), pp. 3–33.

5. Glenn H. Snyder and Paul Deising, *Conflict among Nations: Bargaining, Decision Making, and System Structure in International Crises* (Princeton, N.J.: Princeton University Press, 1977), pp. 462–470; Joshua S. Goldstein and John R. Freeman, *Three-Way Street: Strategic Reciprocity in World Politics* (Chicago: University of Chicago Press, 1990); Robert S. Ross, ed., *China, the United States, and the*

power ushered in not U.S. hegemony, but bipolarity composed of the remaining two powers—China and the United States. Indeed, China was the major strategic beneficiary in East Asia of the collapse of the Soviet Union. Wherever there had been Soviet influence in a third country, China filled the vacuum. This was the case on the Korean Peninsula, where Sino-Soviet competition in North Korea was succeeded by Chinese dominance. The Soviet withdrawal from Vietnam transformed Indochina into a Chinese sphere of influence.

The post–Cold War bipolar regional structure is characterized by Chinese dominance of mainland East Asia and U.S. dominance of maritime East Asia. In Northeast Asia North Korea's location on the Chinese border and its strategic and economic isolation yield China hegemony over North Korea's economy and security. On the Sino-Russian border China enjoys conventional military superiority. Moscow's inability to pay its soldiers, fund its weapons industries, and maintain its military infrastructure has weakened the material capabilities and the morale of the Russian army.[6] Moscow cannot dominate domestic minority movements and numerous smaller neighbors while contending with the better-funded and better-trained Chinese army. China enjoys similar advantages over Russia regarding the new border states of Kazakhstan, Kyrgyzstan, and Tajikistan, and its economic presence in this region yields additional advantages.[7] China dominates mainland Southeast Asia. Burma has been a de facto Chinese protectorate since World War II. Chinese regional influence expanded following the withdrawal of U.S. forces from mainland Southeast Asia in 1975, when Thailand shifted from alignment with the United States to alignment with China. Only Beijing had the credibility to offset Soviet

Soviet Union: Tripolarity and Policy Making in the Cold War (Armonk, N.Y.: M.E. Sharpe, 1993); Lowell Dittmer, "The Strategic Triangle: An Elementary Game-Theoretic Analysis," *World Politics*, Vol. 31, No. 4 (July 1981), pp. 485–515; and R.J. Rummel, "Triadic Struggle and Accommodation in Perspective," in Ilpyong Kim, ed., *The Strategic Triangle: China, the United States, and the Soviet Union* (New York: Paragon House, 1987).

6. See, for example, Aleksey Georgiyevich Arbatov, "Military Reform," *Mirovaya Ekonomika I Mezhdunarodnyye Otnosheniya* 4 [World economy and international relations], July 17, 1997, in Foreign Broadcast Information Service (FBIS), July 18, 1997 (UMA-97–136-S); *Sovetskaya Rossiya* [Soviet Russia], July 9, 1998, in FBIS, July 10, 1998 (SOV-98–190); Interfax, December 4, 1997, in FBIS, December 5, 1997 (UMA-97–338); and NTV (Moscow), February 6, 1998, in FBIS, February 17, 1998 (UMA-98–44). See also Stephen J. Blank, "Who's Minding the State?: The Failure of Russian Security Policy," *Problems of Post-Communism*, Vol. 45, No. 2 (March–April 1998), pp. 3–11.

7. On recent improvement in PLA (People's Liberation Army) training, see June Teufel Dryer, "The New Officer Corps; Implications for the Future," *China Quarterly*, No. 146 (June 1996), pp. 315–335; and Dennis J. Blasko, Philip T. Klapkis, and John F. Corbett, Jr., "Training Tomorrow's PLA: A Mixed Bag of Tricks," ibid., pp. 448–524.

and Vietnamese threats to Thai security.[8] Following the Soviet withdrawal from Vietnam, Hanoi accepted China's terms for peace in Cambodia. Cambodia then developed close relations with China, so that Beijing was content to work with the erstwhile Vietnamese "puppet regime."[9]

Thus by 1991 China had achieved dominance over mainland East Asia. The only exception is South Korea's alliance with the United States. But even here the situation is ambiguous.[10] Because Washington is Seoul's ally and possesses bases in South Korea, it dominates South Korea's strategic calculus. But by the mid-1990s Beijing and Seoul had developed close strategic ties. The two countries share considerable concern for Japanese military potential. Moreover, it is clear that Seoul is pursuing strategic hedging by developing strategic ties with China in preparation for possible U.S. reconsideration of its commitment to South Korea. In addition, in 1997 China was South Korea's third largest export market and the largest target of South Korean direct foreign investment.[11]

The United States dominates maritime East Asia. The U.S. navy lost its bases in Thailand in 1975 and withdrew from its Philippine bases in 1991, but these losses did not weaken either absolute or relative U.S. naval power. In many respects, the United States had secured bases in East Asia because of the poverty of its allies, which could not build and maintain air and naval facilities. For the United States to shoulder the burden, it insisted on possessing the facilities. Now excellent air and naval facilities exist throughout Southeast Asia, so that the U.S. navy is interested in "places, not bases." Washington has access agreements for naval facilities in Singapore, Malaysia, Indonesia, and Brunei.[12]

---

8. On the evolution of Thai security policy, see Sukhumbhand Paribatra, "Dictates of Security: Thailand's Relations with the PRC," in Joyce K. Kallgren, Noordin Sopiee, and Soedjati Djiwandono, eds., *ASEAN and China: An Evolving Relationship* (Berkeley: Institute of East Asian Studies, University of California, 1988); and Khien Theeravit, "The United States, Thailand, and the Indochinese Conflict," in Hans H. Indorf, ed., *Thai-American Relations in Contemporary Affairs* (Singapore: Executive Publications, 1982).

9. On Vietnamese accommodation to Chinese power, see Michael Leifer, "Vietnam's Foreign Policy in the Post-Soviet Era: Coping with Vulnerability," in Robert S. Ross, ed., *East Asia in Transition: Toward a New Regional Order* (Armonk, N.Y.: M.E. Sharpe, 1995). On China's victory in Indochina, see Ross, "China and the Cambodian Peace Process: The Benefits of Coercive Diplomacy," *Asian Survey*, Vol. 31, No. 12 (December 1991), pp. 1170–1185.

10. Walter Lippmann foresaw this development in 1944. See Lippmann, *U.S. War Aims*, p. 93.

11. *Korea Herald*, August 22, 1997, in FBIS, August 26, 1997 (EAS-97–234); and Yonhap News Agency, August 19, 1997, in FBIS, August 21, 1997 (EAS-97–231). On China-South Korea ties, see Victor D. Cha, "Engaging China: The View from Korea," in Alastair Iain Johnston and Robert S. Ross, eds., *Engaging China: Management of a Rising Power* (London: Routledge, forthcoming).

12. For the Pentagon's explanation of its naval strategy, see United States Department of Defense, *East Asia Strategy Report* (Washington, D.C.: U.S. Department of Defense, 1995); testimony of Admiral Charles R. Larson, Commander in Chief, U.S. Pacific Command, to the Armed Forces

Because other powers do not have access to facilities in any of these countries, do not have aircraft carriers, and do not have land-based aircraft that can project power into the region, the U.S. navy dominates maritime Southeast Asia, including the critical shipping lanes connecting East Asia with the Middle East.

Northeast Asia is vastly more complicated than Southeast Asia because Northeast Asian land-based aircraft are within range of important maritime theaters. Nonetheless, the combination of U.S. bases in Japan and superior U.S. air capabilities ensures U.S. dominance of the Northeast Asian naval theater. Despite deployment on the perimeters of Northeast Asia's maritime zones, Chinese aircraft cannot challenge U.S. aircraft in any theater, including over mainland China. Whereas the United States is continuing to develop more advanced aircraft for the twenty-first century, Beijing will rely on Russia's 1970s' generation Su-27 aircraft as the backbone of its early twenty-first-century air force.[13] China is vulnerable to air combat with U.S. aircraft in the East China Sea and the Sea of Japan, and the resulting U.S. air superiority provides for American naval superiority in Northeast Asia.

Rising Powers in East Asia?

Out of the ashes of the Cold War emerged a bipolar East Asia. It is stable because geopolitical conditions determine that no power can challenge it. The only candidates to become poles are Russia and Japan. But given geographic constraints, neither can challenge bipolarity. They are powerful countries that affect the regional balance of power, but they cannot become poles. Rather, they will remain second-class great powers, or, in Randall Schweller's term, "lesser great powers," whose security depends on cooperation with a pole.[14]

Committee, U.S. Senate, March 2, 1994, which includes a discussion of "places" and "bases"; statement of Admiral Joseph W. Prueher, Committee on National Security, U.S. House of Representatives, March 4, 1998. Note also that Washington has reached a status-of-forces agreement with the Philippines, the first step toward access to facilities at Subic Bay. See the statement in Manila by U.S. Secretary of Defense William Cohen, January 14, 1998. The most recent agreement with Singapore is reported in *Jane's Defence Weekly*, November 18, 1998, p. 15.

13. On the Chinese air force, see Kenneth W. Allen, Glenn Krumel, and Jonathan D. Pollack, *China's Air Force Enters the Twenty-first Century* (Santa Monica, Calif.: RAND, 1995); and Paul H.B. Godwin, "PLA Doctrine, Strategy, and Capabilities toward 2000," *China Quarterly*, No. 146 (June 1996), pp. 464–487.

14. Randall L. Schweller, *Deadly Imbalances: Tripolarity and Hitler's Strategy of World Conquest* (New York: Columbia University Press, 1998), pp. 16–19.

SUCCUMBING TO THE WEATHER: RUSSIA AS A NORTHEAST ASIA POWER
Despite Russia's presence in Northeast Asia, its status as a regional pole has been tenuous and rare, primarily because of the inhospitable geography separating the Russian Far East from western Russia. Russians have never migrated east in large numbers. Although the southeast sector of the Far East can sustain agriculture, its isolation from Russia's population and industrial bases obstructs development of the infrastructure needed to support population and financial transfers. Russia's ultimately fruitless effort to establish reliable rail links with the Far East reveals the obstacles posed by the cold and barren Russian heartland.[15] The result has been an enduring lack of manpower and natural resources, both of which are necessary to sustain a large Russian military presence in the North Pacific and to avoid dependency on foreign resources.

One exception to this trend was Russian expansion into the Russian Far East and Manchuria during the late nineteenth and early twentieth centuries. Yet this success reflected the anomaly of Chinese weakness rather than any norm of Russian strength. At times, Russian forces were so overextended that had China knowledge of Russia's situation it could have easily reversed St. Petersburg's advances. At other times, China's preoccupation with other powers compelled it to acquiesce to Russian occupation of its territory.[16] But despite China's weakness, the Russian border remained open to Chinese migration, and the Far East economy remained dependent on foreign suppliers. During the last quarter of the nineteenth century, 80 percent of the civilians in Vladivostok were Chinese and Korean. In 1877 the Pacific Squadron, to avoid total dependence on foreign merchants in Vladivostok, purchased coal in San Francisco and used repair facilities in Japan. In 1885 it still depended on imported coal as well as winter anchorages in Nagasaki. As late as 1912, Russians were a bare majority of the Vladivostok population.[17] These resource and logistical difficulties offset Russia's material advantage vis-à-vis Japan during the 1904–05 Russo-Japanese War. St. Petersburg could not resist Japan's naval blockade

---

15. For an enlightening discussion of Russian frustration in trying to overcome the geographic obstacles to expansion into the Far East, see Walter A. McDougall, *Let the Sea Make a Noise: A History of the North Pacific from Magellan to MacArthur* (New York: Basic Books, 1993).
16. See the treatment of the territorial conflict in S.C.M. Paine, *Imperial Rivals: China, Russia, and Their Disputed Frontier* (Armonk, N.Y.: M.E. Sharpe, 1997), pp. 52–57, 87–88.
17. John J. Stephan, *The Russian Far East: A History* (Stanford, Calif.: Stanford University Press), pp. 57, 84–85; and David Wolff, "Russia Finds Its Limits: Crossing Borders into Manchuria," in Stephen Kotkin and Wolff, *Rediscovering Russia in Asia: Siberia and the Russian Far East* (Armonk, N.Y.: M.E. Sharpe, 1995), p. 42.

of Port Arthur by using land routes to resupply its naval and ground forces, making it easy for the Japanese army to land and defeat the Russian army. The Japanese navy used its readily available harbors, supply depots, and coal supplies to destroy the Russian Pacific and Baltic Sea Fleets.[18]

Russia's strategic position in Northeast Asia quickly eroded during World War I and following the 1917 revolution and ensuing civil war. As late as 1925 Chinese controlled the retail trade in much of the Far East, and Japanese firms dominated the region's banking and shipping and controlled 90 percent of the fisheries. In 1920 Japanese forces moved into northern Sakhalin, withdrawing in 1925 only after the Soviet Union agreed to unfettered Japanese access to Sakhalin's natural resources. The only Russian/Soviet military victory against a major power in East Asia during the nineteenth century and the first half of the twentieth century was in 1939 against Japan at Nomohan. The Soviet army was not fighting in East Asia, however, but on the border of Manchuria and Outer Mongolia in Inner Asia, where Moscow enjoyed better lines of communication and resources, and where Japanese forces were overextended and faced logistical problems. Tokyo could have overcome these obstacles, but in 1939 its forces were fighting a major war with Chinese forces deep in southern China while contending with deteriorating U.S.-Japan relations. Japanese leaders thus assigned Nomohan secondary priority. They knowingly refused to supply the local forces with the minimal manpower and matériel required to contend with Soviet forces and instead unsuccessfully counseled local military leaders to cede ground rather than fight. Given Japan's preoccupation with more pressing issues, the Soviet Union did not need great power capabilities to encourage Japanese caution and to defeat the isolated and unprepared Japanese forces.[19]

Not until the late 1950s did Moscow begin to establish a strong presence in the Far East. In the 1970s it revived the Baikal-Amur Railway project, but it was never fully operative through the end of the Soviet Union. In the 1980s Moscow tried to establish a great power military presence in East Asia. It used Vladivostok to develop its Pacific Fleet and deployed forty-five divisions in the Sino-Soviet border region. But Vladivostok remained isolated from the

---

18. Donald W. Mitchell, *A History of Russian and Soviet Sea Power* (New York: Macmillan, 1974), pp. 204–210, 216–233, chaps. 11, 12.

19. Stephan, *The Russian Far East*, p. 163; and Hara Teruyuki, "Japan Moves North: The Japanese Occupation of Northern Sakhalin (1920s)," in Kotkin and Wolff, *Rediscovering Russia in Asia*. The definitive work on the Japanese defeat at Nomohan is Alvin D. Coox, *Nomohan: Japan against Russia, 1939*, Volumes 1 and 2 (Stanford, Calif.: Stanford University Press, 1939).

western Soviet Union. The Pacific Fleet relied on the vulnerable railway system and on equally vulnerable sea and air routes for supplies, making it the most exposed Soviet fleet. And the maritime geography of Northeast Asia continued to plague Soviet access to blue water: offensive action by the U.S. Seventh Fleet could devastate Soviet naval forces before they could leave the Sea of Japan. Although the Pacific Fleet never achieved parity with the U.S. Seventh Fleet and Moscow maintained only about half of its Far East divisions at full strength, the burden of Soviet Far East deployments significantly added to the overexpansion that contributed to the demise of the Soviet Empire.[20]

Contemporary Russian presence in the Far East is closer to the historical norm. The Far East economy is considerably poorer than the Russian economy east of the Urals. Moscow cannot patrol its perimeters, and its borders can be as porous to Chinese migration and trade as they were for most of the nineteenth and twentieth centuries. China's stronger commercial presence challenges the economic integration of the Far East with the rest of Russia.[21] In short, now that China is no longer weak and internally divided, it enjoys geopolitical advantages over Russia as the result of its large population and industrial centers as well as its agriculture resources in Northeast Asia. In these more "normal" circumstances, Russia is, as it usually has been, a "wanna-be" great power.

Even should Moscow stabilize its authority and the economy greatly improve, Russia will not devote the resources necessary to become a pole in East Asia. Rather, it will focus its limited resources first on the former republics of the Soviet Union and then on the expanded U.S. presence in Eastern Europe. Northeast Asia will likely be of third importance. Moreover, Russia's geography will remain a major obstacle to its presence in Northeast Asia. China

---

20. On the Baikal-Amur railway, see Stephan, *The Russian Far East*, p. 266; and *Delovy Mir* [Business world], July 25–July 29, 1997, in FBIS, August 18, 1997 (SOV-97-0157-S). On Soviet naval facilities, see George W. Baer, *One Hundred Years of Sea Power: 1890–1990* (Stanford, Calif.: Stanford University Press, 1993). On conventional deployments, see Paul F. Langer, "Soviet Military Power in Asia," in Donald S. Zagoria, ed., *Soviet Policy in Asia* (New Haven, Conn.: Yale University Press, 1982); Robert A. Scalapino, "Asia in a Global Context: Strategic Issues for the Soviet Union," in Richard H. Solomon and Masataka Kosaka, eds., *The Soviet Far East Military Buildup: Nuclear Dilemmas and Asian Security* (Dover, Mass.: Auburn House, 1986); Harry Gelman, "The Soviet Far East Military Buildup: Motives and Prospects," in ibid.; and Gelman, *The Soviet Far East Buildup and Soviet Risk-Taking against China* (Santa Monica, Calif.: RAND, 1982).
21. On Sino-Russian border relations, see James Clay Moltz, "Regional Tensions in the Russo-Japanese Rapprochement," *Asian Survey*, Vol. 35, No. 6 (June 1995), pp. 511–527; Gilbert Rozman, "Northeast China: Waiting for Regionalism," *Problems of Post-Communism*, Vol. 45, No. 4 (July–August 1998), pp. 3–13; and Rozman, "The Crisis of the Russian Far East: Who Is to Blame?" *Problems of Post-Communism*, Vol. 44, No. 5 (September–October 1997), pp. 3–12.

would once again have to fragment and Russia consolidate for Moscow to enjoy the relative advantages leading to expanded power. But it is far more likely that Russia will remain divided than it is that China will break up.

JAPAN: ISLAND NATION, SECOND-RANK POWER

Japan also faces geographical constraints. But for Japan the problem is not weather or domestic infrastructure, but size. For Japan to transform its economic and technological capabilities into great power military capabilities will require more than ambition. To become a regional pole, Japan must have the resources to support self-reliant regionwide military deployments. Yet dependency, rather than self-sufficiency, is the rule in Japanese history.

Throughout the twentieth century Tokyo has been acutely aware that Japan's indigenous resources are insufficient to eliminate dependency on great power rivals. A major factor in Japanese interwar expansionism and its drive for regional hegemony was its search for economic autonomy.[22] By the start of World War II, Japan had occupied Korea, much of China, and most of Southeast Asia before ultimately being turned back by the United States. But Japanese successes resemble Russian great power successes insofar as Tokyo benefited from a unique and nonreplicable great power environment. Greater Japanese relative power reflected the declining capabilities of other powers rather than Japanese development of the resources necessary to catch up to its rivals.

The early twentieth century was a propitious time for Japan to begin its expansionist drive. Not only was China suffering from internal divisions, but the region's dominant power, Great Britain, was experiencing relative decline. No longer capable of maintaining its two-power naval standard against Russian and French naval expansion in East Asia, London signed the 1902 Anglo-Japanese alliance to encourage Japan to resist Russian expansion in Manchuria and Korea and to secure Japanese cooperation in defense of British interests in China.[23] And the United States had yet to mobilize its military potential. Thus Japan's only obstacle to Northeast Asian primacy was Russia. With Britain's

22. Akira Iriye, *Across the Pacific: An Inner History of American-East Asian Relations* (New York: Harcourt Brace, 1967), pp. 173–174; and Michael A. Barnhart, *Japan Prepares for Total War: The Search for Economic Security, 1919–1941* (Ithaca, N.Y.: Cornell University Press, 1987). See also Jack Snyder, *The Myths of Empire* (Ithaca, N.Y.: Cornell University Press, 1991).

23. Aaron L. Friedberg, *The Weary Titan: Britain and the Experience of Relative Decline, 1895–1905* (Princeton, N.J.: Princeton University Press, 1988); Ian Nish, *The Anglo-Japanese Alliance: The Diplomacy of Two Island Empires, 1894–1907* (London: Athlone, 1966); and John King Fairbank, Edwin O. Reischauer, and Albert M. Craig, *East Asia: Tradition and Transformation* (Boston: Houghton Mifflin, 1978), pp. 555–556.

assistance and America's blessing, Tokyo defeated Russia in the 1904–05 Russo-Japanese War and achieved preeminence in Korea and in Manchuria, where it acquired Russia's railways, bases, and treaty rights. During World War I and the Russian Revolution, Japan secured German rights and bases in China and consolidated its control over Manchuria. Its further expansion into China and Indochina in the 1930s and early 1940s reflected ongoing Chinese instability and France's preoccupation with war in Europe.[24]

Japanese expansion had achieved impressive results. Nonetheless, paralleling Russia's experience in the Far East, even when enjoying the most opportune circumstances for expansion, Japan was unable to overcome geography. Each new foray into divided China, rather than stabilizing Japan's resource base, led to an expanded front and increased dependency on imported resources, eliciting further expansion to meet the need for additional resources. As late as 1939, Tokyo imported more than 91 percent of the military's commodities and equipment, most of which came from the United States. Japan was critically dependent on the United States for scrap iron, aluminum, nickel, and petroleum products. Continued dependency led to incessant expansion, culminating in Japan's occupation of Southeast Asia and to World War II in the Pacific.[25]

Japan's bid for self-reliance failed not only when the international circumstances were most favorable, but also when its domestic system was uniquely oriented toward strategic expansion. At the height of its expansion, the Japanese government exercised unparalleled control over strategic resources and finished products. Nonetheless, Japan could not simultaneously expand, achieve autarchy, and compete with the United States.[26] Ultimately, its bid for great power stature contributed to its demise. Similar to Russia's experience, Japanese overexpansion taxed Tokyo's ability to compete with a better-qualified great power—the United States—and contributed to Japan's total defeat in World War II.

---

24. Ian Nish, *The Origins of the Russo-Japanese War* (New York: Longman, 1985); Fairbank, Reischauer, and Craig, *East Asia: Tradition and Transformation,* pp. 555–556, 692–693, 755–756; and Barnhart, *Japan Prepares for Total War.* For a discussion of Japanese activities in Manchuria during the Russian Revolution, see James William Morley, *The Japanese Thrust into Siberia, 1918* (New York: Columbia University Press, 1957).

25. Iriye, *Across the Pacific,* pp. 207–208; and Barnhart, *Japan Prepares for Total War,* pp. 91–94, 156, 198–203.

26. Barnhart, *Japan Prepares for Total War,* pp. 67–75, 154. See Robert Scalapino's discussion of the strategic context of Japan's failure in Scalapino, "Southern Advance: Introduction," James William Morley, ed., *The Fateful Choice: Japan's Advance into Southeast Asia, 1939–1941* (New York: Columbia University Press, 1980), pp. 121–123.

Japan will not be able to make a similar bid for full-fledged great power status in the twenty-first century. In the 1930s China was not capable of being a great power, and the United States had not yet decided to become one. Neither of these conditions will likely reemerge in the next quarter century. Domestically, Japan's economy is far more decentralized than it was in the 1930s. Moreover, its trade surplus with the United States makes its dependent on access to the U.S. market. Its dependency on imported energy resources, including petroleum from U.S. allies transported through U.S.-controlled shipping lanes, creates similar vulnerabilities.[27]

In the era of air power, Japan faces an additional geopolitical obstacle to becoming a pole. Prior to the development of aircraft, the English Channel served as a formidable mote insulating Britain's resources and industrial base from attack. But as German bombers and missiles revealed, the English Channel is no longer wide enough to buffer English strategic resources. Japan faces a similar lack of strategic depth. Its economy and infrastructure are vulnerable to attack from the sea—as they were during World War II from U.S. aircraft based both on carriers and on Saipan, Guam, Tinian, and ultimately Okinawa—and from land-based aircraft—such as Soviet aircraft deployed in the Far East in the 1980s (and perhaps Chinese aircraft in the future). Alfred Mahan's observation in 1900 that Japan's size and proximity to other East Asian powers diminish its great power potential is especially relevant for the twenty-first century.[28]

China and the United States: Future Great Power Rivals

The debate over a "rising China" not only obscures the reality that China is already a great power in a bipolar structure, but also the understanding that China can destabilize only by challenging U.S. maritime supremacy. Similarly, American concern for the rise of China obscures the reality that the United States has the potential to strive for and achieve what others cannot—regional hegemony through the erosion of Chinese influence. Whether East Asia re-

---

27. See Michael M. May, "Correspondence: Japan as a Superpower?" *International Security*, Vol. 18, No. 3 (Winter 1993/94), pp. 182–187; and May, *Energy and Security in East Asia* (Stanford, Calif.: Institute for International Studies, Stanford University, 1998).
28. Alfred T. Mahan, *The Problem of Asia* (Port Washington, N.Y.: Kennikat Press, 1970), pp. 106–107. On the role of the navy in the bombing of Japan, see Baer, *One Hundred Years of Sea Power*, pp. 262–272. On the British Channel, see Halford J. Mackinder, *Democratic Ideals and Reality* (Westport, Conn.: Greenwood Press, 1981), pp. 55–57.

mains stable will depend on the evolving strategic capabilities and aspirations of these two powers to penetrate each other's sphere of influence.

CHINA: THE GEOGRAPHY OF HEGEMONIC POTENTIAL

China, unlike Japan, has the natural resources to sustain economic development and strategic autonomy. It is now a major trading country, making extensive use of international markets and capital. China's export industries dominate many of its domestic regional economies and provide much of the capital and technology needed to modernize its industrial base and infrastructure. Nonetheless, *if* Chinese modernization succeeds, it could then be sustained through relatively minimal reliance on imported resources. Although China's use of foreign oil is increasing, it possesses the world's largest supply of coal reserves. These reserves are located in inaccessible interior regions, but should China's infrastructure improve with economic modernization, these reserves will be accessible, reliable, and inexpensive. Coal will remain China's principal energy resource well into the twenty-first century. But with greater capital and advanced technology, China will be able to exploit untapped petroleum reserves in Xinjiang Province.[29]

China complements minimal resource dependency with minimal long-term dependency on foreign markets. Should modernization continue, China's population will have improved purchasing power, which will enable it to sustain high-technology, capital-intensive industries. Moreover, China's large population will enable it to maximize labor productivity with minimal overseas investment. Rather than move abroad as labor costs increase—as the U.S. and Japanese enterprises have had to do—Chinese enterprises, following market forces, will be able to move further into China's interior to exploit an inexhaustible, inexpensive, and relatively reliable labor force.

In addition to possessing the natural and demographic resources needed for strategic autonomy, China also has size and internal lines of communication, providing the strategic depth necessary for a "home base, productive and secure," the "essential" element of naval power.[30] Whereas Japan's insular geography makes its resources and industries open to attack from the sea,

---

29. Jonathan E. Sinton, David G. Fridley, and James Dorian, "China's Energy Future: The Role of Energy in Sustaining Growth," in Joint Economic Committee, United States Congress, ed., *China's Economic Future* (Armonk, N.Y.: M.E. Sharpe, 1997); David Blumenthal and Gary Sasser, "Fuel for the Next Century," *China Business Review* (July–August 1998), pp. 34–38; and Jeffery Logan and William Chandler, "Natural Gas Gains Momentum," ibid., pp. 40–45.
30. Mackinder, *Democratic Ideals and Reality*, p. 55.

China's continental dimensions enable it to develop its industrial base far from its borders and coastline, relatively secure from land-based and sea-based air attacks. Chairman Mao Zedong understood the strategic significance of China's "rear area." During the height of the U.S.-China and Sino-Soviet conflicts from the mid-1960s until the early 1970s, he ordered China's industrial facilities moved to the interior. This industrial "third front" was an integral element of Mao's security strategy.[31]

In this respect, China poses the same potential challenge to stability as Germany and the Soviet Union once did. If Germany had emerged victorious in World War I, "she would have established her sea power on a wider base than any in history, in fact on the widest possible base."[32] During the Cold War, in geopolitical terms, Soviet "control of Western Europe would [have] open[ed] the oceans to Soviet maritime power . . . facilitat[ing] Soviet hegemony in the Mediterranean and its littoral and the Middle East."[33] It is thus inevitable that the United States focus on China as the most likely challenger to regional stability. China is the only country that could conceivably challenge U.S. maritime power and East Asia's bipolar structure.

THE UNITED STATES: ENDURING HEGEMONIC CAPABILITIES

The combination of America's separation from East Asia by the Pacific Ocean and its secure borders neighbored by weaker powers enables the United States to develop military power in strategic isolation and to focus strategic resources on naval power for power projection into distant regions. No other East Asian power has either attribute. Added to these geopolitical factors is the size of the United States and its distribution of indigenous resources. Similar to China, the United States can exploit resources and develop industries in its interior, out of range of an adversary's navy, even should it reach the U.S. coastline. It is an "insular power of continental size." Equally important, similar to China but unlike Russia, the United States' climate and terrain facilitate development of population centers and a dense infrastructure connecting coastal regions with the interior, providing secure interior resources to develop maritime and air power.[34]

---

31. Barry Naughton, "'The Third Front': Defense Industrialization in the Chinese Interior," *China Quarterly*, No. 115 (September 1988), pp. 351–386.
32. Mackinder, *Democratic Ideals and Reality*, p. 62.
33. Gray, *The Geopolitics of Super Power*, p. 71.
34. Ibid., pp. 45, 47.

U.S. strategic assets not only enable maritime power, but also power projection against mainland adversaries. U.S. success in World War II reflected the use of maritime power for land power.[35] Once the U-boat threat had been defeated, secure American ship production provided unlimited supplies for U.S. and Allied forces. But naval power alone did not win the war. U.S. aircraft produced in the security of the United States and based in England bombed German industrial assets, slowing German production and compelling Germany to deploy aircraft in defense of the homeland, thereby reducing air support for German troops on the eastern and western fronts. During the landing at Normandy, 12,000 Allied planes encountered 300 German aircraft, reflecting the relative geographic vulnerability of the German economy to enemy bombing.

But America's secure rear area tells only half of the story of superior power. American economic resources tell the other half. In 1941 the United States produced more steel, aluminum, oil, and motor vehicles than the other industrial powers combined. In 1940, with the exception of naval vessels, U.S. military production was nominal. By 1941 the United States already produced far more aircraft, tanks, and heavy guns than the Axis countries combined. By the end of the war U.S. production of major naval vessels was sixteen times greater than that of Japan. Although a two-front war may have ultimately undermined German power, the United States faced no limitations. Indeed, while Russia, Great Britain and, for much of the war, Germany strained to wage one-front wars, the United States successfully waged a two-front war.

In the aftermath of the Cold War the United States is in a unique historical position to develop great power capabilities on land and on the sea. It should be able to maintain these advantages for at least the next quarter century. Although certain purchasing power parity methodologies forecast considerable relative growth of the Chinese economy, even these methodologies predict continued U.S. economic superiority.[36] Moreover, U.S. self-reliance rests on a secure base. America's large population and high level of development mean

---

35. This paragraph and the next one draw from Richard Overy, *Why the Allies Won* (New York: W.W. Norton, 1995). On maritime power as "facilitator" generally and during World War II, see Colin S. Gray, *The Navy in the Post–Cold War World: The Uses and Value of Strategic Sea Power* (University Park: Pennsylvania State University Press, 1994), pp. 18–20.
36. For the International Monetary Fund's reassessment of China's GDP in 1993 based on purchasing power parity methodologies, see *New York Times*, May 20, 1993; and *Far Eastern Economic Review*, July 15, 1993. For a particularly generous estimate of Chinese growth, see Charles Wolf, K.C. Yeh, A. Bamezai, D.P. Henry, and Michael Kennedy, *Long-Term Economic and Military Trends, 1994–2015: The United States and Asia* (Santa Monica, Calif.: RAND, 1995).

that even should the United States lose access to foreign markets, domestic demand would sustain its industries. In 1997 U.S. exports contributed only 12 percent to the U.S. gross domestic product (GDP). In 1995 only four countries in the world had smaller ratios of trade to GDP.[37] Dependency on imported energy resources is more complex. On the one hand, in 1995 the United States relied on oil imports for approximately 25 percent of energy consumption. But automobiles are the primary consumer of oil products. Critical industries rely on domestic resources, including coal and hydropower. Overall U.S. energy dependency is minimal compared with that of other powers, with the exception of China. Japan, for example, in 1997 relied on imported oil for nearly 60 percent of its energy needs.[38] Finally, U.S. domestic coal and petroleum reserves are significant.

In East Asia the United States is not a declining power in either absolute or relative terms. It is a great power in a bipolar structure and will remain so for the next quarter century. Its strategic depth and isolation as well as its naval power allow it to dominate the coastal waters and to penetrate the air space of any country in the world, including China, with minimal risk to either its navy or air force. These capabilities enable the United States to neutralize the naval capabilities of a great power competitor and to isolate it from offshore allies and resources, while guaranteeing its own access to international resources. Moreover, strategic nuclear superiority allows the United States to carry out such activities with minimal risk of retaliation against the homeland. The United States will possess these resources and capabilities for the next quarter century. It is natural that China focus its suspicions on the United States, just as the United States concentrates its suspicions on China. The United States is the only power that can challenge Chinese territorial integrity.

Peace and Stability in Bipolar East Asia

The United States and China are the two great powers of East Asia. They will not be strategic partners. Rather, they will be strategic competitors engaged in a traditional great power struggle for security and influence. The similarities between the dynamics of the Cold War U.S.-Soviet relationship and the emerg-

---

37. *Economic Report of the President: 1998* (Washington, D.C.: Government Printing Office, 1998), pp. 216–217.
38. U.S. statistics are from U.S. Department of the Census, *Statistical Abstract of the United States: 1997* (Washington, D.C.: Government Printing Office, 1997), pp. 580–582. On Japan, see May, *Energy and Security in East Asia*, p. 11.

ing U.S.-China relationship are striking. Both are bipolar great power relationships. In both situations, the conflict entails a major land power and a major maritime power in which each has the existing or the potential capabilities to challenge the vital interests of the other. In addition, the great power focus in each case is a strategic and economic region with global significance. These similarities suggest that U.S.-China conflict may resemble U.S.-Soviet conflict.

But various bipolar structures do not necessarily exhibit the same great power dynamics. Depending on additional factors, some bipolar rivalries can be more stable than others. Twenty-first-century U.S.-China bipolarity should be relatively stable and peaceful, in part because geography reinforces bipolar tendencies toward stable balancing and great power management of regional order. In addition, the geography of East Asia, by affecting great power interests and by moderating the impact of the security dilemma, offsets the tendency of bipolarity toward crises, arms races, and local wars.[39]

BIPOLARITY, BALANCING, AND GEOGRAPHY

In response to superior U.S. capabilities, China is exhibiting the domestic balancing associated with bipolarity. It has discarded Marxist ideological impediments and overcome significant political obstacles to pursue pragmatic market-based economic policies.[40] Within its limited means, China has improved its ground forces and focused on the technological modernization of its navy and air force. Beijing has also managed great power relations to maximize allocation of resources to domestic growth. It has reached border agreements and developed confidence-building measures with Russia and the bordering Central Asian states. It has developed cooperative economic and security ties with South Korea and encouraged North Korea to moderate its foreign policies. It has also maximized Sino-Japanese economic cooperation. And Chinese leaders have compromised on many issues in U.S.-China relations to diminish the potential for costly conflict with the United States.

These policies assure Beijing access to international economic resources and minimize the likelihood of international conflict that could reorient Beijing's

---

39. On the positive and negative aspects of bipolarity, see Kenneth N. Waltz, *Theory of International Politics* (Reading, Mass.: Addison-Wesley, 1973), chap. 8; and Glenn H. Snyder, *Alliance Politics* (Ithaca, N.Y.: Cornell University Press, 1997), pp. 346–349.
40. On Beijing's economic pragmatism, see Barry Naughton, *Growing Out of the Plan: Chinese Economic Reform, 1978–1993* (New York: Cambridge University Press, 1995); and Nicholas R. Lardy, *Foreign Trade and Economic Reform in China, 1978–1990* (New York: Cambridge University Press, 1992). On the politics of reform, see Joseph Fewsmith, *Dilemmas of Economic Reform in China: Political Conflict and Economic Debate* (Armonk, N.Y.: M.E. Sharpe, 1994).

domestic policies from long-term balancing to short-term defense spending for management of immediate threats. Although Chinese motives for pursuing pragmatic economic development and foreign policies are less important than the systemic affects of its policies, it is significant that Chinese leaders explain that economic modernization is China's key to defense modernization and preparation for the possibility of heightened great power tension in the twenty-first century.[41]

The United States faces no immediate threat in East Asia. But as a maritime power it must look with suspicion on any continental power that achieves preeminence on land. In part in preparation for possible Chinese expansion, Washington maintains a high level of military deployments and alliance development. Ten years after the collapse of the Warsaw Pact, U.S. defense spending is greater than the combined spending of the next six largest defense budgets. U.S. defense priorities reflect concern for China and the corresponding need for maritime power; budget cuts have not reduced American naval deployments in East Asia. Acquisition and research and development also continue, reflected in the 1998 launching of a new aircraft carrier (the *Harry S. Truman*), development of a twenty-first-century warplane and advanced nuclear missiles, and research on missile defense and other advanced technologies. In addition, recent U.S.-Japan agreements put the alliance on more stable political footing and enhance U.S. wartime access to Japanese civilian and military facilities.[42]

East Asian bipolarity also contributes to regional order. In contrast to great powers in multipolarity, great powers in bipolar structures not only have a greater stake in international order, but their disproportionate share of world capabilities gives them the ability to accept the free-riding of smaller states and to assume the burden of order in their respective spheres of influence, so that small states do not challenge the interests of the great powers. This is easier when the allies' contribution to security and their ability to resist are negligible.[43]

In East Asia these dynamics of bipolarity exist. China towers over its smaller neighbors, and the United States towers over its security partners, with the

---

41. On China's management of its regional environment, see Robert S. Ross, "China and the Stability of East Asia," in Ross, *East Asia in Transition*.
42. On the U.S.-Japan alliance, see Mike Mochizuki, ed., *Toward a True Alliance: Restructuring U.S.-Japan Security Relations* (Washington, D.C.: Brookings, 1997). For an authoritative discussion of the China focus of U.S. policy toward Japan, see Joseph S. Nye, Jr., "An Engaging China Policy," *Wall Street Journal*, March 13, 1997.
43. On the advantages of bipolarity versus multipolarity in developing a security order, see Waltz, *Theory of International Politics*, pp. 195–199, 204–209.

partial exception of Japan. Geopolitics reinforces these dynamics. Because Chinese and U.S. spheres of influence are geographically distinct and separated by water, intervention by one power in its own sphere will not appear as threatening to the interests of the other power in its sphere. Freed from the worry of great power retaliation, each power has a relatively freer hand to impose order on its allies. Thus China has intervened in Indochina to achieve both regional order and its security interests without eliciting U.S. countermeasures. In contrast, Soviet military intervention in Eastern Europe led to heightened concern in the North Atlantic Treaty Organization (NATO) over Soviet ambitions and contributed to heightened great power tension.

BIPOLARITY, GEOGRAPHY, AND NATIONAL SECURITY INTERESTS
Positive outcomes of bipolarity appear to be taking place. But neorealism suggests that bipolarity will also have negative repercussions: high threat-perception and unnecessarily high tension and costly foreign policies. In contrast to multipolarity, clarity of threat leads to an intense concern for reputation and repeated "tests of will," resulting in immediate responses to any relative gain by another pole, no matter how peripheral to the balance of power. The Cold War conflict seems to validate this argument, with its superpower arm races, numerous crises, and repeated great power interventions in the developing world.[44] East Asian bipolarity thus suggests that U.S.-China relations in the twenty-first century will be similarly plagued by high tension.

Polarity is a powerful determinant of great power dynamics. But it is not the only determinant nor necessarily even the primary one. Other realist variables complement or even counteract the impact of bipolarity. Geographically conditioned great power interests and corresponding weapons procurement patterns can be equally powerful variables affecting great power relationships in bipolarity and multipolarity. The U.S.-China relationship is one between a land power and a maritime power, each with its own distinct geopolitical imperatives. To the extent that their vital regional interests and military capabilities do not compete, conflict can be restrained.[45]

---

44. For a discussion of why bipolarity produces heightened great power tension, including intervention in the developing world, see Robert Jervis, *Systems Affects: Complexity in Political and Social Life* (Princeton, N.J.: Princeton University Press, 1997), pp. 118–122. See Waltz, *Theory of International Politics*, chap. 8, for the application of bipolar arguments to the Cold War.
45. See Schweller, *Deadly Imbalances*, chap. 1, on realist and neorealist variables in great power dynamics. For the effect of geography on balance-of-power incentives for offensive or defensive military doctrines, see Barry Posen, *The Sources of Military Doctrine: France, Britain, and Germany between the World Wars* (Ithaca, N.Y.: Cornell University Press, 1984), especially pp. 65–71, 78,

U.S. MARITIME INTERESTS AND REGIONAL STABILITY. American interests in East Asia are twofold. First, the United States has an interest in ensuring sufficient strategic presence in regional affairs so that it can militarily resist an effort by any power to dominate the region. To accomplish this objective, it needs cooperation from influential regional states that will offer U.S. forces the facilities necessary to maintain a forward presence. For an extraregional maritime power such as the United States, cooperation with an offshore second-rank maritime power is appropriate, for capabilities are complementary and the regional ally can provide the distant power with forward yet relatively secure naval facilities.

In Europe the United States has traditionally relied on Great Britain as its maritime partner; in post–World War II East Asia it has depended on Japan. But Washington has never been satisfied with relying on Britain to ensure a divided Europe. In the early years of the Republic it required that the great powers on the European mainland be divided so that the United States could cooperate with a continental power. In later years it understood that great power dominance of the European peninsula would exclude U.S. naval presence from the western and southern European maritime perimeter, requiring excessive concentration of U.S. forces in Great Britain. The hegemon's southern ports would be relatively secure from U.S. naval pressure, and it might achieve superiority over U.S. forces regarding naval access to the southern Atlantic and the Mediterranean and, thus, northern Africa and the Middle East.[46]

In contrast, the geography of East Asia allows for maritime balancing. Not only is Japan relatively more powerful than Great Britain in its respective theater, but more important, the dominance of mainland East Asia cannot yield an aspiring hegemon unimpeded access to the ocean. From Japan in Northeast Asia to Malaysia in Southeast Asia, the East Asian mainland is rimmed with

---

237–239. The importance of capabilities and geography for the security dilemma is also discussed in Robert Jervis, "Cooperation under the Security Dilemma," *World Politics*, Vol. 30, No. 2 (January 1978), pp. 167–215; Stephen Van Evera, "Offense, Defense, and the Causes of War," *International Security*, Vol. 22, No. 4 (Spring 1998), pp. 5–43; and Thomas J. Christensen and Jack Snyder, "Chain Gangs and Passed Bucks: Protecting Alliance Patterns in Multipolarity," *International Organization*, Vol. 44, No. 2. (Spring 1990), pp. 137–168. Walter Lippmann argued that the continental interests of China and the maritime interests of the United States do not conflict and that "each can rest in its own element. There is no reason why they should fight." Lippmann, *U.S. War Aims*, p. 103.
46. This is one of the central themes in Samuel Flagg Bemis, *A Diplomatic History of the United States* (New York: Henry Holt, 1936). See also Spykman, *Geography of the Peace*, pp. 55–57. For American strategy following World War II, see Melvyn P. Leffler, *A Preponderance of Power: National Security, the Truman Administration, and the Cold War* (Stanford, Calif.: Stanford University Press, 1992).

a continuous chain of island countries that possess strategic location and naval facilities. Access to these countries enables a maritime power to carry out effective naval operations along the perimeter of a mainland power. The American response to Japanese expansion prior to World War II reflected the United States' strategic interest in maritime East Asia. Washington did not resist Japanese expansion into Korea. Even after Russian and British military decline in East Asia, the United States did not consider Japanese control over China or even Indochina, and its resultant acquisition of the attributes of a continental power, worthy of a military response. Washington's embargoes against Japan and its preparation for war were taken in anticipation that Tokyo would not stop with Indochina but would seek British and Dutch possessions in maritime Southeast Asia.[47]

The United States requires sufficient naval presence in East Asia for maritime containment of a continental power. In effect, this has been the strategy of the United States since its withdrawal from mainland Southeast Asia in 1975, first against the Soviet Union and now against China. Relying on its economic influence and unchallenged maritime power in East Asia, the United States has consolidated strategic alignments with all of the littoral states. As noted above, it has reached arrangements for naval access to facilities in Indonesia, Singapore, Malaysia, and Brunei. With these agreements and its bases and access to facilities in Japan, the United States carries out naval encirclement of China. It can apply air and naval pressure on Chinese access to the ocean along the entire perimeter of mainland East Asia.

Despite advances in military technologies, America's ability to depend on a strategy of maritime balancing will survive for the next twenty-five years. China will undoubtedly try to develop space-based reconnaissance technologies that would enable it to track and target U.S. vessels in the South China Sea. But the United States is not standing still. Its ongoing technology development will allow it to maintain superiority in electronic warfare, enabling it, for example, to hide its fleet from Chinese satellite reconnaissance. Some studies argue that China is falling behind the United States in technology

---

47. A. Whitney Griswold, *The Far Eastern Policy of the United States* (New Haven, Conn.: Yale University Press, 1938); Dorothy Borg, *The United States and the Far Eastern Crisis of 1933–1938* (Cambridge, Mass.: Harvard University Press, 1964); Christopher Thorne, *The Limits of Foreign Policy: The West, the League of Nations, and the Far Eastern Crisis of 1931–1933* (New York: G.P. Putnam, 1973); Iriye, *Across the Pacific*, chap. 7, pp. 201–204; 216–220; and Barnhart, *Japan Prepares for Total War*, chap. 12.

development. Should there be a "revolution in military affairs" (RMA), it will be a largely American revolution.[48]

The requirements of maritime balancing allow the United States to dominate regional shipping lanes and project power wherever necessary in maritime East Asia, and thus achieve its second vital interest: secure access for itself and its allies to regional markets and to strategic resources, including oil in Southeast Asia and the Middle East, in time of war. Even should China develop naval capabilities in its coastal waters, at minimal financial and tactical inconvenience U.S. and allied commercial and military fleets could use secure shipping lanes that are far from mainland aircraft and are dominated by U.S. air and naval forces based in maritime nations.

The United States is an East Asian maritime power with no strategic imperative to compete for influence on the mainland. And the status quo enables it to secure its balance of power interests and its interest in regional shipping lanes through a maritime containment strategy. This contributes to great power stability. Moreover, despite American superiority, U.S. expansionism onto mainland East Asia would face considerable obstacles. Geopoliticians and other international relations theorists have long debated the ease with which maritime power can be used to develop land power.[49] But local geography

---

48. For the Pentagon's assessment of the goals and prospects of China's military modernization program, see the 1998 Department of Defense report to Congress *Future Military Capabilities and Strategy of the People's Republic of China*. For a cross-country analysis of the possession of critical technologies, see Office of the Undersecretary of Defense, *Militarily Critical Technologies List, Part 1: Weapons Systems Technologies* (Washington, D.C.: National Technical Information Service, U.S. Department of Commerce, 1996). For an assessment of China's technological capabilities and prospects, see Bernard D. Cole and Paul H.B. Godwin, "Advanced Military Technology and the PLA: Priorities and Capabilities for the Twenty-first Century," paper prepared for the 1998 American Enterprise Institute conference on the People's Liberation Army, Wye Plantation, Aspen, Maryland, September 11–13, 1998. On the RMA, see Bates Gill and Lonnie Henley, *China and the Revolution in Military Affairs* (Carlisle Barracks, Penn.: Strategic Studies Institute, U.S. Army War College, 1996); and Paul Dibb, "The Revolution in Military Affairs and Asian Security," *Survival*, Vol. 39, No. 4 (Winter 1997–98), pp. 93–116. For a more pessimistic account, see Paul Bracken, "America's Maginot Line," *Atlantic Monthly*, December 1998, pp. 85–93.

49. See the discussions in Mackinder, *Democratic Ideals and Reality;* Paul M. Kennedy, *Strategy and Diplomacy 1870–1945* (London: George Allen and Unwin, 1983), chap. 2; Harold Sprout and Margaret Sprout, *Foundations of International Politics* (New York: D. Van Nostrand, 1962), chap. 10; Sprout and Sprout, *Toward a Politics of the Planet Earth* (New York: D. Van Nostrand, 1971), pp. 269–276, 296–297; Raymond Aron, *Peace and War: A Theory of International Relations* (New York: Praeger, 1968), pp. 192–194; Martin Wight, *Power Politics*, ed. Hedley Bull and Carsten Holbraad (New York: Holmes and Meier, 1978), pp. 76–80; Nicholas John Spykman, *America's Strategy in World Politics: The United States and the Balance of Power* (New York: Harcourt Brace, 1942), pp. 31–34; Spykman, *The Geography of the Peace*, pp. 41–44; and Gray, *The Navy in the Post–Cold War World*, pp. 14–16.

determines the efficacy of capabilities. The American military experiences in Vietnam and Korea revealed how difficult it is to use maritime power to project air and land power onto East Asian terrain, in contrast to maritime-based power projection into the Middle East. The American military continues to have a "no more land wars in Asia" mentality. The difficulty of power projection onto mainland East Asia is a powerful deterrent to any U.S. interest in challenging the status quo.

CHINESE CONTINENTAL INTERESTS AND REGIONAL STABILITY. Just as the United States has secured its vital East Asian maritime interests, China has secured its vital continental interests. China has achieved unique success for a continental power: secure borders on its entire land periphery. But twenty-first-century regional peace will depend on whether China, having secured its continental interests, will turn its attention to developing maritime power-projection capabilities, challenging U.S. interests and bipolarity.

China's status as a continental power not only reflects geography but also the culture of a land power. For more than 2,000 years, Chinese territorial expansion has been led by peasants seeking arable land, followed by a Confucian culture and the administrative and military power of the Chinese state. During this same period, China never carried out territorial expansion across water. Up to the twentieth century, Chinese development of a navy has been, at best, sporadic and brief. Its maritime tradition has focused on commercial exploration.[50] Moreover, threats to Chinese security have originated from the interior. Until the Chinese and Russian Empires met in Central Asia in the nineteenth century and China created the province of Xinjiang, China could never subdue the nomadic armies on the Central Asian steppe. The absence of natural borders made Chinese territory vulnerable to military incursions and enabled nomadic armies to retreat deep into the interior to evade China's retaliating armies. At its worst, nomadic armies established "foreign" dynasties. So persistent was the nomadic threat that during the Ming dynasty (1368–1644) a strategic culture developed regarding relations with the Mon-

---

50. On dynastic expansion, see John King Fairbank, "A Preliminary Framework," in Fairbank, ed., *The Chinese World Order* (Cambridge, Mass.: Harvard University Press, 1968); and Yang Lien-sheng, "Historical Notes on the Chinese World Order," in ibid. On China's maritime ventures, see Jane Kate Leonard, *Wei Yuan and China's Rediscovery of the Maritime World* (Cambridge, Mass.: Harvard University Press, 1984); and Louise Levanthes, *When China Ruled the Seas* (New York: Simon and Schuster, 1994). On China's continental and maritime traditions, see Bruce Swanson, *Eighth Voyage of the Dragon: A History of China's Quest for Sea Power* (Annapolis, Md.: Naval Institute Press, 1982), pp. 1–43.

gols, in which Beijing eschewed all thought of diplomacy and limited victories, seeking total annihilation of its nomadic adversaries.[51]

China's only experience of threat from maritime powers occurred in the nineteenth century. But this exception underscores that land powers pose the primary threat to Chinese security. Although the British navy exacted humiliating defeats on China, Great Britain never attempted to occupy Chinese territory (with the exception of treaty ports). Rather, the greatest threats to China came first from Russia and then from Japan, which used land power to try to conquer China. Japan, following the strategy of the seventeenth-century Manchus, used northeast China as a base to invade the interior. There is no period in Chinese history when a maritime power—as opposed to a land power—posed the greatest threat to Chinese rule or threatened to establish a foreign dynasty.

Two thousand years of continental expansion and of threats from land powers have created a Chinese bias toward the development of land power, just as secure land borders and extensive oceanic frontiers have fostered an American "insular perspective" on international politics. But culture is not immutable. Now that China has secure land borders and is modernizing its economy, its national interests might change—however delayed or mitigated by history and culture. Yet despite China's successes, a continental strategy continues to serve its singular vital interest: borders secure from great power influence.

China remains vigilant to land threats. It is bordered by thirteen countries, second only to Russia. Its most important security concern is its long border with Russia. As Chinese commentators observe, Russia retains the geographic resources required to redevelop formidable military capabilities. This is the case especially in Central Asia, where the theater is close to the Russian heartland but far from China's industrial and population centers and separated by inhospitable desert climate and terrain. China's Central Asian frontier is its strategic vulnerability, just as Russia's Far East is its strategic vulnerability. During the 1930s and 1940s Moscow exploited the weakness of China's

---

51. On China's strategy toward the Mongol armies, see Alastair Iain Johnston, *Cultural Realism, Strategic Culture, and Grand Strategy in Chinese History* (Princeton, N.J.: Princeton University Press, 1995); and Arthur Waldron, *The Great Wall of China: From History to Myth* (New York: Cambridge University Press, 1990). On China's long history of managing nomadic tribes, see, for example, Thomas J. Barfield, *The Perilous Frontier: Nomadic Empires and China* (Cambridge, Mass.: Basil Blackwell, 1989); Joseph F. Fletcher, "China and Central Asia, 1368–1884," in Fairbank, *The Chinese World Order*; and Waldron, *The Great Wall of China*.

Nationalist government by developing dominant political influence in Xinjiang Province. In the early 1960s Moscow used ethnic unrest in Xinjiang to threaten China.[52] The prospect of Sino-Soviet competition for the allegiance of the Central Asian states, in a reenactment of the nineteenth-century "great game" between Russia and Britain, cannot be dismissed. Moreover, many Russians believe that China poses a long-term threat to Russian security. Whereas U.S. territory is protected from China by the Pacific Ocean, Russian territory is vulnerable to Chinese land forces.[53] The fact that Russia and China are neighbors means that China cannot control the Eurasian "heartland" and be confident of secure borders: thus it cannot place strategic priority on maritime power.

China's border concerns are not limited to Russian power. The Central Asian countries adjacent to China have weak governments and could be used by a larger power, such as Russia, to threaten Chinese territorial integrity. China must also consider the long-term prospect for domestic instability in its western provinces, where religious and ethnic minorities identify with the majority populations of China's potentially hostile and unstable neighbors.[54] Southwest China is bordered by India, which has great power aspirations, and southern China is bordered by Vietnam, which still yearns for a great power ally to enable it to come out from under China's strategic shadow. In Northeast Asia Korea could be used by a great power to threaten China's industrial heartland, as Japan and then the United States did for much of the twentieth century.

Given the potential for multifront conflicts and strategic encirclement, China faces greater potential security challenges than those ever faced by dynastic

---

52. Allen S. Whiting and Sheng Shih-ts'ai, *Sinkiang: Pawn or Pivot* (East Lansing: Michigan State University Press, 1958); Linda Benson and Ingvar Svanberg, *China's Last Nomads: The History and Culture of China's Kazaks* (Armonk, N.Y.: M.E. Sharpe, 1998), chap. 3; and June Teufel Dryer, "The PLA and Regionalism in Xinjiang," *Pacific Review*, Vol. 7, No. 1 (1994), pp. 43–44.
53. On Sino-Russian relations, see Jennifer Anderson, *The Limits of Sino-Russian Strategic Partnership*, Adelphi Paper No. 315 (London: IISS, 1997); Stephen J. Blank, "Russia and China in Central Asia," in Blank and Alvin Z. Rubinstein, eds., *Imperial Decline: Russia's Changing Role in Asia* (Durham, N.C.: Duke University Press, 1997; and Blank, "Russia Looks at China," in ibid.
54. See Blank, "Russia and China in Central Asia"; Ross H. Munro, "Central Asia and China," in Michael M. Mandelbaum, ed., *Central Asia and the World: Kazakhstan, Uzbekistan, Tajikistan, Kyrgyzstan, and Turkmenistan* (New York: Council on Foreign Relations, 1994); and Martha Brill Olcott, *Central Asia's New States: Independence, Foreign Policy, and Regional Security* (Washington, D.C.: United States Institute of Peace, 1996), pp. 35, 82, 108–110. On recent instability in Xinjiang, see ITAR-TASS, January 27, 1998, in FBIS, January 29, 1998 (SOV-98–27); *Novoye Pokoleniye* [New generation], January 22, 1998, in FBIS, January 27, 1998 (SOV-98–25); and *Delovaya Nedelya* [Business week], January 16, 1998, in FBIS, January 23, 1998 (SOV-98–21). For a discussion of ethnic and religious discontent and instability in Xinjiang since 1949, see Benson and Svanberg, *China's Last Nomads*, chap. 6.

China. It would have to assume a long-term stable strategic status quo on its land borders to divert substantial resources to naval power. Yet even if China did so, its navy could not approach parity with the U.S. navy. Alfred Mahan went so far as to argue that "history has conclusively demonstrated the inability of a state with even a single continental frontier to compete in naval development with one that is insular, although of smaller population and resources."[55] The challenge to a land power seeking maritime power is even greater in the twenty-first century, when the financial and technology requirements include construction of an aircraft carrier and its specialized aircraft as well as the support vessels and advanced technologies necessary to protect the carrier.

While trying to maintain funding for its land forces, by 2025 China could at best develop a "luxury fleet" similar to that developed by the Soviet Union in the latter stage of the Cold War. Such a second-order fleet might achieve coastal-water defense, pushing the U.S. navy away from the Chinese mainland and interfering with unrestricted U.S. penetration of Chinese air space. It might also be able to disrupt U.S. naval activities further from shore. But, given the United States' ability to respond, Chinese capabilities could not provide the foundation for a great power navy that could challenge U.S. supremacy.[56] Indeed, even if the Chinese navy were able to complicate U.S. naval activities, it would not strike first for fear of a retaliatory strike that would destroy its navy, so that the United States would maintain unrestricted use of maritime East Asia.

China will face the same obstacles to developing naval capabilities vis-à-vis a maritime power that Russia, the Soviet Union, and Germany faced in the nineteenth and twentieth centuries. British maritime supremacy undermined Russia's effort to use naval power to exercise influence in the Ottoman Empire in the mid-nineteenth century, and London took the initiative to destroy the Russian fleet at Sebastopol during the Crimean War. Similarly, the best that Moscow could aim for in the 1950s and 1960s was a "land-oriented" fleet to reduce U.S. ability to strike Soviet territory with carrier-based aircraft. By the

---

55. Alfred Thayer Mahan, *Retrospect and Prospect: Studies in International Relations* (London: Sampson, Low, Marston, 1902), quoted in Gray, *The Navy in the Post–Cold War World*, p. 89. See also Lippmann, *U.S. War Aims*, p. 103.
56. For the concept of a "luxury fleet," see Gray, *The Geopolitics of Super Power*, pp. 49, 92–93. On Chinese maritime power-projection capabilities, see Cole and Godwin, "Advanced Military Technology and the PLA."

1970s it could do no more than "inhibit" U.S. maritime movements. Even in the 1980s, the primary role of the Soviet surface fleet was protection of the homeland and control of coastal waters. Despite the expansion of the Pacific Fleet, Moscow could not develop an adequate response to U.S. "horizontal escalation" against its naval facilities in the Soviet Far East. Overall, the United States could still use its "central maritime position . . . to seize the strategic initiative."[57] Germany was similarly frustrated in its effort to develop naval power. Alfred von Tirpitz's "risk fleet" failed because Germany could never develop sufficient capability to threaten British maritime supremacy, so that during World War I England retained control of the seas without having to engage and destroy the German fleet. For its part, Germany did not dare to initiate hostilities; it understood that Britain would destroy its fleet. Moreover, having diverted funds to the navy, Germany lacked the ability to defeat the French army.[58]

In the absence of compelling maritime interests, Beijing's continental interests and U.S. maritime capabilities should deter China from making naval power a priority. Even continued economic growth and greater energy demand will not lead it to develop maritime capabilities to defend its overseas interests and shipping lanes. Because a Chinese maritime buildup would lead to countervailing U.S. policy, China's energy imports would remain vulnerable to U.S. forbearance. This prospect leads to two policy outcomes. First, given its huge coal reserves, China will continue to prefer coal over petroleum. Second, China will exploit foreign petroleum reserves in regions where its land power has the advantage. China's continental interests are reflected in its effort to secure access to Central Asian oil. Beijing's 1997 investment in Kazakhstan's major petroleum company and its plans to build a pipeline from Kazakhstan to

---

57. On Russian and Soviet naval experiences, see Mitchell, *A History of Russian and Soviet Sea Power,* chap. 8, pp. 510–515, 557–558; A.J.P. Taylor, *The Struggle for the Mastery of Europe 1848–1918* (New York: Oxford University Press, 1954); René Albrecht-Carrie, *A Diplomatic History: Europe since the Congress of Vienna* (New York: Harper and Row, 1973); Baer, *One Hundred Years of Sea Power,* pp. 419–425, 432–434; Michael MccGwire, *Military Objectives in Soviet Foreign Policy* (Washington, D.C.: Brookings, 1987), pp. 179–180, 330–331; and MccGwire, "The Rationale for the Development of Soviet Seapower," in John Baylis and Gerald Segal, eds., *Soviet Strategy* (London: Croom Helm, 1981), pp. 210–254. Paul M. Kennedy, *The Rise and Fall of the Great Powers* (New York: Random House, 1987), pp. 386–387, 510–511, discusses Soviet capabilities in a historical and comparative context. The quotation is from Baer, *One Hundred Years of Sea Power,* p. 421.
58. On German naval strategy, see Paul M. Kennedy, *Strategy and Diplomacy, 1870–1945,* chap. 5; Kennedy, *The Rise of the Anglo-German Antagonism, 1860–1914* (Atlantic Highlands, N.J.: Ashfield Press, 1987), chap. 20; and Andreas Hillgruber, *Germany and the Two World Wars,* trans. William C. Kirby (Cambridge, Mass.: Harvard University Press, 1981), pp. 9–21.

Xinjiang reflect its commitment to developing secure energy resources. Its interest in a natural gas pipeline connecting Siberia to China's northeast provinces also reflects this strategy.[59] The current low international price of oil makes these and other such projects economically very unattractive, but their value is in their contribution to long-term Chinese strategic hedging against dependency on oil controlled by an adversarial power.

Finally, is China a dissatisfied power seeking a "place at the table," so that the politics of prestige could lead to irrational and dangerous Chinese over-expansion?[60] To some extent, the answer will depend on whether Washington will share leadership with Beijing on issues affecting Chinese interests. Recent U.S. policy is encouraging. Moreover, it is worth pointing out that *regionally* China has already secured a place at the table. China's struggle from 1949 to 1989 reflected this objective, and the outcome was a success. In the aftermath of the Cold War, East Asian countries acknowledge that China has legitimate great power interests and that its cooperation is required to secure regional peace. China and the United States jointly manage the Korean Peninsula. China has a leadership role in various regional organizations, including the security-orientated ASEAN (Association of Southeast Asian Nations) Regional Forum and the forum on Asia Pacific Economic Cooperation (APEC). In both organizations Beijing, reflecting its regional authority, has cooperated with local powers to frustrate U.S. policy objectives.[61] Beijing is also gratified by the attention it received during the Asian economic crisis in the late 1990s. China is not a superpower, and its leadership in global issues and institutions is more limited, but its leadership in the East Asian balance of power may satisfy its demands for regional leadership.

---

59. On China's various pipeline and energy investment projects with Central Asian countries and Russia, see Xinhua, June 4, 1997, in FBIS, June 4, 1997 (CHI-97–155); Interfax, June 27, 1997, in FBIS, June 30, 1997 (SOV-97–178); Interfax, February 18, 1998, in FBIS, February 23, 1998 (SOV-98–50); and *Wen Wei Po*, February 18, 1998, in FBIS, February 21, 1998 (CHI-98–50).

60. This is the argument in Richard Bernstein and Ross H. Munro, *The Coming Conflict with China* (New York: Knopf, 1997).

61. On China's role in regional organizations, see Rosemary Foot, "China in the ASEAN Regional Forum," *Asian Survey*, Vol. 38, No. 5 (May 1998), pp. 425–440; and Alastair Iain Johnston and Paul Evans, "China's Engagement with Multilateral Security Institutions," in Johnston and Ross, *Engaging China*. On APEC, see Jiang Xiaoyan, "Dispute over APEC Development Orientation," *Shijie Zhishi* [World knowledge], No. 21 (November 1, 1994), in FBIS/China, November 9, 1995; Chen Fengying, "Growing APEC Resists U.S. Domination," *Xiandai Guoji Guanxi* [Contemporary international relations], No. 8 (August 20, 1996), in FBIS/China, October 17, 1996; Voice of Malaysia, November 15, 1995, in FBIS/East Asia, November 9, 1995; and *The Star* (Malaysia), November 22, 1995, in FBIS, December 11, 1995.

BIPOLARITY, GEOGRAPHY, AND THE SECURITY DILEMMA IN EAST ASIA

The contrasting interests of maritime and continental powers, the strategic characteristics of the regional status quo, and the geography of East Asia all contribute to the prospect of relatively low-level great power tension in the twenty-first century. Nonetheless, even if both China's and the United States' vital interests are satisfied in the current order, the security dilemma in bipolarity could create repeated crises and costly arms races. But in the current strategic environment, preferred weapons programs affect the security dilemma in bipolarity by favoring the defense.

Geographically determined interests lead states to prefer different weapons systems. This can have a profound impact on the security dilemma, for weapons specialization can lead to a defensive bias, mitigating the security dilemma and the effect of bipolarity on the prevalence of crises and arms races as well as reducing the role of nuclear weapons in security. In a confrontation between a land power and a maritime power, each side's specialization is disadvantaged in the other's theater.[62] Thus China will remain inferior to the United States in maritime theaters, and the United States will remain inferior to China regarding ground-force activities on mainland East Asia. This pattern means that the advantage will be for the defense. On the mainland, China's massive conventional retaliatory capabilities allow it to risk a U.S. ground-force attack. U.S. ability to retaliate and destroy Chinese naval assets allows it to risk that China will fire the first shot. Neither side has to fear that the other's provocative diplomacy or movement of troops is a prelude to attack and immediately escalate to heightened military readiness. Tension can be slower to develop, allowing the protagonists time to manage crises and avoid unnecessary escalation.

These dynamics also affect the prospect for arms races. Because each power has a defensive advantage in its own theater, each can resist an equivalent escalatory response to the other's military acquisitions. Each augmentation of China's land-power capabilities does not create a corresponding diminution of U.S. security in maritime East Asia. Similarly, enhanced U.S. maritime presence in the South China Sea, for example, does not create an equivalent decrease in

---

62. On the impact of weapons systems on the security dilemma, see Jervis, "Cooperation under the Security Dilemma." For the assumption of emulation, see Waltz, *Theory of International Politics,* pp. 93, 118. On the relationship between land power and sea power, see also Eugene Gholz, Daryl G. Press, and Harvey M. Sapolsky, "Come Home, America: The Strategy of Restraint in the Face of Temptation," *International Security,* Vol. 21, No. 4 (Spring 1997), pp. 19–25; and Gray, *The Geopolitics of Super Power,* pp. 46–47.

Chinese security on the mainland. The result is that bipolar pressures for a spiraling arms race are minimized. Finally, because each side feels secure with the conventional balance within its respective theater, neither is compelled to adopt a massive retaliation strategy to deter an attack on its own forces or to make credible an extended deterrence commitment. Thus there are reduced fears of a first-strike nuclear attack during a crisis and reduced likelihood of a nuclear arms race reflecting the security dilemma dynamics involving the difficulty in interpreting a counterpart's effort to secure retaliatory capabilities.

The bipolar U.S.-Soviet struggle, which was equally a struggle between a land power and a sea power, did not exhibit similar stability because the geographies of Europe and East Asia are different. In East Asia geography mitigates the pressures of bipolarity; in Europe geography reinforces bipolar pressures to aggravate the security dilemma.[63] Because of geography, the United States could not rely on maritime containment of the Soviet Union to achieve its vital European interests. It required a U.S. presence on mainland Europe to deny Moscow the combination of a secure continental base and access to strategic seas. Thus the Cold War confrontation on the European continent was waged by the army of a continental power and the army of a maritime power. In this setting, because of a widely perceived Soviet conventional force advantage, NATO believed that Moscow would benefit from an offensive attack.[64] Whereas in East Asia geography offsets twenty-first-century bipolar pressures to mitigate the security dilemma, European geography reinforced the effect of bipolarity to aggravate the security dilemma. The result was the rapid spiraling escalation of the Cold War in the 1940s and the Berlin crises.

The Soviet offensive advantage also contributed to the nuclear arms race. Befitting a maritime power, Washington believed that it could not mobilize the resources to maintain sufficient conventional military forces on the European mainland to deny Moscow the benefits of an offensive strategy and thus deter a Soviet attack on Western Europe. Its response was the Eisenhower administration's "new look," whereby the United States would use the threat of massive retaliation against a conventional attack to offset Soviet conventional

---

63. On bipolarity and Cold War tension, see Waltz, *Theory of International Politics*, p. 171.
64. For a careful consideration of how difficult it would be for NATO to resist a Soviet attack, see Richard K. Betts, *Surprise Attack: Lessons for Defense Planning* (Washington, D.C.: Brookings, 1982), chap. 6. Cf., John J. Mearsheimer, "Why the Soviets Can't Win Quickly in Central Europe," *International Security*, Vol. 7, No. 1 (Summer 1982), pp. 3–39. But as Jack Snyder shows, perception is more important than reality in affecting security dilemma dynamics. See Snyder, *The Ideology of the Offensive: Military Decision Making and the Disasters of 1914* (Ithaca, N.Y.: Cornell University Press, 1984), pp. 214–216.

force superiority and to deter an invasion of Western Europe. The United States thus significantly increased its nuclear forces, contributing to the nuclear security dilemma, whereby each superpower feared that its adversary's second-strike capability could be used to destroy its own retaliatory capabilities.[65] The combined result of bipolarity and geography was the nuclear arms race. In contrast, in East Asia geography and the resulting capabilities and defensive advantage held by each pole in its respective sphere of influence diminishes each power's reliance on nuclear weapons for deterrence and, thus, offsets bipolar pressures for an arms race.

Potential Flashpoints: The Spratly Islands, Korea, and Taiwan

The three most prominent East Asian conflicts are the territorial dispute over the Spratly Islands, the prospect for great power conflict on the Korean Peninsula, and the U.S.-China dispute over Taiwan. Of these three, the Spratly Islands conflict is the least significant. Because the disputed islands are in the U.S.-dominated South China Sea, are too small to possess strategic value for power projection, and seem to lack significant energy resources, Beijing has neither the ability nor the strategic interest to challenge the status quo by militarily dislodging the other claimants' forces from the islands.[66] There may be occasional military probes by China or the other claimants, but the United States, because of its advantage in naval warfare, does not need to engage in rapid escalation to deter a possible Chinese offensive.

The Korean and Taiwan conflicts could become sources of heightened tension. They are the exceptions that prove the rule that geography affects the prospects for East Asian conflict. The Korean conflict is a source of heightened tension because it is the sole place in East Asia where the United States has retained a continental military presence. The United States, as a maritime power, like in Europe during the Cold War, has ground forces in South Korea

---

65. See John Lewis Gaddis, *Strategies of Containment: A Critical Reappraisal of Postwar American National Security Policy* (New York: Oxford University Press, 1982), pp. 167–168; Warner R. Schilling, William T.R. Fox, Catharine M. Kelleher, and Donald J. Puchala, *American Arms and a Changing Europe: Dilemmas of Deterrence and Disarmament* (New York: Columbia University Press, 1973), pp. 4–15; and Jerome H. Kahan, *Security in the Nuclear Age: Developing U.S. Strategic Arms Policy* (Washington, D.C.: Brookings, 1975), pp. 12–13. On arms races, see Robert Jervis, *Perception and Misperception in International Politics* (Princeton, N.J.: Princeton University Press, 1976), chap. 3.
66. On the Spratly Islands, see Greg Austin, *China's Ocean Frontier: International Law, Military Force, and National Development* (St. Leonards, Australia: Allen and Unwin, 1998); and Michael G. Gallagher, "China's Illusory Threat to the South China Sea," *International Security*, Vol. 19, No. 1 (Summer 1994), pp. 169–194.

that are vulnerable to a surprise attack. Washington has therefore relied on nuclear weapons to deter an attack, contributing to North Korea's incentive to acquire nuclear weapons. Nonetheless, the status quo has proved resilient for more than forty-five years. Nuclear deterrence has worked with minimal great power tension because China has North Korea as a buffer state and, thus, it has not had a strategic interest in encouraging North Korea to challenge the status quo. On the contrary, with its vital interests satisfied, Beijing has worked with Seoul and Washington to maintain the status quo.

The Korean Peninsula is not a major factor in the balance of power or in U.S. protection of shipping lanes. During the Cold War the U.S. presence on the peninsula denied the Soviet Union a "dagger pointed at the heart of Japan." But this reflected Soviet lack of secure access from the Far East to the Sea of Japan. Because China has a long coast on the East China Sea, the increased threat to Japan from U.S. military withdrawal from the peninsula and greater cooperation between Beijing and Seoul would be marginal. Indeed, just as a twenty-first-century Chinese blue-water navy would be a "luxury fleet," U.S. presence on the Korean Peninsula is a "luxury land force." It gives the U.S. army forward presence on the East Asian mainland, facilitating power projection to China's northeast border. South Korea is a valuable U.S. asset, but it is not a vital interest. It may become politically difficult for the United States to maintain bases in Japan should the Japanese begin to resent that they would be the only Asians with foreign bases on their soil. This is a political problem, however, not a strategic issue requiring belligerent policies.

American military officials are not pleased, but they are reconciled to the likelihood that after unification Seoul will likely request that U.S. ground forces leave Korea. Following unification Seoul may also develop closer relations with China. But Korean unification and closer relations between Beijing and Seoul will not make the United States significantly less secure or the balance of power less stable. It will, however, make East Asia less prone to heightened tension by eliminating a belligerent regime, ending the disruptive conflict between North Korea and South Korea, and reinforcing the dynamics of conflict between a land power and a maritime power.[67]

The Taiwan issue reflects a similar exception to the conflict between U.S. maritime power and Chinese land power. Taiwan lies in both theaters. Because

---

67. See Lippmann's 1944 observation that China will inevitably dominate its "dependencies in the north" and his realist advice that the United States "should recognize that China will be the center of a third strategic system destined to include the whole of mainland Asia." Lippmann, *U.S. War Aims*, pp. 103, 158.

Taiwan is an island, Washington can use superior maritime capabilities, including ships and aircraft, to defend it against China's land-based forces. But Taiwan's proximity to the mainland gives Beijing military superiority to deter Taiwan from attacking the mainland or declaring sovereign independence. Thus, unlike the Korean Peninsula, where North Korean land-power superiority requires U.S. nuclear deterrence strategy to create a stalemate, the Taiwan Strait stalemate is formed by mutual conventional deterrence: the mainland deters Taiwan with its land power, and the United States deters China with its maritime power. Because both theaters are defense dominant, the risk of war is minimal.

Furthermore, similar to the Korean Peninsula, the Taiwan issue does not entail the vital interests of both powers. It is a vital interest to China, mirroring Cuba's role in U.S. security strategy. But despite American support for Taiwan and U.S.-Taiwan ideological affinity, neither U.S.-Taiwan cooperation nor denial of Taiwan to mainland military presence is a U.S. balance-of-power or shipping interest. At no cost to its security, the United States ended military cooperation with Taiwan in the early 1970s. Should Beijing dominate Taiwan, the United States would lose the long-term option of renewed strategic cooperation with an "unsinkable aircraft carrier" near the Chinese coast, depriving it of a beneficial but not vital offensive option regarding China. The United States could still use its bases in Japan and Guam and its access to naval facilities in Southeast Asia to dominate Chinese coastal waters and maintain maritime containment. At worst, should the mainland occupy Taiwan, the difference would be 150 additional miles of Chinese maritime power projection from the southern Chinese coast. During wartime this would require that the United States and its allies move their shipping lanes 150 miles eastward.

The 1995 visit to the United States by Taiwan's Lee Teng-hui and the March 1996 confrontation in the Taiwan Strait were anomalies in an otherwise stable U.S.-China modus vivendi.[68] From the early 1970s to the mid-1990s, the United States and China developed policies on Taiwan that allowed each power to maintain its most important interests while maximizing its cooperation on

---

68. David M. Lampton, "China and Clinton's America: Have They Learned Anything?" *Asian Survey*, Vol. 37, No. 12 (December 1997), pp. 1099–1118; Robert S. Ross, "The 1996 Taiwan Strait Crisis: Lessons for the United States, China, and Taiwan," *Security Dialogue*, Vol. 28, No. 4 (December 1996), pp. 463–470; and Robert G. Sutter, *U.S. Policy toward China: An Introduction to the Role of Interest Groups* (Lanham, Md.: Rowman and Littlefield, 1998), chap. 5. On the strategic significance of Taiwan, it is interesting to note that in 1949 the National Security Council, based on the advice of the Joint Chiefs of Staff, concluded that Taiwan was not a vital interest to the United States. See Thomas J. Christensen, *Useful Adversaries: Grand Strategy, Domestic Mobilization, and Sino-American Conflict, 1947–1958* (Princeton, N.J.: Princeton University Press, 1996), p. 106.

other issues. During this period China denied Taiwan as a strategic asset to the United States. It also isolated Taiwan diplomatically and deterred it from declaring independence, so that Beijing maintained international recognition of its sovereignty over the island. Faced with the U.S. security commitment to Taiwan, Beijing sacrificed actual control over Chinese-claimed territory. For its part, the United States maintained its commitment to Taiwan, deterring a mainland attack and contributing to Taiwan's democracy and economic development. Washington sacrificed its interest in giving Taiwan well-deserved "face" or "dignity"—that is, formal sovereignty—and compelled Taiwan to accept its nonsovereign status in international politics. By 1997 Beijing and Washington had reestablished cooperation based on this long-standing formula, and Taiwan's leaders, despite the pressures from democratic elections, have adopted a more cautious stance toward independence. Allowing for isolated, brief policy deviations from interest-based policies with short-term consequences, as occurred in 1995–96, Washington and Beijing should be able to manage the Taiwan issue for the next quarter century.

The Implications of U.S. Withdrawal

U.S.-China conflicts over the Korean Peninsula and Taiwan are no more than typical great power conflicts. They are not the stuff of cold wars or hot wars. China and the United States will compete for influence in third countries throughout East Asia and elsewhere. This competition will likely entail conflict over "destabilizing" weapons sales, including U.S. arms sales to Taiwan and Chinese arms sales to the Middle East. Such conflict is to be expected in any great power relationship. Beijing and Washington can manage these conflicts without sustained high-level tension. And without Cold War tensions, they can carry out extensive economic relations and normal diplomatic exchanges.

What would happen, however, if the United States downgraded its role as an East Asian great power with balance-of-power responsibilities?[69] Neorealism predicts that another great power would emerge to balance Chinese power. Indeed, Japan has hedged its bets. While relying on alignment with the United States, it has developed advanced-technology defense capabilities, including

---

69. Christopher Layne, "From Preponderance to Offshore Balancing: America's Future Grand Strategy," *International Security*, Vol. 22, No. 1 (Summer 1997), pp. 86–124; Layne, "Less Is More: Minimal Realism in East Asia," *National Interest*, No. 43 (Spring 1996), pp. 64–78; and Gholz, Press, and Sapolsky, "Come Home, America." For an analysis of the American debate over a post–Cold War foreign policy, see Barry R. Posen and Andrew L. Ross, "Competing Visions of U.S. Grand Strategy," *International Security*, Vol. 21, No. 3 (Winter 1996/97), pp. 5–53.

air and naval power, and the foundation for independent power-projection capabilities.[70] But it is not at all clear that Japan can balance China. For almost its entire history, Japan has accommodated Chinese power. Should China successfully modernize in the twenty-first century, Japan, because of its smaller population and industrial base, will be much more dependent than China on imported resources and foreign markets. Some Japanese dependency may well be on China's economy and resources. Equally important, because of its proximity to China and its lack of strategic depth, Japan's economy, including its industrial plant, will be more vulnerable than the Chinese economy to an exchange of air and missile attacks. The difference between Taiwan's and Japan's geographic vulnerability to Chinese missiles is one of degree, not of kind. This asymmetry also undermines Japan's ability to engage in nuclear competition with China.

These disparities might encourage Japanese bandwagoning or ambitious Chinese policy. America's response would be frantic and costly, and contribute to heightened tension, because it would be compelled to belatedly balance expanded Chinese power. In contrast, America's contemporary strategic advantages enable it to balance Chinese power in a relatively stable and peaceful regional order, without a costly and dangerous military buildup.

Alternatively, the United States could reduce its regional presence by sharing balancing responsibilities with Japan. In these circumstances, Tokyo would be expected to develop power-projection capabilities, including aircraft carriers. For two reasons this arrangement would not be as beneficial as the current bipolar balance. First, partial U.S. withdrawal would create a de facto multipolar system, insofar as Japan, albeit a second-rank power, would assume greater weight in the regional balance of power and in the U.S.-Japan alliance.[71] The instability of multipolar balancing suggests that the outcome could be just as costly for the United States as a pure bipolar structure involving Japan and China. Problems of alliance management and balancing, including buckpassing and the ambiguity of threats in multipolarity, could lead to costly last-minute balancing. Moreover, the larger role of second-rank powers would

---

70. See, for example, Richard Samuels, *Rich Nation/Strong Army: National Security and the Technological Transformation of Japan* (Ithaca, N.Y.: Cornell University Press, 1994); Michael J. Green, *Arming Japan: Defense Production, Alliance Politics, and the Postwar Search for Autonomy* (New York: Columbia University Press, 1995); Steven Vogel, "The Power behind Spin-Ons: The Military Implications of Japan's Commercial Technology," in Wayne Sandholtz, Michael Borrus, John Zysman, Ken Conca, Jay Stowsky, Steven Vogel, and Steven Weber, eds., *The Highest Stakes: The Economic Foundations of the Next Security System* (New York: Oxford University Press, 1992).
71. See Schweller, *Deadly Imbalances*, especially chap. 2, on lesser great powers in balancing.

exacerbate free-rider behavior by smaller powers and weaken the ability and the incentives of the great powers to promote regional order.

Second, Japan's buildup could lead to U.S.-Japan conflict. Unlike in U.S.-China relations, U.S. and Japanese capabilities could become competitive—between two maritime powers an offensive strike can be decisive, as Japan almost showed with Pearl Harbor.[72] As long as the United States remains fully engaged, Japan's navy complements U.S. power. But should Washington share naval power with Tokyo, it will likely create security dilemma pressures. Lacking full confidence that Japan would use expanded naval capabilities in support of U.S. interests, Washington may be compelled to balance Japan's naval power through naval expansion. There would also be increased U.S.-Japan competition for influence in the local maritime states and reduced economic cooperation. The result could well be a more expensive U.S. defense policy and a less stable and peaceful regional order.

Finally, both full and partial U.S. withdrawal suffer from a common problem. Each would sacrifice U.S. primacy for the chimera of cheaper balancing. Because the benefits of primacy are many and valuable, the cost of maintaining primacy manageable and the risks of abandoning primacy great, the current balance of power is far preferable to a Sino-Japanese balance of power or a U.S.-China-Japan balance of power.[73] The price of retrenchment would be U.S. security dependence on cooperation with Japan. American access to regional shipping lanes would depend significantly on the Japanese navy. U.S. cooperation with local maritime countries would similarly depend on Japanese forbearance. Japanese politics could have as great an impact on U.S. security as American politics. And this is the positive scenario. Should Japan prove uncooperative or should security dilemma dynamics erode cooperation, the United States would also depend on Chinese cooperation and Chinese politics to secure its interests in East Asia.

A strong American presence maximizes the stability of the balance of power while offsetting the negative consequences of bipolarity through mitigation of the security dilemma. It is less costly than withdrawal. Current defense spending is well below Cold War levels, but it is sufficient to maintain maritime supremacy and a regional balance of power for the next thirty years. Well into the twenty-first century, the U.S.-China bipolar competition will be the most

---

72. See Overy, *Why the Allies Won*, pp. 25–27, 33–44, 60–62.
73. For a discussion of the benefits of primacy, see Samuel Huntington, "Why International Primacy Matters," *International Security*, Vol. 17, No. 4 (Spring 1993), pp. 68–83.

effective and inexpensive strategy for the United States to realize its vital regional interests.

Conclusion

Other factors besides geography and structure affect stability. Democracy, interdependence, and formal multilateral security institutions can contribute to stability, but they are not necessary causes of stability. Nineteenth-century Europe experienced a relatively stable and peaceful order in the absence of widespread democracy, interdependence, and formal institutions. That all three factors are absent from contemporary East Asia does not necessarily mean there will be a greater prevalence of war, crises, and heightened conflict. This article has argued that geography contributes to regional stability and order because it shapes the a priori causes of conflict: capabilities, interests, and the security dilemma.

The prospects for regional peace and stability are good because geography minimizes the likelihood of a power transition and because stable bipolarity encourages timely balancing and great power ability and interest to create order. Geography will further contribute to regional order by offsetting the tendency of bipolarity to exacerbate great power tension. The U.S.-China bipolar conflict is a rivalry between a land power and a maritime power. This dynamic reduces conflict over vital interests and mitigates the impact of the security dilemma, reducing the likelihood of protracted high-level tension, repeated crises, and arms races.

The combination of geography and polarity will contribute to regional peace and order, but neither alone nor in combination are they sufficient causes of peace and order. National policies can be destabilizing. There is no guarantee that the United States will maintain a consistent contribution to the regional balance of power, that China will pursue limited ambitions, or that Washington and Beijing can peacefully manage the Taiwan issue. Despite the positive effects of geography and bipolarity, certain twenty-first-century weapons systems, such as theater missile defense, can exacerbate the security dilemma and contribute to arms races and heightened bilateral and regional tension.[74] The best that can be said is that structure and geography offer policymakers greater

---

74. For a discussion of the destabilizing potential of the Taiwan issue and the impact of theater missile defense on the security dilemma and U.S.-China relations, see Thomas J. Christensen, "China, the U.S.-Japan Alliance, and the Security Dilemma in East Asia," *International Security*, Vol. 23, No. 4 (Spring 1999), pp. 49–80.

confidence in the prospects for a relatively stable and peaceful order and, thus, the opportunity to try to maximize great power cooperation.

Pessimism suggests that America prepare for the prospect of Chinese expansionism and develop a containment-like policy whereby it maintains high military readiness and responds to each Chinese challenge with immediate and costly retaliation. But whereas such a policy may have been appropriate during the Cold War, when Soviet capabilities challenged vital U.S. interests, the combination of geography and structure in post–Cold War East Asia suggests that Washington does not have to be hypersensitive to relative gains issues or to the prospect of Chinese military expansionism. In the twenty-first century, at current levels of defense spending and regional presence, the United States can promote its regional security interests and develop cooperative relations with China on a wide range of security and economic issues, contributing to a relatively peaceful and cooperative great power order.

Part III:
Choices for Policy Toward China

Containment or Engagement of China?

Calculating Beijing's Responses

David Shambaugh

There is little doubt that the People's Republic of China (PRC) is becoming a defining element in post–Cold War international politics, but there is much debate about what this entails and how the world should deal with an ascendant China. China's rise and behavior are particularly bedeviling to the United States, but Beijing also poses substantial challenges to Asian and European nations as well as international regimes. Whether China will become a military threat to its neighbors, an adversary of the United States, a systemic challenge to the global order, or an cultural-ideological challenge to the West remain open questions.[1] But China's sheer size and growing power are already altering the contours of Asian security, international commerce, and the global balance of power.

A robust debate is under way in Western and Asian nations about how best to deal with the awakened dragon. The uncertainties about China's future capabilities and intentions, and the debate about alternative policy options, have spawned a lucrative cottage industry among analysts and pundits in academia, corporations, banks, governments, and the media worldwide. Analysts can reasonably estimate China's economic and military power a decade or more hence based on its present and projected financial, technological and material resources. Far more difficult to predict is China's internal political and social cohesion, and how Beijing will wield its new strength.

Will China be a satisfied mature power or an insecure *nouveau riche* power? Will it become a power at all? Will it flex its muscles or will they atrophy? Will China hold together or fall apart? Will its polity evolve liberally or revert to a dictatorial tyranny? Does Beijing seek regional hegemony or peaceful coexistence with its neighbors? Will the PRC play by the established rules of the international organizations and regimes, or does Beijing seek to undermine and change the rules and institutions? Do China's leaders understand the rules and

---

David Shambaugh is Professor of Political Science and International Affairs and Director of the Gaston Sigur Center for East Asian Studies at the George Washington University. He is Editor of The Journal of Northeast Asian Studies *and former Editor of* The China Quarterly.

---

1. See David Shambaugh, "China's Military: Real or Paper Tiger?" *Washington Quarterly*, Vol. 19, No. 1 (Spring 1996), pp. 19–36. The best case for China as a cultural-ideological challenge is made by Samuel Huntington in "The Clash of Civilizations?" *Foreign Affairs*, Vol. 72, No. 3 (Summer 1993), pp. 22–49.

International Security, Vol. 21, No. 2 (Fall 1996), pp. 180–209
© 1996 by the President and Fellows of Harvard College and the Massachusetts Institute of Technology.

accept their premises? Can China meet its existing bilateral and multilateral obligations? These are some of the pressing questions that fuel the current debates about China and how to cope with it.

This article explores these and related questions by addressing key domestic factors that will shape China's external posture in the near term, and how domestic actors will respond to the international environment and alternative policies pursued by Asian and Western governments. Its central argument is that containment of China is a badly flawed policy option, but that a policy of "engagement"—while preferable from a Western and Asian standpoint—will not be fully reciprocated by Beijing. For numerous reasons, China will be reluctant to respond positively to the policy of "engagement," yet this remains the best option available to the international community at present.

Engagement, in and of itself, should not be the policy goal. Rather, it is a process and a vehicle to the ultimate goal of integrating China into the existing rule-based, institutionalized, and normative international system. Engagement is the means, integration the end. Much work needs to be done both to bring China into international multilateral regimes and to inculcate their norms in Chinese officials and citizens. The evidence presented in this article suggests that such inculation and integration will be extremely difficult at best, and will most likely be resisted for many years to come.

The next section places the current China debates in context, while the remainder of the article examines three domestic variables that will condition China's external orientation in the near to medium term. It concludes by linking each set of variables to potential Chinese responses to policies of engagement or containment.

Debating China

Nearly half a century ago the debate and political witch-hunt over "Who lost China?" raged in the United States, precipitated by the collapse of Chiang Kai-shek's Nationalist government and conquest of Mao's Communist forces. Americans soul-searched over the failure of their nation's missionary effort to "save" and transform China.[2]

---

2. Of the rich literature on America's missionary attempt to remake China, see Barbara Tuchman, *Stilwell and the American Experience in China, 1911–1945* (New York: Bantam Books, 1970); James C. Thomson, Jr., *While China Faced West: American Reformers in Nationalist China, 1928–1937* (Cambridge, Mass.: Harvard University Press, 1969); James C. Thomson, Jr., Peter W. Stanley, and John Curtis Perry, *The American Experience in East Asia* (New York: Harper & Row, 1981); and Michael H.

Embedded in the debate was a brief "recognition controversy" in 1949–50 over the merits of accepting and dealing with the new People's Republic of China.[3] Such considerations were soon dashed with the outbreak of the Korean War and intervention of Chinese forces. This led to two decades of "containment" of an expansionist "Red China," a policy with a profoundly flawed premise that cost the United States nearly 100,000 dead in two wars on the Asian mainland, incalculable losses of commercial and cultural interchange with China, and the polarization of America's relations with Asia. In 1971, President Nixon jettisoned the containment policy in favor of an opening to China. Nixon's reasoning was strategic and tactical, but he also recognized the folly of trying to contain the largest nation on earth. While not using the term, Nixon was the original architect of the policy of "engaging" China—of trying to integrate the People's Republic peacefully into the international order.

Today, a quarter-century after the Nixon opening, another debate over China policy rages. The debate has again polarized into the competing schools of "engagement" vs. "containment"—or what may reminiscently be described as "open door" and "closed door" policies.[4] America's longstanding propensity to see China in a series of extreme images is mirrored in today's policy debate.[5] Often missing in this debate, however, is consideration of China's potential responses to these polarized policies and consideration of the domestic variables inside China that will condition its external orientation. While the debate has tended to be dominated by foreign policy pundits, international relations specialists, and journalists, experts on China's domestic affairs have generally not joined the fray.[6]

Hunt, *Ideology and U.S. Foreign Policy* (New Haven, Conn.: Yale University Press, 1987). For a more contemporary exposition of the American "missionary impulse" toward China, see Richard Madsen, *China and the American Dream: A Moral Inquiry* (Berkeley: University of California Press, 1995).
3. Nancy Bernkopf Tucker, *Patterns in the Dust: Chinese-American Relations and the Recognition Controversy, 1949–1950* (New York: Columbia University Press, 1983).
4. The history of these debates is elaborated in David Shambaugh, "Patterns of Interaction in Sino-American Relations," in Thomas W. Robinson and David Shambaugh, eds., *Chinese Foreign Policy: Theory and Practice* (Oxford: Oxford University Press, 1994), pp. 197–223; and Nancy Bernkopf Tucker, "China and America, 1941–1991," *Foreign Affairs*, Vol. 70, No. 5 (Winter 1991–92), pp. 75–92.
5. See Harold R. Isaacs, *Scratches on our Minds: American Images of China and India* (New York: John Day, 1958), and T. Christopher Jespersen, *American Images of China, 1931–1949* (Stanford, Calif.: Stanford University Press, 1996). For their part, Chinese similarly tend to perceive America in dichotomous images; see David Shambaugh, *Beautiful Imperialist: China Perceives America, 1972–1990* (Princeton, N.J.: Princeton University Press, 1991).
6. One laudable exception is Michael D. Swaine, *China: Domestic Change and Foreign Policy* (Santa Monica: RAND National Defense Research Institute, 1995).

The Western debate over the relative merits of engagement versus containment seemingly treats China as a static entity that will simply have to adjust to whatever policy the other nations pursue. Another characteristic is the proclivity to treat China's economic rise and growing power as an irreversible trend.[7] That China will emerge as a superpower early in the twenty-first century has achieved the status of conventional wisdom, and is repeated regularly in global media and many specialist publications. Yet China's modernization could go off the rails, with potentially disastrous consequences. Even if growth continues unabated, it will breed severe social and political dislocations.[8] Moreover, China has proven its capacity to reverse course and slip quickly into domestic strife due to unpredictable leaders and opportunistic citizens. A sober note of caution should thus be part of any prediction that China will be a global power in the next millennium.

Not all observers are convinced of China's inexorable path to power. Economists note severe fiscal distortions and half-achieved reforms, with many hiccups ahead. Political scientists see vulnerability in the state and volatility in society. Sociologists and anthropologists observe an increasingly complex and stratified society. Humanists point to an eclectic mix of values, ideas, and fads that percolate through the populace. Military specialists identify numerous weaknesses amid progress in the armed forces. An increasingly complex China breeds an array of predictions about China's future. As the end both of the century and the era of Deng Xiaoping approaches, there is no shortage of prognostications. Assessments by knowledgeable observers run the gamut from an expansionist economic and military superpower led by a repressive authoritarian and highly nationalistic Chinese Communist Party (CCP); to a modernizing and incrementally democratizing society under "soft authoritarian" CCP rule; to a splintered nation permeated with corruption and convulsed by civil conflicts; and possibly the implosion and overthrow of CCP rule. There exist various permutations of these and numerous other alternative futures, and each has different consequences for China's interlocutors.[9]

---

7. Typical of this tendency is the analysis of William Overholt, *China: The Next Economic Superpower* (London: Weidenfeld & Nicolson, 1993); and Overholt, "China After Deng," *Foreign Affairs,* Vol. 75, No. 3 (May/June 1996), pp. 63–78.

8. See Samuel Huntington, *Political Order in Changing Societies* (New Haven, Conn.: Yale University Press, 1968).

9. Among the many prognostications, see Richard Baum, "China After Deng: Ten Scenarios in Search of Reality," *China Quarterly,* No. 145 (March 1996), pp. 153–175; Swaine, *China;* Robert G. Sutter, *China in Transition: Changing Conditions and Implications for U.S. Interests* (Washington, D.C.: CRS Report No. 93–1061 S, 1993 and updated annually); Nicholas Lardy, Kenneth Lieberthal, and

To a significant extent, China's external behavior will be shaped by international institutions, forces, and balances of power beyond its control. Consequently, many China specialists and foreign policy practitioners advocate enmeshing China in as many international regimes and binding commitments as possible so as to minimize its potential for disruptive behavior and maximize the smooth integration of China into the international order. A consensus exists among the governments of the European Union, Japan, Korea, Association of Southeast Asian Nations (ASEAN), Australia, Canada, and the United States that this is the wisest way to deal with an emerging China. The Clinton administration defines this policy as "comprehensive engagement." However, differences exist among Western and Asian nations over the tactics to pursue, particularly with regard to the use of penalties and sanctions. Different variants exist: e.g., "constructive engagement," "conditional engagement," "coercive engagement." The differences depend on the degree of punitive measures advocated for Chinese violation of U.S. laws and of international rules and norms.[10]

There is strong merit to the engagement argument. It offers the best chance of integrating China into international rule-based regimes while at the same time maintaining open channels to press bilateral national interests. Such a contemporary version of *ostpolitik* also offers the greatest leverage to influence the domestic evolution of Chinese society in a more liberal and open direction. There is a likely correlation between China's domestic liberalization and its ability and readiness to comply with international rules and norms.

But a competing school of thought advocates containing China. This vocal minority sees China as a disruptive threat to regional security and the interna-

---

David Bachman, *The Future of China* (Seattle: National Bureau of Asian Research, 1992); Yoichi Funabashi et al., *Emerging China in a World of Interdependence* (New York: Trilateral Commission Report, 1994); David Shambaugh, "China's Fragile Future," *World Policy Journal* (Fall 1994), pp. 41–45; Shambaugh, *Political Dynamics in Transitional China: Implications for the United States* (Carlisle Barracks, Penn.: U.S. Army War College National Strategy Institute, 1996); Maria Hsia Chang, "China's Future: Regionalism, Federation, or Disintegration," *Studies in Comparative Communism* (September 1992), pp. 211–227; Gerald Segal, *China Changes Shape: Regionalism and Foreign Policy*, Adelphi Paper No. 287 (London: International Institute of Strategic Studies [IISS], 1994).

10. The case for "conditional engagement" is made in James Shinn, ed., *Weaving the Net: Conditional Engagement with China* (New York: Council on Foreign Relations, 1996). The case for "constructive engagement" is best articulated in Audrey and Patrick Cronin, "The Realistic Engagement of China," *Washington Quarterly*, Vol. 19, No. 1 (Winter 1996), pp. 141–170. In addition to presenting a comprehensive and thoughtful summary of the debates, the case for "coercive engagement" is offered in Michael J. Mazarr, "The Problems of a Rising Power: Sino-American Relations in the 21st Century," *Korean Journal of Defense Analysis*, Vol. 7, No. 2 (Winter 1995), pp. 7–40. The case for "comprehensive engagement" has been made by many U.S. officials of the Clinton administration, and is well argued in Kenneth Lieberthal, "A New China Strategy," *Foreign Affairs*, Vol. 74, No. 6 (November/December 1995), pp. 35–49.

tional system, and advocates balance of power tactics to either "deter," "contain," or "constrain" China.[11] This school argues that engagement is naive and wishful thinking that constitutes a modern form of appeasement. Proponents of this view implicitly view China as a classic rising power with potentially aggressive intent—similar to post-Meiji Japan, Wilhelmine or Nazi Germany, and the former Soviet Union. They argue that interdependence is insufficient to condition China's behavior and that more traditional *realpolitik* methods of power and pressure are required to restrain and contain China.

The current debate on managing China's emergence is both well-timed and necessary. Modern communications afford a rare opportunity to learn from history, anticipate the pending profound change in the world order that will result from China's rise a decade or more in advance, and fashion a strategy for dealing with this eventuality. Our predecessors in the nineteenth and twentieth centuries lacked such an opportunity, and paid dearly for it. Today the international community has the opportunity to anticipate change in China and to formulate strategies that may integrate the state that represents one-quarter of humankind into the international system peacefully and with minimal disruption.

What is worrying about China's rise is historical precedent. Both history and scholarship clearly suggest that nations in economic transition tend to be assertive externally,[12] and that accommodating a rising power into the established order has proved difficult and disruptive.[13] Recent research by Edward Mansfield and Jack Snyder also indicates a strong correlation between states in political transition from authoritarian to democratic systems and the incidence of war.[14] While there are certain political and economic similarities between China's current rise and those of Wilhelmine and Nazi Germany, post-Meiji

---

11. See, for example, Arthur Waldron, "Deterring China," *Commentary*, Vol. 100, No. 4 (October 1995); Gideon Rachman, "Containing China," *Washington Quarterly*, Vol. 19, No. 1 (Winter 1996), pp. 129–140; Gerald Segal, "East Asia and the 'Constrainment' of China," *International Security*, Vol. 20, No. 4 (Spring 1996), pp. 107–135.

12. See A.F.K. Organski and Jacek Kugler, *The War Ledger* (Chicago: University of Chicago Press, 1980); Charles Doran and Wes Parsons, "War and the Cycle of Relative Power," *American Political Science Review* (December 1980), pp. 947–965; Nazli Choucri and Robert C. North, "Lateral Pressure in International Relations: Concept and Theory," in Manus I. Midlarsky, ed., *Handbook of War Studies* (Ann Arbor: University of Michigan Press, 1989), pp. 289–326.

13. See Karl W. Deutsch and J. David Singer, "Multipolar Power Systems and International Stability," *World Politics* (April 1964), pp. 390–406; and J. David Singer et al., *Capability Distribution, Uncertainty, and Major Power War, 1820–1965* (Beverly Hills: Sage Publications, 1972).

14. Edward D. Mansfield and Jack Snyder, "Democratization and the Danger of War," *International Security*, Vol. 20, No. 1 (Summer 1995), pp. 5–38; and Mansfield and Snyder, "Democratization and War," *Foreign Affairs*, Vol. 74, No. 3 (May–June 1995), pp. 79–87.

Japan, and the former Soviet Union—strong political authoritarianism, rapid industrialization, and military modernization—there are also significant differences in traditional statecraft, military traditions, and scientific establishments that suggest China may be more benign.[15] But the sheer magnitude of China—its population, economy, and armed forces—combined with its intense nationalism and irredentist claims have given the historical comparisons and concomitant policy debates contemporary currency.

Today a third key variable is at play: the international order itself is highly fluid and undergoing profound systemic change. China is a rising power at the very time that the post–Cold War international system is itself in great flux. Absorbing a rising power into a structurally rigid and hierarchical system could prove especially disruptive to that established system. The currently dynamic global system, with dispersed polarity, might therefore prove more accommodating to China. On the other hand, in the post–Cold War order the international agenda and balance of power are increasingly dominated by global issues and transnational regimes, which China finds onerous given its emphasis on strict state sovereignty and non-interference in what it deems "internal affairs." By this criterion, absorbing the PRC may prove difficult.

In either case, the global systemic variable is cause for concern given the findings of A.F.K. Organski and other scholars that there is a high correlation between global system transition and war.[16] Organski and his associates concluded that the important fact was that war correlated positively with transition from one system to another.

Challengers [to the existing international system] are those powerful and dissatisfied great nations who have grown in power after the imposition of the existing international order. Their elites face circumstances where the main benefits of the international order have already been allocated. The conditions for conflict are present. Peace is threatened when challengers seek to establish a new place for themselves in the international order, a place to which they believe their increasing power entitles them.[17]

Organski and Kugler could hardly have described present-day China better. China today is a dissatisfied and non–status quo power which seeks to change the existing international order and norms of inter-state relations. Beijing is not

---

15. See John Garver, *Will China Be Another Germany?* (Carlisle Barracks, Penn.: U.S. Army War College National Strategy Institute, 1996).
16. A.F.K. Organski, *World Politics* (New York: Knopf Publishers, 1958, rev. ed. 1968).
17. Jacek Kugler and A.F.K. Organski, "The Power Transition: A Retrospective and Prospective Evaluation," in Midlarsky, *Handbook of War Studies*, p. 174.

satisfied with the status quo, sees that the international system and its "rules" were created by Western countries when China was weak, and believes that the existing distribution of power and resources is structurally biased in favor of the West and against China. It does not just seek a place at the rule-making table of international organizations and power brokers; it seeks to alter the rules and existing system. Beijing seeks to redress historical grievances and assume what it sees as its rightful place as a global power. Above all, China seeks to disperse global power and particularly to weaken the preponderant power of the United States in world affairs. In this regard, Beijing is encouraged by the trends towards multipolarity and power dispersion in the post–Cold War world. It relishes every disagreement that Japan and European countries have with Washington, and is adroit at playing one off against the other. China's primary foreign policy goal today is to weaken American influence relatively and absolutely, while steadfastly protecting its own corner. This goal stems from a number of historical considerations as well as contemporary aspirations.

Beijing also seeks to redress the Asian regional subsystem balance of power. History does not suggest that China seeks to conquer or absorb other countries in the region (except Taiwan and claimed territories in the East and South China Seas), but rather to place itself at the top of a new hierarchical pyramid of power in the region—a kind of new "tribute system" whereby patronage and protection is dispensed to other countries in return for their recognition of China's superiority and sensitivities. International relations scholars recognize this as a classic benevolent hegemonic system, although China adheres to a more coercive definition of hegemony (*bachuanzhuyi*). This is not to say that the PRC is unwilling to use force to achieve its aims in Asia; it has done so at an alarmingly frequent rate since 1949, by teaching punitive "lessons" to one neighbor after another, and China has fought more border wars than any other nation on earth over the last half century. But Chinese divisions marching into Asian capitals does not conform to traditional Chinese statecraft, even if it did lie within People's Liberation Army (PLA) capabilities. China's preferred tactic is to command respect and obeisance through patronage and preponderant power.

As China's economic and military power grows, the international community can expect it to make more forceful challenges to existing norms and rules of international behavior. The PRC will prove a truculent partner and a stubborn opponent. Nonetheless, in the coming years the world will shape China more than China will shape the world. Certainly China's internal demographic, economic, environmental, political, and military profiles will affect the global community to no small extent. But China's global influence will not likely become that of a superpower.[18] It is difficult to imagine China commanding the global influence of the United States or Soviet Union after World War II, which would require both substantial economic and military prowess and moral and ideological appeal.

As China develops, there will be increasing pressure from abroad for it to become part of international structures and behave by established rules and norms. China's response to these pressures will be strongly conditioned by a series of domestic factors. As is the case with all nations, direct causal linkages between domestic sources (inputs) and external behavior (outputs) are not easily identified. Rather, the foreign policy and external behavior of the Chinese state is the product of a complex mix of contextual, historical, political, institutional, and temporal variables.

At present, three principal clusters of variables interact to shape Chinese foreign policy and external relations: domestic politics, the decision-making milieu, and the elite's worldview. These clusters subsume numerous discrete elements and go beyond a conventional listing of individual actors and institutions that participate in the policymaking process. Opening the "black box" of decision-making to identify influential participants is only part of the story. More important are the multiple influences that these individuals embody, and that are brought to bear upon them as they make decisions. Many of these are cognitive, subjective, affective, and unconscious. Many involve the perceptual prisms through which participating elites screen information and calculate decisions. Others are broad systemic and social forces that shape an overall policy agenda and the political environment in which politicians must operate. Still others are temporal and situation-specific in nature. It is therefore important to understand both the objective environment and the subjective framework in which foreign policy elites make decisions.

Domestic Politics

Chinese politicians, like politicians anywhere, do not leave their domestic concerns and constituencies behind when they go into a meeting to consider foreign policy or national security issues. Three elements of domestic politics

---

18. Chinese leaders have repeatedly stated that China will never behave like a superpower even if it possesses the requisites of one.

particularly influence China's external behavior: (1) succession politics; (2) systemic fragility; and (3) the devolution of central political control to subnational actors and units.

SUCCESSION POLITICS

Under conditions of succession politics, various issue areas become sensitive barometers of political maneuvering among the elite; foreign and national security policy are such policy realms. They provide opportunities for succession contestants to prove their worthiness and test their mettle. Risk-taking is generally not rewarded at a time of political indeterminacy, when the pressures for consensus and continuity are strong. Political compliance confirms loyalty and party discipline. Deviation from established positions can prove politically costly. Yet, at the same time, taking high-profile positions or actions that appeal to nationalistic sentiment can accrue positively to contestants in the succession sweepstakes. Conversely, if such initiatives fail, they can cost a leader his job. Succession politics thus tends to produce a contradictory atmosphere of caution and conservatism on the one hand, but risk-taking on the other. In the succession to Deng Xiaoping there have been elements of both.

Elite factionalism has been kept to a minimum since the purge of the Yang brothers in 1992.[19] The Deng succession has to date been managed with considerably less overt factionalism than the succession to Mao. While Deng's two previous anointed successors, Hu Yaobang and Zhao Ziyang, were sacked for being soft on democracy, the post-Tiananmen leadership has adopted a hard line internally and externally. Deng's third designated successor, Jiang Zemin, has tried to build up a power base in the Politburo by promoting loyal lieutenants from Shanghai and Shandong to key positions, and he has taken some criticism for this. But it does not seem to have endangered Jiang, and on balance seems to have strengthened his hand as those promoted have proved

---

19. President Yang Shangkun and his half brother Yang Baibing were both PLA generals and both had senior positions on the Central Military Commission. Yang Baibing also headed the General Political Department of the PLA. Yang Shangkun had been Deng Xiaoping's close associate since the mid-1950s; together they masterminded the Tiananmen massacre. The precipitating cause of their purge following the Fourteenth Party Congress in October 1992 was their alleged attempt to dominate the military hierarchy through an extensive factional network. Yang Baibing was also accused of convening several secret meetings to plan a seizure of power in the aftermath of Deng Xiaoping's death. Deng Xiaoping apparently thought these meetings premature and inappropriate, and ordered the Yangs' removal. See Willy Wo-lap Lam, *China After Deng Xiaoping* (Singapore: John Wiley & Sons, 1995); and David Shambaugh, "China's Commander-in-Chief: Jiang Zemin and the PLA," in James Lilley, ed., *China's Military Modernization* (London: Routledge, Kegan Paul, forthcoming).

capable administrators (particularly Politburo members Wu Bangguo, Huang Ju, and Central Committee General Office Head Zeng Qinghong). Jiang has also strengthened his ties with the military, although his relationship with the People's Liberation Army (PLA) is one of mutual need and benefit.[20] Jiang's major rivals are Premier Li Peng and National People's Congress Chairman Qiao Shi. Both have tried to bolster their stature through foreign travel and involvement in the foreign affairs arena, but neither is a player in the national security and military policy domains.

Foreign policy has generally not been an object of factional competition among civilian elites during the Deng succession, although it has been between civilians and the military.[21] By taking tough positions, Chinese leaders demonstrate their nationalist credentials and win vitally important domestic political support. Foreign analysts would do well to remember that strident Chinese posturing is directed more at home than abroad. For Chinese leaders, there might be greater room for cooperation and compromise in the absence of succession politics, but under such conditions compromise is often cast as capitulation. To make concessions would leave leaders open to charges of selling out sovereignty, which is political suicide in the Chinese system. No Chinese politician can afford to appear soft on "hegemony" or "imperialism" and expect to stay in power. Relatively little leeway has been available to civilian Party leaders on litmus-test issues like Hong Kong, Taiwan, the South China Sea, and pressure from the United States because the military High Command has defined the parameters of policy options by defining these issues as core to national sovereignty.

The bullying of Taiwan with provocative military exercises and missile tests in 1995–96 is a case in point. Foreign Minister Qian Qichen and the Foreign Ministry had been perceived by the PLA brass as being "soft on hegemony" since the Gulf War. He was further embarrassed when, after promising to the Politburo that he had received assurances from U.S. Secretary of State Warren Christopher that no U.S. visa would be granted to Taiwan's President Lee Teng-hui, the visa was granted. Qian and paramount leader Jiang Zemin were both forced to make self-criticisms to the Central Military Commission.[22] It also reflected particularly badly on Jiang, who, in February 1995, had made a conciliatory initiative towards Taiwan with the so-called "eight points." When

20. See Shambaugh, "China's Commander-in-Chief."
21. See John Garver, "The PLA and Chinese Foreign Policy," in Lilley, *China's Military Modernization,* forthcoming.
22. Interview with knowledgeable military sources in Beijing, July 16, 1995.

failure of his "carrot" policy was demonstrated by Lee's trip to America, Jiang had no choice but to acquiesce to the "stick," backing the provocative exercises in July 1995 and March 1996 advocated by the PLA brass.

In this supercharged nationalistic atmosphere, Chinese diplomats must attempt to manage bilateral relationships and to make necessary adjustments in international negotiations in such varied issue areas as the Nuclear Non-Proliferation Treaty (NPT); the Comprehensive Test Ban Treaty (CTBT); entry into the World Trade Organization (WTO); the Missile Technology Control Regime (MTCR); intellectual property rights; and resolution of conflicting South China Sea disputes.

SYSTEM FRAGILITY

The second way in which domestic politics affects China's external behavior is social instability and the political system's incapacity to address growing public needs. While this does not necessarily have a direct influence on foreign policy decision-making, the Chinese leadership cannot easily disassociate its domestic environment from its foreign relations. Indeed, there is no more important foreign policy goal than facilitating China's continued modernization and emergence as a world economic power, with accompanying international status and national security. For a nation with a long history of autarchy and weakness, simply keeping the investment and credit lines open to international capital is considered a major foreign policy accomplishment. In China, too, "*Shi jingji, benren!*"[23]

As China has pursued its Open Door Policy in pursuit of rapid economic modernization, various socio-economic fissures have had political consequences for the nation's foreign relations. Pent-up economic, social, and political demands are not being adequately addressed by the state. Given the Communist Party's zero-sum view of state-society political relations—any gain on society's part is a loss for the party-state—formal and informal channels of interest aggregation and articulation are not being created. Civil society is repressed or co-opted, while all forms of protest are seen as seditious dissent.

China is following the well-worn path of other developing countries whereby, at a certain level of economic development and consumer satisfaction, citizens begin to seek improved social services and public policies. The concern is not with democracy, but rather with crime, corruption, health care, education, the environment, unemployment compensation, and delivery of other

---

23. "It's the economy, stupid!"

social services. If the political channels for articulating these demands—or for aggregating these interests via civic or political non-governmental organizations (NGOs)—are unavailable or closed off by the state as they are in China, the split between state and society widens with explosive potential.

China's rulers are nervous about social, economic, and political "instability" (*bu wending*): they would not otherwise have significantly tightened controls over the military and security services, and dealt so harshly with social deviance.

China's economy remains in a halfway house between plan and market.[24] Prices continue to be heavily subsidized and arbitrarily set.[25] The banking sector faces a crisis of insolvency with crippling "chain debts" that make the U.S. savings and loan fiasco pale by comparison.[26] Although approximately 700 million still live in rural areas, the rural sector suffers from severe underemployment. More than 200 million peasants have moved out of agriculture into light industrial manufacturing, or have joined the migratory exodus to coastal cities. Urban governments cannot cope with this influx. The state's biggest economic conundrum, though, is state-owned enterprises (SOE). These socialist behemoths account for nearly 50 percent of China's industrial output and employ at least 50 million workers, yet two-thirds of the 12,000 large and medium-sized state factories lose money. It is estimated that 70 percent of factories are unable to meet payroll on a regular basis.[27] Most people who do draw income stay at home while production lines lie idle due to lack of demand for unsellable goods; it is a classic case of disguised unemployment. Keeping the SOEs afloat severely strains state coffers.[28] Urban unemployment is growing, but due to its fear of adding millions to the unemployment rolls, the government has repeatedly postponed action.

---

24. See Barry Naughton, *Growing Out of the Plan: Chinese Economic Reform, 1978–1993* (New York: Cambridge University Press, 1995); and Andrew G. Walder, ed., *China's Transitional Economy* (Oxford: Oxford University Press, forthcoming 1996).
25. Inflation reached 47 percent in 1994, but has been curtailed through the reimposition of old-style communist price controls, thus delaying the inevitable reckoning that will accompany the phasing out of price and state industrial subsidies.
26. See Nicholas Lardy, *China's Economic Transformation* (Carlisle Barracks, Penn.: U.S. Army War College National Strategy Institute, 1996).
27. Citing internal PRC government documents, Willy Wo-lap Lam, "Unrest on the Cards," *South China Morning Post International Weekly*, December 16, 1995, p. 7.
28. In May 1995 the Chinese government announced that SOEs had total assets of $300 billion and $200 billion in debt. Default on this debt could well cause the collapse of the banking system. The agricultural debt burden is at least as severe. Nicholas Lardy of the Brookings Institution is currently making the first major study of the Chinese banking system. For a discussion of the looming crisis see Lardy, *China's Economic Transformation*.

Politically, the legitimacy of the Chinese Communist Party has seriously weakened. Despite Deng Xiaoping's successful economic reforms, the Party has never really recovered from the damage done by the Cultural Revolution. In recent years, respect for authority has waned and communist ideology has been discredited. Political directives are ignored or compliance is feigned. Many of the old organs of the Leninist state—the Propaganda, Organization, United Front departments—have atrophied.[29] Recruitment into the Communist Party has fallen off; membership is no longer seen as *entrée* into the elite or a guaranteed avenue of upward mobility.

Another telltale sign of eroding Party legitimacy is rampant official corruption. Local Communist Party officials are deeply engaged in *"nomenklatura capitalism."* Given the pivotal role played by the local state in financing development,[30] this problem is systemically rooted in China's economic reforms and is therefore not about to disappear as the result of the government's periodic anti-corruption campaigns.

China's social fabric is fraying. Crimes, drug use, smuggling, prostitution, and other vices are increasing. Secret societies and criminal triads operate nationally and internationally. Alienation is rampant among youth, intellectuals are distraught, and many ethnic minorities chafe under Han chauvinism. The nuclear family is fracturing: divorces rose nearly 100 percent between 1984 and 1994. "Money worship" pervades society and there is a crisis of morality. The general decline in state authority and moral community is the root of the problem, but the erosion of the public security system outside the capital, the opportunities for graft, rising social tensions, and increased access to weapons have all contributed.

While China's leaders are confronted with systemic weaknesses and an array of domestic problems, many social problems do appear to have subsided compared with a year ago. The economic growth and inflation rates have come down to manageable levels (10 and 12 percent respectively), leading some economists to conclude that China has managed the desired "soft landing."

---

29. They are by no means ineffective. The CCP Propaganda Department's control over the media and the Organization Department's control over personnel remain near total. For the effectiveness of the United Front Work Department, one need only examine the CCP's infiltration of Hong Kong. The control of the CCP's political commissar and party committee systems in the military is another example of the continued effectiveness of the Chinese Leninist state. See Kenneth Lieberthal, *Governing China* (New York: W.W. Norton, 1995), chapter 7.
30. See Jean C. Oi, "The Role of the Local State in China's Transitional Economy," *China Quarterly*, No. 144 (December 1995), pp. 1132–1149.

The leadership succession seems more stable than it did a year or two ago, and China's foreign relations show strength in many cases.

However, as long as social and political problems pressure the Chinese government, they will have a bearing on the nation's foreign relations. First, China's leadership will be preoccupied with pressing domestic issues. No government in history has had to cope with the dislocations of modernization on such a massive scale. Second, there has always existed an essential linkage in Chinese thinking between internal disorder and external pressure (*neiluan waihuan*). Further, in traditional Chinese thought the concept of security has always had more of a domestic connotation than an external one.[31] Since coming to power in 1949, Chinese Communist leaders have feared political subversion from outside forces. Since the days when John Foster Dulles first spoke of promoting the "peaceful evolution of Communist China," Chinese leaders have been fearful of American subversion.[32] Such paranoia is exacerbated during times when the regime faces internal unrest and other challenges to its rule.

There is thus a tendency for the Chinese leadership to look for "hostile foreign forces" behind domestic unrest and even deviance within the Communist Party, and a suspicion that other nations have ulterior motives in dealing with China. Thus, foreign demands to change Chinese behavior internally—such as to improve human rights conditions or enforce intellectual property rights—are usually viewed by Chinese leaders as instruments of subversion rather than constructive proposals in their own right. This reinforces China's sensitivities to infringements of sovereignty and its distinction between internal affairs (*neizheng*) and external affairs (*waishi*).

Thus China today has a political system with weak institutions and atrophied mechanisms of control within the context of hegemonic rule. The ruling elite are undergoing wholesale generational turnover and a political succession. The new elite is a conglomerate of *apparatchik*-technocrats who, thus far, pursue incrementalist policies intended above all to preserve their power and maintain

---

31. See David Shambaugh, "Growing Strong: China's Challenge to Asian Security," *Survival*, Vol. 36, No. 2 (Summer 1994), pp. 43–59; and Wang Jisi, *Comparing Chinese and American Conceptions of Security*, Working Paper No. 17 (Toronto: North Pacific Cooperative Security Dialogue [NPCSD], 1992).

32. See David Shambaugh, "Peking's Foreign Policy Conundrum Since Tiananmen: Peaceful Coexistence vs. Peaceful Evolution," *Issues and Studies* (November 1992), pp. 65–85; and Shambaugh, "Patterns of Interaction in Sino-American Relations."

social order. They continue to reform the economic system, but since 1989 have shown little sign of fostering political reforms.

The Chinese Communist Party is riddled with corruption, draws upon shrinking sources of legitimacy, and maintains its rule through coercive power, bargains with local power brokers, and appeals to strident nationalism. The analogy of the current regime to moribund imperial dynasties is apparent to many. When the booming economy suffers the inevitable downturn and living standards stagnate, the most positive tool in the regime's arsenal will disappear. China's current robust growth and international image as a juggernaut economy could quickly turn sour.

While fragile, however, China's political system is not about to implode.[33] Decay is a gradual process. The instruments of statecraft grow dull before they become blunt. Many Chinese dynasties endured in despotic epochs for several generations, and many nations "muddle through" with problems far more acute than China's. Unlike North Korea, China's government is capable of carrying out certain social responsibilities, delivering economic growth, and protecting national security. These are not signs of a system on the verge of collapse. Yet they should not mask underlying systemic weaknesses in the system and the profound challenges facing it in the future.

THE DEVOLUTION OF CENTRAL CONTROL

As central political authority and control has atrophied and decentralized in post-Mao China, it has affected every realm of Chinese governance. Some argue that it has affected China's foreign relations.[34] This is correct with regard to foreign economic relations, scholarly and cultural exchanges, and even arms transfers, but the management of foreign and national security policy is still monopolized by central authorities in Beijing; there is no such thing as a Xinjiang or Shandong foreign policy. Nor do individual Military Regions (MR) have the independence to undertake "neo-warlordism." Since 1989 the command and control structure of the PLA has been significantly recentralized to decrease the possibility of renegade regional commanders. The old distinction between main force units, controlled by the Central Military Commission (CMC), and regional force units controlled by individual MR commanders, has been eliminated; the movement of any troops larger than a battalion must now

---

33. See the exchange between Jack Gladstone ("The Coming Chinese Collapse"); and Huang Yasheng ("Why China Will Not Collapse") in *Foreign Policy*, No. 99 (Summer 1995), pp. 35–68.
34. Segal, *China Changes Shape: Regionalism and Foreign Policy*.

be authorized specifically by the CMC via the PLA General Staff Department, and in no case can troops be moved across Military Region boundaries without CMC approval. Access to weapons and munitions has also been recentralized by the PLA General Logistics Department.

Thus, discussions of the impact of "regionalism" on foreign policy and the supposed emergence of neo-warlordism in China lack an empirical basis. However, provincial and sub-provincial authorities or entrepreneurs do engage in direct foreign trade, play the foreign capital markets, and deal directly with foreign investors or international aid agencies. Local universities, research institutions, and cultural troupes also exchange personnel and participate in international activities. Chinese companies linked to the military-industrial complex have sold and transferred weapons and nuclear materials abroad without the knowledge or approval of central military or civilian authorities.

These activities are all part of China's foreign relations. It means that when Beijing enters into bilateral or multilateral international agreements, it some- times cannot enforce them at home. This has been the case with piracy of software, compact discs, videotapes, and other goods; the sale to Pakistan of ring magnets for plutonium enrichment by China's state nuclear corporation; and the smuggling into the United States of automatic weapons supplied by leading arms export companies. Local authorities erect non-tariff barriers and other impediments to market access that violate World Trade Organization provisions, and private companies export goods made by prison labor. Some naval and border control units are deeply involved in smuggling activities. The Ministry of Space and Aeronautics has placed satellites in orbit in violation of internationally agreed orbital bands.

Numerous other examples exist of external behavior by sub-central units and individuals that contravene Beijing's directives. As China continues to modern- ize, economic power will continue to devolve, and the reach of the central state decline. In terms of China's foreign relations, this means that domestic compli- ance with bilateral and international agreements will be more difficult.

The Decision-making Milieu

Despite decentralization, much of China's behavior on the world stage is still the product of calculated decisions taken by civilian and military elites in Beijing. The decision-makers and their institutional milieu are a critical domes- tic source of China's external behavior.

INSTITUTIONS AND INDIVIDUALS

Foreign policy is normally the preserve of a small handful of leaders and senior officials in the Foreign Ministry, while national security and military policy is even more concentrated in the Central Military Commission and General Staff Department of the PLA. This concentration is accentuated during times of political succession, when foreign policy becomes a sensitive barometer of elite cohesion. Few policy areas in China are as sealed and unsusceptible to societal influences or "raiding" by other bureaucracies than foreign and national security policy. It is generally a closed system not open to domestic lobbying or checks and balances by the National People's Congress.[35] No matter how many domestic constituencies have a vested interest in a given foreign policy outcome, policy deliberations involve relatively few institutions and individuals. This is not the place to delve in depth into the organizational dynamics of the foreign and military policymaking communities, but a brief description of each is in order.[36]

At the apex of the system is the Communist Party Politburo and its Standing Committee (PBSC). The Politburo and PBSC are both proactive and reactive bodies in policy formation.[37] In practical terms the PBSC is the locus of authority over foreign affairs, but it draws in certain members of the broader Politburo when necessary. The PBSC sets the "direction" (*fangzhen*) and "general line" (*zonghe luxian*) for Chinese diplomacy, and adjudicates major diplomatic problems or inter-bureaucratic disputes. In an earlier era, Chairman Mao and Premier Zhou Enlai dominated foreign policy decision-making, but during the 1980s there emerged a more collective division of labor among PBSC members. This division of labor was defined geographically with various members holding different country and region-specific portfolios. It is unclear if this geographic division of labor is still in effect, as Premier Li Peng has seemingly

---

35. The Foreign Affairs Committee under the Standing Committee of the National People's Congress has no decision-making authority and is generally staffed with retired diplomats; its work is restricted to ratification of international treaties and agreements.

36. See Michael D. Swaine, "The PLA and Chinese National Security Policy: Leaders, Structures, Processes," *China Quarterly*, No. 146 (June 1996), pp. xxx-xxx; Carol Lee Hamrin, "Elite Politics and the Development of China's Foreign Relations (especially "Appendix: Structure of the Foreign Affairs System") in Robinson and Shambaugh, *Chinese Foreign Policy*, pp. 70–114. For a more anecdotal and general account see George Yang, "Mechanisms for Foreign Policy Making and Implementation in the Ministry of Foreign Affairs," in Carol Lee Hamrin and Suisheng Zhao, eds., *Decision Making in Deng's China* (Armonk, N.Y.: M.E. Sharpe, 1995), pp. 91–100.

37. Defense and national security policymaking is more concentrated in the Central Military Commission. This policy sphere is detailed in Swaine, "The Role of the PLA in China's National Security Policy Process."

taken preeminent control over the foreign policy–making machinery and particularly policy towards the United States, Russia and former Soviet states, and Europe. Jiang Zemin apparently still oversees Taiwan policy, via his chairmanship of the Taiwan Affairs Leading Group, but has substantial input from Li Peng and military circles. No doubt Jiang also has a significant input into general and specific foreign and national security deliberations, but his role is not preeminent. PBSC member and National People's Congress Chairman Qiao Shi also influences the foreign policy process, and quite likely retains overall responsibility for relations with Asia, Africa, the Middle East, and Latin America. Qiao also retains oversight responsibility for foreign intelligence operations as well as the activities of the Central Committee's International Liaison Department. PBSC member and Vice-Premier Zhu Rongji oversees the international trade and finance sphere (including relations with international organizations and lending agencies) along with Vice-Premier Li Lanqing. Central Military Commission Vice-Chairman Admiral Liu Huaqing, a PBSC member, has overall responsibility for defense policy.[38]

Thus decision-making authority is concentrated among members of the Politburo and its Standing Committee, with responsibility for implementation delegated to the Foreign Ministry, Ministry of Defense, and Ministry of Foreign Trade and Economic Cooperation (MOFTEC). Each member of the Politburo is conscious of each other's turf and generally defers to the individual concerned. Only Jiang Zemin, Foreign Minister Qian Qichen, and Premier Li Peng have authority to speak on a range of foreign policy matters, while only Jiang Zemin, Liu Huaqing, CMC Vice-Chairman Zhang Zhen, and Defense Minister Chi Haotian are licensed to comment on military affairs.[39] In general, however, it appears that Premier Li Peng has unrivaled responsibility for overall management of foreign policy since recovering from his heart attack in 1994. Prior to that time, Deng Xiaoping, Yang Shangkun, and other party elders would frequently intervene, but with Deng physically incapacitated and Yang politically sidelined, Li has moved to centralize control in his hands.[40]

---

38. Liu delegates responsibility for defense intelligence to Vice-Chief of General Staff General Xiong Guangkai.
39. This does not preclude official spokesmen of the Foreign Ministry from commenting in public or civilian and military specialists from expressing views in print or privately.
40. This has reportedly caused some friction with Jiang Zemin and Qiao Shi, but confirming empirical evidence is lacking.

Beneath the PBSC and Central Committee Secretariat there exists a Central Foreign Affairs Leading Small Group (FALSG or *Waishi Xiaozu*).[41] Established in 1958, it is the central leadership's "coordination point" (*kouzi*) to coordinate the management of foreign affairs. Similar Leading Groups exist in other policy spheres and serve as horizontal "interagency" policymaking mechanisms.[42] The FALSG has its own staff office that coordinates paperwork with the General Office and Secretariat of the Central Committee and the Ministry of Foreign Affairs. Its membership is generally composed of several Politburo members plus officials from the State Council and General Staff Department of the PLA. In the past, retired diplomats have also been members (e.g., Ji Pengfei, Zhu Muzhi, Pu Shouchang). While it appears that membership on the FALSG is flexible and changeable, there are some indications that membership is *ex officio*.[43] The Premier of the State Council is normally the chairman of the FALSG, although the Leading Group straddles the Communist Party and State Council hierarchies.

There are some reports that Jiang Zemin seized the FALSG chairmanship from Premier Li Peng when the latter was ill during 1993–94, but all sources now concur that after Li's return to active work he has retaken control.[44] Of course, as president and CCP general secretary, Jiang Zemin is often in the

---

41. For further discussion of the FALSG, see Swaine, "The Role of the PLA in China's National Security Policy Process"; A. Doak Barnett, *The Making of Foreign Policy in China* (Boulder, Colo.: Westview, 1987), p. 44; and Hamrin, "Elite Politics and the Development of China's Foreign Relations: Appendix," pp. 110–112.

42. The importance of the Leading Group system in Chinese policymaking cannot be overstated, although foreign scholars have only "discovered" their importance in recent years. For further discussion of Leading Groups in the Chinese policy process see Carol Lee Hamrin, "The Party Leadership System," in David M. Lampton and Kenneth Lieberthal, eds., *Bureaucracy, Politics, and Decision Making in Post-Mao China* (Berkeley: University of California Press, 1992), pp. 95–124; Wei Li, *The Chinese Staff System: A Mechanism for Bureaucratic Control and Integration* (Berkeley: Institute of East Asian Studies, 1994); and Kenneth Lieberthal, *Governing China* (New York: W.W. Norton, 1995), pp. 192–194. Few openly published Chinese sources even mention the role of Leading Groups, but one recently published source identifies 278 Leading Groups since 1949. See Wang Jingsong, *Zhonghua Renmin Gongheguo Zhengfu yu Zhengzhi* [Government and Politics of the People's Republic of China] (Beijing: Zhonggong zhongyang dangxiao chubanshe, 1995), p. 378–441.

43. FALSG includes, in addition to relevant PBSC members, the premier, foreign minister, director of the State Council Foreign Affairs Office, director of the Central Committee International Liaison Department, defense minister or chief of PLA General Staff, minister of foreign trade and economic cooperation (MoFTEC), director of the Xinhua News Agency International Department, the minister of state security, and a small number of advisers. I am indebted to Michael Swaine for this information.

44. Interviews with knowledgeable officials in Beijing (April 1994) and London (November 1994). However, Lieberthal claims in that "as of 1994 Li Peng remained in charge [of the foreign affairs *kou*]"; Lieberthal, *Governing China*, p. 193.

position of authority to negotiate directly with foreign leaders, but by 1995 the premier's dominance of the FALSG (and the foreign policy machinery more generally) appeared unparalleled.[45] One should not underestimate the role of Foreign Minister Qian Qichen in this process, given his statutory position and membership on the Politburo and FALSG, but it is also clear that Qian has his political weaknesses (especially *vis-à-vis* the PLA).

The FALSG can call on the State Council's Office of Foreign Affairs (*Guowuyuan Waishi Bangongshi*) and Center for International Studies (*Guoji Wenti Yanjiu Zhongxin*) for policy input.[46] The China Institute of Contemporary International Relations (CICIR) also provides the FALSG with research assessments and policy studies, although this large intelligence analysis organization is formally subordinate to the Ministry of State Security (MSS). The MSS and the Propaganda Department of the Party apparently came to play an increasing role in formulating China's policy towards the United States during 1995, and together with representatives of PLA have constituted a dominant coalition in formulating a hardline policy towards the United States.[47]

The policy impact of the FALSG has varied over time. Interview sources indicate that during Mao's lifetime it was rarely convened and performed little more than staff functions to implement the chairman's dictates.[48] During the 1980s, and particularly under Zhao Ziyang's tenure as premier, the FALSG (like other Leading Groups) took on an increasingly advisory function. During the 1990s, under Li Peng's chairmanship, the FALSG has become much more of a deliberative and decision-making body.

While Chinese foreign policy is made at the highest levels of the Chinese party-state, the Ministry of Foreign Affairs (MoFA) has responsibility for day-to-day management of China's foreign affairs. The MoFA's bureaucratic stature has grown during Qian Qichen's tenure as foreign minister. This is the result both of China's further integration into the international community, and of Foreign Minister Qian's increased political standing (he was promoted to the

---

45. Interviews with knowledgeable officials and scholars in Beijing, July 1995; and Swaine, "The Role of the PLA in China's National Security Policy Process."
46. Since 1994 and the appointment of Vice Foreign Minister Liu Huaqiu as director, the State Council Office of Foreign Affairs has reportedly assumed considerable influence and input in the policy formation process. Liu is said to wield considerable influence in the foreign policy process at present, and is reported to be Premier Li Peng's right-hand man in this domain. The State Council Center for International Studies has dramatically declined in influence in recent years since the death of Huan Xiang.
47. Interview with international relations specialist, July 16, 1995, Beijing.
48. Interview with Lin Ke, Mao's personal secretary (*mishu*) for foreign affairs, Beijing, April 24, 1994.

Politburo in 1992) and close ties to Premier Li Peng. In many policy areas the MoFA need not take instructions from the FALSG or higher levels, but it seems to defer on major bilateral relationships. On the other hand, the MoFA and Qian have also come under sharp attack from the military in recent years.

Thus foreign policy is dominated by a handful of Politburo-level officials. Defense and national security policy is handled entirely by the Central Military Commission. During the Deng succession period, decision-making has become even more centralized and concentrated than usual. The tight control and insularity of this decision-making system, and the relative lack of foreign intelligence and information flowing to top policymakers, suggests that Chinese foreign policy is often made in a vacuum where bureaucratic and interest group pressures are minimized, but so are policy options.

Worldview

It is, of course, not just a matter of who makes decisions, but more importantly the perspectives that these individuals bring to policy deliberations. Several operational elements in the worldviews of the current leadership affect how they interpret international events and behavior of other nations and, in turn, condition China's responses and activities on the world stage: (1) the socialization of the key policymakers; (2) the impact of the Tiananmen demonstrations and massacre; and (3) Chinese nationalism.

SOCIALIZATION

Many members of China's principal decision-making elite belong to the generation trained in the Soviet Union during the 1950s. Jiang Zemin, Li Peng, Qiao Shi, Liu Huaqing, Zhu Rongji, Qian Qichen, and Li Lanqing all lived and studied in the Soviet Union during the 1950s. Russian-trained bureaucrats have also risen to the top of many ministries under the State Council. The dominance of this Soviet-trained generation has important implications for Chinese foreign and defense policy, not the least of which is the growing closeness of the Sino-Russian relationship—proclaimed a "strategic partnership" by Jiang Zemin and Boris Yeltsin during the latter's April 1995 visit to China.[49] These leaders do not presently perceive Russia to threaten China's territorial, cultural,

---

49. Patrick Tyler, "With Eye on U.S., Chinese Welcome Yeltsin's Embrace; Jiang Says Beijing and Moscow Forge a 'Strategic Partnership'," *International Herald Tribune*, April 25, 1996; Joseph Kahn, "China, Russia Flaunt New Comradery in an Apparent Warning to the U.S.," *Wall Street Journal*, April 26, 1996.

or political integrity. This set of perceptions helps to explain the relative ease with which the bilateral relationship has adjusted to the collapse of the Soviet Union, and the extraordinary expansion of ties since that time.[50] The Chinese leadership were very distrustful of Gorbachev, but find in Yeltsin a man they "can do business with."[51] They also see allies in Russian Foreign Minister Yevgeny Primakov and the "Eurasian clique" that has come to dominate Russian foreign policy.[52]

Since the abortive *coup d'état* in Moscow in 1991, the Sino-Russian relationship has grown apace in the military, diplomatic, commercial, and science and technological fields. More than 100 bilateral accords have been signed; the 2,580-mile common border has been demarcated and demilitarized; a variety of security confidence-building measures have been implemented, and the relationship is expanding in all spheres. Part of this expansion is restoring a dormant relationship to normal levels, but it has exceeded all expectations. China's leaders also see a willing partner in Moscow at a time when Beijing's ties with Washington are fragile and antagonistic. The PRC can gain access to sensitive technology and weaponry from Russia that the West still embargoes for sale to Beijing. Thus far this has included Sukhoi-27 fighters (with an agreement for co-production of more), Ilyushin-76 transport aircraft (some of which are being refitted to serve as in-flight refueling tankers), Kilo attack submarines, SA-10 surface-to-air missile batteries, AA-8 Aphid air-to-air missiles, and defense technology cooperation in a variety of areas including anti-ballistic missile defense, nuclear submarine technology, tanks and conventional artillery, and anti-submarine warfare.[53]

The Russian orientation of this generation of Chinese leaders, as well as *realpolitik*, motivates Beijing to develop a close partnership with Moscow. Their predecessors had a more hostile experience with the Soviet Union. Conversely, this generation of Chinese leaders is more distrustful of the West, and the

---

50. For an excellent overview see Lowell Dittmer, "China and Russia: New Beginnings," in Samuel Kim, ed., *China and the World*, 3rd ed. (Boulder, Colo.: Westview Press, 1995), pp. 94–112.
51. In political and economic terms, Chinese leaders would feel more comfortable with a new communist government, but they are quite troubled by his calls to restore the former Soviet empire and its borders. For the same reason, Chinese leaders and analysts are even more wary of the ultra-nationalists led by Vladimir Zhirinovsky. These views were conveyed in discussions with Russian specialists and Chinese officials in Beijing during July 1995 and January 1996.
52. See Bilveer Singh, "Russia and East Asia," paper presented at the conference on "Strategic Cultures and Security in East Asia," Ebenhausen, Germany, May 1996.
53. See Bates Gill and Taeho Kim, *China's Arms Acquisitions From Abroad: A Quest for "Superb and Secret Weapons"* (Oxford: Oxford University Press, 1995); and Shambaugh, "China's Military: Real or Paper Tiger?"

United States in particular. The Soviet-trained generation will dominate Chinese politics for some years to come. Now largely in their sixties, they constitute a substantial portion of ministerial-level officials as well as senior leaders. If mandatory retirement regulations are implemented, they could produce early elite turnover, but the fact that China's Cultural Revolution generation is next in line will discourage early retirement. This places the Western-trained generation of the elite even further behind in the queue, even if the majority who have elected to remain abroad return.

Socialization is an important indicator of proclivities and leanings, but ultimately the external orientation of China's leadership depends on what best suits China's quest for modernity and independence. China's leaders will tilt their nation toward any other that does not threaten Chinese sovereignty or security, and that helps modernize China without strings attached. Nationalism and how elites have been taught to understand Chinese history are the most important variables shaping their worldview.

THE ENDURING IMPACT OF 1989

The second element affecting the *weltanschauung* of China's current elite is the experience of the 1989 mass demonstrations, massacre, international isolation, and the collapse of Communist Party rule elsewhere. These events left an indelible mark on the psyche of these elites,[54] and the siege mentality that resulted has by no means fully abated despite the new confidence deriving from China's international rehabilitation and growing economic power.

The events of 1989 convinced the leadership of the potential for social "instability" and they have been warning about it ever since. It also reinforced in their minds the presumption that "hostile foreign forces" will try to cause or take advantage of such instability for their own political purposes. Some see in the United States a government implacably hostile to their own. Since 1989 they have seen not only a concerted campaign of "peaceful evolution" led by the United States,[55] but a broader tendency to isolate and contain an emerging China. The events of 1989 also reinforced in China's leaders a sense of the vulnerability of their own rule, and the critical need for the appearance of unanimity. They believe that overt factionalism—as was evident in the spring of 1989—fuels dissent and encourages foreign forces to take advantage. They

---

54. See, for example, the secret and classified speeches by Chinese Politburo members in *Chinese Law & Government* (Spring 1992).
55. See Shambaugh, "Peking's Foreign Policy Conundrum Since Tiananmen: Peaceful Coexistence vs. Peaceful Evolution."

remain convinced that it was correct to use force to quell the demonstrations, although they appear equally convinced that less drastic riot control methods should have been used if possible. Above all, the events of 1989 increased in their minds the linkage between internal and external subversion.

THE IMPACT OF NATIONALISM

The third and probably most important element in shaping the worldview of China's elite is nationalism. Many recent writings on the subject question the extent to which Chinese even have a "national" identity.[56] As Lucian Pye aptly observed, "China is a civilization pretending to be a state."[57] National consciousness in China today derives from the past, and it promises a future that will restore past glory and dignity; this is what Allen Whiting calls "affirmative nationalism."[58] The Chinese Communist regime has a vested interest in playing up the history of weakness in the face of Western imperialism, territorial division, unequal treaties, invasion, anti-Chinese racism, social chaos, etc., phenomena collectively referred to as "the century of shame and humiliation." The CCP's interest derives from its role in eliminating them in 1949 and during the early years of the People's Republic; hence they are at the heart of a principal claim to Party legitimacy today.

They also have implications for China's future external behavior. One lesson of the past is a particular sensitivity to infringements on territorial integrity or national sovereignty. Another is a wariness of dependency on foreign sources of supply. Thus entry into binding relationships that oblige China to certain behavior domestically will likely be eschewed. When China encounters difficulties in its international interactions today, CCP propagandists are quick to draw parallels to past encounters with imperialism (today labeled "hegemonism"). Widespread indignation about past inequalities and lost great-

---

56. See Lowell Dittmer and Samuel S. Kim, eds., *China's Quest for National Identity* (Ithaca, N.Y.: Cornell University Press, 1993); James Townsend, "Chinese Nationalism," *Australian Journal of Chinese Affairs*, January 1992, pp. 97–130; John Fitzgerald, "The Nationless State: The Search for a Nation in Modern Chinese Nationalism," ibid., January 1995, pp. 75–104; Lucian W. Pye, "How China's Nationalism Was Shanghaied," ibid., January 1993, pp. 107–133; George T. Crane, " 'Special Things in Special Ways': National Economic Identity and China's Special Economic Zones," ibid., July 1994, pp. 71–92; and Wang Jisi, *Comparing Chinese and American Conceptions of Security*.
57. Lucian W. Pye, "China: Erratic State, Frustrated Society," *Foreign Affairs*, Vol. 69, No. 4 (Autumn 1990), p. 54.
58. Allen S. Whiting, "Chinese Nationalism and Foreign Policy After Deng," *China Quarterly* (June 1995), pp. 295–316.

ness, reinforced by a half-century of intensive patriotic propaganda, has resulted in little tolerance for criticism from abroad.

As China has grown economically more powerful, in recent years, nationalism has increased exponentially. One often encounters strident anti-American lectures and denunciations from officials and intellectuals in the foreign policy community in Beijing in recent years, what Whiting describes as "aggressive nationalism."[59]

I would, instead, characterize current Chinese posturing as "defensive nationalism." It is assertive in form, but reactive in essence. It appears self-confident, but really reflects insecurities. It affirms China's glorious past but emphasizes transgressions against its weaknesses. It is occasionally pragmatic, but usually uncompromising. It has a strong moralistic tone. It does not seem imperious or imperial in aspiration, but is arrogant in its singularity and dismissal of others' views and positions. Defensive nationalism reflects basic insecurities about China's society and place in the world. Psychologists quickly recognize such bravado as overcompensation for an insecure ego, and note that it can cause rash behavior.

Increased Chinese nationalism affects the PRC's external dealings in virtually all realms. The stronger China becomes, the more virulently nationalistic will be its external posture. It is unlikely that increased strength will produce a quiet confidence and moderate behavior; rather, it is likely to result in increased defensiveness and assertiveness.

Dealing With China: External-Internal Linkages

These domestic variables suggest a range of pressures on China's foreign relations. How these variables will evolve and interact domestically in China, and how they will respond to various policies of other nations toward China, is impossible to predict with any precision. But they do suggest certain features

---

59. Whiting further distinguishes "assertive nationalism" as more generally xenophobic in nature; other scholars see signs of "confident nationalism" or "pragmatic nationalism" in contemporary Chinese foreign policy. Ibid.; Allen S. Whiting, "Assertive Nationalism in Chinese Foreign Policy," *Asian Survey* (August 1993), pp. 913–933; Michel Oksenberg, "China's Confident Nationalism," *Foreign Affairs*, Vol. 65 (Winter 1986–87), pp. 501–523; Wang Jisi, "Pragmatic Nationalism: China Seeks a New Role in World Affairs," *Oxford International Review*, Vol. 6, No. 1 (Winter 1994), pp. 28–30, 51, 64.

that will be present and will influence how China may respond to policies of containment or engagement.

THE IMPACT OF DOMESTIC POLITICS
The Chinese leadership will be preoccupied with complex domestic issues for some time to come. Foreign relations are not likely to rate high on the policy agenda; when they do, they will tend to be viewed in the context of linkages to the domestic economy, society, and polity. Given the significant systemic weaknesses detailed above, the Chinese leadership will tend to interpret all foreign relations through a domestic political prism: Will they enhance or undermine CCP rule? Will they strengthen or weaken China?

The uncertainties of succession politics and perceived external threats to CCP rule combine with profound elite fears of internal social instability to produce a regime that is insular, paranoid, and reactive. Thus, Chinese leaders will not be capable of taking major initiatives on the world stage, nor of compromising with foreign (particularly American) demands. They will be highly suspicious of the agendas of Western nations and international organizations, and will generally be a truculent partner in international dealings. Their intense nationalism only stiffens their spine and emboldens their resolve.

ENGAGEMENT. The Western policy of engagement will be treated suspiciously. That the implicit policy goal of engagement is to transform China's international and domestic behavior based on rules and norms largely set by Western nations and organizations is not lost on the Chinese. The Chinese leadership, Foreign Ministry, military, and international relations institutes strongly suspect that engagement is merely a form of "soft containment" or "peaceful evolution." It was no accident that Jiang Zemin asked President Clinton during their October 1995 meeting in New York, "Are you trying to contain China or not?" President Clinton reportedly responded, "No, no, I am trying to engage, I don't want to contain you."[60]

Strict Chinese definitions of state sovereignty and proclivities toward *realpolitik* further incline Chinese elites to be wary of multilateralism, internationalism, and interdependence. Nations or global institutions that pursue universalistic agendas, particularly those based on Western liberal principles, are largely unacceptable to the Chinese government. China's strong preference is to deal with nation-states bilaterally, rather than with international regimes multilat-

---

60. The conversation, leaked by the Clinton administration, was reported by Thomas Friedman in the *New York Times*, April 17, 1996. The White House Press subsequently confirmed this exchange.

erally. China will cooperate only when it is in its specific national interests to do so, not because of a commitment to international behavioral norms.[61] Beijing is a ruthless and hard bargainer that intensely guards its sense of sovereignty and national interests. It bends only when the *quid pro quo* is financially worthwhile (such as reform policies that bring World Bank and IMF loans) or when the penalties of not compromising or complying are unacceptably high. The Chinese government generally eschews binding obligations that commit China to enforce international treaties and agreements inside of its borders.

Because of its domestic politics, China cannot and will not reciprocate the Western policy of "engagement" because, on the one hand, the regime views it as a policy of subversion and, on the other, the costs of adapting to international rules and norms are too high.

CONTAINMENT. A policy of containment would certainly confirm Chinese elite suspicions about Western subversion and hostility to the Communist regime. A containment policy would work directly against Western desires to improve human rights, stimulate civil society, and pluralize politics in China. All leverage would be lost and China would have no incentives to cooperate in these or other realms; indeed, it would be free to act with impunity. A China unconstrained by the global system would be far more dangerous and injurious to Western (and Asian) interests. Nor would containment be practically viable; Asian, European, and North American countries could not forge a united front to pursue such a policy. Japan, ASEAN, and the European Union have already made it quite clear that they have no interest in containing China.[62]

Thus, a policy of containing China is a non-starter. It could not be effectively implemented even if the United States sought to do so; even if it were, it would consume incalculable resources. The West tried to contain China for two decades after the Communists came to power. The policy failed badly. Since Nixon abandoned containment in 1971, U.S. administrations and G-7 governments have engaged the People's Republic, with substantial benefit to China and the world. A policy of engaging and opening China has proved to stabilize Asian

---

61. Samuel Kim and others disagree, and argue that China accepts interdependence and embraces multilateralism. While it is true that China has now signed more international agreements and participates in more multilateral bodies that ever before, I do not believe that this *ipso facto* sustains Kim's view. For further elaboration on this subject see Harry Harding, ed., *China's Cooperative Relations* (forthcoming).

62. See David Shambaugh, *China and Europe, 1949–1995* (London: Contemporary China Institute, School of Oriental & African Studies, 1996); and Shambaugh, "China and Japan Towards the Twenty-first Century: Rivals for Preeminence or Complex Interdependence?" in Christopher Howe, ed., *China and Japan: History, Trends and Prospects* (Oxford: Oxford University Press, 1996).

security, while a policy of containing and isolating China had the opposite effect. It would be foolhardy, dangerous, and morally irresponsible to return to a failed policy abandoned a quarter of a century ago.

With either engagement or containment, Chinese domestic politics suggest that Beijing is unlikely to be very cooperative. But there is far better chance of eliciting modest cooperation through engagement.

CENTRALIZED DECISION-MAKING

The nature of the decision-making system affects how China responds to Western policies of engagement or containment. Centralization and the influence of the military make the actors particularly attuned to any hint of containment, and contribute to the predisposition to see a containment policy where none exists.

The highly centralized nature of the system also means that the nuances and complex rationale for the engagement policy are probably not explained to, or digested by, Chinese leaders. They are puzzled by the whole concept. Interviews with Chinese international relations and America specialists indicate a severe case of cognitive dissonance, in that many see engagement as another form of "peaceful evolution" or "soft containment." There is even difficulty in defining the term "engagement" and conveying its meaning in Chinese. The common translation for engagement is *jiechu,* which does reflect the verb "to engage" (as in "engaging the enemy"), but its more common usage simply means "contact."[63] Interviews with China's leading America specialists indicate that they have a better understanding of the policy debates that have led to the engagement policy, but are still puzzled by its significance and suspicious of its intent. "Why shouldn't America engage China? We are a great power," said one.[64]

PERCEPTIONS

The prevailing worldview of Chinese elites undergirds the insular effects of domestic politics, creates several "screens" through which external information is filtered, and brings a strong dose of nationalism to bear on policy responses. The Soviet socialization of China's current generation of ruling elites, their Leninist discipline, and the experiences of 1989–91 combine with a distrust of

63. Beijing Foreign Languages Institute English Department, ed., *Han-Ying Cidian* [Chinese-English Dictionary] (Beijing: Commercial Press, 1985), p. 344.
64. Interview with member of the Institute of American Studies, Chinese Academy of Social Sciences, July 18, 1995.

international interdependence and foreign agendas to produce a strong defensive nationalism in China's dealings with the Western world.

Nationalism will make it very difficult for foreign interlocutors to elicit cooperation on issues that trigger historical sensitivities. Contemporary Chinese nationalism is not really self-confident. It recalls ill-treatment at the hands of Japan and Western powers during the "century of shame and humiliation"; many present-day challenges to Chinese policy are filtered through this historical prism. One might have expected China's growing power to help overcome this insecurity and defensiveness, but in fact it seems to have fueled it.

China's strict sense of national sovereignty and concomitant distrust of interdependence and multilateralism will further fuel fears of engagement, as transnational issues, multilateral regimes, and integration into the international system play such a central role in the strategy.

Conclusion

These three sets of domestic sources reinforce each other and suggest that, no matter how fine-tuned or well-intended the Western and Asian policy, China will be difficult to engage in the years to come. The insular and defensive character of Chinese politics and nationalism suggests that China will be reluctant and difficult to engage and to integrate into the existing international order. However, there is no alternative but to try. The potential costs of not doing so are too high. China's capacity to disrupt and destabilize international security, the world economy, global environment, and human welfare are substantial. The world and China will be far better off if one-quarter of mankind becomes a cooperative partner in the international community.

East Asia and the "Constrainment" of China

Gerald Segal

$\mathbf{T}$he remarkable economic growth in East Asia depends on further modernization of political and social systems throughout the region. Stability and growth also depend on the development of an international system that restrains non–status quo powers and develops mechanisms for managing and resolving conflicts short of war. There is little doubt that the single most important state in East Asia is China: a China that collapses in chaos, or is aggressive in the region, can wreck the prosperity of the region.

Is regional security in East Asia impossible when China is strong? Is regional insecurity especially likely when a rising China is insecure about whether it can sustain its rise, and whether others will allow it to rise? How should other states deal with the state that may be the single largest force for change in the global balance of power?

Sadly, the debate on these questions is often unsophisticated. On the one hand the dominant "engagement" school argues that China can be neutered as a challenge to the status quo, by giving it incentives to join regional and global society. The engagement school believes that there is no need to think in terms of a balance of power because stability will be provided by states anxious not to lose the benefits of economic interdependence.[1] There is another school of

Gerald Segal is a Senior Fellow at the International Institute for Strategic Studies, Director of the Economic and Social Research Councils Pacific Asia Programme, and Co-chairman of the European Council for Security Cooperation in Asia-Pacific.

This work is the result of extensive interviews in nearly every country in East Asia in 1994–95. All interviews were on a confidential basis. But the author would like to thank the following people for commenting on all, or parts of an earlier draft of this article: Sidney Bearman, Barry Buzan, Bates Gill, Paul Godwin, Harlan Jencks, Ellis Joffe, Gary Klintworth, Michael Leifer, Paul Monk, Jonathan Pollack, Michael Swaine, David Shambaugh, Allen Whiting, and the anonymous reviewers for *International Security*.

1. For example see Kishore Mahbubani, "The Pacific Impulse," *Survival*, Vol. 37, No. 1 (Spring 1995); James Richardson, "East Asian Stability," *The National Interest*, No. 38 (Winter 1994–95); Morton Abramowitz, "Pacific Century: Myth or Reality," *Contemporary Southeast Asia*, Vol. 15, No. 3 (December 1993). Some of the engagement school is struggling with ways to add a dose of realism. See the notion of "conditional engagement" and "virtual alliances" as discussed in a study program on China currently underway in the Council on Foreign Relations. I am grateful to Jim Shinn of the Council for an opportunity to see the work in progress.

International Security, Vol. 20, No. 4 (Spring 1996), pp. 107–135
© 1996 by the President and Fellows of Harvard College and the Massachusetts Institute of Technology.

thought that China must be "contained." The containment school argues that the balance of power in East Asia is becoming dangerously unstable.[2]

The notions of "engagement" and "containment" are left over from the Cold War, and for that reason alone they are insufficient categories of analysis for the special problem of coping with a rising China. Instead, this article argues that engagement is a vital, necessary but insufficient policy towards China. China is a powerful, unstable non–status quo power.[3] Those states whose interests are in conflict with China should defend those interests by constraining China where they can. Formulating a policy of "constrainment" requires an assessment of whether China's neighbors and powers further afield are strong enough to resist China. I argue that they are, but that it also requires the will to do so. The evidence presented below suggests that most states lack the will to constrain China. A careful look at recent trends, and especially responses to China's activity in the South China Sea, reveals that China is not constrained by concerns that it might damage its increasingly important economic interdependence with East Asia. I identify the risks of a policy that engages China through interdependence but does not also constrain its undesired behavior, and suggest the possibilities for the success of a more constraining policy.

China and East Asia: Balancing Room?

Balancing and constraining China in East Asia might appear at first glance to be an impossible task. China is 68 percent of East Asian territory and some 65 percent of the East Asian population (See Figure 1.)[4] These fundamental bases

---

2. Paul Dibb, *Towards a New Balance of Power in Asia*, Adelphi Paper No. 295 (London: International Institute for Strategic Studies [IISS]/Oxford University Press, May 1995). See related arguments in Richard K. Betts, "Wealth, Power and Instability: East Asia and the United States after the Cold War," *International Security*, Vol. 18, No. 3 (Winter 1993–94); Aaron Friedberg, "Ripe for Rivalry: Prospects for Peace in a Multi-polar Asia," ibid.; and Barry Buzan and Gerald Segal, "Rethinking East Asian Security," *Survival*, Vol. 36 No. 2 (Summer 1994). These issues have become a trendy and sometimes vibrant focus of debate. See, e.g., Shannon Selin, *Asia-Pacific Arms Buildup*, Working Paper No. 6 (Vancouver: University of British Colombia, Institute of International Relations (1994); Andrew Mack and Pauline Kerr, "The Evolving Security Discussions in the Asia-Pacific," *The Washington Quarterly*, Vol. 18, No. 1 (1995); and Jonathan Pollack, "Sources of Instability and Conflict in Northeast Asia," *Arms Control Today*, November 1994.
3. Gerald Segal, *China Changes Shape*, Adelphi Paper No. 287 (London: IISS/Oxford University Press, March 1994). On the optimist side see William Overholt, *The Rise of China* (New York: Norton, 1993); and most recently, Jim Rohwer, *Asia Rising* (New York: Simon & Schuster, 1995). For a range of academic views see Thomas Robinson and David Shambaugh, eds., *Chinese Foreign Policy* (Oxford: The Clarendon Press, 1994).
4. Figure 1 and Table 1 were produced by Digby Waller, the Defence Economist at the International Institute for Strategic Studies.

Figure 1. Percentage of East Asia by population, land, GDP, defense spending, exports.

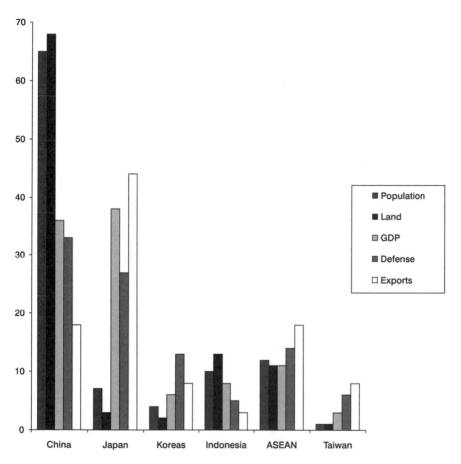

NOTE: All figures are for 1994, except exports (1993). ASEAN figure does not include Indonesia; China figures include Hong Kong.

of power are relatively unchanging. The only other region in the world where the balance of power is so dominated by a single state is North America. The contrast to the far more balanced European condition is striking.[5]

5. Perhaps it is precisely because the European theater seems so susceptible to complex balances, and East Asia seems so unsuited, that the European balances have received so much analytical attention, and East Asian balances are virtually virgin analytical territory. Henry Kissinger, *Diplo-*

The imbalances in terms of size and population in East Asia have existed for centuries—indeed longer in East Asia than anywhere else in the world. The result has been a centuries-old, distinctly unbalanced pattern of international relations. Before the coming of European imperialism (only in strength in the seventeenth century), the political units were rarely engaged with one another. When they were, the nature of the balance of power depended overwhelmingly on whether China was strong. A strong China cast a long shadow over its smaller neighbors. When China was weak, the neighbors were far more free to engage in relations with only parts of China and were not subject to significant Chinese pressure. Some of China's neighbors, most notably Japan and Korea, did manage to develop the basis of healthy, strong and independent political cultures, but they knew that their independence depended overwhelmingly on China remaining weak. The peoples of Southeast Asia were far less successful in organizing strong and persistent political entities, and therefore this region was much more deeply affected by the patterns of interaction set during the era of European domination and then by the overlay of the Cold War in the second half of the twentieth century. When the Cold War overlay was lifted (much earlier in East Asia than in Europe), both the relatively strong states of Northeast Asia, and the much weaker ones in Southeast Asia, knew that the future pattern of international relations in their region depended on whether they had a strong or weak Chinese neighbor.[6]

The Chinese empire spent most of the twentieth century in tatters. In 1850 China was still, nominally, the world's largest economy, but by the end of the nineteenth century it was losing territory all around its rim to rapacious foreigners. By the end of the twentieth century, China has regained only a little of what it lost. Apart from offshore islands taken from Taiwan, islands in the South China Sea, and the prospect of regaining Hong Kong in 1997, the boundaries of the Chinese state are little changed from the late nineteenth century. The result is an irredentist China with a boulder rather than just a chip on its shoulder.

China can afford to shoulder the boulder because in the intervening century China has gone from basket case to economic boom. As geo-economic histori-

---

macy (New York: Simon & Schuster, 1994); Richard Rosecrance, "A New Concert of Powers," *Foreign Affairs*, Vol. 71, No. 2 (Spring 1992), pp. 64–82; Coral Bell, *The Post-Soviet World* (Canberra: Strategic and Defence Studies Centre, 1992); John Mearsheimer, "Back to the Future: Instability in Europe After the Cold War," *International Security*, Vol. 15, No. 1 (Summer 1990), pp. 5–56. See also William Pfaff, *The Wrath of Nations* (New York: Simon & Schuster, 1993).
6. Gerald Segal, *Rethinking the Pacific* (Oxford: The Clarendon Press, 1990).

Table 1. Countries as a Percentage of East Asia.

	Population	Land Surface	GDP 1994 (1992)	Military Spending 1994 (1992)	Exports 1993 (1992)
China & HK	65.2	68.3	35.7 (33.8)	33.3 (32.5)	18.1 (17.6)
Indonesia	10.4	13.4	7.6 (8.0)	5.4 (5.0)	3.3 (3.3)
Japan	6.8	2.7	37.5 (38.3)	27.0 (26.7)	44.4 (45.3)
Vietnam	3.9	2.4	0.7 (0.7)	1.3 (1.4)	0.3 (0.2)
Philippines	3.6	2.2	2.1 (2.3)	2.3 (2.2)	0.9 (1.5)
Thailand	3.2	3.7	4.6 (4.7)	5.4 (6.1)	3.9 (3.7)
S. Korea	2.4	0.7	5.6 (5.8)	9.9 (9.1)	7.9 (7.9)
Taiwan	1.2	0.2	2.8 (2.9)	6.4 (6.3)	8.3 (8.5)
N. Korea	1.2	0.9	0.3 (0.4)	3.2 (4.0)	0.1 (0.1)
Malaysia	1.1	2.4	2.1 (2.1)	3.3 (4.4)	4.3 (4.0)
Singapore	0.2	0.0	0.8 (0.9)	1.8 (1.6)	8.2 (7.7)

SOURCES: International Institute for Strategic Studies, World Bank, IMF. Gross domestic product (GDP) and defense spending rates are purchasing-power parity (PPP). Exports are for merchandise and invisibles.

ans have pointed out, there does seem to be some strong correlation between economic power and the ability of empires to satisfy their territorial claims. But China's sustained economic growth is still in its early stages. As Table 1 shows, China is far from being a dominant power in East Asia according to many measurements of power. It is true that its relative economic and military power is increasing, but sustained economic growth in China only seems possible in a very decentralized political and economic system.[7] China is also hobbled by weak leaders, massive social problems, and internal migration said to number between 100 and 150 million people.[8] In short, China is much weaker than it appears at first glance.

Nevertheless, China still feels that it has legitimate claims to territory and to increased status in East Asia and the wider world. The challenge for East Asia and the wider world is whether China should be allowed to take the territory, power and status that it claims, or whether it should be constrained while it is still relatively vulnerable.

East Asia need not travel "back to the future," if only because so many East Asian states, most notably Japan, are much stronger than they were in pre-

---

7. The process and problems of Chinese decentralization are discussed in David Goodman and Gerald Segal, eds., *China Deconstructs* (London: Routledge, 1994).
8. Paul Smith, "The Strategic Implications of Chinese Emigration," *Survival*, Vol. 36, No. 2 (Summer 1994).

European times. The international system is also very different. China's growth depends to a great degree on being economically and perhaps even politically interdependent with the international system, and that openness might well be put at risk by aggressive irredentism. China's prospects for growth depend on other states providing markets for its goods, raw materials and investment for its economy, and information and technology for its development. Thus there clearly is a basis for East Asians and the wider world to manage a growing China, but East Asian powers must be prepared to take steps to do so.

WILL EAST ASIA BALANCE?

Objective conditions for balancing China are not the same as real policies to do so. In the nineteenth century the key to ensuring a balance against a strong adversary was developing a sufficient commonality of interests to hold together a coalition. The strategy also depended on there being a core of relatively strong states who were prepared to articulate and then act upon such a commonality of interests. In East Asia there may be a commonality of interest, but there seems to be little will to articulate let alone act upon shared interests.

The fracture lines in East Asia are clear enough. First, in East Asia a wide range of capabilities confronts China. As Figure 1 and Table 1 show, there are few states that might qualify as a great power, but a large number of middle or smaller powers. Only two countries have more than 100 million people (Japan and Indonesia). Only Australia and Russia have huge territories on China's scale, but both have small populations. Russia is a great power, but only to someone looking from Europe.[9] Its backside in Asia is vulnerable, especially given the fact that, apart from Japan, it was the last to seize large swaths of territory from a weak China. Koreans are still divided, but even if united would still be the smallest state in Northeast Asia. The Association of South-East Asian Nations (ASEAN) states are mostly aspiring middle powers and in any case their combined gross domestic product (GDP) is less than that of Australia and New Zealand combined. Indonesia is the only substantial ASEAN power, and it is the most distant from China.

9. Michael Bradshaw, *The Economic Effects of Soviet Dissolution* (London: Royal Institute of International Affairs, 1993); and Bradshaw, *Siberia in a Time of Change*, No. 2171 (London: Economist Intelligence Unit, 1992). See also Andre Voskressenski, "Current Concepts of Sino-Russian Relations and Frontier Problems in Russia and China," *Central Asian Survey*, Vol. 13, No. 3 (1994); and Gerald Segal, *The Soviet Union and the Pacific* (London: Unwin Hyman for the Royal Institute of International Affairs, 1990).

Second, the East Asians have a range of different interests regarding China. In some cases, some people raise questions about the loyalty of large parts of the population that are ethnic Chinese.[10] Because ethnic Chinese are a majority of the population in Singapore, many in the region suspect any Singaporean keenness on close co-operation with China on Chinese terms. On the other hand, in Taiwan there is also a majority ethnic Chinese population, but because many of them fled the communist take-over of the mainland and value their current prosperity and independence, they generally are more hostile towards mainland China. The attitudes of Koreans towards China are dominated by their perception of how it affects the conflict over the unification of Korea.

Alone among the major players, Japan has no significant ethnic Chinese population, but it does have a tradition of independence from and rivalry with China. Indonesia has a more powerful (but still small) ethnic Chinese population, but a less consistent, albeit sometimes intense worry about China.[11] These two countries might have been expected to work more closely together in thinking about China, but both have had their eyes on other challenges. Indonesia has seen itself as playing a leading role on the ASEAN or Non-Aligned stage, while Japan has remained bound into an alliance with the United States and sees its role as on the global and most notably the G-7 stage. It is almost as if Japan, because of its behavior in China in the 1930s and 1940s, has avoided thinking long and hard about how to handle China.[12] Indonesia has, until recently, simply considered China as not much constraint on its behavior.

Because of these different positions towards, and interests in China, the states of East Asia have interacted with China in very different ways. Japan and Korea have found that their trade and investment relations are increasingly focused on China's northern coastal areas. Russia does most of its business with Northeast China, while Hong Kong and Taiwan focus on southern coastal China.[13] States farther from China have less clear-cut regional relationships. Singapore, much like the European or "Anglo-Saxon" states of the Pacific rim, does a great

---

10. Tim Huxley, *Insecurity in the ASEAN Region* (London: Royal United Services Institute, 1993); and Amitav Acharya, *A New Regional Order in South-East Asia,* Adelphi Paper No. 279 (London: IISS/Oxford University Press, May 1993). See also Michael Leifer, *ASEAN and the Security of Southeast Asia* (London: Routledge, 1989).
11. Michael Leifer, *Indonesia's Foreign Policy* (London: Allen and Unwin for the Royal Institute of International Affairs, 1983).
12. Kenichiro Sasae, *Rethinking Japan-U.S. Relations,* Adelphi Paper No. 292 (London: IISS/Oxford University Press, December 1994).
13. Goodman and Segal, *China Deconstructs,* on different regions.

deal of business with central coastal China. In short, there are signs that the decentralization within China is reflected in the more fragmented relationship that the outside world is developing with China.

The fragmented attitude to China is also evident on key East Asian issues. Concern over the proliferation of nuclear weapons in North Korea affects China's relations with other states in Northeast Asia, but has little resonance in Southeast Asia. Concern over ethnic Chinese populations is a factor in China's relations in Southeast Asia, but has no role in Northeast Asia. China's difficult negotiations regarding entry into the World Trade Organization (WTO), or its violation of international copyright agreements, are of primary interest to states with the most developed service sectors, and have little role in Sino–Southeast Asian relations. Thus there is a clear tendency for states to take different views of China, and for China to be able to play on such differences.

Because East Asia is generally fragmented, the result, in a third feature of the region, is the relative lack of East Asian institutions or even a clear sense of regional international society.[14] The ability to balance and constrain China does not only depend on the existence of such institutions. Nevertheless, most East Asians understand that it is in China's interest that such institutions do not develop, especially in the security sphere. As the strongest and rising power, it is in China's interest to deal with its neighbors bilaterally, and to seek to reduce any efforts to "internationalize" aspects of foreign policy that would result in more actors being capable of working together to balance China.

China is not the main reason for the slow development of APEC (Asia-Pacific Economic Cooperation), but it is an important factor in the long term. In the shorter term, a primary problem has been the tension between those who wish to see what is essentially a non-white East Asian group (Malaysia's proposal for an East Asia Economic Caucus, or EAEC), and those who see the benefit of a more open trans-Pacific APEC.[15] Obviously an EAEC has less chance of remaining economically open, and certainly less ability to resist a growing China that in 1995 became the largest economy in the region, according to World Bank purchasing power parity (PPP) calculations of GDP.

The very tentative nature of East Asian regionalism is even more evident in the security realm. The ASEAN Regional Forum (ARF)—an informal collection

---

14. David Dewitt, "Common, Comprehensive and Cooperative Security," *The Pacific Review*, Vol. 7, No. 1 (1994); and Paul Evans, "Building Security," *The Pacific Review*, Vol. 7 No. 2 (1994).
15. "ASEAN and Regional Security," *Strategic Survey 1994–1995* (London: IISS/Oxford University Press, 1995).

of states in Asia-Pacific (as well as the European Union)—makes no pretense of seeking to shape the security policy of member states. Even its most ardent supporters acknowledge that the ARF will not begin to consider matters of conflict resolution for many years. Cynics may see the ARF as little more than a gentleman's dining or golf club, because no one is willing to articulate the nature of the primary security concern: China. Even in the parallel, non-governmental track-two process of CSCAP (Council on Security and Cooperation in Asia-Pacific), China has been able to block significant membership for Taiwan. From the Chinese point of view, it is advantageous not to have an effective collective or even co-operative security system, for it is inevitable that such a system would be primarily intended to constrain the largest power.[16] As one ASEAN official put it, China and its neighbors know that if East Asians do not hang together, they will certainly hang separately.

Does Interdependence Restrain China?

The analysis so far suggests that there are objective conditions, but little propensity, for China to be balanced and restrained by East Asians. One reason for the lack of will to constrain China is the assumption, as stated by the "engagement" school, that China will be restrained by the need for economic interdependence. In 1993–94 this question was tested on the anvil of Hong Kong policy. The answer seemed to be that Chinese behavior was to some extent constrained, but for a complex and perhaps unique series of reasons.[17]

---

16. For some indication of Chinese thinking, unofficially, see the *Kyodo* report of a high-level Chinese policy document reportedly opposed to regional security schemes. January 29, 1995, in British Broadcasting Corporation (BBC), Summary of World Broadcasts (SWB), Far East (FE/) 2216/G1. See also Huang Fan-zhang, "East Asian Economics: Development, Cooperation Prospects, and China's Strategy" in Barbara Bundy, et al., eds., *The Future of the Pacific Rim* (London: Praeger, 1994). A good Western analysis appears in Bonnie Glaser and Banning Garrett, "Multilateral Security in the Asia-Pacific Region and its Impact on China's Interests: Views from Beijing," *Contemporary Southeast Asia*, Vol. 16 No. 1 (June 1994). The author is also grateful for insights from Susan Shirk based on her "track two" dialogue with the Chinese on these issues. See also Denny Roy, "Hegemon on the Horizon? China's Threat to East Asian Security," *International Security*, Vol. 19, No. 1 (Summer 1994); John Garver, "China's Push Through the South China Sea," *The China Quarterly*, December 1992; Harry Harding, "A Chinese Colossus," *Journal of Strategic Studies*, Vol. 18, No. 3 (September 1995).
17. See a wide-ranging discussion in the UK House of Commons Foreign Affairs Committee in *Relations Between the UK and China in the Period up to and Beyond 1997* (London: HMSO, March 1994). See also Percy Cradock, *Experiences of China* (London: John Murray, 1994); and Gerald Segal, "A Clearer Fate for Hong Kong," *The World Today*, February 1994.

When the new British Governor, Chris Patten, proposed democratic reforms in defiance of Chinese wishes, China's first instinct was to shout and threaten dire consequences, seemingly in disregard of its economic interests in a stable Hong Kong. At first glance, China's policy offered scant support for the notion of restraint through interdependence. And yet China soon found that the bluster failed to cow the people of Hong Kong into rejecting the Patten proposals, and Beijing was unwilling to carry through on most of its dire threats. In effect it adopted a wait-and-see approach and took part in local elections, hoping that it might do well enough to undermine Patten in a more subtle fashion. When it failed to do so in the elections to the Legislative Council in September 1995, China still did not revert to its dire threats, and instead carefully tried to isolate Governor Patten.

Beijing's bite amounted to something less than its bark, in part because policy towards Hong Kong was no longer simply a matter of central government fiat. Too many people in the more decentralized Chinese political and economic system have a stake in stability in Hong Kong. Whether due to the "Red Princes"—the wealthy and powerful children of senior leaders—or the local authorities in southern coastal China, the result was a more fragmented and pragmatic Chinese policy. To the extent that these decentralized forces in China drew some of their power from their international connections, the Hong Kong case provided evidence that China's hand was stayed by interdependence. More accurately, this was evidence of how China can be constrained by interdependence, even in the teeth of opposition from the central government.

While the Hong Kong case is often explained away as unique, it was far more difficult to dismiss the importance of the next major test of the notion that China could and would be constrained by economic interdependence.

The South China Sea Case

China has never hidden its claim to complete sovereignty in the South China Sea. Ever since China emerged from the distractions of the Cultural Revolution, it has sought carefully to extend its control of these disputed waters.[18] China has insisted on its unshakable legal claim to the region, although it has frustratingly never explained the legal basis of its policy nor defined the precise limits of its claim. China signed but has not yet ratified the 1982 United Nations

---

18. Lo Chi-kin, *China's Policy Towards Territorial Disputes* (London: Routledge, 1989); Mark Valencia, *China and the South China Sea*, Adelphi Paper No. 297 (London: IISS/Oxford University Press, July 1995); Michael Gallagher, "China's Illusory Threat to the South China Sea," *International Security*, Vol. 19, No. 1 (Summer 1994).

Convention on the Law of the Sea. Beijing has given no indication that it would accept international arbitration of its claim to sovereignty over every bit of territory in the region. China has been reluctant to take the issue to the International Court of Justice (ICJ) in part because, like all the other claimants (Taiwan, Vietnam, Malaysia, Philippines, Brunei), its claim to sovereignty is weak.[19] China has applied the continental shelf principle in defining its maritime claims in the Yellow and East China Sea, but claims the South China Sea on the basis of "historic use and administration."[20] However, China has clearly not had continuous and effective control, administration, and governance of the territory, as the latter principle calls for. And even if some sovereignty claims would be upheld by the court, the tiny outcrops in the sea do not appear to be legally qualified to justify exclusive economic zones of 200 nautical miles or even more extensive con- tinental shelves. Only 26 features in the Spratly group are above water at high tide and the largest has a land area of less than half a square kilometer. None has ever sustained a permanent population. Continental shelf claims from states surrounding the Spratlys are likely to be seen as much stronger by the ICJ.

It appears, as Michael Swaine of the RAND Corporation has suggested, that Chinese claims "have more to do with power than law."[21] Clearly the Chinese do not feel that they have to negotiate with anyone about this issue. The furthest reaches of the South China Sea stretch some 1800 km from undisputed Chinese territory on Hainan island, and touch Natuna island (in the south of the South China Sea) held by Indonesia.[22] China moved south in stages, taking the Paracel islands from Vietnam in 1974, and then building an airstrip on the islands capable of handling fighters and transport aircraft. In the 1980s China extended its control into the more southerly Spratly group. The most publicized clash in the Spratlys came in 1988, when several Vietnamese ships were destroyed in one engagement.

---

19. Valencia, *China and the South China Sea;* and Mark Valencia with Jon M. Van Dyke and Noel Ludwig, "The Solution for the Spratly Islands Ought to Look Like This," *International Herald Tribune,* October 10, 1995.
20. In June 1995, in the midst of a new period of anxiety in Southeast Asia about the South China Sea, Chinese archaeologists claimed to have found porcelain fragments there dating back to the Song Dynasty (960–1279). *Xinhua* (China's News Agency) on June 13, 1994, in SWB FE/2332/G7.
21. Michael Swaine quoted in *Far Eastern Economic Review,* April 13, 1995, p. 25. For a classic example of the Chinese line of argument see the interview with a Chinese State oceanographic official in *Wen Wei Po,* April 17, 1995, in SWB FE/2284/G1–3. See also *Ta Kung Pao,* February 26, 1995, in SWB FE/2241/G/1–2.
22. For a careful analysis of the legal issues, see Daniel Dzurek, "China Occupies Mischief Reef in Latest Spratly Gambit," *International Boundary Research Unit Boundary and Security Bulletin* (London), April 1995, pp. 65–71.

By the early 1990s, the six rival claimants were all busy reinforcing their postures and seeking contracts with foreign firms to explore for oil and gas. In August 1990, Chinese Premier Li Peng declared in Singapore that China was prepared to put aside the question of sovereignty and jointly develop the Spratlys. But it soon became clear that China was not in fact interested in anything that might "internationalize" the problem, and refused any serious efforts at multilateral negotiations.[23] China's position was far better pursued in bilateral relations where it could pick off one rival after another. In October 1991, at an unofficial but Indonesian-sponsored (and Canadian-financed) meeting of the claimants to the Spratlys, China joined in the agreement to resolve matters peacefully and to avoid unilateral action. It seemed as if China would be constrained from extending control of the South China Sea by its concerns about appearing to be a regional bully and about losing the benefits of economic interdependence.

In February 1992 China promulgated the "Law on Territorial Waters and Adjacent Areas," but this was more a political symbol than a necessary legal procedure in the pursuit of territorial claims.[24] In 1992 Chinese officials appeared to accept the terms of a July 22 five-point ASEAN declaration on the South China Sea, which agreed that force should not be used to change the status quo.[25] Beijing agreed that opportunities for joint development should be explored, although China made clear that it agreed to nothing that would constrain its sovereign rights in the region. Various discussions were held, many of the most important ones under the auspices of Indonesia (a non-claimant to the Spratly group), but no agreements were reached.

By 1994 both China and Vietnam were becoming more adept at developing contacts with Western countries and corporations. Vietnam even began to modernize its armed forces, including the acquisition of SU-27 aircraft.[26] Vietnam also grew bolder in asserting its right to explore for oil and gas, and evidence seemed to be growing that there were exploitable reserves in the area.[27] Vietnam was set to join ASEAN (by July 1995) and was feeling far less

---

23. This has been a steady refrain. See *Xinhua*, May 11, 1995, in SWB FE/2301/G/1.
24. Michael Leifer, "Chinese Economic Reform and Security Policy: The South China Sea Connection," *Survival*, Vol. 37 No. 2 (Summer 1995); and Esmond Smith, "China's Aspirations in the Spratly Islands," *Contemporary Southeast Asia*, Vol. 16, No. 3 (December 1994).
25. *The Straits Times* (Singapore), July 31, 1992.
26. *Jane's Defence Weekly*, May 20, 1995, p. 3; *Flight*, May 24, 1995, p. 24.
27. Michael Richardson, "Strategic Signpost for Asia" in *Asia-Pacific Defence Reporter Annual Reference Edition*, Vol. 21, No. 6–7 (December 1994–January 1995), pp. 49–51. See also Ho Limpeng, "The Spratly Islands: Asian Flashpoint," *Navy International*, September 1994, pp. 257–259. On oil finds see *International Herald Tribune*, May 25,1995.

of a pariah. In August 1994 China grew concerned about Vietnam's oil pros-
pecting activities with foreign companies in the Spratlys; in several incidents
in the summer and autumn, Vietnamese forces chased off Chinese boats operating in Vietnamese-controlled waters in the Spratlys.[28] Vietnam was clearly
seeking to tie its fate in the South China Sea to that of Western oil companies,
hoping thereby to add to its strength and deter China. This was not so much
a policy of constraining China through China's interdependence with the
outside world, as constraining China through a mixture of precise use of
military force and use of Vietnamese interdependence with the outside world.
The question was whether this clever strategy was too clever by half, and
whether China would be constrained.

The end of 1994 was also a time when China was finding itself in deeper
conflict with the West, and the United States in particular, over trade disputes
and entry into the WTO. But China got into this problem in part because it
was feeling less constrained by the international system. Some Chinese officials
had incorrectly calculated that because the United States had recently abandoned the linkage of trade and human rights, Western powers would no longer
use the linkage of foreign policy issues to constrain Chinese behavior. But the
late 1994 trade disputes demonstrated that China was set for a much longer
and more complex dispute with the United States on trade issues. This was a
difficult time for China, because it was being asked to accept that from now
on it would be more, not less, bound by the international system. The Chinese
were aware that they were soon to become a major food and fuel importer and
thus ever more dependent on the global market for vital supplies.[29] As it could
see the implications of becoming more dependent on the outside world, China
chose to resist the process as much as it could. The decision to acquire at least
10 (and possibly as many as 22) Kilo-class submarines from Russia was part

---

28. *Xinhua*, October 17, 1994, in SWB FE/2130/G/2; and *South China Morning Post International
Weekly*, August 27, 1994, p. 6. See also Mark Valencia, "Dancing with the Chinese Dragon" in *Trends*,
August 27, 1994; and *Far Eastern Economic Review*, October 13, 1994, p. 29.
29. Reports in 1994 suggested that China became a net oil importer in November 1993. It turned
out that these initial assessments were premature. In the first quarter of 1995 Chinese oil exports
were 4m tonnes, down from 4.2m in the same period in 1994, but still higher than China's import
total of 2.45m tonnes which was up from 2.43m. See *Reuters*, May 8, 1995. Estimates suggest China
will need to import 100m tonnes by 2010. See Valencia, *China and the South China Sea*. On China's
food dependence see a report by The Worldwatch Institute cited in "Malthus Goes East," *The
Economist*, August 12, 1995. In that context, it is significant that whereas the Spratly islands
proven to be rich in marine resources, oil has not yet been found in major quantities. The Natuna
gas field in the south of the region is the world's largest. See GMA-7 Television (Philippines), June
18, 1995, in SWB FE/2335/B/4; and *World Resources 1994–95* (Oxford: Oxford University Press,
1994).

of a much wider program to modernize Chinese naval forces and extend their power-projection capability.[30] And so, in September 1994 when the Philippine armed forces detained 55 fishermen from China who tried to set up structures on one of the islands claimed by the Philippines, China felt it had to respond. As in the past when China used force to defend what it defined as its national interest, Beijing found itself making policy on the fly.[31]

Although the Spratly islands themselves might not have been very important, the region provided a real test of whether China would be constrained by economic interdependence. While it may not be surprising that China felt it needed to deliver a message that it would not be pushed around, it surprised most observers that China would, for the first time, come into conflict with an ASEAN member. The conventional wisdom in East Asia was that China would no doubt continue to take territory claimed by Vietnam, but it would not encroach on territory claimed by ASEAN states. The argument was that China needed to be on good terms with ASEAN states in order to keep the flow of investment and technology from these states. Any use of force against such pro-Western states would also threaten relations with the developed world as a whole. But the conventional wisdom was wrong.

There is little evidence upon which to reconstruct China's decision-making process, but it seems likely that the general propensity to use force to regain territory claimed by China would not have caused much dispute in Beijing. What might well have been more disputatious was the timing and the target. It seems that the specific operation was launched by the Guangzhou Military Region and South China Fleet, even though some, such as the Foreign Ministry, might have been expected to oppose such action at that time. But at a time of uncertainty in Beijing leadership politics, and with some parallels to the 1974 Paracels incident and the 1988 clash with Vietnam in the Spratlys, it would have been more possible for local commanders to operate under what they thought were standard procedures and strategies that did not require formal approval in Beijing.[32]

---

30. *Janes Defence Weekly*, March 18, 1995, p. 3. More generally see Jun Zhan, "China Goes to the Blue Water," *Journal of Strategic Studies*, Vol. 17, No. 3 (September 1994).
31. The pattern of Chinese action in such circumstances is discussed in Gerald Segal, *Defending China* (Oxford: Oxford University Press, 1985).
32. This is a difficult subject and I am grateful for the views of Paul Godwin on the matter. For some additional insights see *Kuang Chiao Ching* (Hong Kong) No. 271 (April 16, 1995) in SWB FE/2301/G/1–3. See also the view of Admiral Lanxade who was in China in the relevant months, in *Cols Bleus* (Paris), May 6, 1995.

In choosing to take on an ASEAN state in the South China Sea, China was taking a political risk of souring relations with ASEAN and scaring off foreign investors. On the other hand, in choosing the weakest ASEAN member, the Philippines, China chose the softest target. In choosing the state that had ejected American forces from their bases, it also tested American intentions in the most cautious manner. Thus sometime in the three months before the end of January 1995, China sent at least nine naval vessels to Mischief Reef.[33] This was not the most southerly territory taken by China, but it was the first time it had seized territory claimed by an ASEAN state. Chinese forces arrested Philippine fishermen, built structures on the island, and left troops in place to guard what many analysts expect will turn into a Chinese naval facility and possibly even an airstrip. Philippine forces confirmed the action on February 8 and found they could do nothing to reverse the situation.

What is the significance of the mischief on the reef? The most obvious change in the status quo was that China had unambiguously violated the 1992 ASEAN understanding by using force against an ASEAN member.[34] China claimed that it was only acting in keeping with its sovereign claims; at least for public consumption, it insisted that it had only erected shelters for fishermen. When Western intelligence resources were finally focused on Mischief Reef, it became clear that China had built military structures and stationed People's Liberation Army (PLA) units on a long-term basis. Although Chinese officials admitted in private to Western governments that these were indeed PLA units, in public China continued to assert that this was the benign action of Chinese fishermen and that using force to eject Filipino fishermen was not the same as an attack on an ASEAN member. In any case, China asserted that this was a form of self-defense because the territory was its own. Some Chinese even suggested that the lesson to be learned was the need to expand Chinese forces very rapidly in order to seize the region quickly and thereby avoid such political inconveniences as China would endure in the first half of 1995.[35] China was clearly taking a risk in taking on an ASEAN member and it also risked feeding the sense in the wider world that China would sacrifice economic relations if

---

33. Aptly named by the British Admiralty, Mischief Reef is more than 1,100 km from Hainan, and less than 240km from the coast of the southern Philippine island of Pauline.

34. Those who seek to minimize the importance of the incident on Mischief Reef note that China did not "use force" in the sense of the 1988 clash with Vietnam where troops were killed. But China clearly did "use force" to eject the Philippine fishermen and then placed naval forces on the Reef to deter counter-attack.

35. *China News Digest*, April 26, 1995; and *Xinhua* on April 20, 1995, in SWB FE/2284/G/1; and *Kuang Chiao Ching* (Hong Kong) No. 271 (April 16, 1995), in SWB FE/2301/G/1–3.

this were the only way to satisfy territorial claims and obtain vital energy resources. The main question, and the test of the significance of the Mischief Reef operation, depended on the way in which other people reacted to the Chinese operation and whether China had indeed put at risk the benefits of interdependence.

The initial reaction from ASEAN states was stunning silence, or at least the nearest thing to it that diplomats can muster. In private, ASEAN officials were furious that they had been humiliated by China. The Philippines fumed, in part at their own failures, and soon took out their anger by destroying some Chinese markers on other reefs elsewhere in the Spratlys. But what was most striking was the absence of any formal ASEAN complaint that blamed China for breaking the 1992 understanding. Various countries in the region issued statements regretting the rise in tension and calling for all parties to avoid the use of force: hardly statements of robust deterrence. Behind closed doors, ASEAN officials concluded that they could do little about Chinese activity and that therefore discretion was the better part of valor. They saw no reason to issue statements that condemned China if they could do nothing to back them up. If "Finlandization" described a state that constrained its policies because it lived next door to a neighbor too powerful to challenge, then the states of Southeast Asia were "ASEANized." Of course, this ASEAN version of Finlandization was a self-fulfilling strategy: if no concern were articulated, then no one could be asked to help. If no one helped, then nothing could be done.

ASEAN foreign ministers issued a joint statement that expressed concern about recent activities but declined to identify either the problem or the fact that China was the one who had seized territory. Even these limited moves were made only because the Philippines "made a diplomatic scene" and demanded that something be said to China.[36] China apparently did not even have to pay a public relations price. When China humiliated Vietnam in 1974 and 1988, the Vietnamese had shouted from the moral high ground about Chinese aggression. In 1995, however, meetings of ASEAN officials suggested that there was no unanimity on how to handle China and great reluctance to criticize China explicitly for its actions on Mischief Reef.[37] China found that it could more easily defeat ASEAN members than it could Vietnam.

On April 2–4, 1995, at an already planned meeting with Chinese officials behind closed doors in Hangzhou, the Chinese were apparently presented with

---

36. *Far Eastern Economic Review,* April 6, 1995.
37. *International Herald Tribune,* April 21, 1995.

a unified ASEAN expression of concern over Chinese actions (informally over dinner). Beijing was "asked" to cease building military structures on disputed islands.[38] The ASEAN officials had asked for the issue to be considered formally at the meeting, but China refused and ASEAN backed down. From China's point of view, the fact that the meeting was routine and secret, and that the message was only delivered informally over dinner, meant that China could feel that it had little price to pay for its actions.

However, while China had humiliated ASEAN, in so doing it may have stimulated forces that it had rather left dormant. As Vietnam had shown after the setback of 1988, a Chinese triumph can stimulate the vanquished to work on a better strategy. After defeat by China, Vietnam sought the benefits of interdependence with Western oil companies, turned itself into a target of opportunity for Western multinationals rather than a target for abuse by Western governments, and sought support by joining ASEAN. The new Vietnamese strategy of deterrence appeared to cause China to avoid taking on Vietnam in 1995 and to seek instead a more vulnerable and less costly target.

The states in the cross-hairs were those ASEAN countries that suddenly found that China was prepared to take them on directly. China was apparently unconstrained by economic interdependence. The action on Mischief Reef demonstrated that engaging China was not a sufficient strategy.

IS ANYONE LEARNING LESSONS?

The initial reaction to Mischief Reef and subsequent events in ASEAN and beyond was low-key. But as 1995 developed, the main actors tried to come to terms with the fact that their hope in the restraining qualities of interdependence was misplaced. Difficult choices now had to be made. As different states groped for a policy, they went off in different directions. In the process, there were signs that while most were not prepared to try to constrain Chinese behavior by organizing a more effective counter-balance of power, such a strategy, if adopted, might have some effect.

THE UNITED STATES. U.S. policy towards China, as in many other aspects of American foreign policy in the 1990s, was hard to judge.[39] There were obvious flip-flops—none more glaring than the case of the Clinton administration's temporizing and then refusal in 1994 to link Most Favored Nation trading

38. Philippines GMA-7 Television, April 10, 1995, in SWB FE/2276/B1. See also *Far Eastern Economic Review*, April 20, 1995, p. 12.
39. Harry Harding, "Asia Policy to the Brink" in *Foreign Policy*, No. 96 (Fall 1994).

status to an improvement of China's human rights record. On the other hand, this same American administration took a tougher line on trade issues, and even liberalized relations with Taiwan.

In the defense field, there was also a range of policies on view. On the one hand, the United States resumed military-to-military contacts, including ship visits. And yet the war games played in American defense academies pitted U.S. forces against China (with a 2010 scenario).[40] When an American aircraft carrier jousted with Chinese military units on October 27–29, 1994, off the Chinese coast, this demonstrated that at least some influential people in the Department of Defense were concerned about how to deal with a rising Chinese military power.[41] Following events on Mischief Reef, Stanley Roth of the National Security Council was quoted as expressing support for the Philippines' efforts to stop "Chinese intrusions," American officials looked for ways to bolster security ties with Japan, and the new Marine Corp commandant, General Charles Krulak, expressed deep concern about China's long-term intentions.[42]

On the other hand, Admiral Richard Macke, then commander of American forces in the Pacific, said in Singapore in March 1995 that Asia and the West must accept the fact that China will develop a modern navy including aircraft carriers intended to project power overseas.[43] In May 1995, U.S. Chief of Naval Personnel Admiral Zlatoper, when rejecting the argument of a study suggesting that China was the main challenge to the Asian balance of power, reportedly argued that China might even be part of a Gulf War–style joint defense strategy to deal with regional crises.[44]

The confused state of American policy in East Asia and towards China was encapsulated in the somewhat contradictory content of the newly revised American strategy for Asia-Pacific published in February 1995. It argued for a greater concentration on traditional friends in the region, but one had to read between the lines to appreciate that China was seen as the main challenge to the regional balance of power. Therefore, implicitly, increased U.S. reliance on its allies would show increasing concern about Chinese intentions.[45]

---

40. *Defense News*, January 30, 1995, pp. 1, 26.
41. *International Herald Tribune*, December 15, 1994.
42. Associated Press, April 2, 1995; *International Herald Tribune*, June 23, 1995; *Far Eastern Economic Review*, September 28, 1995, p. 32.
43. *International Herald Tribune*, March 8, 1995; Richard C. Macke, "A Commander in Chief Looks at East Asia," *Joint Forces Quarterly*, Spring 1995, esp. pp. 12–13.
44. *Reuters*, May 3, 1995, referring to Dibb, *Toward a New Balance of Power in Asia*.
45. *U.S. Security Strategy for the East Asia–Pacific* (Washington, D.C.: Office of International Security Affairs, Department of Defense, February 1994). See also William Perry speech to China's National Defense University in Beijing on October 18, 1994, in *Defense News*, Vol. 9, No. 81 (1994).

In effect the United States stayed on the sidelines while the security situation deteriorated. It was fully five months after the incident on Mischief Reef that the United States managed to cobble together a formal statement on the incident. The State Department declined to single out any state in the region as the main problem, and instead issued a general statement of "concern" about the freedom of navigation.[46] But by then Sino-American relations were in a tailspin, triggered by the granting of a visa to the Taiwanese president so he could receive an honorary degree at Cornell University. When Sino-Taiwanese relations subsequently deteriorated so badly that China closed air and sea lanes in the Taiwan Straits in order to test-fire missiles, it had become clear that the Spratly issue was only part of a much wider worry about China's propensity to use force, relatively unconstrained by the risks that it might damage economic interdependence in East Asia. It remained unclear, and indeed a major uncertainty for the future, whether China was constrained from attacking Taiwan by an understanding that the United States would help Taiwan resist. The United States remained ambiguous about whether it was offering Taiwan such balance-of-power protection, but for the time being even such an uncertain deterrent seemed to be holding China at bay. Not even such a limited strategy was on offer for those who might wish to resist China in the South China Sea.

JAPAN. The East Asian country that seemed to be having the most significant debate about China was the only other indigenous major power in East Asia, Japan. Well before the events on Mischief Reef, Japanese officials were expressing increasing concern, mainly privately, about Chinese intentions and the resolve of the United States to guarantee East Asian security. With signs that China seemed increasingly willing to throw its weight around, Japan became willing to express its concerns more explicitly. Even in the midst of chaotic Japanese domestic politics and debates about whether it should identify more strongly with Asia or the West, officials in Tokyo were speaking more openly of the need for a robust attitude towards China.[47]

Japanese officials helped nudge the United States in 1995 to revise its strategy in Asia-Pacific and in particular to place far greater stress on working with traditional allies. U.S. officials pointed out to Japanese officials that the litany of challenges to security in the report were mostly identified with China. When the Japanese prime minister visited China in May 1995, Japan edged closer to

---

46. *Reuters*, May 10, 1995; and *Korea Times*, May 15, 1995.
47. These points are in part based on discussions at a closed seminar at the UK Foreign Office in March 1995. See also "A Question of Balance," *The Economist*, April 22, 1995.

a full apology for its wartime behavior, but the talks, heavily leaked in the Japanese press, were robust in raising difficult security issues where Japan felt China was not acting in the best interests of regional and global security.[48] Japan's reaction to the incident at Mischief Reef drew a warning from Japanese officials, especially in terms of Japanese anxiety to keep the sea lanes in the region open.[49] Japan's Defense White Paper published in June expressed explicit concern with China's more aggressive policy in the South China Sea and called for an improvement in the quality of Japanese forces as a result.[50] In August, Japanese fighters attempted but failed to intercept Chinese fighters that overflew the disputed Senkaku islands.[51]

When China tested a nuclear device in May 1995 just after the renewal of the Nuclear Non-proliferation Treaty (NPT), Japan took the opportunity to send a more general warning to China that if it took action opposed by its neighbors and the international community, it should expect punishment. Japan reduced its grant aid to China by a symbolic amount, but the action was, especially for the usually cautious Japanese, a loud signal of serious worries about Chinese behavior. At the time of the fiftieth anniversary of the surrender of Japan in 1945, Japan and China engaged in increasingly nasty exchanges, each accusing the other of being the greater risk to regional stability. Japanese officials expressed increasing concern that China was trying to exert pressure in new forms. China tried to tell Japan what terms it could use for dealing with the Taiwanese, as the host for the 1995 APEC summit in Osaka. Coupled with increasing frustration over China's blocking of progress on the negotiation of an zero-level comprehensive nuclear test ban treaty, Japanese officials in various ministries found China increasingly difficult to handle.[52]

AUSTRALIA. Perhaps the most thoughtful assessment of the changing balance of power in Asia came from Australia. As the architect of APEC, Australia was worried about what it saw as a stubborn impulse in ASEAN to set the Asia-Pacific agenda and to relegate the Anglo-Saxon countries on the rim to a more marginal role. In public, Australian officials spoke of the need to join Asia; even

---

48. *UPI*, May 1, 1995. See various reports on the visit in SWB FE/2295/G/1–6.
49. *Agence France Presse* from Tokyo, March 8, 1995; and *International Herald Tribune*, April 4, 1995.
50. *Reuters*, June 30, 1995; *South China Morning Post Weekly*, July 8, 1995, p. 9.
51. *China News Digest*, August 30, 1995.
52. For evidence on these issues in the public domain see *Xinhua*, July 3, 1995, in SWB FE/2347/G/1; *Kyodo*, August 30, 1995, in SWB FE/2396/E/1; Liu Jiangyong, "Distorting History will Misguide Japan," *Contemporary International Relations*, Vol. 5, No. 9 (September 1995); *Kyodo* on pro-Taiwan forces in *Daily Yomiuri*, September 22, 1995; and Ryuichi Otsuka on the test ban in the *Daily Yomiuri*, September 21, 1995.

the normally outspoken Australian Foreign Minister, Gareth Evans, was careful not to condemn China's seizure of Mischief Reef.[53] But the new Australian defense strategy in December 1994 was even more explicit than the 1995 revision of American strategy in identifying China as the major challenge to regional security. In a more detailed presentation of the case, the architect of the Australian review, Paul Dibb, set out the case for concern in a less diplomatic form of words.[54] Implicit in the Australian approach was a sense that its opening to Asia was perhaps misjudged in its undue emphasis on ASEAN states.[55] While it was necessary to work with Indonesia in particular, the Australians increasingly felt that most other ASEAN states were especially hostile to a more important Australian role in Asia. Australians were finding that their closest friends (and most important trade partners) were in Northeast Asia and their closest ally was still the United States. Like the Americans, Australia worried that ASEAN was drifting towards the temptation of a non-white EAEC in which a more powerful China would be far less constrained and far more able to set an anti-Western agenda. Thus in December 1995, when Indonesia unexpectedly signed a defense accord with Australia, departing for the first time from its "non-aligned" posture, there was evidence that at least some of the middle powers of East Asia were beginning to grow seriously worried about China.

TAIWAN. Of the East Asian states, it was always assumed that Taiwan would take the toughest line towards China because it was defending its *de facto* independence. It was certainly true that Taiwanese officials were consistently among the firmest in warning about the consequences of a rising China. Yet when the attention turned to the South China Sea, Taiwan was caught between its desire to resist Chinese pressure and its view that the South China Sea belonged to China.[56] In the PLA operation in 1988 in the Spratlys, a Taiwanese military station had reportedly supplied fresh water to Chinese forces, and on March 25, 1995, Taiwanese forces fired on Vietnamese supply vessels. In April 1995, Taiwan announced meetings with Chinese officials about co-operation in oil exploration in the East and South China Sea, and cancelled a naval patrol

---

53. Gareth Evans was in Malaysia at the time. See Malaysian Television on February 17, 1995, in SWB FE/2232/B/2.
54. Dibb, *Towards a New Balance of Power*.
55. Gareth Evans on March 20, 1995, reported by *Reuters* from Sydney on March 20, 1995. On the defense White Paper, see *Far Eastern Economic Review*, December 15, 1994, pp. 18–20.
56. Various reports in mid-April 1995 from Taiwanese media in SWB FE/2276/F1; and *Far Eastern Economic Review*, April 13, 1995, p. 29.

in the South China Sea when the tension surrounding Mischief Reef seemed to be rising. In August 1995, the number of mainland Chinese fishermen working on Taiwanese-owned boats was reported to be rising sharply.[57]

The root of Taiwan's ambivalence toward the Spratlys was the gradual emergence of a stronger sense of self-definition. This drew Taiwan's concern away from the Spratlys, and much closer to home. Following President Lee's 1995 pre-election campaign trip to Cornell University, relations between Taiwan and China took a sharp turn for the worse. Beijing rattled its missiles in a summer and autumn of tension, and yet Taiwan received no support from anyone in the region.[58] China's leaders resorted to ultra-nationalist policies, in large part for domestic consumption, at a time of weak leadership in Beijing. China seemed to be paying little attention to the fact that a Taiwan Straits crisis might hinder the flow of investment and trade across the straits. Like the Spratly case, the Taiwan crisis demonstrated the extent to which China seemed unconstrained by either a balance of power or the logic of economic interdependence.

ASEAN. The policies of the ASEAN states were the most fluid. Although their formal response to events in 1995 was to avoid public attacks on China, it was clear that ASEAN officials felt the need to demonstrate that they could constrain Chinese behavior at least in some symbolic fashion. What they achieved was not much, but perhaps just enough of a sense that China was listening, even if it was not prepared to change its behavior.

When China's relations with the United States deteriorated over Taiwan, and Japans relations with China went sour because of nuclear tests, ASEAN found that China was more willing than before to listen to appeals for good behavior. Beijing needed to avoid antagonizing everyone at the same time.[59] Ahead of the ARF meeting in Brunei on August 1, 1995, ASEAN officials persuaded China to promise at least cosmetic changes in policy. While in Brunei, China's Foreign Minister Qian Qichen insisted that China still had sovereignty over the entire South China Sea, but declared that China was willing to resolve disputes according to the Law of the Sea. Qian also agreed to discuss the issue in a

---

57. In 1994, some 21,000 mainland fishermen sailed on Taiwanese fishing boats. *International Herald Tribune*, April 5, 1995; *The Economist*, April 29, 1995. On fishing boats, see *China News Digest*, August 30, 1995.
58. "Tensions Across the Taiwan Strait," *China News Analysis*, No. 1543 (September 15, 1995).
59. For the formal Chinese statement, and evidence of its linkage of the ARF to the poor state of relations with the United States, see *Xinhua*, August 1, 1995, in SWB FE/2371/G/5; and *Wen Wei Po* on August 1 in SWB FE/2372/G/1.

multilateral forum with ASEAN. While none of this was strictly new—China had already signed the 1982 Law of the Sea convention and had discussed the Spratly issue in Hangzhou in April 1995—the tone at least reflected a recognition of the need to ease ASEAN worries. China agreed to a bit more transparency on military matters, although its officially published defense data is notoriously unreliable.[60] Perhaps most importantly, China seemed prepared to sign agreements with Indonesia for gas supplies from the Natuna field in the southern Spratly islands, thereby apparently putting a practical end to its claim of ownership, at least in the short term.[61]

The more cooperative behavior from China showed that Beijing worried about a coalition being built against it, and that if the states of East Asia could begin to articulate and act upon a shared concern with China, then Beijing might well alter its policies. Signs of the depth of concern in ASEAN before the ARF meeting were not as coherent as they might have been, but ASEAN states certainly showed that China had crossed an important line.

THE PHILIPPINES. The Philippines, having been shocked by the initial Chinese action in January 1995, was also among the most vociferous in warning about the long-term threat. The Philippine armed forces were in no position to take on China on their own, but in the aftermath of the incident on Mischief Reef, Manila did authorize an increase in defense spending. Philippine naval units also destroyed seven Chinese markers on other islands in territorial waters just east of Mischief Reef, although they did not take on Chinese forces remaining on Mischief Reef, nor did they challenge Chinese naval vessels operating in disputed waters.[62] The Philippine navy arrested 62 Chinese fishermen just south of Mischief Reef on March 25, 1995, and charged them with illegal possession of firearms and explosives, and illegal entry.[63] In the months following the incident there were exaggerated worries among Philippine leaders about China posing a threat to the main islands of the Philippines,[64] at the same time as the Philippines engaged in mostly clever diplomacy intended to

---

60. China published a "White Paper" on arms control in November 1995 that suggests it does not feel it needs to be any more transparent, only that it must pretend to be so. See the text in *Xinhua* on November 16, 1995, in SWB FE/2463/S1/1–10.
61. *Kyodo*, August 1, 1995, in SWB FE/2372/S1/1 for the ARF statement. Also *Financial Times*, July 31, 1995; *Business Times* (Singapore), August 2, 1995; *The Economist*, August 5, 1995; *International Herald Tribune*, August 4; and ibid., October 7, 1995. For further details on the ARF see *PacNet*, No. 29 (August 18, 1995); *PacNet*, No. 31 (September 1, 1995).
62. Philippines GMA-7 Television on April 24, 1995, in SWB FE/2287/B/1.
63. Philippines GMA-7 Television on April 11, 1995, in SWB FE/2277/B/3.
64. *UPI*, April 19, 1995.

raise consciousness among ASEAN partners about the need to take a more robust line towards China.

China agreed to discuss a "code of conduct" with the Philippines, but refused to do so on a multilateral basis. As China realized that the Philippines was scoring diplomatic points, China warned that others should not "misinterpret" its intentions, an ambiguous remark that could cover a multitude of possible reactions in the future.[65] Other Chinese comments warned the Philippines that it "would bear all the consequences" if it continued to "cling obstinately to its course."[66] But it was Beijing that shifted ground at the ARF meeting, agreeing at least to discuss the Spratly issue in a multilateral dialogue with ASEAN, among other things. Oddly, the Philippines then proceeded to undermine its good efforts in raising consciousness about China by negotiating a "code of conduct" bilaterally with Beijing.[67] Perhaps lessons had not been learned after all.

MALAYSIA. Of course, ASEAN states were not immediately attracted to the notion of multilateral negotiations about territorial disputes because they had so many unresolved disputes among themselves. ASEAN states also had a range of other reasons for turning a deaf ear to Philippine concerns. Malaysia, with its large ethnic-Chinese minority, might have been expected to take a firm line against an extension of Chinese power. But as Prime Minister Mahathir has grown more confident about his ability to manage the Chinese majority at home, he has been happy for them to seek economic benefits from new trade ties with China. He has also seen China as a crucial anti-Western ally in his struggle to develop an EAEC and to shut out the Anglo-Saxon states across the Pacific. China has been more than willing to support this aspiration and happy to hear Mahathir say that "we no longer regard China as a threat."[68]

SINGAPORE. As Malaysia shifted to a more sympathetic stance towards China, Singapore viewed the change as a vindication of its own more long-standing pro-China tilt. As a tiny, mainly ethnically-Chinese state in a sea of non-Chinese, Singapore has natural worries about its survivability. Thus it in effect (but never formally) welcomes a degree of worry by its ASEAN neighbors about China's intentions. It has taken a special role in helping China modernize, and in providing China with oil processing and other facilities in

65. *Reuters*, May 10, 1995; *Xinhua*, May 16, 1995, in SWB FE/2306/G1.
66. *Ta Kung Pao*, May 17, 1995, in SWB FE/2310/G/1–2.
67. *Xinhua* on August 11, 1995, in SWB FE/2381/G/9; GMA-7 Television (Philippines) on August 9 and *Xinhua* on August 9, both in SWB FE/2379/B/3. See also *Financial Times*, August 11, 1995.
68. *Financial Times*, February 10, 1993.

the region.[69] It is also one of the few ASEAN states that has no real or even potential territorial disputes with China. Singapore appreciates, however, that it is in a vulnerable position and must take care not to be seen to be too sympathetic to China's position. Hence, Premier Goh Chok Tong suggested in Beijing that China's rising power, arms spending, and activities in the South China Sea were "stirring anxiety" in the region. Although this was a belated response, Singapore felt that it could not afford to be seen to be silent when China was picking on a fellow member of ASEAN.[70]

INDONESIA. Perhaps the most important and firm response in ASEAN to China's moves in the South China Sea came from Indonesia. The Indonesians were always the most likely leaders of ASEAN and simply by virtue of their size stand as a middle power without their ASEAN colleagues. But because of various factors in post-war regional politics, Jakarta has seen fit to take a back seat in ASEAN. Yet everyone knows that Indonesia has an uneasy relationship with China. As China worked its way down through the Spratly group, and seemed undeterred about taking on an ASEAN member, it looked likely that China would carry on to the southernmost reaches of the South China Sea. As Chinese aspirations in effect reached Natuna island and the proven natural gas reserves (said to be the world's largest) in the region, Jakarta began to wake up to the threat it had allowed to develop unhindered. At a workshop in Surabaya in 1993 organized by Indonesia to discuss Chinese claims to the Spratly islands, China presented a map showing that the southern reaches of its claim included the Natuna gas field. Indonesia now realized that it was no longer neutral in the discussions about the South China Sea. In preparation for the ASEAN Regional Forum in July 1994, Indonesia asked its ASEAN partners to support a formula that would have cut back the area of the Chinese claim in the South China Sea. But Indonesia's supposed partners turned it down, preferring to take the immediate benefits of good trade relations with China rather than risking confrontation.[71] Indonesia grew more concerned.

In July 1994, Jakarta asked China to clarify whether its territorial claims extended to the Natuna region, but China refused to respond. After the Mischief Reef incident, Indonesia decided that the silence meant that China did claim the gas fields, and in April 1995 Indonesia began air patrols in the region around Natuna. Indonesian officials had been reluctant to characterize China

---

69. For example as reported by *Reuters* on January 6, 1995.
70. *Dow Jones News Service*, May 15, 1995; *Reuters*, May 14, 1995.
71. *Far Eastern Economic Review*, August 11, 1994, p. 18.

as a threat,[72] but in a marked change of tone, the commander of the Indonesian armed forces said in April that it was especially important to modernize Indonesia's air force in order to deal with the Chinese challenge in the South China Sea.[73] Thereafter the Indonesian Foreign Minister Ali Alatas was reported to have obtained Chinese clarification that its South China Sea claims did not include the Natuna gas field, and that China would apply the UN Law of the Sea Convention to the entire South China Sea.[74]

AND CHINA AGAIN. While it remains uncertain just how much China is constrained by its ARF declaration in August 1995, China clearly felt sufficiently constrained by a wave of protest and signs of increased vigilance in East Asia to moderate its diplomatic position. Events in the Taiwan Straits and the South China Sea did not appear to support the notion that Chinese expansionism would be constrained by fear of damaging economic interdependence, but it did seem that China was worried about what looked like early steps in building a regional, anti-China coalition. China seemed to understand that it could be the target of a balance of power, and that it had to alter policy accordingly.

Conclusion: Constructing a Constrainment Strategy

This analysis tells us some important things relevant to the three main questions in the China debate.

First, what is the nature of the China that interacts with the outside world? It is clear that China is a far more complex actor than ever before. Reforms in all their splendor and squalor have ensured that, for all China's authoritarian features, it makes less and less sense to talk of a single Chinese foreign policy. The timing and nature of Chinese activity in the South China Sea during 1995 have been seriously complicated by regional economic interests and regional military forces. Divisions in policy making in Beijing have also been evident, most especially in the linked tensions concerning Taiwan and even Sino-American relations. While those doing economic business with China have known it for a while, those in the diplomatic business are learning that talking to a handful of Chinese leaders in Beijing does not provide a sure sense of Chinese policy.[75]

---

72. *Far Eastern Economic Review,* April 27, 1995, p. 28.
73. *Suara Karya* newspaper (in Indonesian) on April 11, 1995, in SWB FE/2277/B2–3. See also tough comments by the armed forces commander cited by *Reuters* on May 31, 1995.
74. *Antara* (Jakarta) newsagency, on July 21, 1995, in SWB FE/2363/B/1–2.
75. Michael Swaine, *China: Domestic Change and Foreign Policy* (Santa Monica: RAND, 1995); Susan Shirk, *The Political Logic of Economic Reform in China* (Berkeley: University of California Press, 1993);

Precisely because Beijing recognizes that the outside world is learning to appreciate the complexity of modern China, there has been a marked tendency for Chinese leaders to resort to increasingly extreme nationalism in order to build unity in a post-ideological age. Chinese, whether they be dissidents or Party bosses, believe that, in the pithy phrase of Geremie Barme, "to screw foreigners is patriotic."[76] And yet many foreigners do not recognize the new nationalism as a sign of China's weakness. It should be recognized that China is an incomplete great power, with all the uncertainties that we learned to live with in the case of that incomplete superpower, the Soviet Union.

Second, is China learning to live with the constraints of interdependence? The optimists would have us believe that it is: witness its eventual signature on the NPT. But even if China is learning, it only does so under serious pressure. It certainly is a slow learner who is far too keen to rewrite the textbooks. China's determination to change the WTO before the WTO changes China is a case of how hard China fights to reject the constraints of economic interdependence. China's behavior in the South China Sea and across the Taiwan Straits in 1995 also suggests either that China does not feel that the fruits of economic interdependence are at risk when it pursues its irredentist agenda or seeks greater international status, or else that these are short-term prices worth paying for a greater good.[77] In short, economic interdependence does not seem to constrain China as much as many might have hoped.

Third, does China bend to pressure? Can it be constrained? It is remarkable how often one hears that we must understand the Chinese point of view in order to recognize why they are unwilling to bend to external pressure. We are told that China is unique and the Chinese strategic culture simply does not operate like that of other powers. According to this notion, China will never play by the rules of international society or be constrained by a balance of power.

But the evidence from East Asia in 1995 suggests a central conclusion of this article, that Chinese behavior can be moderated by concerted pressure. It was

Richard Yang and Gerald Segal, eds., *Chinese Economic Reform and Defence Policy* (London: Routledge, forthcoming 1996).
76. Geremie Barme, "To Screw Foreigners is Patriotic," *China Journal*, No. 34 (July 1995); and Allen Whiting, "Chinese Nationalism and Foreign Policy After Deng," *China Quarterly*, Summer 1995. For an earlier version of the argument see Michel Oksenberg, "China's Confident Nationalism," *Foreign Affairs*, Vol. 65, No. 3 (Winter 1986–87).
77. It is worth noting that in 1995 China shocked those supporting the notion of a Mekong river development zone, and those who thought China was learning to play by the rules of economic interdependence, by suddenly and sharply reducing flows of water to the delta. *The Economist*, November 18, 1995.

fear of such a concert of power that led China to soften its line at the ARF. In earlier years China signed the NPT because the international community kept up the pressure. China does sign arms control agreements—for example with Russia—when it feels it is dealing with a powerful and tough adversary.

China's policy will remain softer only if pressure is maintained. That is a lesson of trade disputes with China, for once the pressure is off, Chinese leaders go back to doing what they want to do. Thus, for example, if the Japanese and others want China to accept a full Comprehensive Test Ban Treaty, they will have to keep forcing China to pay a price in terms of loss of aid if it continues testing or blocking the negotiations. If Indonesia wants to keep its Natuna gas fields, or keep China from threatening Jakarta in order to keep prices low, then Indonesia will have to galvanize its ASEAN colleagues to keep criticizing undesired Chinese actions, and to do so in even clearer terms.

Emphasis on pressuring China and skepticism about the immediate constraining power of economic interdependence are not meant to suggest that it is necessary to embark on a confrontational strategy towards China. The goal is to integrate China into the international system. Most people would like to see a stable, secure, pluralist, and peaceful country. Sadly, China is none of those things at the moment, in part because it has not yet accepted the constraints inherent in real interdependence with the outside world.

A policy intended to constrain China, much like the one that managed relations with the Soviet Union, is intended to tell China that the outside world has interests that will be defended by means of incentives for good behavior, deterrence of bad behavior, and punishment when deterrence fails. In 1995, China was offered only the first element regarding the South China Sea, and hints of the second element. The result was an unconstrained China. In the same year, when China rattled missiles at Taiwan, there was far more deterrence, although the haziness of the signals left China free to carry on threatening Taiwan. On trade issues in 1995, China was forced to improve its terms for entry into the World Trade Organization as the West held firm to its demands. When China faced punishment for violation of intellectual property agreements, it capitulated to American demands. Constrainment of China can work, but its neighbors and powers further afield need to appreciate that they must act in a concerted fashion both to punish and to reward China; they must use elements from a strategy of engagement as well as the balance of power.

Learning to constrain China is a necessity for all great powers, but most immediately for the East Asians. The ASEAN states seem the least prepared for the difficult task. The largest among them, Indonesia, has the most important role in deciding whether ASEAN is Finlandized. Japan, which dominates a very different configuration of power in Northeast Asia, once looked likely to be similarly Finlandized. But in recent years Japan has begun to move, often surprisingly adroitly, to treat China as a risk that must be constrained and trained.

The key to constraining China is of course the United States. But American policy towards China and East Asia has been and still is incoherent. The longer-term indicators are not for anything much better. Of course the United States cannot be expected to "hold the ring" in East Asia unless the states of the region want and help it to do so. Northeast Asians have made some strides in this direction, but Southeast Asians, apart from Indonesia, have not. For the time being, it is the United States that provides the oxygen of security for the maritime states of East Asia. But without a serious debate in East Asia and the United States about how to constrain China, doubts are bound to grow about whether the United States will continue to keep maritime East Asia from asphyxiation.

Suggestions for Further Reading

The literature on the implications of China's growing power is vast. We have selected a few recent books and articles on topics addressed in this volume. In making these choices, we decided to emphasize recent English-language sources that would be readily accessible. We did not include Chinese-language sources or government documents from the United States and other countries. These materials are obviously important, but are too diverse and numerous to list here. Readers also should note that journals such as *China Quarterly*, *Asian Survey*, and the *Journal of Contemporary China* contain many more relevant articles than could be listed here.

Overviews of China's Foreign Policy and International Outlook

Christensen, Thomas J. "Chinese Realpolitik." *Foreign Affairs*, Vol. 75, No. 5 (September/October 1996), pp. 37–52.

Johnston, Alastair Iain. *Strategic Culture and Grand Strategy in Chinese History*. Princeton, N.J.: Princeton University Press, 1995.

Kim, Samuel, ed. *China and the World : Chinese Foreign Policy Faces the New Millennium*. Boulder, Colo.: Westview Press, 1998.

Lampton, David, ed. *The Making of Chinese Foreign and Security Policy in the Era of Reform*. Stanford, Calif.: Stanford University Press, 2000.

Nathan, Andrew J., and Robert S. Ross. *The Great Wall and the Empty Fortress: China's Search for Security*. New York: Norton, 1997.

Waldron, Arthur. "After Deng the Deluge: China's Next Leap Forward." *Foreign Affairs*, Vol. 74, No. 3 (September/October 1995), pp. 148–153.

Assessing China's Capabilities and Intentions

Allen, Kenneth W., Glenn Krumel, and Jonathan D. Pollack. *China's Air Force Enters the Twenty-first Century*. Santa Monica: RAND, 1995.

Bernstein, Richard, and Ross H. Munro. *The Coming Conflict with China*. New York: Knopf, 1997.

Gallagher, Michael G. "China's Illusory Threat to the South China Sea." *International Security*, Vol. 19, No. 1 (Summer 1994), pp. 169–194.

Gill, Bates, and Michael O'Hanlon. "China's Hollow Military." *The National Interest*, No. 56 (Summer 1999), pp. 55–62.

Godwin, Paul H.B. "From Continent to Periphery: PLA Doctrine, Strategy, and Capabilities Toward 2000." *China Quarterly*, No. 146 (June 1996), pp. 464–487.

Kristof, Nicholas D. "The Rise of China." *Foreign Affairs*, Vol. 72, No. 5 (November/December 1993), pp. 59–74.

Lampton, David. "Think Again: China." *Foreign Policy*, No. 110 (Spring 1998), pp. 13–27.

Lilley, James, and Carl Ford. "China's Military: A Second Opinion." *The National Interest,* No. 57 (Fall 1999), pp. 71–77.

Mulvenon, James C., and Richard H. Yang. *The People's Liberation Army in the Information Age.* Santa Monica: RAND, 1999.

Pillsbury, Michael, ed.. *Chinese Views of Future Warfare.* Washington, D.C.: National Defense University Press, 1997.

Ross, Robert S. "Beijing as a Conservative Power." *Foreign Affairs,* Vol. 76, No. 2 (March/April 1997), pp. 33–44.

Segal, Gerald. "Does China Matter?" *Foreign Affairs,* Vol. 78, No. 5 (September/October 1999), pp. 24–36.

Shambaugh, David. "China's Military: Real or Paper Tiger?" *Washington Quarterly,* Vol. 19, No. 2 (Spring 1996), pp. 19–36.

Shambaugh, David, and Richard H. Yang, eds. *China's Military in Transition.* Oxford: Clarendon Press, 1997.

China's Economic Future

Economy, Elizabeth. "Reforming China." *Survival,* Vol. 41, No. 3 (Autumn 1999), pp. 21–42.

Lardy, Nicholas. *China's Unfinished Economic Revolution.* Washington, D.C.: Brookings Institution, 1998.

World Bank. *China 2020: Development Challenges in the New Century.* Washington, D.C.: World Bank, 1997.

Domestic Politics in China

Goldstone, Jack. "The Coming Chinese Collapse." *Foreign Policy,* No. 99 (Summer 1995), pp. 35–52.

Huang, Yasheng. "Why China Will Not Collapse." *Foreign Policy,* No. 99 (Summer 1995), pp. 54–68.

Lieberthal, Kenneth. *Governing China.* New York: Norton, 1995.

Pei, Minxin. "Is China Democratizing?" *Foreign Affairs,* Vol. 77, No. 1 (January/February 1998), pp. 68–82.

Pei, Minxin. "Will China Become Another Indonesia?" *Foreign Policy,* No. 116 (Fall 1999), pp. 94–109.

Segal, Gerald. *China Changes Shape: Regionalism and Foreign Policy.* Adelphi Paper No. 287. London: International Institute for Strategic Studies/Brassey's, 1994.

Chinese Nationalism

Oksenberg, Michael. "China's Confident Nationalism," *Foreign Affairs,* Vol. 65, No. 3 (Winter 1986–87), pp. 501–523.

Sautman, Barry. "Racial Nationalism and China's External Behavior." *World Affairs,* Vol. 160, No. 2 (Fall 1997), pp. 78–95.

Unger, Jonathan, ed. *Chinese Nationalism.* Armonk, N.Y.: M.E. Sharpe, 1996.

Whiting, Allen S. "Chinese Nationalism and Foreign Policy after Deng." *China Quarterly*, No. 142 (June 1995), pp. 295–316.

China and Regional Security in East Asia

Betts, Richard K. "Wealth, Power, and Instability." *International Security*, Vol. 18, No. 3 (Winter 1993/94), pp. 34–77.
Feigenbaum, Evan A. "China's Military Posture and the New Economic Geopolitics." *Survival*, Vol. 41, No. 2 (Summer 1999), pp. 71–88.
Friedberg, Aaron L. "Ripe for Rivalry: Prospects for Peace in a Multipolar Asia." *International Security*, Vol. 18, No. 3 (Winter 1993/94), pp. 5–33.
Nye, Joseph S. "China's Re-emergence and the Future of the Asia-Pacific." *Survival*, Vol. 39, No. 4 (Winter 1997/98), pp. 65–79.

Chinese Views of the Region and the World

Deng, Yong and Feiling Wang, eds., *In the Eyes of the Dragon: China Views the World and Sino-American Relations*. Boulder, Colo.: Rowman and Littlefield, 1999.
Garrett, Banning, and Bonnie Glaser. "Chinese Apprehensions about Revitalization of the U.S.-Japan Alliance." *Asian Survey*, Vol. 37, No. 4 (April 1997), pp. 383–402.
Li, Rex. "Partners or Rivals? Chinese Perceptions of Japan's Security Strategy." *Journal of Strategic Studies*, Vol 22, No. 4 (December 1999), pp. 1–25.
Shambaugh, David. *Beautiful Imperialist: China Perceives America, 1972–1990*. Princeton, New Jersey: Princeton University Press, 1991.
Whiting, Allen S. *China Eyes Japan*. Berkeley: University of California Press, 1989.

Taiwan

Garver, John W. *Face-Off: China, the United States, and Taiwan's Democratization*. Seattle: University of Washington Press, 1997.
Lee, Bernice. *The Security Implications of the New Taiwan*. Adelphi Paper, No. 331. Oxford: International Institute for Strategic Studies/Oxford University Press, 1999.
Roy, Denny. "Tensions in the Taiwan Strait." *Survival*, Vol. 42, No. 1 (Spring 2000), pp. 76–96.

Policies Toward a Rising China

Gill, Bates. "Limited Engagement." *Foreign Affairs*, Vol. 78, No. 4 (July/August 1999), pp. 65–76.
Johnston, Alastair Iain, and Robert S. Ross, eds., *Engaging China: The Management of an Emerging Power*. London: Routledge, 1999.
Lieberthal, Kenneth. "A New China Strategy." *Foreign Affairs*, Vol. 74, No. 6 (November/December 1995), pp. 35–49.
Perry, William J., and Ashton B. Carter, *The Content of U.S. Engagement with China*. Stanford, Calif. and Cambridge, Mass.: Center for International Security and Coop-

eration, Stanford University, and Belfer Center for Science and International Affairs, Harvard University, 1998.

Shambaugh, David. "Sino-American Strategic Relations: From Partners to Competitors." *Survival*, Vol. 42, No. 1 (Spring 2000), pp. 97–115.

Shinn, James, ed. *Weaving the Net: Conditional Engagement with China* (New York: Council on Foreign Relations, 1996).

Vogel, Ezra, ed. *Living with China*. New York: Norton, 1997.

Waldron, Arthur. "Deterring China." *Commentary*, Vol. 100, No. 4 (October 1994), pp. 17–21.

International Security

The Robert and Renée Belfer Center for
Science and International Affairs
John F. Kennedy School of Government
Harvard University

Articles in this reader were previously published in **International Security**, a quarterly journal sponsored and edited by The Robert and Renée Belfer Center for Science and International Affairs at the John F. Kennedy School of Government at Harvard University, and published by MIT Press Journals. To receive subscription information about the journal or find out more about other readers in our series, please contact MIT Press Journals at Five Cambridge Center, Fourth Floor, Cambridge, MA, 02142-1493.